BELVA LOCKWOOD

JILL NORGREN

BELVA LOCKWOOD

The Woman Who Would Be President

FOREWORD BY U.S. SUPREME COURT JUSTICE
RUTH BADER GINSBURG

New York University Press • *New York and London*

NEW YORK UNIVERSITY PRESS
New York and London
www.nyupress.org

Library of Congress Cataloging-in-Publication Data

Norgren, Jill.
  Belva Lockwood : the woman who would be president / Jill Norgren.
  p. cm.
Includes bibliographical references and index.
ISBN-13: 978-0-8147-5834-2 (cloth : alk. paper)
ISBN-10: 0-8147-5834-7 (cloth : alk. paper)
1. Lockwood, Belva Ann, 1830-1917. 2. Lawyers—United States—Biography.
3. Women lawyers—United States—Biography. [1. Lockwood, Belva Ann, 1830–1917.
2. Lawyers. 3. Women lawyers.] I. Title.
KF368.L58N67   2007
340.092—dc22
[B]   2006034486

New York University Press books are printed on acid-free paper,
and their binding materials are chosen for strength and durability.

Manufactured in the United States of America
10 9 8 7 6 5 4 3 2

for Ralph Norgren, Sheila Cole, and Philippa Strum
whose passion for the written word has enriched my life

Contents

All illustrations appear as an insert following p. 154.

Foreword
Ruth Bader Ginsburg
Associate Justice, Supreme Court of the United States

In 1973, when I first appeared before the United States Supreme Court to present oral argument, nearly a century had elapsed since the Court first heard a woman's voice at counsel's lectern. At the start of the 1970s, law remained a dominantly male profession, but the closed door era had ended. Given the impetus of antidiscrimination legislation, women lawyers were beginning to appear in court as more than one-at-a-time curiosities. Principal among way pavers in days when women were not wanted at the bar was a brave pioneer named Belva Ann Lockwood.

In this meticulously researched and moving account, Professor Norgren has rescued Lockwood's extraordinary story from relative obscurity. Once compared to Shakespeare's Portia by her sister suffragist Elizabeth Cady Stanton [p. 74], Lockwood resembled Shakespeare's character in this respect: Both were individuals of impressive intellect who demonstrated that women can hold their own as advocates for justice. Like Shakespeare's Portia, Lockwood used wit, ingenuity, and sheer force of will to unsettle society's conceptions of her sex. Portia, however, succeeded in her mission by impersonating a man. Lockwood, in contrast, used no disguise in tackling the prevailing notion that women and lawyering, no less politics, do not mix: She became the first woman admitted to the Bar of the Supreme Court, and she ran twice for the office of President of the United States. Her enduring legacy, however, is the path she opened for women who later followed the tracks she made.

Her front-runner status was achieved by persistent effort. In 1869, as a mother of two approaching her thirty-ninth birthday, Lockwood gained no easy entrance into what was then a nearly all-male profession. Initially denied a legal education on the ground that her presence "would be likely to distract the attention of the young men" [p. 41], she persevered until she found a law school willing to admit her. She encountered yet another obstacle when that school refused to issue the diploma she had earned.

Throughout her life, Lockwood continued to wear down barriers society placed in women's way. When the U.S. Supreme Court refused to admit her to its Bar, she accelerated her efforts to persuade Congress to grant her plea. After years of lobbying, she gained passage of a bill that required the High Court to relent. In 1879, she became the first woman admitted to practice before the Supreme Court, and, twenty-one months later, the first woman to participate in oral argument at the Court. She next and last argued before the Court in 1906. Then age seventy-five, she helped to secure a multi-million dollar award for Cherokees who had suffered removal from their ancestral lands and relocation, without just compensation.

Lockwood was not content to rest on her personal achievements. She sought full political and civil rights for women and became a prominent leader in the suffrage movement. Though she could not vote for President, she ran for the office herself, pointing out that nothing in the Constitution barred a woman's eligibility. As she wrote in a letter to her future running mate, Marietta Stow: "We shall never have equal rights until we take them, nor respect until we command it" [p. 129]. In 1884 and 1888, during her two campaigns as the presidential nominee of the Equal Rights Party, Lockwood drew attention to a range of issues important to Americans. For example, she urged protection of public lands, called for reform of family law, and advocated use of tariff revenues to fund benefits for Civil War veterans. She was an activist in the international peace movement and became a leading proponent of international arbitration.

So much has changed for the better since Belva Lockwood's years in law practice. Admissions ceremonies at the Court nowadays include women in numbers. It is no longer unusual for women to represent both sides in the cases we hear. Women today serve as presidents of bar associations, federal judges, and elected representatives on the local, state, and federal level. Still, the presence of only one woman on the current High Court bench indicates the need for women of Lockwood's sense and steel to see the changes she helped to inaugurate through to full fruition.

Professor Norgren deserves high commendation for recognizing Lockwood's rightful place in United States history by writing this biography, the first for adult readers. Norgren's effort is all the more impressive because so many of Lockwood's personal papers have been destroyed. The story told in the following pages reminds us that ideas once taken as fixed can be changed. Resilience, wit, and good humor, Lockwood's work and days reveal, can turn put-downs and slights into opportunities. With optimism and tenacity, may we continue to strive as she did to advance in our Nation and World the ideals of liberty, equality, and justice for all.

Prologue and Acknowledgments

Belva Lockwood seldom told stories on herself but she did like to describe her childhood obsession with the imitation of biblical miracles: she tried to walk on water, to move mountains, and to raise the dead. At age fifty-eight, having become the first woman admitted to practice law before the United States Supreme Court and the first woman to run a full campaign for the American presidency, she repeated the story of her would-be miracles in an autobiographical article, observing soberly that while she had failed to raise the dead, she had "awakened the living."[1]

Lockwood was born Belva Ann Bennett in the Niagara County town of Royalton, New York, on October 24, 1830, the second daughter, and second of five children, of farmers Lewis J. and Hannah Green Bennett. Unlike the famous transcendentalist writer Margaret Fuller, or women's rights advocate Elizabeth Cady Stanton, at birth she had neither social standing nor the promise of a fine education. Like Abraham Lincoln, she was self-made, and invented herself as a middle-class professional woman. Had she been a man, her life would have resembled a conventional nineteenth-century plot: ambitious and talented chap walks off the farm, educates himself, seeks opportunities, and makes a name. But because she was not male, in striving for the equal opportunity to compete, Belva became a radical. Her story flows from the denial of opportunity that men took for granted.

In her time, Lockwood commanded the attention of presidents, congressmen, and columnists as she adopted bold positions in support of equal opportunity for women. She did not hesitate to confront the male establishment that kept women from voting and from professional advancement. When the Supreme Court refused to admit her to its bar, she lobbied Congress until that body passed "An act to relieve the legal disabilities of women." In March 1879 she became the first woman admitted to the high court bar and, months later, the first woman lawyer to argue a case there. Her bids for the presidency in 1884

and 1888 startled the country and infuriated other suffrage leaders. She
was a steadfast member of the international peace and arbitration
movement and was not above thinking herself, or her organization, the
Universal Peace Union, a worthy candidate for the Nobel Peace Prize.

Lockwood exuded ego. She openly chose fame, reveled in public
notice, and offered herself as a model of female accomplishment and independence. She endured scorn and ridicule but also found, and cultivated, communities of women and men who shared her passion for reform. A person of great energy, she made her last trip to Europe at the
age of eighty-three in order to lobby for the cause of women and international peace. She did not close her private legal practice until the following year.

Some years ago, while helping my younger daughter find books to read
at the public library, I stumbled across a biography of Lockwood written for children. I realized immediately that I knew nothing about the
woman or her accomplishments. As it turned out, I was not alone; virtually none of my university colleagues knew her name. A bit of scholarly snooping confirmed that historians had indeed lost the thread of
Lockwood's long life, which had been devoted to nurturing democracy
and individual rights.

I reached this conclusion after reading a handful of essays written
by twentieth-century women writers who had attempted to rescue
Lockwood from anonymity. Julia Davis, Madeleine Stern, and Julia
Hull Winner each had sketched intriguing portraits of a woman who
believed, with Jefferson and Adams, in "self-evident" truths, but who
dared to imagine a more vibrant Republic in which women had equal
rights and conflict could be resolved without war.[2] How had we lost the
story of this extraordinary life and of an event as important as a nineteenth-century woman running for the presidency? It would be easy to
say that she fell out of history because she was a woman and women,
particularly in politics, have had to struggle for notice. But Lockwood's
obscurity results from many factors, of which a preference in history
books for Founding Fathers and fighting generals is only one.

Late in her life, Lockwood agreed that a nephew's wife, Lella Gardner, could write her biography.[3] Curiously for someone given to self-
promotion, Lockwood did not throw herself into the project. She was
often too busy to give her niece the hours needed to recall a life rich in
events and personalities, or to find the documents and correspondence

Lella needed to write the book. Lella lived at some distance from Washington. She was not a professional author and had begun the project when her aunt was eighty. When Belva died six years later, the biography was nowhere near complete. Lella struggled for thirty years to write a complete biography but did not succeed.

Lockwood's slide into obscurity also occurred because, at the time of her death in 1917, few libraries collected the papers of women activists. Family members had to be relied upon to save the correspondence, diaries, and documents of respected relatives, and here fate conspired against Lockwood. She had suffered financial reversals three years before her death and was forced to leave her large house on Washington's F Street. She had outlived her daughters and buried her second husband. Her closest relative, grandson DeForest Ormes, was in his twenties with no permanent home. Her books and files, including a full library of peace literature, did not fit easily in the new apartment, but apparently she was not ready to give them to Lella. Her niece wanted the collection; she understood its importance to the completion of the biography, but when her aunt's death was announced she reached Washington too late to claim what she said had been promised to her.[4] Before she arrived, DeForest took away several cartons of papers from the apartment: active legal files, partial sets of lecture notes, a few letters, campaign memorabilia, and at least one scrapbook.[5] Insufficiently appreciative of his grandmother's place in history, or unable to make room for this life-bulk, he then arranged for the Salvation Army to take the rest of her papers, later telling Swarthmore College curator Ellen Starr Brinton that they were probably "sent direct to a paper mill" and made into pulp.[6]

In 1998, knowing only some of these facts, I weighed the probability that sufficient documents had survived and plunged into the writing of this biography, gambling, with decent odds, that a woman as accomplished as Lockwood had left footprints.

And she had. Lockwood was a consummate publicist who used newspapers as a public diary. The staff of the Washington *Evening Star* could not print enough about her. Newspapers in New York City, upstate New York, and the Midwest also thought her good press. *Harper's* wrote about her, cartoonists for *Puck* drew her, and daredevil journalist Nellie Bly sought her out for a feature interview. Lockwood herself wrote autobiographical articles and for many years her daughter, Lura McNall, published "Our Washington Letter." This column, appearing principally in the *Lockport* (New York) *Daily Journal*, offered an insider's view of the nation's capital and, not infrequently, reported on "Mrs. Lockwood, Washington's lady lawyer."

The National Archives was another treasure trove filled with details of Lockwood's life. Her law practice was based in Washington and the records of the courts in which her cases were tried are housed at the Archives. At the Library of Congress, I unearthed her letters to presidents, leaders of the woman suffrage movement, and World City enthusiast Henrik Andersen. Colleagues and new websites helped me track down other correspondence and memorabilia. Certain finds demanded weeks of sleuthing. One summer afternoon, after a long search, I telephoned an elderly woman in California. "Yes, my deceased husband was a Lockwood relative. . . . Years ago he framed a letter that she wrote and a funny little stock certificate with her picture and hung them on our living room wall." The letter provided new insight into family relations while the handsome stock certificate gave me the surprising news that Lockwood had tried to start a homeopathic remedies business.

Together, the letters, case files, government documents, reform movement newsletters, personal memorabilia, and newspaper articles are more than enough material from which to write a woman's life. And yet, large pieces of Lockwood's life and soul are missing. No original documents or artifacts—letters, diaries, school copybooks—survive from her childhood. With enormous frustration, I realized that a narrative of her early life was not possible. Much as I longed to explain the actions of the adult woman through the lens of compelling childhood events, or charismatic role models, I lacked the necessary evidence. Lockwood had little interest in future generations knowing about the home she shared with her parents and siblings, or the one she established with her first husband, Uriah McNall. She was a person who lived in the present and for political purpose. Even when given the opportunity, she chose not to write in detail about her family, and in autobiographical articles she recycled the same carefully selected stories: miracle making, discriminatory pay, Uriah's mill accident. The accident is all we ever learn about Uriah. We do not know whether she loved him, whether he encouraged her dreams, or what they felt when their child, Lura, was born.

Lockwood became a more accessible biographical subject when, after her move to Washington, D.C., she entered public life. She lobbied for women's rights, argued civil and criminal law cases, campaigned for the presidency, spoke at international peace conferences, and delivered paid lectures. She was old-fashioned as a public figure, disliking the confessional mode. She laughed off her second marriage to the elderly Ezekiel Lockwood with a dismissive sentence; she argued equal opportunity for women but never spoke about her aspirations for the grown daughter who was always—loyally—at her side, or about Lura's husband, who remains a cipher. She did not deny domestic life, but the law, politics, and social reform were her abiding interests. The life that Lockwood intended to be inscribed, the one that I have written, contemplates those interests. For me they are more than enough. Lockwood withheld from posterity the tools of psychological biography. She did not want us boring into her soul or psyche. That was for her Methodist god.

Lockwood, by then a 36-year-old widow, arrived in the nation's capital in 1866. She was curious and ambitious but also poor and without connections. In seven years, against all odds, she would earn a law school degree and open a Washington law office; in eighteen years, she would be an announced candidate for the presidency of the United States. She came to the capital for the same reasons that many men—and a few women—flooded into the city at the end of the Civil War. She was fascinated by politics and quietly entertained the idea that she might transform her life in a city bustling with adventurers and office seekers. Emerging from rural New York, she radically altered the course of what had been an unsatisfying life. She chose a public stage. It suited her forceful, resolute personality. From that platform, as an advocate for women's rights, a presidential candidate, and a peace activist, she demonstrated an unyielding faith in the promise of American ideals.

This book has been a joy to research and write in no small measure because of the people who also believe that Lockwood deserves a biography. Wendy Chmielewski guided me through Lockwood's papers as well as those of the Universal Peace Union at the Swarthmore College Peace Collection, and has become a friend. Robert Ellis has patiently steered me through the extraordinary collections housed at the National Archives and has demonstrated an unflagging interest in Lockwood's life. The National Endowment for the Humanities, the Woodrow Wilson International Center for Scholars, the National Museum of American History, John Jay College, and the PSC-CUNY Research program generously provided travel and fellowship support without which this project would not have been possible. I am enormously grateful for the help provided by the library staff of the Wilson Center as well as student interns Bill Elliot, Sara Farrokhzadian, Lika Miyake, Sarah Rackoff, Gemma Torcivia, Julie Watson, and Stefanie Yow. I owe a special debt of gratitude to Russell Menyhart who, while a law student, unraveled many of the mysteries of Lockwood's work on the Cherokee Nation case. Andrea Horowitz, Amy Leonard, and Jane Fuller also aided the project as research assistants.

I have been privileged to give numerous talks about Lockwood and am particularly grateful for the invitations received from John Jay College, Wayne State University, the New York Women Writing Women's Lives Seminar, and the Wilson Center. Many people have discussed the project with me or read parts of the manuscript. The advice of Barbara Allen Babcock, Cecelia Cancellaro, Wendy Chmielewski, John Ferren, Elisabeth Gitter, Ann D. Gordon, Sarah Barringer Gordon, Miriam Levin, Ralph Norgren, Steve Tullberg, and Mel Urofsky, along with anonymous reviewers, has strengthened this biography in innumerable ways. Philippa Strum provided a home away from home during my many research trips to Washington, D.C., and read the entire manuscript. My debt to her is very large. I am grateful to New York University Press for publishing this biography and to Deborah Gershenowitz, my editor, for helping me to shape Lockwood's story. My thanks go also to copy editor Emily Wright and managing editor Despina P. Gimbel, who have been loving friends of this manuscript.

Friends and family have encouraged me in this project and listened with goodwill to my endless talk of Belva. I thank Norma Wollenberg, Jacob Marini, Blanche Wiesen Cook, Sheila and Michael Cole, Deborah Klimburg-Salter, Tiana Leonard and John Kuldau, Serena and Robin Nanda, Jayne and Ted Merkel, Alice and Tim Stroup, Stephanie Cooper and Howard Weinberg, Simon Thornton and Marie-Dominique Even, Ruth O'Brien, Janet Pickering, Anneka Norgren and Luis Garzon, Tiana Norgren and Chris Rohner, and the three granddaughters, Elena, Ilomai, and Isabel, born during this book's gestation. I wish for these granddaughters lives as interesting and accomplished as that of Mrs. Lockwood, Washington's lady lawyer.

1

Early a Widow

I ask no favors for my sex. . . . All I ask our brethren is, that they will take their feet from off our necks, and permit us stand upright on that ground which God designed for us to occupy.

Sarah Grimké, women's rights advocate, 1837

Belva's mother, Hannah, was a Greene. Family histories describe the Greenes as descended from Magna Carta barons. An early forefather, John, is said to have sailed from England in the 1630s to the British West Indies, found it "Godless," and shipped out for the Massachusetts Bay colony.[1] He and others from whom Hannah was descended were also said to be followers of the religious dissidents Roger Williams and Anne Hutchinson.

Sometime after the War of Independence, Belva's branch of the Greene family began a journey westward. A son of this clan, William, took his wife and children as far as Washington County, New York. Hannah, the youngest of six children, was born there in 1812. In 1814, wanting better farmland, William joined family members in another trek to the far western corner of New York State, where several of the men had purchased property from the Holland Land Company.

Hannah's family settled in a frontier region some twenty-odd miles east of Niagara Falls. This had long been the land of the Iroquois Nation (Seneca), but in 1669 the French explorer, Robert Cavelier de La Salle, had established a post on what was then called the Niagara Frontier, and was followed by French traders and missionaries. In 1759 English forces expanded into the area following their capture of Fort Niagara. Later yet, warfare and politics placed the region in the hands of the United States, which sold much of it to financier Robert Morris. Seeking quick profits, he arranged the sale of a million and a half acres of western New York to Dutch bankers who capitalized the Holland Land

Company, one of the many speculative investment groups that carved up the late-eighteenth-century frontier. Using newspaper ads, hand-bills, and tavern talk, company agents put out the word that good land was available on liberal terms of credit. Special incentives were estab-lished to encourage extended families, or networks of friends, to make the move together.[2] Buoyed by dreams, Hannah Greene's family be-came a client of the Holland Land Company, and after that, farmers and manufacturers of potash.[3]

Belva's father, Lewis J. Bennett, was also born in Washington County, New York. His people were Scots. Late in life Belva proudly wrote to a niece that Lewis's ancestor Nathan High fought in the Revolution, "so we have a part in the foundation of the Govt."[4] Lewis was five years older than Hannah. It is possible that the Greenes and Bennetts moved west to Niagara County at the same time, but Ben-nett lore was scarce; Belva always knew more about her mother's people.

The Greenes claimed their lands from the Holland Company and started the hard work of clearing acreage. They sowed wheat, corn, and barley. Dairy farms were started, and then fruit orchards. Next came the gristmills and sawmills, powered by the plentiful local stream water. Rising from this industry were clusters of small farming communities. Royalton, in the southeastern corner of Niagara County, was one such village. The first town meeting was called within a few years of the Greenes'—now spelled "Green" by some—arrival. Hannah's father, a respected Baptist elder, was elected to the post of inspector while Solomon Richardson, husband of Hannah's older sister, Ruth, took up duties as constable.[5] Royalton looked to its civic organization none too soon. A rural community needed law and order, roads and schools, and a sensible plan for dealing with the blessings, and problems, of the Erie Canal.

In 1814, when the Greens emigrated west, it took weeks to cross New York State. To obtain goods from the port city of New York, or to sell farm produce, or timber, from the center of the state required long, arduous, and expensive journeys across bad roads, and then ship pas-sage on the Hudson River. Market expansion and westward movement cried out for a quick and inexpensive means of connecting the Atlantic Coast to the Great Lakes. Spurred on by future governor DeWitt Clin-ton, the New York State legislature agreed to support the building of an "artificial river."[6]

Begun in 1817, and completed in 1825, the Erie Canal transformed the landscape and economy of northern New York. Hundreds of laborers and artisans flooded the route of the planned waterway, and remained after the canal was completed. They brought new cultures and a stronger cash economy. Water-powered manufacturing spread from the path of the canal, as did villages and towns servicing the needs of merchants and travelers. At Lockport a series of locks had been built to breach the Niagara escarpment, permitting the canal to continue west to Buffalo. When the canal opened in 1825, Lockport's population equaled that of Rochester and Buffalo. It was a bustling hub whose cosmopolitan resources nourished the residents of surrounding villages like Royalton.

Hannah Green married Lewis Bennett at Royalton on December 11, 1827. She was fifteen; the groom, twenty. It appears that the newlyweds lived with a maternal aunt and her husband, the John Layton family. Belva and her older sister, Rachel, were born at the Laytons', and it is probable that Lewis Bennett labored for Layton and neighboring farmers.[7] Lewis never succeeded as a farmer. He moved his family around the county for twenty years, owning property briefly but never prospering.[8]

The five Bennett children, Rachel, Belva, Warren, Cyrene, and Inverno, born between 1828 and 1841, shared a close relationship with one another and the numerous members of Hannah's extended family who lived nearby. Belva had mixed feelings about a childhood in which her accomplishments and ambitions were not particularly valued. She complained that she did the work of a boy caring for the farm animals but did not get proper credit.[9] She chafed when her father did not encourage her schoolwork because of her sex. But she had a strong ego and later remembered personal feats of running, rowing, jumping, and horseback riding that she immodestly described as "proverbial."[10]

The Bennett children attended country schools near Royalton when they were not needed for farm work. Belva was a good student and at fourteen was offered an instructor's position by the local school board. With the family in need of money, she ended her formal education and took up the life of a rural schoolteacher. She boarded with the parents of her students and had her first taste of independence—and sex prejudice. As a female instructor, she received less than half the salary paid to her male counterparts. She called this treatment "odious, an indignity not to be tamely borne," complaining to the wife of a local minister who counseled her that such was the way of the world.[11] As the daughter of a poor family she had little choice but to accept the pay that was offered.

While teaching Belva began to imagine a life different from that of her mother and aunts—the life of a great man. She asked her father's permission to go back to school, but Lewis refused her request. He was a man of limited means and did not believe that women needed a higher education.[12] Defeated, his daughter did what was expected of her: on November 8, 1848, at the home of her parents, Belva Bennett, eighteen years old, married Uriah McNall.[13]

In her fifties Belva recalled the decision to marry: "The daughter of a poor farmer, I followed the well-trodden road, and was united in marriage to a promising young farmer of my neighborhood."[14] Uriah was twenty-two. His father, John, had come to Royalton from Canada and was one of the most respected men in Niagara County. The senior McNall farmed, ran the red brick tavern at McNall's Corners, and shouldered his share of civic responsibilities, serving for many years as justice of the peace and town supervisor.[15] His son was a sober young man. Belva had married well. By the new year, she and Uriah were settled on land a few miles north of their families, near the village of Gasport, where they farmed and operated a sawmill.[16]

Uriah and Belva married four months after the revolutionary stirrings of women, in July 1848, at Seneca Falls, New York. Here, ninety miles from the home of the newlyweds, sixty-eight women led by Lucretia Mott and Elizabeth Cady Stanton, and thirty-two men, including Frederick Douglass and James Mott, signed a "Declaration of Sentiments." The short document, echoing the natural-law language of the Declaration of Independence, proclaimed the patient suffering of women denied an equal station in life by the government under which they lived. The facts submitted "to a candid world" included the denial of their right to vote, submission to laws in whose making they had no voice, a double standard in matters of morality, and limited access to education and well-paying employment. The declaration took particular care to spell out the abuse of women in marriage, condemning a system of law that gave husbands the power to deprive their wives of liberty, property, and wages.

Upstate New York newspapers reported on the extraordinary gathering, and it is likely that Belva, who loved to read newspapers, had seen the document. She thought about these provocative issues and later wrote that Uriah had joined with an unconventional wife who found contemporary marital customs loathsome. She believed that the marriage of an ordinary woman, clearly not including herself in that category, "is the end of her personality, or her individuality of thought and action." A woman, she said, "is known by her husband's name, takes his standing in society, receives only *his* friends, is represented by him, and becomes a sort of domestic nonentity, reflecting, if anything, her husband's religious, moral, and political views, and rising or falling in the world as his star shall go up or down."[17] She resisted this "ordinary" life by reading widely and producing articles for literary magazines and local newspapers. She proudly described her interest in books and writing as "unwomanly habits."[18]

As Mrs. McNall, Belva had little time to find the permanent direction of her domestic star. Not long into their marriage, Uriah was injured in a mill accident that weakened his health. By the spring of 1853, four and a half years after their wedding, the young husband was dead. He left behind his 22-year-old bride and a three-year-old daughter, Lura, born July 31, 1849. He owned real estate, most probably mortgaged, valued at slightly less than three thousand dollars.[19]

Had Uriah not died, Belva's life might have followed a course similar to that of Harriet Beecher Stowe, or Elizabeth Cady Stanton, who, as mothers of small children, stormed the world using household writing tables. Tragedy, however, freed Belva McNall from these constraints, stealing from her the comforts of a settled arrangement and challenging her to act on long-buried ambitions. Initially, her husband's death and the responsibility of caring for Lura made her indecisive. She contemplated the conventional possibilities: retreat to the home of her parents or her in-laws, engage in farm work, and undergo an appropriate period of mourning, perhaps followed by remarriage, even though she later revealed that after Uriah's death she wanted to become independent, to throw off "a woman's shackles," but was ridiculed by friends.[20] For a short while she "submitted," made no decisions, found life "aimless and monotonous," then, finally, determined to "take destiny into [her] own hands."[21] Her first step was to return to school, believing that education would be the road to independence.

Drawing on the limited capital left in Uriah's estate, she enrolled at neighboring Gasport Academy. Her purpose was "to fit myself for some active employment whereby I could earn a livelihood for myself and child."[22] She was twenty-three and thought her plan reasonable but encountered "impudent" criticism from neighbors who commented that her behavior was "unheard of and unusual," snidely questioning what the young widow expected to make of herself.[23] Her father joined this chorus of nay-sayers: quoting St. Paul, he insisted that her desire for education was improper and unwomanly.[24]

Belva had yielded at eighteen but now she persisted. She finished the academic term and asked the school trustees for a job teaching the winter session, when boys typically enrolled and men taught. The trustees replied that a male instructor had been engaged. Then, fate stepped in. The teacher was fired and the trustees asked the young widow if she would take over his class, which she did, bringing Lura to school each day.[25] She taught several short terms, saving enough money to move forward with a truly subversive scheme: Lura would be given over to the care of her parents, who were about to move to Illinois, while she pursued a ladies' seminary degree. Years later Belva admitted that all of her friends and advisers objected to this idea, and that she "was compelled to use a good deal of strategy to prevent an open rupture."[26] But she prevailed. In September 1854 she packed her modest and much-mended wardrobe and in the company of two young women companions undertook the sixty-mile trip east to Genesee Wesleyan Seminary in Lima, New York. This was her first journey, and it was, she wrote, "a matter of a good deal of moment."[27]

Belva arrived at Lima and enrolled at the Methodist seminary in a program that offered a "ladylike" curriculum for young women, as well as preparatory work for young men hoping to matriculate at Genesee College, which shared its campus. When she learned that the college was engaged in the radical experiment of coeducation, she applied to transfer after presenting herself to an examining board.[28] She believed that the more demanding curriculum as well as the prestige of a college degree was an opportunity she could not afford to lose, one that would "gratify" the ambitions of her youth.[29] She gave up a lady's "finishing" in music and the arts and, without consulting her family, began Genesee's "Scientific Course," a program in politics and science. Her transfer earned a "half remonstrance" from the preceptress of the seminary, who told her she could expect to be a more highly cultured person if she stayed with the ladies' program.[30] The president of the college welcomed her, but did not hide his concern that she, a poor single mother, would not finish the longer course of study.

The Genesee program imposed a strict code of behavior, one that emphasized long hours of study and rote classroom recitation. The cloistered students were not allowed newspapers, and were encouraged not to mix with the citizens of Lima. Belva said that as a result of these policies she and her classmates were a "blank" with respect to contemporary politics.[31] On campus, informal social conversation between the sexes was also discouraged. At meals, men and women sat on opposite sides of long tables without speaking. Belva had no callers at the dormitory parlor, something of a trial for a gregarious person.

Genesee had a "decidedly religious cast," with male students and teachers dominating the school: "The only thing that the young ladies pretended to run themselves," Belva wrote, "was a literary society, which gave opportunity for the display of such genius as had not been exhausted by the rigorous study of the week."[32] Although the college nourished her in many ways, she occasionally slipped away in order to widen her perspective. She attended law lectures conducted by a local attorney. She said this was frowned upon by the Genesee faculty, who considered it an intrusion upon their rights, but her fascination with the law was already strong, and she went as often as possible.[33] On at least one occasion she also left campus in order to hear Susan B. Anthony lecture on women's rights. Anthony made the radical argument that society must permit women to work in stores and offices, a proposal Belva described as "startling heresy" to the public of the time.[34]

Belva graduated with honors on June 27, 1857. Forty years later, she confided that the discipline and thought "awakened" by the Genesee faculty was as important as the knowledge imparted by these teachers; and that the education "has been . . . like a cash capital in bank, giving reputation and standing in the community, and a constant desire for greater knowledge."[35] She had risked the love of her family for a degree that did, in fact, change her life.

While she may have dreamed about finding an attorney bold enough to apprentice her, immediately after graduation Belva headed home to take up work at the Lockport Union School. In 1857 teaching was virtually the only profession open to women. Schools were enrolling an increasing number of female students, and women instructors were being sought to teach them.[36] After the quiet of her life with Uriah, and the isolation of Genesee, she would be living in the county seat, a prosperous transportation and manufacturing town with a population of several thousand. Again, however, she faced the problem of wage discrimination. Although the school board knew she was a widow with a child to support, she was offered a salary lower than the one paid to her male colleagues. She complained, unsuccessfully, and then began the work of educating some of the school's six hundred students, anxious to earn enough salary to be reunited with her daughter.[37] In the late autumn she collected her pay and made the journey to her parents' home in Onargo, Illinois. She saw Hannah and Lewis for the first time since leaving for college in 1854 and was reunited with Lura, to whom she was a stranger. After a visit of some weeks, she gathered up her six-year-old daughter and her teenaged sister, Inverno, and traveled back to New York. She set up housekeeping at Esther Comstock's boarding house, grateful for the presence of her sister, who was close to Lura. Both girls were enrolled at the Lockport Union School, Lura in the lower division and her aunt, already a high school student, in the Senior Department.

Historians describe the decades before the Civil War as an "age of great movements." Men joined in organized campaigns, at first religious but later secular, to bring the "good news" that society could be reformed. Women's activism labored under the general belief that women belonged in the home, that they were intellectually inferior to men and should defer to them. But there was something sufficiently permissive in the culture of western New York where Belva grew up and had returned to teach that women could, and did, claim a place in changing society. With men, they became a voice against slavery and drink and, at Seneca Falls, they publicized the peaceful suffrage revolution that was taking shape in a number of communities through talk and petitioning.[38]

Cloistered college life had been confining for Belva, an enthusiast, but the move to Lockport freed her to join the highly charged world of upstate New York reform, to read newspapers, and to catch up on the politics of the day. Her religion drew her to benevolent-society activity, while her experience with sexual discrimination and the tragedy of widowhood gave her a natural sympathy for women's rights.

The social ferment in western New York was the product of many influences, including "fires of the spirit" that had burnt with particular intensity twenty years earlier during a period of religious revivals, giving the region the nickname, "the Burned-Over District."[39] By the time Belva returned to Lockport in 1857, this religious excitement had matured into a culture of spiritual and secular optimism that embraced the hoped-for second coming of Christ and the practice of benevolence.

The year before moving to Lockport, Belva had been converted to Methodism by the preaching of her college president, Joseph Cumming, and had been baptized by him. She had read the Bible as a child and un-doubtedly attended the revival meetings that broke the tedium and iso-lation of farm work, but before 1856 she never spoke about membership in a church. The Methodists' belief in individual responsibility, divine love freely bestowed upon humankind, and faith confirmed by good works nurtured Belva's inherent sense of her own worth and encouraged her desire to improve the world. Through her conversion she gained focus. She became, she wrote, "an earnest, zealous laborer in the cause of Education, Sabbath School and Missionary work and an indefatigable advocate of the Temperance Cause."[40] It was a public role encouraged by a church that, since the early days of John Wesley's preaching in England, had been progressive on the question of women. In western New York Methodist women had been known to preach at meeting, publicly af-firming Wesley's particular message of salvation and charging others to share the good news of the Gospels.[41] By 1857 this part of the state, once a storm center of personal religious fervor, had turned outward with cit-izens now stoking the fires of social and political reform in matters of temperance, abolition, and women's rights.

Western New York was a good place for Belva, who was empow-ered by her religion and by a thousand changes, large and small, that were working their way into the secular culture that also defined women's lives. An increase in commerce, transportation, urbanization, and female literacy reshaped mid-nineteenth-century America, intro-ducing new ideas about what was right and proper. Belva also bene-fited from the slow but dramatic transformation in women's civic life that had begun in the 1830s. Once welcomed and celebrated in politics only for their role as mothers of the Republic, ordinary women had seized a greater role and stepped out into the community, as Belva had, performing benevolent and missionary work. In this coming out, they saw their communities and governments in a new light and concluded that the perfection of society required their participation in politics.[42] Although they could not vote, women sized up parties and candidates, concerned themselves with the business of school boards, and began lobbying state educational appropriations, married women's property rights, and observance of the sabbath.

This activism was aided by a handful of courageous women who proved to be exceptionally able theoreticians, agitators, and organizers. In Belva's civic genealogy, they are the mothers: African-American Maria Stewart; Quaker minister Lucretia Mott; southern abolitionists Angelina and Sarah Grimké. Each asserted the right of respectable women to talk in public even when what they had to say was controversial. They argued that all women, not only preaching women who spoke from an "Inner Light," had the right and duty, as equals to men, to speak on matters of public importance. The Grimkés wrote essays on women's unequal status. Their work anticipated the writing of Margaret Fuller, one of America's great intellectual figures, who made the radical argument that men "could never reach [their] true proportions while [woman] remained in any wise shorn of hers."[43] In her too-short life, Fuller championed women's intellectual (rather than domestic) development, insisting that women must be taught rigorous critical thinking. She offered private classes, "Conversations for a circle of women in Boston," that were eagerly attended and later became a model for women's clubs and organizations.[44] At a time when advice books told women to be domestic, pious, and submissive, to "avoid a controversial spirit, to repress a harsh answer," these women challenged orthodoxy and were objects of curiosity and occasional violence.[45] Newcomers did not make lightly the decision to join their ranks.

Like these women, Belva did not shy from controversy. Once established in Lockport, she did not hesitate to collaborate with New York women reformers, who radiated "controversial spirit," most significantly with Susan B. Anthony, who was ten years older than Belva and had already earned a reputation as a peripatetic activist who would not brook sex discrimination. In 1852 she bolted from a Sons of Temperance meeting in Rochester when the chairman, saying women delegates were only present to listen, refused to let her speak. With her new friend Elizabeth Cady Stanton, Anthony organized the Women's State Temperance Society, an association run by women. Five hundred delegates attended its first meeting in April 1852 where they heard Stanton argue that male drunkenness as well as adultery should be grounds for divorce under state law.[46] Stanton and Anthony also linked temperance to woman suffrage, insisting that men could not be relied upon, as proxies for women, to vote against alcohol. In public Anthony urged the wives of drunks not to allow their husbands "to add another child to the family." This message from "a maiden lady" was taken as effrontery and Anthony, who faced the public more in these years than the often-pregnant Stanton, found herself viciously attacked by newspaper editors protective of liquor interests and male prerogatives. In one editorial she was demeaned as "personally repulsive," a woman who labored "under feelings of strong hatred toward male men, the effect we assume of jealousy and neglect."[47]

Anthony, like Belva, had begun teaching while in her teens. She left the profession to work as a paid organizer for the Anti-Slavery Association but continued to use educators' forums for her advocacy. Belva encountered her most often at teachers' conventions held in Lockport. In a message warmly received by Belva, Anthony repeatedly encouraged women teachers to agitate for equal professional status and pay. The message provoked contention. At an August 1858 New York State Teachers Association meeting, a cranky male delegate admonished Anthony for practicing "every dodge," constantly bringing in this question of woman's rights. He pronounced the topic now "a stench in the nostrils of many prominent educational men."[48] Anthony refused to back down and Belva watched with admiration as she insisted upon the appointment of women to association committees.

Anthony also opposed many elements of the traditional "girls'" curriculum. During one convention, at Anthony's suggestion, she and Belva were placed on a committee charged with determining whether it would be appropriate and beneficial for young ladies to be taught public speaking. The two women were given the length of a school term to submit a report. Belva worked quickly, anxious to demonstrate, "with my usual practicality," that the curriculum for girls, which emphasized domestic arts, underestimated their mental abilities.[49] In an experiment, she assigned a weekly public talk to her students and found, over the course of a quarter, that they greatly improved with practice, so much so that "declamation for the girls became the standing order for the school forever after."[50] Flush with success, she urged the school association to recommend a similar change in curriculum throughout the state. When she became an attorney, she praised this liberalization and said such training would have benefited her in the courtroom.[51]

While they would later quarrel over policy and strategy, in the 1850s Belva and Anthony had a warm relationship, nurtured by their shared profession, work on curriculum reform, and mutual interest in the expansion of coeducational schooling.[52] Belva described "this"

Susan as a young and handsome woman, whose "spirit of aggressive-
ness" made her a marked figure, always far ahead of her competitors.[53]
Profession, family, and finances kept Belva in Lockport, but without
Lura and Inverno to care for she might well have emulated Anthony
and left teaching to become a field organizer and public speaker for
temperance and woman suffrage. She had left Lura once, however, and
now felt she had no choice but to remain where she was and to teach,
particularly after 1859 when Inverno graduated and returned to Illinois,
where she became a teacher and later married.[54]

When the Civil War started in April 1861 Belva, an abolitionist but
also a pacifist, experienced a struggle of the spirit. She was not yet for-
mally affiliated with the American peace movement but, like many
northern pacifists, she found it necessary to choose between principle
and politics. Reluctantly, she gave Lincoln her support and became
president of the Aid Society, organizing the girls in her school, along
with the older women of the community, into groups that made clothing and lint bandages for several companies of local volunteers. Like
many people, however, she never made peace with the cruelties and
cost of this war. Years after the bloodshed ended, she wrote that she had
been opposed to slavery "from the first moment that I was able to lisp
my school reader" but would have preferred peaceful arbitration "to
the sad carnage."[55]

Belva resigned her position in Lockport in the summer of 1861 and
moved the small McNall household southeast to Wyoming County,
New York, where she took up a teaching position at the Gainesville Female Seminary. Aged thirty-one and restless, Belva hoped shortly to
buy a small ladies' seminary where she could experiment further with
education whose transforming powers she appreciated as a democrat,
a Methodist, and an advocate of equal opportunity for both sexes. Like
influential women educators before her, including New Yorker Emma
Willard, she thought that a rigorous education could alter women's
lives and make them financially independent.[56] She had read about
Mary Lyon's Mount Holyoke Seminary, founded to prepare rural
women to work as teachers and missionaries, and was devoted to the
exercise regimens advocated by Catharine Beecher of the Hartford Female Seminary.[57] Respectable but radical, these mentors sought to open
a wider sphere of public influence to their students, claiming for
women teachers a share of the life-shaping authority that traditionally
had rested with family and church. Belva had accepted this role when

she went to Lockport, making a number of changes in the curriculum for girls, including the introduction of a program of calisthenics devised by Beecher. She hoped that the move to Gainesville would afford her even more independence and the chance to mold a new generation of women students.

Initially the move produced little more than frustration and failure. Although Belva was looking for a school of her own, for two years she had to settle for being an employee and endure the opposition of a principal who rejected her suggestions for reform. They clashed over the introduction of Beecher's calisthenics. When ponds near the seminary froze over, Belva recommended that the girls be encouraged to skate, but her employer forbade it, saying that the innovation would be immodest and irreligious.[58] The two were spared further argument when the seminary building burned down, forcing Belva to take Lura and move on. They went to nearby Steuben County, where, in the town of Hornell, Belva obtained a new teaching position at a private academy.

In 1863 the nomadic pair set off again, to the south-central New York State town of Owego, where Belva used her savings to buy the small Owego Female Institute, located on Front Street near the Susquehanna River. Owego was the county seat and the commercial center of a prosperous agricultural and lumbering district. Various teachers had operated a woman's seminary in the vicinity since 1828, typically not staying more than a few years. Princeton graduate George H. Burroughs and his wife preceded Belva. In 1863 they sold the building to her. Announcement of the change was made in the *Owego Times*, where an advertisement commended Belva McNall to the citizens of the village as "an earnest and efficient teacher."[59] She and three women assistants operated the institute as a day and boarding school. She made no record of her professional work and after three years, again restless, made the decision to risk an uncertain future in order to explore unspoken ambitions.[60] She sold the school property for double her original investment and enrolled Lura, sixteen, at the Genesee Wesleyan Seminary.[61] And then, because of her fascination with national politics, she decided to visit Washington, D.C.

2

In Search of a New Identity

Madame de Staël said to Napoleon Bonaparte, when asked why she meddled with politics: "Sire, when women have their heads cut off, it is but just they should know the reason."

Anonymous nineteenth-century French-Swiss writer

Belva McNall went to Washington and forged a new identity. By luck, or design, the capital turned out to be the perfect place for a woman whose secret dream was to live the life of a great man.

In 1866 the District was a frontier, a town in search of its identity. Boston, New York, and Philadelphia were long-settled cities, defined in their character. But Washington, in the view of Boston Brahmin Henry Adams, was "a mere political camp, as transient and temporary as a camp-meeting for a religious revival."[1] Transience was the hallmark of District life. The men who were the government, and men having business with the government, lived in boarding houses and hotels. Their families remained at home in places other than Washington. Office seekers came and went with changing administrations, and with the seasons. Those who could do so escaped what Adams called the "brooding indolence" of Washington's sultry summers.[2]

Journalists had few kind words for the city Belva decided to make her new home. Mary Clemmer Ames described Washington as a third-rate southern town, physically crude and dirty.[3] New York newspaperman Horace Greeley cautioned that "the rents are high, the food is bad, the dust is disgusting, the mud is deep, and the morals are deplorable."[4] The view up Pennsylvania Avenue to the Capitol was impressive, but the avenue itself had no majesty. Low brick and wooden buildings housing saloons, pawn shops, second-class hotels, and the offices of lawyers and newspapers filled the space that connected the White House to the Capitol. Adams remarked that the city lacked high society or an intelligentsia.[5] Nevertheless, there was, he said, an ease to life and one could not stay a month without, inexplicably, growing to love "the shabby town."[6]

During the Civil War former slaves, soldiers, and clerks had poured into the city, which struggled to accommodate a population that grew from seventy-five thousand in 1860 to double that number in 1864. The unkempt city smelled. Sewage was everywhere, as the streets were neither drained nor graded; most were not paved. In 1870 Senator William Stewart discouraged the efforts of local businessmen to organize an international industrial fair in the District: "None of us are proud of this place, " he said, arguing that the city had neither grandeur nor power to display.[7] Still, the victory of the Union signaled the possibility of an awakening. A District commissioner later said that it was not until the capital had been fought over that Congress showed an abiding interest in it.[8]

Belva McNall went to Washington because it was the seat of expanding national power. She was intrigued by politicians, and by their power. Psychologically, the move from Owego to the nation's capital was far less charged than her journey to college. She was thirty-six, had acquired a small amount of capital from the sale of her Owego school, and, with Lura nearly grown, was free to decide what to do next. In her autobiographical *Lippincott's* article, Belva wrote, perhaps disingenuously, that she "came to Washington, for no other purpose than to see what was being done at this great political centre,—this seething pot,—to learn something of the practical workings of the machinery of government, and to see what the great men and women of the country felt and thought."[9] She also said that she had not come to the capital with any idea of making it her home.[10] Something about Washington, however, proved addictive. The city throbbed with political ego and the demands of a wounded nation. Perhaps the outspoken schoolteacher sensed that in this place she could break the restraining bonds of custom.

Belva arrived in Washington during the winter of 1866. It was an extraordinary moment. Members of Congress had assembled in December for the first time since the end of the Civil War, ready to consider President Andrew Johnson's plan for the nation's recovery and reconciliation. Questions quickly developed over Johnson's use of pardons in the South as well as his wavering commitment to freedmen's rights. Although many legislators were quick to denounce Johnson, neither the

House nor the Senate had developed a firm plan of reconstruction. Eventually Congress would pass civil-rights and military-reconstruction acts, and approve constitutional amendments guaranteeing civil and political rights, but in these months the direction of postwar programs was uncertain.

Belva decided to spend a few months in the capital before going to see her parents in Illinois. She accepted a teaching position at the Young Ladies' Seminary run by Margaret and Mattie Harrover. The school, at Thirteenth Street, NW, between G and H Streets, was advertised as a boarding and day school.[11] Although the position did not pay well, it fit her needs as it was located in downtown Washington and she was free to leave each day at one o'clock.[12]

Day after day, indulging her passion for politics, she strode up the hill to the Capitol. At the Senate's new chamber she sat in the recently opened "Ladies Gallery."[13] Here, and in the House gallery, she listened to wide-ranging discussions, which included renewal of the Freedmen's Bureau bill, naval appropriations, pension reform, proposals to amend the federal Constitution, and the heated response to the president's veto of a ground-breaking civil rights bill. She also observed the hallway lobbyists and, when it was in session, went to the chamber of the U.S. Supreme Court, tucked away in a corner of the Capitol building, perhaps finding a seat when General Benjamin Butler, the "beast" of New Orleans, argued in defense of presidential authority and martial law in *Ex parte Milligan*.[14] She took long walks. It is not difficult to imagine the athletic newcomer striding along, indulging her dreams as she visited neighborhoods and dodged into public buildings. Young, ambitious men cultivated political mentors. Women like Belva had a more solitary journey.

Belva left Washington temporarily in the summer of 1866. She traveled south to Richmond to see the former capital of the Confederacy, then turned north and sailed to New York City, journeying on to meet one of her sisters. Together, they went to Chicago and on to their parents' home in Onarga. Belva, a 36-year-old widow with no financial security, had promised them that she would think about settling in Illinois, joining her brother and sisters who now lived in the Midwest. She inquired about teaching positions in several towns near Onarga, but found none that satisfied her. By summer's end, despite her attachment to Hannah, Belva abandoned the idea of moving west.[15] Putting rural Illinois behind her, she traveled back to the District by way of Harper's

Ferry, shaping two plans of action. One was easily and openly discussed: in order to support herself she would establish a small school. The second plan was less clear and more radical: she would pursue a life thought unsuitable for a lady, a life in government or law.

Belva had long been fascinated with law and lawmaking. Like most schoolchildren of her generation, she had been assigned the essays and speeches of American statesmen Daniel Webster, John Quincy Adams, and Henry Clay.[16] As a child she had eagerly read books describing the lives of important men, and later reported having discovered that "in almost every instance law has been the stepping-stone to greatness."[17] Perhaps for this reason, while at Genesee College she had taken the unusual step—for a woman—of studying the Constitution, the law of nations, and political economy. Standing at Harper's Ferry, the site of tragic insurrection, she must have considered her own rebellious dreams. She had been born a woman "with all of a woman's feelings and intuitions," but, she acknowledged, she "had all of the ambitions of a man, forgetting the gulf between the rights and privileges of the sexes."[18]

Belva proved daringly ambitious, but she was no fool. While she shaped her dreams into a concrete plan, she went forward with the task at hand: opening the new school. Early in the autumn of 1866 she placed an advertisement in the education column of the *Evening Star*: McNall's Ladies' Seminary, in the Union League Hall, Ninth Street, would begin classes on October 8, "Terms Moderate."[19] She planned to teach most of the subjects, but Lura, seventeen, home from Genesee Wesleyan Seminary, would be her assistant, conducting Latin and French recitations. The two women rented one floor of the Union League building, keeping the main section for the seminary, while making the east end their living quarters.[20] Belva also earned money as a rental agent at the Union League, Commercial, and Temperance Halls.[21] She said very little about the school except to suggest that teaching no longer engaged her. For practical reasons she could not stop, but her mind was elsewhere, engaged by other, more provocative projects.

One of these endeavors, in which she failed completely, involved an effort to open the American Foreign Service to women.[22] She had been told about a vacancy at the U.S. consul's office at Ghent and rushed to brush up on her German, while searching the musty basement library of the U.S. Supreme Court for books on international law. Through a member of Congress she obtained a copy of the Consular Manual and memorized its contents. When she felt herself competent to perform the services required of a consular officer, she submitted her job application to President Johnson and his secretary of state, William H. Seward.

To her "chagrin and disappointment," the application was not acknowledged. Belva later wrote that she had not stopped to consider whether the Europeans would receive a woman officer. Still a novice in the game of politics, she let the matter drop, later criticizing herself as having been "weak-kneed."[23] But she was harsh in this judgment. She had, after all, *acted*, fearlessly taking aim at the federal government, defying custom and risking ridicule. The President had ignored her—Belva attributed the inattention to his messy entanglement in Reconstruction politics, a prelude to his 1868 impeachment trial—but he could not undo the challenge, the direct action that would become the signature of her politics. For this reason, the application was an important milestone, and one she often mentioned. Before this test she had been a woman who jousted verbally with local school boards engaged in shameless wage discrimination. Now, with a few pieces of paper, she had challenged the hiring practices of the United States government.

Belva came to Washington knowing only her mother's nephew, William G. Richardson, and his wife, Sarah. Richardson was a ship captain, four years older than Belva.[24] His presence eased the transition to life in the capital. When Lura arrived, she and her mother joined the Wesley Methodist Church at Fifth and F Streets, NW, a few blocks' walk from their rooms at the Union League Hall.[25] Although church and family provided the first network of friends, reform activism endowed them with community. In the ensuing years these new friends and acquaintances would include people of influence, notoriety, and modest rank: government clerks and members of Congress, many women, and more than a few men.

The women that Belva met were an unconventional vanguard, ladies intent on public and professional lives. Josephine Griffing was among the first of Belva's acquaintances.[26] She was an established figure in the National Freedmen's Relief Association, as well as the fledgling national woman suffrage movement. Griffing had made a name for herself as an outspoken abolitionist. Earlier, while living in Ohio and Indiana and despite the responsibilities of motherhood, she had toured the Midwest as a paid agent of the Western Anti-Slavery Society. She had come to Washington near the end of the war to work for freedmen's relief and, later, to lobby on behalf of a federal intervention program, the Freedmen's Bureau.

Griffing and Belva may have become acquainted at Washington temperance meetings, as both women sang the praise of abstinence. It is also possible that they met late in 1866 when Belva and other Washington activists began to talk about forming a local woman suffrage organization. As they puzzled out strategy, Julia Archibald Holmes joined the circle and became the first president of the women's rights group that they launched, the Universal Franchise Association (UFA). Holmes had lived in the New Mexico Territory and, against local advice, had been the first white woman to climb the 14,000-foot Pike's Peak. She and her husband were active in the Republican Party and operated a printing office that, against custom, employed women as typesetters.[27] UFA meetings also gave Belva the opportunity to make the acquaintance of Sara Spencer, who ran the woman's department of the Spencerian Business College, as well as doctors Susan Edson and Caroline Winslow. J. Hamilton Willcox, a statistician in the Treasury Department, and Andrew J. Boyle, a congressional clerk assigned to the Committee on Education and Labor, each came to meetings and became friends. These men had political expertise that Belva was quick to appreciate. From her earliest days with the UFA she saw the benefit of working for change with sympathetic men.

Belva also came to know several powerful Washington women journalists. Emily Briggs, who wrote under the pen name "Olivia," was the first woman to obtain news regularly from the White House. Northerner Mary Clemmer Ames had flirted with writing before the breakup of her marriage opened the way for a move to the District, where, in 1866, she launched her career as a political commentator. She could be observed for long hours in the ladies' gallery of the House and Senate taking notes for her column. Like Briggs, she wrote about the problems encountered by women government clerks.[28]

Dr. Mary Walker was a friend of a different stripe. In the eyes of the world, she was an eccentric who, despite her medical degree, sacrificed respectability by wearing male clothing. Walker had emerged as a notorious figure during the Civil War when, against all odds, she won an appointment as an assistant surgeon for the 52nd Ohio Regiment.[29] She scandalized the troops by wearing the uniform of a male medic. She served at the front and was captured by Confederate soldiers. Imprisoned for four months, she was released in exchange for a Confederate officer. After the war, she adopted the habit of wearing a man's frock coat and pantaloons, accompanied by a high silk hat and a slender cane. As the years rolled on, she cast off the pantaloons and frilly shirt collars, and wore strictly male attire. Newspaper editors seldom lost the opportunity to mock her. Lura, more parochial than her mother, was also given to belittling Walker.

Belva liked the doctor. The two women met sometime after September 1867, when Walker returned from a year of lecturing in England and France. They formed a lifelong friendship, though the two women could not have been more different in matters of family life and physical appearance. Walker was a divorced loner with no children. She lived far from her upstate New York relatives and seldom kept house, while Belva followed many of the conventional domestic routines of the day. The friendship rested upon the experience of two independent women who shared a love of ideas and writing, each of whom needed to earn a living, each of whom believed in the movement for women's rights.

These Washington women had a profound effect on Belva. As professionals and as reformers, they were tough, assured, and accomplished. Before Washington Belva had known hard-working and caring women, her mother chief among them. But during her New York State days, with the exception of Susan B. Anthony, at best an acquaintance, she had lived outside the world of influential women leaders. She needed a circle of friends and associates who would be political confederates, people who would encourage her, educate her and, critically, respect her. In Washington she found that community and a life in equal rights politics.

It is a startling fact that the United States Constitution ratified in 1789 did not guarantee Americans the right to vote. Out of a desire to protect states' rights, established property interests, and traditional cultural values, the Framers of the Constitution remained virtually silent on a matter that we now agree lies at the heart of democratic government. Hoping to escape the oppressive heat of Philadelphia with a document that would be approved, the convention delegates decided to leave the determination of who could vote to the states, whose laws, in the first decades of the nineteenth century, limited participation in national and local elections to white men who met property qualifications.[30] Free African Americans and women rarely qualified. By 1850, most white men had been granted suffrage regardless of their economic status, the result of practical concerns, including the recruitment of militia as well as political-party competition for voters. Women of all races remained disfranchised while, at the outbreak of the Civil War in 1861, African-American men could vote in five New England states and, with qualification, in New York.[31]

Free blacks had protested their limited voting rights before the Civil War. After the victory of the North, they resumed this agitation, joined by the new freedmen of the South and a small group of white allies, in particular the Radicals of the Republican Party. Some women also disputed their exclusion from full political citizenship and had been lobbying state legislatures on the question of suffrage at least since the mid-1840s. When Belva arrived in Washington in 1866 Congress was debating the question of African-American voting rights. Within months, much to her surprise and pleasure, a proposal that would enfranchise the women of Washington, D.C., also came before the legislature. The bill provoked a heated discussion of universal suffrage. It also strengthened Belva's identity as an advocate of women's rights.

Universal suffrage embodied the simple but, at the time, radical idea that neither race nor sex could be used as a bar to voting. In December 1866, following a Republican victory in the midterm election, the Radicals, in alliance with party moderates, seized the moment, believing that they could enact legislation that would expand African-American manhood suffrage. As a preliminary measure, they introduced S.1, "An act to regulate the elective Franchise in the District of Columbia," legislation that would extend the right to vote without regard to race to "male persons" living in the capital.[32]

Pennsylvania Senator Edgar Cowan, who thought it was dangerous to give freedmen the vote, and who was no particular friend of women, immediately stepped forward with an amendment that he hoped would defeat the bill.[33] His proposal struck out the word "male," changing S.1 into universal suffrage legislation that he assumed would meet an early death—and perhaps humiliate the Radicals.

The Cowan amendment created an uproar. It also produced an unexpected opening for the discussion of woman suffrage, a cause that had been shunted aside by the Radicals in spite of lobbying by activist women. Seeing this opportunity, local suffragists, including Belva, visited the Capitol, where they encouraged members of Congress to speak out in support of women's right to vote. Cowan's colleagues also stepped forward, happy to denounce his "prank." Rhode Island Republican Henry Anthony said that he supposed "the Senator from Pennsylvania introduced this amendment rather as a satire upon the bill itself, or if he had any serious intention it was only a mischievous one to injure the bill."[34] "Injury," of course, was exactly what Cowan had in mind. He had not anticipated, however, that his proposal would unleash three days of earnest debate on the issue of women's rights. On December 11, 12, and 13, a handful of senators rose to praise the talents of women leaders, to give lessons in political theory (citing John Stuart Mill and Herbert Spencer), and to assert that women were every bit as entitled as men to the natural right to vote. Several representatives challenged the idea that politics must be a rude and disorderly sport, insisting that women's involvement would reduce strife. Without meaning to, Cowan had ignited one of the earliest congressional deliberations on voting rights for women.

Senators opposed to woman suffrage responded with standard arguments, noting woman's failure "to bear the bayonet" and the desirability, in a republic, of making the family rather than the individual the "foundation upon which to rest suffrage."[35] One opponent argued poetically that "the domestic altar is a sacred fane [temple] where woman is the high and officiating priestess" whose need for purity required that she be "separated from the exercise of suffrage and from all those stern and contaminating and demoralizing duties that devolves upon the hardier sex—men."[36] He warned against making "noble woman a partisan, a political hack."[37] Other senators condemned Cowan for distracting them from the "pressing necessity" of protecting freedmen. When the presiding officer finally called for a vote, nine members supported the universal suffrage amendment, while thirty-seven cast their ballots in opposition. Having held Belva and her confederates at bay, the Senate recessed for the Christmas holiday. After the New Year, the members reconvened, with both houses of Congress taking up S.1 in its original form. The legislation passed quickly, and was repassed over the veto of the president, enfranchising "every male person over the age of 21" in the District while making no change in the political status of women.[38] Despite the defeat, Belva said that the amendment had served "a good purpose for all disfranchised classes, as [it] called out a notable debate."[39]

Belva and her colleagues were both maddened by the vote and optimistic. Full of fight, after watching the newly enfranchised freedmen vote at a May 1867 District election, a small group decided to organize in behalf of D.C. woman suffrage. Late in the spring Belva and Griffing, among others, met at the home of James and Julia Holmes and founded the Universal Franchise Association. The vote on S.1, as well as the recently broken alliance with the abolitionist movement, had convinced them that in order to recruit more supporters, and win legislative battles, they needed to hold regular public meetings where universal suffrage could be defended.

This decision was not made lightly. Open meetings courted ridicule and assault. Animosity toward women's rights was intense. Not infrequently a "woman shrieker" speaking in public required police protection and even then, according to one journalist, "she was in danger of being bombarded with addled hen fruit, and very sure to hear the world's estimate in language profane and nasty."[40] Tough and resolute, the UFA women, with their male supporters, faced their fears and made their plans public. At the first association meeting they discussed how to reopen the question of woman suffrage in the District, and announced support for the work of the American Equal Rights Association (AERA), a newly formed national organization whose members were campaigning for a constitutional amendment that would guarantee universal suffrage.

In 1867 37-year-old Belva McNall made the acquaintance of a 65-year-old gentleman. His name was Ezekiel Lockwood and, in less than a year, he would become Belva's second husband.

Lockwood was a Washington dentist whose advertisements promised "Teeth extracted without pain."[41] He belonged to the E Street (Thirteenth Street) Baptist Church and, for some time, had also worked as a lay minister.[42] Beyond that, he was a mysterious figure. Forty-five years after their marriage, Belva told her nephew's wife that she knew little about Dr. Lockwood's life: "I cannot give a very comprehensive account," she said, "and his last son died 2 years ago."[43] Pension records show that Ezekiel was born in 1802 in Jay, Essex County, New York. Like Belva, he came from a farm family. In the 1820s he followed his older brother James west and later won appointment as the postmaster in Galena, Illinois.[44] He and James bought land.[45] There was a wife, who died, and decades of middle-aged life about which he was silent. In February 1862, he joined the Union Army as chaplain to the 2nd Regiment, D.C. Infantry. Wartime records describe a decent but aging soldier who won praise for his "comforting words" at the second battle of Bull Run and the battle of Antietam.[46]

Belva and Ezekiel left little record of their courtship. They met at the Union League Hall where Belva and Lura lived and conducted their classes. Like Belva, Ezekiel earned income as a rental agent. Courting was a simple matter as he boarded a few blocks away, near his Pennsylvania Avenue dental office. Few of their friends were aware of the courtship until the couple sent out wedding invitations.[47] In an autobiographical sketch, Belva introduced the fact of her second marriage humorously, perhaps apologetically: "In the midst of these labors [reading legal treatises], I committed the indiscretion so common to the women of this country, and, after fifteen years and more of widowhood, married the Rev. Ezekiel Lockwood."[48]

The couple wed on March 11, 1868, in an evening ceremony held at the Union League building. Two local clergymen, the Reverend Dr. George W. Sampson, president of Columbian College, and his colleague, the Reverend Dr. Abraham D. Gillette, had been invited. Each cleric offered prayers and comments before Gillette performed the marriage service. Margaret Renshaw, a widow who lived at Twelfth Street, served as Belva's matron of honor; Dr. O. A. Daily, a fellow dentist, joined Ezekiel as best man. Lura and her cousins, the Richardsons, stood in line to congratulate the couple, along with the many friends who had been invited for an evening of food and music.[49] A neighbor described Ezekiel as "a spare man and tall, quite aged yet spry."[50] That he did not shine when compared with his wife is suggested by the later comment of passing acquaintance James Densmore, who portrayed Ezekiel as "a man much her inferior in force and ability."[51]

Ezekiel was sixty-six when they married, twenty-eight years older than his bride (and four years older than her father). He was a pious man, which pleased Belva, who attended church regularly and supported temperance. He was hard working and cultivated opportunity. In addition to managing the League Hall, and practicing dentistry, sometime in the late 1860s Ezekiel joined the corps of men who, at the conclusion of the Civil War, offered their services as veteran-pension claim agents.[52] Shortly after this, he won a public commission as notary public. Although modest, this was the kind of striving that Belva expected and admired. It was also work that could be shared with a wife.

Before their marriage Belva told Ezekiel that she was bored with teaching. She had been reading law books at night and hoped for a new occupation. Although careful not to say as much in public, she imagined a jointly operated claims office with Ezekiel offering respectable cover at the front desk. Beyond that, it is not unreasonable to think that she envisioned Lockwood & Lockwood as a stepping stone to a career as an attorney. Although Belva knew very little about Ezekiel's past she gambled, correctly, that he was a man who would not be threatened by her life as an activist, or her barely suppressed dreams of breaking occupational barriers. Widowed for most of her adult life, Belva had found companionship and the promise of a new vocation. She understood that the family's financial well-being would ultimately fall on her shoulders. She accepted this reality. Ezekiel, in turn, won an interesting bargain: the company of a smart woman whose radical challenges to society would make the last years of his life anything but quiet.

The couple continued their work as rental agents for several public halls, including the Union League building. This hall, situated in the center of downtown Washington at Ninth Street and Pennsylvania Avenue, stood at a good location, and the Lockwoods were able to fill it daily with social and civic groups, including four separate temperance lodges.[53] Veterans' groups also rented space, as did the Universal Franchise Association. This work, however, caused the neighbors to talk. They said it was a strange business for a woman. Belva disliked the gossip, and she disliked the work, which she found distasteful. Her duties kept her up late at night and placed her, she wrote, "constantly in contact with people with whom [I] had no affiliation."[54] But the Lockwoods needed the agent fees and continued in the business for five or six years.

When they married, Ezekiel moved in with Belva and Lura at the Union League building. In addition to managing the building the couple continued, with Lura's help, to run the school, but only for a few months. Belva had become pregnant. Married in March 1868, Belva knew about the pregnancy some time late in May. Although it was the custom of the day for middle-class women who were "expecting" to withdraw from public life, Belva maintained her active schedule of benevolent and political work. In late September, five months pregnant, she was among the speakers at a UFA meeting called upon to welcome U.S. Senator S. C. Pomeroy as the group's honorary president.[55] Four months later, on January 28, 1869, Belva gave birth to a daughter, named Jessie Belva. Marriage and motherhood did not cure her "mania for the law."[56] She had finished the British jurist William Blackstone's *Commen-*

taries on the Laws of England and now spent any time Jessie spared her reading James Kent's commentaries on American law.[57]

Belva and Ezekiel forged a relationship based upon the creation of a household economic unit and shared interests in social reform. They were relative newcomers to Washington, inhabiting the hard-working world of the emerging urban middle class. Such people resided in boarding houses, toiled as clerks and teachers, and experimented with small enterprise. Belva and Ezekiel entered the radical politics of women's rights, but the form of their partnership was quite conventional. They were not attracted to the example of the prominent Lucy Stone and Henry Blackwell, who, when they married in 1855, read aloud at their ceremony, and signed, a "Marriage Protest." Stone, a nationally known abolitionist and women's rights activist, had agreed to marry Blackwell only after he accepted a contract in which the couple renounced the social and legal disabilities imposed on women. Their "Protest" decreed not only that Stone would retain ownership of her property but also that she would have complete control of her body and determine if, and when, she would become pregnant.[58] She also refused to take Blackwell's last name.

Belva asked nothing so scandalous. She married Ezekiel without any particular concern that he would limit her independence. She remained a member of her Methodist church but also visited his congregation, E Street Baptist.[59] She adopted his last name, but signed letters and documents "Belva Ann Lockwood" rather than "Mrs. Ezekiel Lockwood." The new couple participated together in women's rights and temperance activities. Ezekiel sometimes chaired suffrage meetings that were held at the League building at the far end of their living quarters.

The newlyweds did not always agree. Although Ezekiel supported women's right to vote, a young friend remembered that Dr. Lockwood took issue with the idea of women governing, insisting that "it would be too sudden a change."[60] Belva glossed over these differences, and in 1876 wrote stiffly, "Dr. Lockwood fully sympathized with his wife in her ideas in regard to woman's enfranchisement, and together they valiantly battled for the Woman's Suffrage cause."[61]

3

Apprenticeship

The notion of political equality for women was so radical that for a
long time it was virtually impossible even to imagine woman suffrage.

Ellen Carol DuBois, 1987

The Universal Franchise Association first met at a Pennsylvania Avenue
building known as Spiritualists Hall but later moved to the space that the
Lockwoods provided at the Union League building. The UFA welcomed
men as members, but the elected positions of chair and secretary were
filled by women who managed the association and represented it in public.[1] After Julia Holmes and Josephine Griffing each served as president,
Belva took office in 1870. Holmes was a widely traveled woman whose
husband had finessed a political appointment from Lincoln but, in the
late 1860s, in their group, Josephine Griffing was the star, an activist with
years of experience who regularly corresponded with other influential
reformers.[2] Lockwood was the less knowledgeable partner, a newcomer
on the periphery of suffrage and temperance politics.

The women started the UFA hoping for a measure of positive influence on public opinion. The congressional debate over S.1 had been respectful, but the behavior of the public and the press was another matter. Rowdy opponents could, and did, reduce public UFA meetings to
chaos. Men came just to hiss and boo speakers. As a child, Allen Clark,
a Lockwood family friend, watched as bystanders threw vegetables and
rolled metal plates among the chairs.[3] He developed great admiration
for the bravery of these "suffragettes," then a term of derision. Lockwood and her reform colleagues were, he wrote, "martyrs without
seeking credit for their martyrdom. They endured the abuse in silence
[and] were of strong spirit which ridicule could not swerve."[4]

Belva thought that the press wanted to "break" the UFA. She wrote
that as soon as the regular meetings of the association took on a "seri-

ous air," reporters began to show a "special talent in ridicule."[5] They described the heckling and rolling tinware with smug satisfaction and threatened to print the name of any woman who attended a meeting of the UFA.[6] This bullying, along with what Lockwood called the "fusilade of ludicrous reports," scared away many ladies who were curious about suffrage reform but afraid to have their husbands come to the breakfast table and learn from newspaper gossip that their wives were inclined toward women's rights.[7] What was apparently not remarkable was the racially integrated nature of UFA membership. Local newspapers noted, without comment, the presence of "ladies and gentlemen of both colors."[8]

UFA officers bore the insults directed at them with dignity and continued to call meetings although it was also difficult to draw diffident women to gatherings that spun out of control when the police "join[ed] hands with the mob."[9] Reluctantly, the officers decided to impose an admission fee, hoping to put a check on the "rabble." "Strangely enough," Lockwood reported, "so great had the interest become, the crowd increased instead of lessening, and night after night Union League Hall was crowded, until the coffers of the association contained nearly $1000."[10] In 1869 the association's executive committee passed a resolution to spend this money on a lecture series devoted to the question of equal political rights for women. Lockwood, UFA secretary, and Griffing, then president, organized the series, beseeching leading personalities of the day to "favor" them with a talk. They succeeded in scheduling the much sought after Anna Dickinson, "queen of the lyceum," humorist-satirist Petroleum V. Nasby (David Locke), author Bret Harte, Stanton, Anthony, and Belva's future boss, newspaperman Theodore Tilton.[11]

Lockwood adopted a practical attitude toward the press. She believed that editors could be won over with goodwill. To enhance the group's reputation, as well as her own, she became adept at producing a steady stream of news items for the daily papers. Although many of Lockwood's contemporaries disparaged journalism, she never mocked the men of the newsroom. Living in downtown Washington, close to the offices of the *Star* and other papers, she was able to visit with editors and staff, and to befriend them. At national suffrage conventions she offered resolutions of gratitude to local reporters "for their courtesy."[12] She had a natural feel for the art of public relations, and her attention to the press paid off. Increasingly, reporters and editors treated her and the issue of women's rights with deference.

At the end of the Civil War women like Lockwood expected that the significant energy of the abolitionist and women's movements would be jointly focused upon winning national legislation, or a constitutional amendment, barring the use of race or sex in the determination of voting rights. For more than two decades members of the antislavery and women's movements had worked closely, sharing leaders and the common language of natural rights. But in 1865, only weeks after the victory of the North, Elizabeth Cady Stanton learned that prominent advocates of African-American citizenship and voting rights planned to abandon the fight to enfranchise women, limiting their campaign to black manhood suffrage. Wendell Phillips, president of the Anti-Slavery Society, declared that the "hour belongs to the negro" and that Reconstruction politics could not bear the weight of women's aspirations.[13] Stanton, a long-time friend, quickly fired off a letter in which she asked, "Do you believe the African race is composed entirely of males?"[14]

For the next five years a fight to define the terms of this suffrage-reform debate enveloped these two civil rights movements. Initially, Stanton, Anthony, Lucy Stone, and Lucretia Mott, along with male allies, including Theodore Tilton, tried to win back the support of their antislavery society colleagues with a renewed appeal for the "equal rights of all." In May 1866 they formed the American Equal Rights Association (AERA), with Stanton asking whether the time had not come "to bury the black man and the woman in the citizen?"[15] Within a month of its founding, however, Congress approved a constitutional amendment, the Fourteenth, which established modest guarantees of male African-American voting rights while ignoring the question of women.[16] AERA members protested, sending to Congress petitions that legislators refused to introduce into floor debate. The amendment assailed women's sense of justice but, with a bitter irony, it also disappointed many male reformers who had hoped for a stronger statement of impartial male voting rights.

The limitations of the Fourteenth Amendment, which was ratified by the states and made part of the federal Constitution in 1868, meant that the nation's examination of its political conscience continued through the elections of 1867 and 1868. Christmas 1868 brought the bold decision of congressional Republicans that, despite recent setbacks at the polls, they would support a Fifteenth Amendment to enfranchise African-American men.[17] Proponents of woman suffrage immediately pressed their former allies to reject anything other than a universal suffrage amendment, again to no avail. With violence against African Americans rising in the South, and the Republican Party leadership envisioning a greatly expanded base of voters if the more than one million freedmen were enfranchised, virtually no member of Congress was willing to jeopardize passage by asking that women be added to the list of citizens to be protected in their political rights.

Stanton and Anthony came into this fight with tarnished reputations. Stanton, in particular, was increasingly spoken of as a radical critic—of religion, men, and the laws of marriage and divorce. The two women vociferously opposed the Fifteenth Amendment, debated in Congress during January and February 1869 and sent out to the states for ratification in March. But in speaking against the "aristocracy of sex" that the amendment would establish, Stanton abandoned measured language.[18] Anthony defended her friend. She wrote the editor of the *New York Times* that Stanton did not object "to the voting of ignorant men *per se*, but that she most strenuously protests against the principle and the practice that gives them civil and political superiority over . . . women."[19]

Recognizing the likely ratification of the Fifteenth Amendment, in the early spring of 1869 the Stanton-Anthony faction prevailed upon Radical Republican George Julian to introduce into Congress a Sixteenth Amendment that would enfranchise women. In May these women, a group that included Lockwood's colleague Josephine Griffing, traveled to New York City for a meeting of the near-moribund AERA. At the convention hall they presented a plan: their faction would discontinue its effort to block the ratification of the Fifteenth Amendment if the association would pledge its immediate support of Julian's bill.[20]

The convention was a contentious meeting of friends who had fallen into hopeless bickering over interpretations of democratic theory, strategy, and ego. Delegates who championed the Fifteenth Amendment refused to endorse the Julian initiative, still arguing that debate on the woman suffrage question could threaten ratification of African-American manhood suffrage.[21] Frederick Douglass was one of several speakers who insisted that woman's cause was not as urgent as "the shield of suffrage" needed by freedmen facing the violence of the "Ku-Kluxes."[22] Exasperated, Anthony told him he would not "exchange his sex & color, wronged as he is, with [the woman] Elizabeth Cady Stanton."[23]

The Equal Rights Association had been tottering, and now it fell. Stanton, Anthony, Griffing, and a number of other reformers, impatient, bitter, and fearful that the power of the Radical Republicans was waning and that the delay demanded by the Douglass faction would defer woman suffrage indefinitely, quit AERA, determined to form an independent women's rights organization. Two days after the close of the AERA convention, they announced the creation of the National Woman Suffrage Association (NWSA). These break-away delegates pledged to work for a federal woman suffrage amendment and to do everything in their power to block ratification of the Fifteenth Amendment. Six months later AERA members who supported the Fifteenth Amendment formed the American Woman Suffrage Association (AWSA). Built around the leadership of several notable New Englanders, including Julia Ward Howe, Lucy Stone, and Henry Blackwell, the "Americans" committed themselves to woman suffrage only after ratification of the manhood suffrage amendment, and to the recruitment of men in the "management" of the association.[24] After the ratification of the Fifteenth Amendment, the efforts of AWSA members focused on reform of state constitutions. Twenty-one years would pass before the two factions reunited as the National American Woman Suffrage Association.

Lockwood did not join the anti–manhood suffrage lobby in the winter of 1869 or participate in the meetings that led to the creation of the NWSA. She was sidelined, being nine months pregnant and then busy with her young daughter, Jessie, born January 28. She relied on Josephine Griffing to represent the UFA and to bring news to her. When the time came to declare loyalties, she became a member of the National Woman Suffrage Association. While she supported voting rights for freedmen, she had personal ties to Griffing and Anthony and believed, as they did, that female citizens should not have to wait any longer for their political rights. This group also attracted her because its founding members championed equal educational and employment opportunities for women, and for a number of years had lobbied for the reform of laws that gave husbands absolute control of their wives' assets and earnings. Lockwood liked their willingness to bundle social, economic, and political rights. As she later told an interviewer, she had first taken an interest in woman suffrage because of the "inequality that prevailed between the payment of men and women for identical work."[25]

For an energetic woman who liked to be in charge and in the thick of things, Lockwood's "confinement" must have been a trial. She curtailed her public activities for as short a period as was respectable and then, with paid household help as well as support provided by Lura and Ezekiel, she resumed her life as an activist. She wrote that the baby, her "little blossom," did not prevent her from doing "a great amount of work in benevolent causes."[26] Temperance figured in this "benevolence" but, curiously, she seldom referred to her advocacy of prohibition laws.[27] She also resumed work on the reform of the District's married women's property laws, and by summer 1869 she was participating in discussions of how to overcome employment discrimination with her UFA colleagues as well as her friend Mary Walker. The UFA had an ambitious plan to attack the inequities experienced by women working for the federal government, while Lockwood and Walker, perhaps with the support of Julia Holmes, who employed women typesetters, were exploring the possibility of collaboration with the new trade union movement.

The new mother was not yet traveling. In August she wrote a letter of introduction for Walker to take to the National Working Men's Convention in Philadelphia: "This is to certify that Dr. Mary E. Walker is connected with the Woman's Labor Movement in this City and is an accredited Delegate for the Working Women of Washington."[28] Lockwood and Walker left no record attesting to a local labor movement; quite possibly, they invented it at Belva's writing table. Still, their concern with improved salary and working conditions for women reached back to their teenage years. They were undoubtedly encouraged by the knowledge that several women, including Susan B. Anthony, were trying to create a bridge between the women's movement and labor reform. Anthony had been seeking influence within the National Labor Union but Walker, apparently with Lockwood's blessing, hoped to win credentials from the more radical-socialist Working Men's Association.[29] Their correspondence is silent as to whether she succeeded.

With her confinement behind her Lockwood learned that the fledgling National Woman Suffrage Association planned to hold its first annual convention in mid-January. She had missed several important suffrage meetings because of the pregnancy and was pleased that this gathering would be in the capital, only a few blocks from her residence and eleven-month-old Jessie. The year, 1870, would be an important one for her: she was about to step into greater prominence as the president of the Universal Franchise Association, and she was now giving greater thought to becoming a lawyer. The convention of the Nationals was a good start: for the first time she came face to face with accomplished women from across the United States, many of them ready to take up the mantle of progressive reform leadership.

In a world without radio, television, telephone, or internet, the annual meetings of the National provided suffrage women with the opportunity to boost one another's morale and to inform public opinion. The women met in January because Congress was in session. Founding member Matilda Gage told delegates that the meeting had been called in Washington "to impress more fully upon members of the National Legislature the claims of the women of the land."[30] Grabbing a few headlines was also part of the plan.

The record of the annual NWSA meetings held in the 1870s and early 1880s tells the story of respectable middle-class women with a remarkable commitment to free and open debate. Lockwood was attracted to this spirit of inquiry and argument. She also enjoyed hobnobbing with the country's leading reform women and quite quickly realized that she could carve out a niche for herself, privileged by her Washington residence and, later, by her status as a woman lawyer. She was repeatedly chosen as a member of the important resolutions committee through which convention policy was expressed, served as convention coordinator, and was a regular speaker until her falling out with the Anthony faction in the mid-1880s.

NWSA delegates met for two days, in a setting that, for some, must have resembled a revival jamboree. People came and went in easy fashion, with talks occasionally interrupted to applaud a late arrival whose reputation was greater than that of the speaker. Members of the audience were asked to stand up for suffrage and promised a better world when, according to Stanton, women's votes would bring "moral power into the political arena."[31] The speeches were sober, full of urgency, encouragement, and, occasionally, bitterness. Most speakers concentrated on the issue of woman suffrage, but Matilda Gage and Lockwood were not alone in urging the membership to lobby for equal educational, employment, and property rights.[32]

Stanton opened the convention with an enthusiastic speech. She rejoiced in the decision of the Wyoming territorial legislature granting women the right to vote and said that the hour of universal woman suffrage throughout America was near. In the hours that followed, in quick succession, the audience heard comments from several men who had joined the meeting as well as letters from absent supporters, including one, read by Stanton, from the English philosopher John Stuart Mill. Delegate Pauline Davis delivered a lengthy history of the women's rights movement in the United States, Britain, and Europe. For many of the convention participants, this talk was the first opportunity to hear the details of their as-yet-unwritten struggle. Primed with history and exhortation, the delegates listened next as Anthony enumerated four resolutions presented for approval. If accepted, they would guide the association's lobbying effort in the coming months. Predictably, the first resolution requested that members of Congress submit a woman suffrage (Sixteenth) amendment to the states. A second resolution asked that Congress strike the word "male" from the federal laws governing the District of Columbia, while a third urged officials to enfranchise the women of Utah Territory as a "safe, sure and swift means to abolish the polygamy of that Territory."[33] Lockwood's influence, felt in the D.C. resolution, was also expressed in the final resolution, which petitioned Congress to amend federal law to provide equal pay for women government employees. All of the items received approval. Before a dinnertime adjournment, Anthony said the hour had come "to pass the hat," to cover the expenses of the rental hall. In a rare moment of playfulness she said that women delegates were not expected to make much of a contribution as their husbands still held the purse strings, "but the men were expected to give liberally."[34]

Speaking at these meetings was not an easy task. Audiences were unpredictable, and could be apathetic or overstimulated. In Washington the sessions became *events* that, according to one reporter, attracted large crowds of young ladies, drawn more "from curiosity than a desire to be instructed."[35] As a matter of policy the public could enter much of the time without paying a fee, leaving the men and women at the podium with the challenge of addressing simultaneously believers, cynics, and social gadflies.

Lockwood left the convention full of plans. In addition to the public sessions where speakers exhorted the audience to take action, there had been opportunities to talk about the future during informal conversations. She had been particularly interested in meeting Phoebe Couzins, who, along with Lemma Barkaloo, had started law school at St. Louis's Washington University. Three months earlier the faculty of the law department of the District's Columbian College had denied Lockwood's application to become a student. She was stung by their decision but had resolved to apply to other law schools, and to join Barkaloo, Couzins, and Illinois resident Ada Kepley as one of America's first women law students.[36] Nothing she learned at the convention changed her mind.

Lockwood felt good about the future. Shortly after the NWSA convention, she took over as UFA president, an opportunity that may have come to her because Josephine Griffing was showing signs of the illness that would lead to her death in 1872.[37] Lockwood was a logical choice to head the association. She had joined the organization as an inexperienced newcomer but had apprenticed successfully with Griffing, who had taught her the ropes and who appreciated that Belva's personal fearlessness made her a valuable spokeswoman for an unpopular cause. As she left the NWSA convention Belva had the confident feeling that she could duplicate her rise to prominence in the UFA within the national women's movement. Perhaps to prove this, she took up work on two UFA-backed initiatives: a renewed drive for female suffrage in the District and a campaign to initiate equal employment legislation for women employees of the federal government.

Lockwood brought experience and passion to the question of employment discrimination. Throughout her teaching career she had been paid less than her male colleagues. In Washington she had quickly learned that the federal government also discriminated in the salaries paid to women. Friends told her it was not unusual for a female clerk to be promoted to the vacant place of a man, to do exactly the work he had performed, and yet to receive half the "male" wages. She also discovered that the government limited the number of clerking positions open, through hiring or promotion, to women. As a result, before the Civil War, domestic service and prostitution were the only reliable, ready sources of employment for women.[38]

The Treasury Department was the first federal agency to recruit women employees, after the department had been ordered to print more paper money as a means of financing the war. Processing the new currency was a labor-intensive activity. Fresh notes had to be cut and counted, while old currency had to be checked for counterfeits, recounted, and then destroyed. According to local lore, Treasurer Francis Spinner arrived on the job at the beginning of the war and found dozens of healthy men busy with scissors. He suggested to Secretary of the Treasury Salmon P. Chase that the men could be sent off to fight, to be replaced by women, who would be more productive and who could be paid half the twelve-hundred-dollar salary of the men.[39]

Chase, reluctant to violate Victorian customs concerning women's proper place, was won over when a trial group of women outperformed all expectations. Congressmen also gave their approval. While they shared Chase's concern for the "proper and tender" nature of women, they were quick to see economic advantage in the new arrangement. These decisions opened government work to women, beginning what one historian has described as a bold experiment, "avant-garde . . . bordering upon scandalous."[40] The "ladies," happy for respectable, white-collar work, accepted the lower wages, pay that increased to nine hundred dollars with the passage of the 1866 Appropriations Act.[41]

According to Lockwood, in 1868 officials at the Treasury Department again urged Congress to approve higher salaries for its women employees, but the legislators, concerned with the government's expanding postwar budget, said no.[42] This result infuriated her and she decided to get involved. New to writing legislative proposals, she turned to Andrew Boyle, a friend from the UFA. Boyle was clerk to the House Committee on Education and Labor, headed by Tennessee Representative Samuel M. Arnell. He helped her to draft an antidiscrimination law. They took their proposal to Arnell, who, in the winter of 1870, signaled his support, perhaps after visits from NWSA delegates.

On March 21 Arnell introduced "A bill to do justice to the female employees of the Government, and for other purposes." Numbered H.R. 1571, it was read twice and assigned to his committee for preliminary debate.[43] In its original form, the proposal attacked all forms of employment discrimination and forbade the use of discriminatory hiring practices in any branch of the civil service, requiring that departmental examinations "be of the same character for persons of both sexes." The Arnell bill was the first major legislation introduced in the Congress of the United States that addressed sex discrimination in the federal departments. Lockwood had reason to believe that it might succeed. The government had been flooded with demands for action on pension, patent, and homestead filings. Federal departments were desperate to keep up with the flood of business and pressed to hire good workers. Lockwood thought that this bill would bring forward the best people and show that the federal government could influence employment practices around the country for the better. To her mind, it was a perfect example of the kind of reform that a Radical Republican Congress should foster, as it embodied fundamental principles of fairness and equal opportunity.

Working with Boyle and Arnell, the former teacher and would-be lawyer fashioned a campaign to win passage of the bill. She quickly discovered a mix of viewpoints among Arnell's colleagues. A number of representatives supported equalizing the salaries of male and female clerks, but other legislators were skeptical on the question of equal pay, and completely opposed to giving women fair consideration in hiring and promotion. Lockwood had two strategies: she lobbied her position in private meetings on the Hill, while drumming up public support through a petition drive. As was common practice among activists, she placed notices in various newspapers describing the legislation. Interested readers were requested to cut out the notice, sign it, and then circulate it among friends and coworkers.

Lockwood also thought that the endorsement of both woman suffrage organizations would be important, and arranged to travel to New York, where the National and the American were each meeting. She gathered hundreds of signatures and, in separate interviews, asked leaders of the two groups for backing.[44] Consistent with Stanton and Anthony's interest in labor reform, the National readily endorsed the bill. She struck out with the Boston-based AWSA, writing later that Lucy Stone had turned her down because "the proposition did not come from Boston."[45]

House and Senate members debated the bill throughout the spring of 1870. Laughter had accompanied the introduction of the radical proposal, but the discussion devoted to its various measures was lengthy, serious, and revealing.[46] Three questions dogged the debate: Was it just to pay women less than men for the same work? Was it only fair to open all grades of clerkship to women? Could the government afford to compensate women at the same rate as men? Lockwood was disappointed when, in marking up the bill, the House Education and Labor Committee axed several of its key provisions. By June the bill had been transformed into an amendment attached to the federal government's general appropriations act.

The proposal fared better in the Senate, where the legislation was also reworked into an amendment but one that would more explicitly equalize salaries and prohibit sex discrimination in hiring and promotion. When the House again took up the matter on June 10 and 11, Lockwood's most constant supporters acknowledged that the Senate amendment (a reasonable approximation of the original bill) would cost the government hundreds of thousands of dollars. Demonstrating a commitment to human dignity and justice, these legislators insisted that the final voting should be guided by fairness, not economy. Illinois Representative John Farnsworth stated the case: "Whether it involves an expenditure of $400,000, or twice that amount, I propose that a woman doing just the same work as a man shall receive just as much money for her work—I do not care whether the amount be billions or dimes."[47]

But New Hampshire Republican Jacob Benton disagreed, laying out his own blunt statement of the issue: "As I understand the matter, a large number of female clerks have positions in various Departments of this Government, in the interest of economy, and for the purpose of saving the public money. That is the reason why they have got these offices."[48] He argued that nowhere in America were women compensated as well as these clerks. Other opponents of the bill took up this claim in the next day's debate. Women government clerks employed at an annual salary of nine hundred dollars a year received seventeen dollars each week, and Arkansas's Anthony Rogers said that if northern factory girls earned only two and three dollars a week, female government clerks in Washington should be content.[49]

Arnell responded with a speech that affirmed the breadth of the issue and the depth of the discord. Lockwood listened in the gallery as he said that his bill did have a wider object "than merely to serve the interests of these female clerks."[50] The question affected the interests of all of the working women of the country: "The mere recognition on the part of the American Congress of the legal right of women to equal work and equal pay for that work cannot be overestimated. It will indirectly increase the pay and wages of the factory girls." The 37-year-old congressman, one of the truest champions Lockwood would ever find, continued with a stark and radical assessment of social relations:

> Man has been unjust to woman. What we call civilization from age to age has brought to man wider freedom, yet has but little relaxed the iron subjugation of woman. None but women are treated as political pariahs; and now that we are engaged as a nation in breaking up the serfdoms of the world I would have this injustice and barbarism of the past consigned to its tomb. Yet I am gravely told that this will upset our social system. My opinion is that it will correct great and long-standing evils. The poor pay of woman is an undervaluation of her as a human being.

In the end the conservatives prevailed. The Senate amendment that would have raised the salaries of women clerks to those of men doing similar work was defeated in favor of one proposed by the House Committee on Appropriations, which stated

> [t]hat the heads of the several departments are hereby authorized to appoint female clerks, who may be found to be competent and worthy, to any of the grades of clerkships known to the law, in the respective departments, with the compensation belonging to the class to which they may be appointed, but the number of first, second, third, and fourth class clerks shall not be increased by this section.[51]

For Lockwood lobbying the Arnell bill had been a difficult but thorough immersion in congressional politics. Through Boyle and Arnell she had gained access to members of the House and Senate, and had won their respect for her advocacy work. Eight years later several of these congressmen would prove important in her fight to win women lawyers the right to practice in federal courts. Most critically, during the nearly four months in which the Arnell bill moved through Congress, she observed the game of political compromise first-hand. She learned that large principles often did not survive the play of politics but that a savvy representative could maneuver and win enactment of a more limited measure. This is just what Arnell had done. Broad principle was sacrificed in the name of a modest but nonetheless affirmative statement by Congress in the matter of equal employment rights.

Lockwood spoke of the Arnell legislation as an important contribution to the lives of working women. Salary figures collected by the Treasury and Interior Departments suggest that the legislation did, in fact, help women. In the decade of the 1870s, the percentage of women in positions at Treasury paying more than nine hundred dollars increased from 4 to 20 percent.[52] Yet while the new law urged that fair consideration be given to women's employment, a culture of patronage and patriarchy continued to nourish the discretionary powers of politicians and federal agency officials. In September 1875, Lura McNall told readers of her *Lockport Daily Journal* column about Washington that the government needed a better merit system and that she had recently heard it rumored that the new U.S. treasurer was as likely as his predecessor to hand out jobs according to the looks and charms of female applicants.[53]

4

Becoming a Lawyer

No woman shall degrade herself by practicing law ... if I can save her. I think the clack of these possible Portias will never be heard at Dwight's moot courts. "Women's Rights-women" are uncommonly loud & offensive of late. I loathe the lot.

George Templeton Strong, a founder of Columbia
University Law School, Diary entry, October 9, 1869

In antebellum America the profession of law belonged to men, who, in accordance with tradition, passed on their knowledge through legal apprenticeships held by their sons and nephews and neighbors' boys. When the Lockwoods married in 1868 there were no women attorneys in the District. Belva had begun her private study of law shortly before the marriage and found that she loved reading legal commentaries. She could not, however, find a lawyer willing to take her on as an apprentice.[1] In October 1869, Ezekiel's fellow parishioner, the Reverend George Samson, invited the couple to attend his lecture at Washington's Columbian Law School, where he was president. This invitation marked the beginning of Lockwood's public struggle to become an attorney and to join the small sorority of pioneers still unknown to her— Barkaloo, Couzins, Kepley, Myra Bradwell, Arabella Mansfield, and Charlotte E. Ray—who had also set out to open the profession of law to women.[2]

Columbian College had been founded by Baptists in 1821. The Law Department, abandoned in 1828, had been revived and in 1869 was offering lectures in the late afternoon and evening in order to encourage the enrollment of government clerks.[3] Samson's decision was part of a national movement to institutionalize legal training by moving apprentice education out of law offices and into university classrooms.

On the day that Lockwood visited Columbian, she was approaching her thirty-ninth birthday, the mother of two daughters, one barely a toddler. She described herself to a census taker as "keeping house," although she worked as a rental agent and helped her husband with his claims business.[4] She told people that she had "wearied" of teaching, and believed that law "offered more diversity, more facilities for improvement, better pay, and a chance to rise in the world."[5] While the profession was closed to women, Lockwood had, as she put it, a "mania" for law and counted, among her friends and UFA colleagues, many unconventional professional women who no doubt urged her on.

The Lockwoods went to Samson's lecture at a time when, with regular discipline, Belva was reading the major legal authorities of her time, William Blackstone and James Kent. She gave herself daily assignments, having set her sights on winning admission to one of the new law school programs like Columbian that were hungry for students.[6] After listening to Samson's lecture, she returned to the school a second time and then, before a third lecture, presented herself for matriculation, ready to pay the entrance fee.[7]

Her radical act quickly became a matter of public attention. An article in Washington's *Morning News* describing the law school's opening exercises observed, "the noticeable feature of the evening was the presence in the school of the irrepressible Mrs. Lockwood, of Union League Hall—women's rights discussion notoriety. It is understood that she is anxious to study for the bar, and will endeavor to be admitted to the school."[8] Many people thought her rash and provocative, and once again, as with her application for the consul position, she found her way blocked. The entrance fee that she offered was refused on the pretext that the question of her admission needed review by the faculty.

On October 7, 1869, a brief note arrived from President Samson: "Madam,—after due consultation [the faculty] have considered that such admission would not be expedient, as it would be likely to distract the attention of the young men."[9] Belva later described Samson's action as a slap in the face, a dismissal of her rights and privileges because they were thought to conflict with those of men.[10] At the same time, officials at Columbian refused the offer of Mrs. Maria M. Carter to endow scholarships for female students in the undergraduate program, a gift that would have initiated coeducation at the school.[11]

Samson's letter put Ezekiel in the difficult role of supporting his wife's ambitions while not antagonizing his church colleague. He counseled Belva to keep silent, but reporters got hold of the story—quite possibly from the rejected candidate—and came around to speak with her, and to see the letter. Ezekiel protested but his wife, asserting her independence and her cause, read Samson's reply to the local press, who published it.[12] It went out on the wire service. Two days later the *Evening Star* reprinted an article from the *New York Commercial* agreeing that coeducational law school was a poor idea, although suggesting that "an exception might be made in favor of these ladies on the shady side of forty, who are classed under the head 'Rawboned,' and wear spectacles."[13] A flurry of talk continued but eventually the furor, and hard feelings, died down.

Lockwood was anxious to study for the bar but, not wishing to leave Washington and the family claims office, she continued to face the problem of *where*. Hearing Couzins and achieving a certain success with the Arnell bill only increased her "irrepressible" interest in the law. But only weeks after the final vote on the bill, tragedy struck the Lockwood home when eighteen-month-old Jessie sickened and died. In the Victorian idiom of her time, Belva memorialized her "little blossom," writing that Jessie had been a comfort and blessing "and had awakened . . . maternal love to a depth that an uncultivated individual can never comprehend. But the flower wilted, and . . . the immortal gem of purity was set by the Eternal Jeweler in his own coronet to be worn eternally."[14]

Lockwood faced tragedy and disappointment throughout her life. Her genius, first demonstrated after Uriah's death, lay in accepting misfortune and moving ahead with new plans. Jessie's death was no different. Determined to be resilient, she resumed her public activities, using the well-being of the community to justify a short period of mourning: "[O]ther people's children were soon to be worse than dead, if a prohibitory law were not passed in the District."[15] She joined the acrimonious debate over proposals to regulate alcohol and obtained seven hundred signatures on a petition to be presented to the government. She never again wrote publicly about Jessie, whose death seemed to increase her desire to become a lawyer.

Sometime in 1870, she thought she had found a way. In that year officials of the District's new National University Law School, perhaps in order to lard enrollment in the program, invited a number of women, including Lockwood, to attend classes. She later insisted that the offer was "part of [their] plan to admit women to membership on the same terms as men," and that the program would be coeducational.[16] Early in

1871, fifteen women, including Belva and Lura, enrolled in National's law program.[17] Most of the ladies, Lockwood wrote, matriculated "as a novelty . . . certainly without any adequate idea of the amount of labor involved."[18] They believed that the school's administrators sympathized with the idea of equal rights, but when they came to class, the women discovered that while they would be permitted to attend certain lectures with the male students, their regular recitations would be sex-segregated. Lockwood called this a compromise between prejudice and progress that the women accepted.[19]

The male students, however, were locked into their old-fashioned ideas. They rebelled at any presence of the opposite sex, sending up what Lockwood described as a "growl," with some of them declaring they would not graduate with women.[20] The administration capitulated and the female students were notified that they could no longer attend the lectures. Under pressure, the officials gave them the option of completing their studies in a completely segregated program. The rancor and the work prompted most of the women to leave at the end of the first quarter. A few ladies, including Lura, stayed for a year and then resigned. Only Lockwood and Lydia Hall, a government clerk who was also a member of the UFA, completed the course of study.

Despite the behavior of the male students, the two women finished their studies with the expectation of being granted a law degree. If officials had ever said otherwise, Lockwood did not let on, and she was furious when the faculty told the two women that because they had not studied long enough they were not going to receive diplomas, or be permitted on the stage with the men on graduation day.[21] Lockwood was already giving legal advice to friends and neighbors and called the school's decision "a heavy blow to my aspirations, as the diploma would have been the entering wedge into the court and saved me the weary contest which followed."[22] She knew that, as a matter of diploma privilege, the successful candidates of a graduating law class would be presented as a group for admission to the District of Columbia bar. Without their diplomas, she and Hall would be excluded, and would not become members of the bar.

Bar admission was a contentious issue in post–Civil War America. In the late eighteenth century, following the Revolutionary War, the American legal profession had begun—state by state, sometimes county by county—to shape a system of training and accreditation distinct from the one used in England. American lawyers settled upon apprenticeship, and later law schools, rather than replication of the ancient English "juridical universities," the Inns of the Court and Chancery.[23] The course of implementation of this American system was not smooth. Early law schools were founded and became insolvent; apprenticeships varied in length and quality of supervision. Legal knowledge was frequently considered to be insufficient, and practitioners bankrupt in their personal conduct. As a remedy, lawyers established bar associations hoping to regularize expectations concerning professional knowledge and moral character. This system of professional licensing became popular, although in some states legislators tried to limit the growth of such associations, describing them as undesirable protectionist leagues.[24]

Hall and Lockwood refused to be defeated by the denial of diploma privilege. In late April 1872 they turned to Francis Miller, a colleague from the Washington women's suffrage movement, and asked him to press their cause before the local bar examination committee. As a result of his intercession, the committee agreed to administer oral tests to the two women, who appeared before a panel of local practitioners. The men tested the two women and declared each proficient in the law. Apparently without warning, however, anonymous members of the bar spoke against the admission of the women to the D.C. bar and successfully blocked their admission.[25]

For a time Lockwood yielded "quite ungracefully to the inevitable," while Hall, a woman past forty, "solaced" herself by marrying and soon after left the city.[26] Lockwood wrote caustically of Hall's defection, saying she supposed her friend had become "merged" in her husband but that she would not be so easily squelched.[27] After a respectable interval, Lockwood visited Miller and again requested that he nominate her for the bar. In late July the sympathetic attorney petitioned for her admission, and her application was referred, once more, to an examining committee. She said that the members came together "with evident reluctance," administering an oral examination that lasted three days.[28]

Several weeks passed, days of unrelenting summer heat, but the committee did not submit the necessary evaluation. Lockwood filed a complaint with D.C. Supreme Court Justice David K. Cartter, but still nothing happened. Cartter may have requested a third committee, or he may have pressed the second group to make its report, reminding its members that the judges of his court recently had urged that the word "male" be struck from local bar qualifications.[29] The applicant, full of fury, had nothing but stinging words for the men of Washington's bar. They were, she said, old-time conservatives and culprits "opposed to innovation."[30] In the matter of sex, these men had created a protection- ist league. Name calling, however, did not assuage her misery: she told friends that she felt "blocked" and "discouraged." But she was also "the irrepressible Mrs. Lockwood," who quickly declared that she "had not the remotest idea of giving up."[31] Becoming a lawyer was a dream that she had nurtured for a long time and, as one of Washington's notorious women's rights ladies, she felt great pressure not to look foolish. Ezekiel's health was beginning to fail. That, too, weighed on her, mak- ing her all the more anxious to take over support of the household. But without bar membership she could do little more than file pension claims and chase small cases in police court. She wanted to establish a full general legal practice, and had come too far to let go of the idea that a qualified woman should have the same rights and privileges accorded men. At summer's end, however, even the irrepressible Mrs. Lockwood seemed to have been stopped.

Fate stepped in when New York newspaper editor Theodore Tilton of- fered her a temporary job, one few women would consider. He wanted her to make a three-month tour of the South as a canvassing agent and correspondent for his newspaper, *The Golden Age*. She would travel alone, make her own arrangements, and be responsible for finding local informants. The trip would take her, a northerner, to some of the most socially conservative towns in America, where her solitary traveling, college education, and support of woman suffrage would mark her as a very different sort of person.

Tilton and Lockwood knew one another from suffrage circles. He was a respected journalist who, the year before, had started the news- paper he called "a free parliament," open to all points of view.[32] She had engaged him for a lecture sponsored by the Universal Franchise Asso- ciation, and had met him again when she joined the loosely organized group supporting the presidential aspirations of New York publisher Victoria Woodhull.

In these meetings Lockwood must have impressed Tilton as some- one who could handle a tough assignment. Despondent over her stalled legal career, she accepted his offer, saying she was "desperate enough for any adventure."[33] She also calculated that this trip might launch her as a journalist or lecturer, salaried work that could be combined with a legal career. Although technically not a law school graduate, Lockwood felt that her unique status as a woman attorney would play to her advantage. She had already drawn on this notoriety in the spring of 1872 when she delivered several paid lectures in upstate New York. Writing had long appealed to her and working for Tilton would give her the chance to break into journalism with a national paper.

Before she headed south, Tilton made another request: in addition to writing and canvassing for his paper, he asked if she would campaign for Horace Greeley, the presidential candidate backed by *The Golden Age*. Greeley, a well-known reformer and New York *Tribune* newspaper editor, had won the nomination of the newly formed Liberal Republican Party at its Cincinnati convention. He was a controversial candidate, criticized for his lack of experience in elective office, his support for a conciliatory policy toward the former Confederate states, and his refusal to endorse woman suffrage.[34]

Lockwood agreed to Tilton's request despite her otherwise outspoken support for women's right to vote. She did not discuss her reasons. Other reformers had already joined the Greeley camp. In addition to Tilton, who was managing the candidate's campaign, the famous Anna Dickinson had abandoned the Republicans for the upstart editor. Senator Charles Sumner, the great voice of racial justice, also had endorsed Greeley. But woman suffrage leader Elizabeth Cady Stanton had not minced words when she said she would rather see "Beezlebub (*sic*) President than Greeley."[35]

Funds were low in the Lockwood household, and she and Ezekiel were uncertain whether she would ever win the fight to become an attorney. Like other activists, she may have found it necessary to compromise her politics for financial reasons. After all, Stanton and Anthony had accepted funds for their newspaper from the notorious racist George Train. Trying to accommodate her commitment to women's rights, during the tour she focused on Greeley's "soft peace" proposals to end Radical Reconstruction and his long history as a temperance man and remained silent on the subject of his opposition to woman suffrage.

The trip began in late July. Lockwood was expected to solicit subscribers, to find opportunities to speak in support of the Greeley-Brown ticket (Benjamin Gratz Brown, governor of Missouri, was the vice-presidential candidate), and to conduct informal political polling. She went first to North Carolina, then went on to northern Georgia, and then swept across Alabama and Mississippi, turning north into Tennessee. From Memphis, she traveled to Nashville, and then went north again to Louisville, Kentucky, on to Indianapolis, east to Columbus, Ohio, and, finally, home to Washington through West Virginia and past Harper's Ferry. The trip and the work provided her with an apprenticeship in the rigors of travel and the basics of grass roots campaigning.

In each new town, Lockwood would arrive, visit the owner or editor of the local newspaper (seeking an endorsement for Greeley and information about the community), sell pictures of the candidates, and canvass informally for the Greeley-Brown ticket. Where possible, she gave a campaign speech. In some towns the local press mocked her. The editor of the Republican-controlled New Bern, North Carolina, *Times* offered up an extravagant denunciation, telling his readers that this newcomer was a "women rights mulatto Democrat Greeleyocrat Spiritualist free-love agent."[36]

Elsewhere, however, she was shown considerable courtesy. In Huntsville, Alabama, she was offered the use of the courthouse for her campaign talk, causing the northern suffrage newspaper, *The Woman's Journal*, to remark that the revolution was still going on.[37] The Huntsville audience had never before heard a woman speak in public. Lockwood reported that they listened with interest and respect and that she was later received by the town's prominent citizens. In other states she met with governors and mayors. If these officials thought a northern woman touring the South for Greeley a bit "mad," they kept it to themselves.[38]

Tilton published a dozen of Belva's articles. They were travel accounts in the style made popular by Dickens, de Tocqueville, and Fanny Trollope in their antebellum romps across America. But unlike the Europeans Lockwood had a campaign to report, requiring that she mix the pleasantries of travel with political observation. In Raleigh she described maturing corn and full-blooming cotton fields, scarce money, and a dull economy. Everywhere, she revealed her good feelings for the people of the South. In North Carolina she was happy to find "almost every white man and woman are for Greeley." He had been an enemy during the war and she thought it "magnanimous" that these Americans were now willing to support him.[39] Given that she was an emissary of the "reconciliation" candidate, this was the appropriate stance to adopt, an attitude that was also consistent with her own deepening opposition to war and conflict. She also reported on the "colored voters" who, she wrote, having heard the inflammatory scare talk of Republican politicians, could be expected to support Grant.[40]

Tilton published her most interesting article, "Southern Immigration," in mid-October. Written in Memphis, and very much mirroring Greeley's reconciliation and migration policies, the entire column was a plea for northerners to invest in, and move to, the South, particularly the fertile country she had just crossed on the Memphis and Charleston Railroad. These states, she wrote, "cry out for *capital* and *labor*."[41] They were "desolated and impoverished" by the war but have rich natural resources. "It is false!" she told her readers, for northerners to believe that they are not wanted, or would not be safe in the South. She acknowledged the Ku Klux Klan's six-year reign of terror but argued that violent incidents were now isolated and exaggerated, and that "the spirit of a whole people" could not be judged by exceptional instances of wrongdoing: "Southerners are not all doves and lambs, but they are not hyenas, nor are they donkeys."[42]

While Greeley's name was never mentioned, the logic of his "soft peace" policy flowed naturally from Lockwood's argument, and from her closing words: "There are as many true-hearted men and women, in proportion to the population at the South as in the North. Human nature is the same here as in the North. Kindness begets kindness, and charity leads to charity. The issues of the war are settled. Why not come together . . . Americans once more."[43] "Southern Immigration" was the most political column that Lockwood contributed to *The Golden Age*, safe in its support of Greeley but disappointing in its failure to explain that a tense, and not infrequently violent, struggle for control raged across much of the former Confederacy six years after the armistice.[44] She consciously chose to present an optimistic picture, failing to discuss the growing exclusion of freedmen from the polls and betting on hard work and market forces to revive the South and promote well-being for former slaves. She did not avoid the discussion of race but was cautious, perhaps feeling herself insufficiently knowledgeable to say more, or concerned about contradicting Greeley in some way.

In November Lockwood completed the tour, saying little more about the campaign and nothing about the women's issues that were otherwise so important to her. Back in Washington, however, she forced the issue, presenting Tilton with a column devoted to the accomplishments of the professional women of the capital. In "Women of Washington" she identified and praised women who dared to think and act on their convictions, an "advance guard" in public opinion.[45] She named doctors, teachers, writers, journalists, and government clerks. She denounced as ridiculous the idea that the few American women who had been permitted to train as physicians were "unsexed" because of exposure to dissecting rooms and hospital wards. Without raising the question of suffrage, Lockwood made her point: Washington (and by implication, the nation) was full of ordinary women and extraordinary women—educated, sensible, independent—deserving of the vote.

After incumbent Ulysses S. Grant was declared president, Lockwood decided to resume her effort to obtain a law school diploma. She applied to matriculate in the law program at Georgetown College but was bluntly notified by officials that the school was not a coeducational institution.[46] After this rebuff, she began to attend lectures at Howard University's law school but then stopped, saying that "the fight was getting monotonous and decidedly one-sided."[47]

Lockwood presented the fight as one-sided but, in fact, the men of Washington were divided over the question of women's rights. Debate of various franchise bills, the fair employment legislation sponsored by Arnell, and male membership in the UFA attested to support of women's aspirations and rights in certain quarters. This included a number of the judges of Washington's lowest courts. Lockwood had been giving legal advice and occasionally arguing in court. The first notice of this lawyering appeared in one of Lura's column's for the *Lockport Daily Journal*, where she reported that "Mrs. Lockwood" had appeared in early February 1872 at a District court "as attorney for her husband, and plead [sic] and won her suit amid many congratulations."[48] In a later account Lockwood wrote that when she had "ventured to bring suit on a contract in a justice court" the procedure was considered so "novel" that it was telegraphed all over the country by the Associated Press.[49] Practical, persuasive, and likable, she had won to her cause several men of the bench: the justices of the peace in the District, Judge William B. Snell of the Police Court, and Judge Abram B. Olin of the Probate Court had notified her that she would be recognized as counsel in the trial of any case in their courts.[50]

This encouragement pleased her, but it was not enough. She wanted her degree. Only after she held a diploma could she make the point that women were entitled to, and could succeed at, equal educational and professional opportunities. In the late summer of 1873 Lockwood decided to renew the fight with officials of the National University, an institution, she later wrote, that "shut up like an oyster" after admitting her and one or two African-American men.[51] Instead of petitioning the university's chancellor or faculty, she wrote to President Grant, who, by virtue of his political office, was president, ex officio, of National University. Two letters went out on September 3 under her signature. In one, presumably the first to be written, she documented the facts of her case, and the "manifest injustice" experienced by the fifteen women matriculants. The tone reflected a sober supplicant while the text observed the rules of decorum:

> Sept. 3, 1873
>
> Dear Sir: . . . . Sometime in February 1871 I was invited to enter this Institution as a student . . . and to use my influence to induce other ladies to join, with the assurance, that if faithful to the recitations, we should receive diplomas at the same time with a class of young men. . . . We went regularly to the recitations, and for two or three times were admitted to the lectures, when this means of knowledge was denied us, without any explanation being given. . . . [O]nly two, Miss Lydia S. Hall (now Mrs. Graffam) and myself completed the Course. We continued faithfully, patiently, and with the deepest interest so long as the recitations were continued; studying through the long hot days of Summer. . . . Judge our disappointment when diplomas were refused us on the ground that we had not studied long enough. . . . Having received a liberal education, and graduated in a College composed mostly of young men in the State of New York as far back as 1857 . . . I cannot appreciate or understand this (to me) manifest injustice. I am not only wounded in my feelings, but actually deprived of an honest means of livelihood, without any assignable cause.[52]

Apparently, only hours after posting this letter, she again wrote Grant. The envelope addressed to the president contained nothing more than a note, short and alarmingly rude.

> September 3, 1873
>
> Sir,—You are, or you are not, President of the National University Law School. If you are its President, I desire to say to you that I have passed through the curriculum of study in this school, and am entitled to, and demand my diploma. If you are not its President, then I ask

that you take your name from its papers, and not hold out to the world to be what you are not."[53]

President Grant did not answer her, but two weeks later the university chancellor presented Lockwood with her long-denied diploma.

Obtaining the diploma was the key to bar admission. On September 24, 1873, the "culprits" so opposed to innovation stepped aside and Belva Lockwood was admitted to the District of Columbia bar. She became the second woman attorney in the capital, and one of the very few in the nation, to be licensed to practice law. Ironically, the first woman admitted to the District bar, Charlotte E. Ray, had enrolled at Howard Law School in 1870, completed the course of study, and won admission to the District bar in March of 1872, when the names of her entire class were forwarded to the bar committee. Ray was the daughter of the nationally prominent African-American minister Charles B. Ray. Had Lockwood attended Howard, she might never have had to endure "the weary contest." She never said why she had not started law school at Howard or why, when she attended lectures there after working for Tilton, she chose to quit. It seems less likely that "the fight was getting monotonous" than that she and Ezekiel could no longer afford the tuition. She did, however, maintain good relations with the faculty at Howard. She later received invitations to speak there and saw at least one of her female acolytes graduate from its law program.

In the nineteenth century most Americans felt that women would "unsex" or degrade themselves if they undertook professional work. Female brains were thought to be unfit for the strain of mental exercise. Wombs, it was also believed, could be weakened by mental exertion. Women first broke through the barriers of workplace prejudice in the field of teaching. With greater struggle, before the Civil War, Elizabeth Blackwell and a handful of her sisters opened American medical education to members of their sex. They faced resistance from male physicians but they succeeded, in part, because of the belief that women doctors should attend female patients.[54] In the 1850s Jennie Jones invented women's-interest news for the daily newspapers and was thought to be the first woman to work in a newsroom.[55] Organized religion also resisted women's importuning. Olympia Brown matriculated at St. Lawrence Theological School in Canton, New York, and was ordained to the Universalist ministry in June 1863, but she was a lonely pioneer.

The hostility toward women with professional aspirations was so great that only the very brave voiced their interest in public. Lockwood was not apprehensive about her place in the vanguard, and while she strongly supported women's rights, she did not enter the field of law specifically to plead the cause of her sisters. Rather, she expressed a love for reading law and desired greater professional status and financial security. She loved the fact that law was a man's game and that it could be "a stepping stone to greatness." But she would always smart at the way she had been treated. Nearly three decades after she had been barred from graduation she retold, with unvarnished sarcasm, the story of her first months as a woman attorney improperly denied a license. "I had," she wrote, "already booked a large number of government claims, in which I had been recognized by the heads of the different Departments as attorney: so that I was not compelled, like my young brothers of the bar who did not wish to graduate with a woman, to sit in my office and wait for cases."[56]

5

Notorious Ladies

We cannot forget, even in this glad hour, that while all men of every race, and clime, and condition, have been invested with the full rights of citizenship, under our hospitable flag, all women still suffer the degradation of disfranchisement.

Declaration of Rights of the Women of the United States
by the National Woman Suffrage Association, July 4, 1876

On July 4, 1876, Richard Henry Lee stood in Philadelphia's Independence Hall and read aloud the Declaration of Independence. As he sat down Susan B. Anthony, barred from participating in the centennial celebration, rose from her seat and marched past foreign guests and American officials to the speaker's stand, where she thrust a copy of the "Declaration of Rights of the Women of the United States by the National Woman Suffrage Association" into the hands of President Grant's representative. Followed by a small group of supporters, Anthony retraced her steps while scattering copies of the offending document among the invited guests. As the women had planned, she then mounted a platform erected at the front of Independence Hall. With Matilda Gage holding an umbrella to protect her friend from the intense noonday sun, she read the declaration "to an immense concourse of people."[1]

The hour was sorely needed political theater. After repeated defeats in legislatures and in the courts, the cause of woman suffrage had stalled. NWSA members had hoped to revive interest on the occasion of the nation's hundredth birthday by issuing an attention-grabbing declaration. They had asked for, and had been denied, a place on the official centennial program. General Joseph Hawley, president of the organizing committee, told the NWSA that their "slight request," if granted, "would be the event of the day—the topic of discussion to the exclusion of all others."[2]

Lockwood waited for Anthony a few blocks away at the First Unitarian Church, where the Nationals had arranged to hold their own celebration of the nation's birthday. She had signed the declaration and now sat at the front of the church, one of several speakers scheduled to tell a warmly approving audience about "the tyranny and injustice of the nation toward one-half its people."[3]

In its official record, the editors of the *History of Woman Suffrage* proclaimed the meeting a great success. Still, the fact remained that, despite a great deal of lobbying, public demonstration, and a test of woman's disfranchisement that had been heard by the U.S. Supreme Court, in July 1876 Americans showed little inclination to tackle the question of women's rights. Equality challenged settled arrangements with which most citizens were content to live.

If, in 1876, Americans were satisfied with the arrangements that disadvantaged women it was not because the notorious suffrage ladies of Lockwood's acquaintance had not done everything in their power to educate them, and to change the law. And in a startling declaration on April 2, 1870, one of the most notorious announced herself as a candidate in the 1872 presidential campaign. Her name was Victoria Woodhull, and she wanted to create a new reform party that would challenge the power and corruption of the Republicans.

Like Lockwood, Woodhull was a work in progress. At the age of fifteen, she had stepped out of a chaotic childhood into a hard-luck marriage to an alcoholic. In her twenties, however, encouraged by her sister Tennie Claflin's success as a spiritual medium, and urged forward by James Harvey Blood, her second husband, Woodhull became a medical clairvoyant.

The sisters were good at their vocations, earning substantial fees. In 1867 they decided to move to New York City, where they hoped to solicit the backing of Commodore Cornelius Vanderbilt. In the spring of 1868, the sisters presented him with engraved business cards. Beauty, brains, and business credentials won them his immediate attention, and the three formed an extraordinary relationship that brought the two women fame, wealth, and, for Victoria, the opportunity to speak forcefully on the subject of woman's unequal status.

Woodhull made her first recorded visit to a woman suffrage convention in January 1869. She traveled to Washington, D.C., where she listened to Senator Pomeroy argue that the existing Constitution granted to all citizens, including women, the right to vote. In the months that followed she heard about Francis and Virginia Minor, two activists from St. Louis who, like Pomeroy, were making the case that women already had the right to vote and that no amendment specifically to guarantee woman suffrage was necessary. The Minors contended that if, under the U.S. Constitution, women had not always been entitled to elective franchise, the recently ratified Fourteenth Amendment enfranchised them as a right of national citizenship. In stating that "all persons born or naturalized in the United States" were "citizens of the United States and of the State wherein they reside," the Fourteenth Amendment established a national definition of citizenship that, when joined to subsequent clauses prohibiting states from making or enforcing "any law which shall abridge the privileges or immunities of citizens of the United States," forbade the denial of suffrage.

Most suffrage women knew nothing about Woodhull until early 1870 when the New York newspapers and Stanton and Anthony's suffrage paper, *Revolution*, began covering Woodhull, Claflin & Co., America's first female stockbrokers, a business established with Vanderbilt's help.[4] Woodhull worked quietly in the first months of 1870, pulling together a team of advisors that included Blood, radical philosopher Stephen Pearl Andrews, and Massachusetts congressman Benjamin Butler. In April, pronouncing herself "the most prominent representative of the only unrepresented class in the republic," she declared herself a presidential candidate, saying, "While others of my sex devoted themselves to a crusade against the laws that shackle the women of the country, I asserted my individual independence. . . . I proved it by successfully engaging in business. . . . I boldly entered the arena of politics. . . . I therefore claim the right to speak for the unenfranchised women of the country."[5]

Woodhull was the first woman to enter an American presidential race. Suffrage activists were electrified by her decision, but nervous about her radical social views. She supported sweeping change in relations between capital and labor as well as between the sexes. Reporters charged her with advocating free love. She made no effort to hide her personal and political philosophies, voicing them in *Woodhull & Claflin's Weekly*, the newspaper that she had established, which covered finance, culture, and politics. Woodhull used the publication to promote her candidacy and to write about women's rights, including the argument made by the Minors and her own view that suffrage was a civil right of all citizens.[6]

Late in 1870 Woodhull traveled to Washington, prepared to test her ability to influence the suffrage debate. She had learned from her friend Benjamin Butler that Julian's Sixteenth Amendment bill, viewed as a pesky piece of business, would never come out of committee. The news pleased her because, like the Minors, Woodhull thought that the Fourteenth and Fifteenth Amendments made a woman suffrage amendment superfluous. She had come to Washington to argue that Congress now only needed to pass "enabling legislation" similar to the Enforcement Act of May 31, 1870 (prohibiting state officials from discriminating against voters on the basis of race).[7]

Woodhull presented this written argument in "The Memorial of Victoria C. Woodhull." Four days before Christmas, members of the House and Senate received copies of the document along with the request that the question of a declaratory bill be referred to each chamber's judiciary committee. And then, in a blunt test of her star power, the publicity-savvy candidate arranged to make a personal plea for action before the House Judiciary Committee. Woodhull's January 11, 1871, appearance, organized with the help of Butler, was a coup for her, and for the suffrage movement. Despite the increasing frequency with which women lobbied members of Congress, as Lockwood had done in support of the Arnell bill, women's public testimony in one of the Capitol's smoky committee rooms remained unusual.

Lockwood, invited to be present along with other leaders from the UFA, was fascinated by Woodhull's argument.[8] She listened a second time when Woodhull crossed town and repeated her presentation before delegates attending a national woman suffrage convention. The delegates agreed to make the Minor-Woodhull position their "New Departure." The new strategy had considerable appeal with its call for direct action rather than a long, uncertain wait for a woman suffrage amendment. An agenda took shape that emphasized passage of enabling legislation, efforts to register and vote, and court challenges when local officials refused to register women or to accept their ballots.

Lockwood immediately saw the possibility of using the Woodhull-Minor theory of woman suffrage to influence Senate debate on a new District of Columbia governance bill. Only days after Woodhull's presentation, in collaboration with UFA colleagues Caroline B. Winslow and

Susan A. Edson, she prepared two memorials intended to convince members of Congress that District women had the right to vote. They had met defeat in 1867 when the universal suffrage bill was voted down. Now, however, they had the carefully constructed New Departure argument to work with.[9]

It is likely that Lockwood, having just entered law school, authored most of the text. In the first memorial she argued that the original Constitution and Bill of Rights gave women the right to vote although she acknowledged that the constitutional text was ambiguous. She told the senators that they could not know the intentions of the Framers, and must construe the rights and obligations of citizenship from the document's language. She then repeated the much-observed fact that the Constitution, as originally written, contained no "negative declaration," no language that prohibited women from voting. Therefore, she wrote, any state or territorial government, or Congress on behalf of the District of Columbia, could enact declaratory legislation granting women the right to vote. Wyoming had done so and, in 1870, so had the territorial government of Utah. Like any good lawyer, she did not rest her case on one theory. American constitutional law, she observed, now embraced the additional guarantees of the Fourteenth and Fifteen Amendments, which must be read to include women in the national community of citizens entitled to vote, and to be protected in that right by the federal government.[10]

A second memorial outlined the cultural and political reasons for woman suffrage. Answering opponents who misrepresented man's greater position outside of the home, and contributions in war, Lockwood and her colleagues described woman's role as producer and taxpayer, and as a class that suffers under the "responsibilities and dangers of maternity."[11] Yet, despite these contributions to society the law treats her as "a mere chattel." Countering the nineteenth-century belief that women lacked the ability to reason, and thus to participate responsibly in the political life of the country, the memorial insisted that "[w]oman possesses the faculty of government, and cannot be deprived of its advantages without damage to the body politic." Pursuing this utilitarian political argument, they concluded the sober but hopeful lecture: "Man, deprived of female society degenerates rapidly, as may be seen in all communities composed of men alone. Doubtless the same would be true of woman. A perfect government can only come of a perfect manhood and womanhood with their efforts united for the common good."

Senator Pomeroy, honorary UFA president, arranged for the memorials to be introduced into the record on January 23, but Congress could not be persuaded to side with the women, and the attempt to win "impartial suffrage" in the District of Columbia failed. On February 27, 1871, the new law, locally referred to as the Organic Act, went into effect, with District voting still limited to men.[12] Perhaps inspired by Woodhull's candidacy, Lockwood responded to this defeat by trying to win a delegate's position at the nominating convention that was to select a District representative to sit in the Congress. She delivered a short speech and came within one vote of winning a place.[13]

While women in the territories of Wyoming and Utah had won the right to vote from their territorial governments, the experience of the women of Washington in the struggle for suffrage was far more typical. In general, there was little progress in the matter of woman suffrage. Julian's Sixteenth Amendment bill was dead in committee, and the declaratory act strategy had resulted in little gain. On January 30, 1871, a majority of the House Committee on the Judiciary, having considered Woodhull's "Memorial," issued a report that rejected the Minor-Woodhull argument in its entirety. Chairman John A. Bingham of Ohio wrote that neither the Fourteenth nor the Fifteenth Amendment granted women the right to vote and that, therefore, "it is not competent for the Congress of the United States to establish by law the right to vote without regard to sex in the several States of the Union."[14] It was the opinion of the committee that women could expect to be enfranchised only when public opinion deemed reform advisable and the people altered state constitutions and laws, or "if established in the courts."[15]

The failure of the federal enabling legislation strategy left movement leaders with little choice but to test the power of "New Departure" theory in the courts. In January 1871 Washington lawyer Albert G. Riddle, a staunch supporter of woman suffrage, told NWSA members that he would handle a test case of women's right to vote, appealing, if necessary, to the U.S. Supreme Court.[16] The National put out the message that women should attempt to register and to vote. "This action," said the NWSA principals, "not only serves the purpose of agitation of the whole question of suffrage, but it puts upon men, our brothers, the onus of refusing the votes of their fellow citizens, and compels them to show just cause for such proceeding."[17]

Washington women settled on a twofold test of their rights. They would appear before D.C. election officials and attempt to register and, on a local election day in April, they would try to vote. They believed that if the authorities refused to register them as voters, or to let them cast official ballots, they would have grounds for a test of their constitutional rights in a court of law.

On April 14, 1871, the late edition of the D.C. *Evening Star* announced that earlier in the day "a number of ladies of this District" had entered the City Hall. Once inside, the racially mixed group of women presented a petition to the president of the Board of Registration asking that their names be registered as qualified voters in the Territory of the District of Columbia.[18] It was the second time that week that suffrage women had appeared before the members of the board, seeking to register for an upcoming election. On this afternoon, Lockwood led the "advance guard" of men and women.[19] Her friend, Mary Walker, walked beside her. The two women, neither averse to publicity, carried bouquets, ready to bestow flowers on any board member who was prepared to approve the registration of women. Ezekiel stood behind his wife along with a Who's Who of Washington's professional and activist women. Frederick Douglass joined the demonstration. The suffragists crowded around the registration desks for two hours, taking down the names of the registrars and making speeches. At four o'clock the women received permission separately to approach the registrars. Dozens did so and, one by one, each application was rejected on the grounds that "under the law [Section 7 of the Organic Act] of the Territory [the District] none but males are entitled to register."[20]

The women had marched on City Hall, in part, to orchestrate an *event* that, by provoking the attention of the press, would keep the issue of woman suffrage alive and before the public. The *Evening Star*, loyal to the aspirations of women, was respectful, while articles published by the *National Republican* sported complaint and sarcasm.[21]

To recruit additional supporters and maintain the interest of the press, the women organized an information and strategy meeting. Notices were placed in the Washington newspapers inviting "Ladies of the District" to attend a gathering on April 18 at the Ladies Department of the business college run by activist Sara Spencer and her husband.[22] Sara Spencer opened the meeting by introducing A. G. Riddle. Washington was a small town, and it is likely that most of the people in the room knew him. Riddle, a former congressman, began with words of encouragement and then outlined the legal issues. He asserted that in returning their applications to the protesters, the Board of Registration had not only violated their constitutional rights but had also, he believed, committed a breach of the 1870 Enforcement Act. The act, passed out of concern for the political rights of freedmen, permitted an applicant who had been prohibited from registering to vote to go to the polls on Election Day with an affidavit stating that there had been wrongful action by the registrars. Riddle now urged the women to take copies of the affidavit that he had prepared, and to present themselves at their proper voting districts at the election on April 20.

Spencer and Lockwood each knew women who had been fired by the federal government after participating in the April 14 demonstration at City Hall.[23] And while the women had protested at City Hall as a group, their lawyer was now asking the would-be voters to go out on their own to their respective polling places. Despite the honored place of voting in the United States, polling was often carried out in taverns and other places considered inappropriate for women. Politicians spoke about "[h]igh party excitement" that led to violence and rude speech at the polls.[24] Ironically, *men's* election day behavior had become part of the argument against women's right to vote. One husband insisted that the polls were so vile that *he* would not go there to vote.[25]

Lockwood and her friends considered the possibility of heckling and violence, and decided they were willing to risk public ridicule. Sara Spencer made the practical suggestion that in each precinct as many ladies as possible get together "and present themselves as a body."[26] Riddle was relieved. He wanted at least some women to present themselves at the polls so that he would have two possible lawsuits, one against the Board of Registration for its refusal to register the women, and a second to challenge the anticipated rejection by the judges of election of the protesters' ballots.

On April 20, the women headed out to their precincts, hoping to join local men in voting for the District's delegate to Congress and member of D.C.'s governing council. Lockwood went to her polling place in the 12th District. The presiding official would not take her ballot but she stayed long enough to deliver a speech in support of women's rights.[27] As agreed among the women at their earlier meeting, she departed after saying, "I have done my duty."[28] She then accompanied her friend Lydia Hall to the 15th District, where her ballot was also refused.[29] The following day the *National Republican* praised the citizens of Washington for the chivalry that they showed in the face of "the un-womanly conduct of the applicants," whose action, wrote the editor, had been premeditated, "with the avowed object of testing in a court of law, the right to vote."[30]

Within days Riddle and his law partner, Francis Miller, had filed two cases at the District of Columbia Supreme Court: *Sara J. Spencer vs. Martin et al.* (The Board of Registration) and *Sarah E. Webster vs. Griffin et al.* (The Judges of Election).[31] Writs were served and pleadings entered. Money damages as provided by law were asked for each woman.[32] Although the lawyers acted quickly, the case was given a court date for mid-September. Meanwhile, Lockwood and her friends resumed their political appeals, this time to local officials. On July 14, 1871, Lockwood appeared before the District Committee of the House of Delegates on Laws and the Judiciary. She wrote Mary Walker, temporarily out of town, with an account of the meeting where the proposed equal pay bill for women employees of the District, as well as possible changes to the Organic Act, were to be discussed. The meeting had gone well. She had delivered a short speech and, by her reckoning, "completely annihilated the 7th Sec. [the males-only clause] of the Organic Act."[33] The committee members had not been argumentative and, after listening to Lockwood's talk, two representatives had come out in support of woman suffrage. The *Morning Chronicle* echoed the sentiments of her letter, describing Lockwood as having "marked ability and an earnest eloquence."[34]

This talk introduced themes that would become standard fare in Lockwood's lectures and sidewalk stumping. She quoted from English law and precedent and then recounted women's accomplishments, one moment drawing on the examples of Elizabeth I, Catherine the Great, and Joan of Arc while in her next breath praising American women professionals. She said that women were recognized as citizens and that true government depends upon self-government by each individual. Lockwood not only advocated women's right to vote but also prophesied the contributions women would make if elected to legislatures, where they would bring "their peculiar wisdom to bear upon the law."[35] The *Morning Chronicle* gave the talk a "good report," after which friends suggested that it be published. Lockwood did this, writing Walker that she had "two thousand struck."[36]

Summer over, the District Supreme Court resumed its business, hearing argument the second week of September in the *Spencer* and

Webster cases. Riddle acknowledged the problematic language of the Organic Act's seventh section ("all male citizens shall be entitled to vote") but argued that "the language of the statute does not exclude women . . . that in the presence of the first section of the Fourteenth Amendment, which confers elective franchise upon 'all persons,' this word 'male' is as if unwritten, and that the statute, constitutionally, reads, 'That all citizens shall be entitled to vote.'"[37] The Organic Act did not comport with the law of the Constitution.

Riddle also advanced what had become the standard natural rights argument that consent of the governed preceded the creation of the Republic. "I contend," he said, "that under our system the right to vote is a natural right [that] supposes that all joined in and consented to the government."[38] Returning to the force of the Fourteenth as well as Fifteenth Amendment, he argued that the first section of the Fourteenth removed "all hindrance" to the exercise of suffrage, while the Fifteenth "is a solemn mandate to all concerned not to deny this [suffrage] right."[39] The two amendments, he continued, harmonized and supported the women's claim that they were entitled to vote.

The members of the District of Columbia Supreme Court, however, did not agree. Writing in the manner of a gentle father lecturing his child, District Supreme Court Chief Justice Cartter told the women plaintiffs that he and his colleagues on the bench had "listened patiently and with interest to ingenious argument . . . but have failed to be convinced of the correctness of the position."[40] He dismissed the natural rights argument as likely to involve the destruction of civil government and concluded that Congress, as the legislative power of the District, was within its rights in not issuing a declaratory act enfranchising the women of Washington. It was the opinion of the court that the women would have to return to Congress to win the right that body had patently denied in 1867 and, again, in February 1871: "The constitutional capability of becoming a voter created by this [Fourteenth] Amendment lies dormant, as in the case of an infant, until made effective by legislative action. Congress, the legislative power of this jurisdiction, as yet, has not seen fit to carry the inchoate right into effect, as is apparent in the law regulating the franchise of this District."[41] Cartter denied the suits and assigned court costs against the women.

The outcome was not unanticipated and did not discourage other members of the NWSA from similar challenges. Woodhull, the flamboyant rising star of the suffrage movement, repeated the dare in the

November 1871 New York City elections. Susan B. Anthony went to the polls in November 5, 1872, cast a ballot, and two weeks later was arrested by a United States marshal for "knowingly voting without having a lawful right to vote."[42] Federal authorities hoped to intimidate Anthony, who, refusing to be quieted, traveled throughout New York State criticizing the Republican Party for blocking the popular democratic movements excited by emancipation and black manhood suffrage.[43]

In this hostile climate, the Washington women were fortunate to have the services of male attorneys who were willing to risk professional reputations as well as public notoriety. The number of women lawyers in the United States could be counted on one hand, but Riddle and Miller appeared to be the ideal surrogates. They worked closely with their UFA clients, and when the disappointing Cartter decision was handed down in September 1871, they requested a rehearing.

When they were refused the two men filed an appeal with the United States Supreme Court, and on February 23, 1872, Chief Justice Salmon P. Chase announced that the Court would hear the appeal. It appeared that through *Spencer* and *Webster* the high court would address the question of women's right to vote and that Riddle and Miller would be associated with a landmark decision. But the *Spencer-Webster* cases were never argued. Records show that the Supreme Court of the District of Columbia, as ordered by Chase, sent the trial transcript to the high court. And then the attorneys on one, or both, sides failed to appear for argument, not once, but twice. As a result, on October 16, 1874, Morrison R. Waite, the new chief justice, issued a short memorandum: "This is the second term at which this case has been called for argument, and . . . neither party is now prepared to argue the same."[44] He ordered that the cases be dismissed.

What happened to keep Riddle and Miller from appearing at the U.S. Supreme Court? In 1871 the *Spencer-Webster* cases advanced cutting-edge legal theory and offered the first opportunity for the Supreme Court of the United States to address the question of woman suffrage. The women of the District continued to anticipate their day in court, reasoning that Riddle and Miller, having already argued before Cartter, were fully prepared to make the appeal at the high court. Given the importance of the issue of voting rights, and the expectations of their clients, it is difficult to believe that the attorneys stepped aside or back. But it appears that this is what they did.

The simplest explanation is that Riddle and Miller decided to delay their appeal while following the progress of two other women's rights cases destined for the U.S. Supreme Court. *Bradwell v. Illinois* challenged the authority of a state to deny a woman the right to pursue a legal career. Myra Bradwell, a Chicago attorney who founded and published the *Chicago Legal News*, had been denied membership in the state bar solely on the grounds of her sex, a decision upheld by the Illinois Supreme Court. Through her lawyer, the prominent politician Matthew Carpenter, Bradwell argued that this was a violation of the privileges of citizenship guaranteed as a federal right under the new Fourteenth Amendment.[45]

Bradwell was decided by the Supreme Court in April 1873. The ruling was a stunning defeat for women's rights, with eight of the nine justices siding with Illinois. Writing for the majority, Justice Samuel F. Miller said that "the right to control and regulate the granting of license to practice law in the courts of a State is one of those powers which are not transferred [by the Fourteenth Amendment] for its protection to the Federal Government."[46] The decision signaled the Court's restrictive reading of the Fourteenth Amendment's privileges or immunities clause and meant that women would have to wrestle state by state to become licensed lawyers in lieu of a federally recognized right.[47]

The resounding defeat in *Bradwell* may have discouraged Riddle and Miller. On the other hand, the nature of Carpenter's argument on behalf of Bradwell might have urged them forward.[48] Although a staunch advocate of woman suffrage, Carpenter had concluded that the Supreme Court was certain to hand down an adverse ruling in Bradwell's case unless the question of a woman's right to earn a living was separated from the issue of her right to vote. He had, therefore, distinguished his client's constitutional right to practice law from the establishment of women's right to vote, arguing that unlike the right to work, voting was not a privilege protected by the Fourteenth Amendment.[49] When she learned about Carpenter's strategy, a furious Susan B. Anthony wrote that his words amounted to "a school boy pettifogging speech—wholly without a basic principle."[50]

Carpenter's tactics must have made Lockwood and her friends all the more anxious for Riddle and Miller to appear at the Court, and to argue that, under the Fourteenth Amendment, women were entitled to vote. But still the two attorneys hung back, perhaps as an act of courtesy based on their learning that Francis and Virginia Minor, the original theoreticians of New Departure, had initiated what they hoped would be *the* test case of women's voting rights.

In 1872 the Minors had sued the St. Louis registrar, who, acting under the state constitution, had refused to register Virginia as a voter. In August 1873, after losing in the lower courts, they appealed to the U.S. Supreme Court. Although the justices agreed to hear the case, *Minor v. Happersett*, the Court put off argument until February 9, 1875. Appearing with cocounsel, Francis Minor presented the legal claim he first made in 1869: "Since the adoption of the fourteenth amendment, a woman who is a citizen of the United States and of the State [in which she lives] is a voter in that State."[51] A month later, Chief Justice Waite handed down a decision that ended the short life of New Departure theory. "The Constitution of the United States does not confer the right of suffrage upon any one," he wrote, "and the constitutions and laws of the several States which commit that important trust to men are not necessarily void."[52] With this ruling, the Supreme Court declared that suffrage was not a privilege of citizenship and that the Fourteenth Amendment, despite its guarantees of equal protection of the law and privileges of citizenship, did not shield women from the political decisions of state governments about the right to vote.

The *Minor* decision ended the movement to enfranchise women by legal fiat. Riddle and Miller may have felt that, as the authors of the New Departure, the Minors had the greater right to bring the issue before the Supreme Court. They certainly understood that *Minor*, appealing state action, should it be won, would have broad value as a precedent. Still, in the end, the two attorneys, Washington insiders, apparently feared a loss. At the New Year of 1874 Riddle wrote Susan B. Anthony that he would not argue the *Spencer* case because "he would be beaten" and because "he is not ready to make his argument before that last tribunal."[53] His action anticipated the defeat that was, in fact, forthcoming in *Minor*.

The Supreme Court's decision in *Minor* was only one of the many disappointments endured in the first half of the 1870s by the notorious suffrage ladies. Virtually every aspect of their legal and political action failed, including Woodhull's short-lived presidential candidacy. She had courted labor as well as supporters of woman suffrage throughout 1871 and engineered a nominating convention in May 1872 only to be brought down that summer by her radical social and economic views, and lack of funds. After the miscalculation of exposing in print the sexual infidelities of the Reverend Henry Ward Beecher, the charismatic head of Brooklyn's Plymouth Church, Woodhull was deserted by most of her supporters. In an extraordinary reversal of fortune, she was prosecuted, under the new Comstock Act, for sending obscene materials (the newspaper article about Beecher) through the federal mail, spending Election Week 1872 in jail!

Like the women's movement, the path of Lockwood's professional life in the early 1870s was uncertain and filled with struggle. Yet despite the social and legal climate that produced the defeats in *Spencer*, *Bradwell*, and *Minor*, Lockwood refused to abandon her faith in the possibility of bringing about change. With Matthew Carpenter, she believed that courts and legislatures would support women's right to work and, in spite of the decision in *Bradwell*, in 1874 set out to succeed where he, a man of considerable renown, had failed.

6

A Tougher Fight

The Justices of the Supreme Court saw, in imagination, great crowds of females, all learned in the law, trooping into the court-room and occupying the best seats in the semi-circle, now sacred to the Bar. The dignity of the court would take itself wings and fly away when two feminine legal lights would converse audibly and at long range on such standard works as "Worth on the Female Costume." . . . But none of these things have come to pass.

Anonymous, c.1890

A downtown law office proved an ideal location from which to pursue civil and criminal work in the local courts. It also afforded access to clients doing business with the federal government. Ezekiel Lockwood worked as a private agent, filing papers for claimants against the government, and his wife was quick to see the possibilities of legal work involving veterans' pensions and property claims as a source of steady income. But in order to plead cases in a U.S. district court, the U.S. Court of Claims, or the U.S. Supreme Court, Belva Lockwood needed to be admitted to each court's bar. She had won her fight to join the D.C. bar, and if she were admitted to the other bars she would no longer have to relinquish good cases, or to share them—and fees—with attorneys with bar status.[1] She hoped, having prevailed with the District bar, that admission would be a simple matter. But it was not.[2] In the end the struggle required five years and became the crusade of a novice attorney who wanted the full opportunities of her profession.

The new contest began when Charlotte Van Cort engaged Lockwood to file a claim against the navy for the use and infringement of a patent, an action that led client and attorney to the U.S. Court of Claims. Lockwood wished to be the attorney of record, so she asked a local lawyer, A. A. Hosmer, "a reputable member of that court," to sponsor her for admission to the Claims Court bar.[3] Early in April 1874, the two walked up the hill to the Capitol building where the court held its sessions, and presented themselves.

Hosmer made the required introduction, describing his colleague's legal credentials and vouching for her good character. There was stunned silence as the five judges turned toward the applicant. Then Court of Claims Chief Justice Charles Drake announced the obvious: "Mistress Lockwood, you are a woman."[4] Somewhat amused, Lockwood did not deny the charge and waited for him to continue. The silence, she said later, was painful. When Drake finally spoke he said that his court had not consided her application as its Rule 13 specifically referred to the admission of *men* of good moral character.[5] He refused to act on Hosmer's motion, announcing a one-week continuance.

The small drama was too much for Hosmer, who left the room, vowing not to come back. Lockwood thought him a coward, writing that he did not have "backbone enough to keep up the fight."[6] She, however, was not intimidated. Along with Ezekiel and some local friends, she returned to court on the designated day, standing when her case was called. Drake wasted no time with formalities. He looked up and now charged her with being "a *married woman*!"[7] The chief justice very much wanted to be rid of her and hoped that a blunt reference to Lockwood's marital status would chase her from his court.

Drake was not making a social observation. Rather, he believed that Lockwood's application was legally burdened by her marital status. Under the centuries-old principle of coverture, brought to the United States from England, a man and woman, upon marriage, became one legal entity, with the husband responsible for himself and his wife. At the altar, a woman accepted the status of feme covert, a woman "covered" by her husband, a person whose legal existence was incorporated into that of her husband, under whose protection she performed everything.[8] A feme covert yielded control of her property to her husband, and could not legally enter into contracts without his consent (a feme sole, a single woman, retained her personal rights and obligations). Lockwood listened to Drake, then stood her ground, telling the judges that the application had been made with Ezekiel's consent. She hoped this would resolve the matter, but Drake and his colleagues still refused to act, and ordered another continuance.

The Lockwoods plotted their next move as they walked down Capitol Hill toward their home. Within a day, they had enlisted the help of two respected Washington attorneys, Thomas J. Durant and Charles W. Hornor. The two men prepared a written brief and, a week later, appeared in Drake's courtroom.

Hornor made the initial presentation, starting with the reaffirmation that his client met the qualifications stated in Rule 13 that she believed to be relevant—age, moral character, and a license in the highest court of the District. He acknowledged that the admission of attorneys to practice before the court fell within the discretion of the judges but insisted that this power, a legal trust, should not be executed "arbitrarily, nor irregularly exercised, nor be flagrantly improper."[9] Then he turned to the matter of his client's status as a married woman.

Lockwood and her attorneys felt that Drake's position was easy to attack. The Supreme Court of the District of Columbia had admitted her to its bar without raising the issue of coverture. It had done so because in 1869 Congress had enacted legislation, a District of Columbia married woman's property act, that "exploded" the old common law notion of coverture.[10] The act secured to a married woman in the District the absolute right to hold property, to convey, devise, and bequeath her property, and to contract and sue and be sued in her own name.[11] In other words, as the result of this act, since 1869 Washington women were free from this particular "subjection" of the common law. Congress had restored to them the right to enter into independent legal relations, including contractual actions essential to the work of an attorney.

There remained, however, the fact that she was a *woman*. Hornor and Durant feared that the Court of Claims could ground an adverse decision in the language of Rule 13, with its specific reference to males. To fight this possibility, the attorneys cited new congressional legislation providing rules for the construction of statutes: "in all acts hereafter passed . . . words importing the masculine gender may be applied to females . . . unless the context shows that such words were intended to be used in a more limited sense."[12] They argued that this rule was applicable and that "the tendency of the age [was] to throw open and not to close up the so-called learned professions; to offer to women new modes of livelihood and new spheres of activity."[13]

The judges of the Claims Court, however, were not inclined to grant this right. Drake announced another continuance, and several weeks elapsed before the court prepared its ruling. Lockwood wrote that during these weeks of waiting she "pondered upon the vast disparity between the sexes" and observed, "if I possessed any nice discrimination, [I would have seen] the utter folly of my course."[14] And folly it was. A unanimous court rejected her application. She was forty-three years old and the very model of a proper and ambitious attorney.

The job of writing the court's opinion in *Mrs. Lockwood's Case* fell to 46-year-old Charles Nott. Judge Nott was a transplanted New Yorker with a strong sense of civic duty. He had opposed slavery. Wanting to open the profession of law to freedmen, while on the bench, he also taught classes at Howard University's law department.[15] In the matter of *Mrs. Lockwood's Case*, however, Nott proved himself a conservative jurist content to rest his opinion on tradition-bound common law. Drake had ordered that Nott read the full opinion during the court's session. His first words signaled defeat and Lockwood's face flushed with anger as she endured the ninety-minute disquisition, which included a hypothetical situation not posed by her case and the judges' stubborn insistence that the Married Women's Act made no express admission of women to the bar and, therefore, must be ignored.[16]

Lockwood wrote that the decision was a "squelcher" and that anyone with an "ordinary female mind" would have yielded to fate.[17] Still, she remained polite when asked about the ruling while 25-year-old Lura, possibly acting as her mother's naughty alter ego, tossed Nott a bouquet of sarcastic sass. In her May 20 newspaper column, Lura questioned his erudition and laughed at the idea that he was protecting the male bar from lady lawyers "with their taking ways."[18]

Lockwood admitted to being crestfallen but went back to work. She had filed Charlotte Van Cort's case with the Claims Court clerk and had been promised a large fee. She proceeded to take Van Cort's testimony and to prepare a brief. She then returned to court with Van Cort and asked leave for her client to read the brief: "This, they had no power to deny, as it is the privilege of every applicant to plead his own case, and [I] sat by Mrs. Van Cort until the hearing was completed."[19] It was a modest victory. Elsewhere she admitted working at a disadvantage: "My clients lacked the confidence in me that I would have commanded had I stood fairly with the court."[20]

Whether she should have been prepared for the rejection of her application is an open question. That she was a member of the District bar, that she conducted legal business with many federal departments, and that she contracted with clients might have given pause to the Claims Court bench. But whatever reflection the judges devoted to these facts was outweighed by their reading of the law as well as the prevailing cultural belief that, with the exception of teaching and nursing, women were not fit for professional work. Nott had said as much when he wrote that it was not the business of the judiciary to "intermeddle" with the question of woman's proper sphere.

Lockwood found Nott's reasoning extraordinary and quite probably inspired by the concurring opinion U.S. Supreme Court Justice Joseph P. Bradley had written the year before when he voted to uphold attorney Myra Bradwell's exclusion from the Illinois bar: "Man is, or should be, woman's protector and defender. The natural and proper timidity and delicacy which belongs to the female sex evidently unfits it for many of the occupations of civil life."[21]

Lockwood had worried about the impact of Bradwell's case. The two women knew each other from suffrage circles and Lockwood had read the majority and concurring opinions with great care. In some ways, Bradwell had less at stake than her friend. She was married to a lawyer and had used knowledge acquired from him to establish a newspaper in 1868. Under her direction, the *Chicago Legal News* had become the most widely circulated legal trade publication in the nation.[22] When the United States Supreme Court ruled against her she could, and did, abandon the fight to practice law, putting all of her energies into editing the *Legal News*, whose pages were filled with the conventional subject matter of a legal trade paper as well as the less common news of her "sisters-in-law" and the prejudice they endured. A May 1872 item took note of Lockwood: "We had the pleasure this week of welcoming Mrs. Belva A. Lockwood, the woman lawyer of Washington, to our sanctum." At Myra's invitation, she had come to the Bradwells' Congregational church, where she delivered a lecture, "Woman and Her Relations to the Law."[23]

The *Bradwell* decision created a poor psychological climate for women's professional aspirations but, at least in Lockwood's case, it could not be cited as precedent against her at the Court of Claims. *Bradwell* addressed the reach of the Fourteenth Amendment in the face of discriminatory state action, while Lockwood's application involved a federal court. Still, the ruling in the earlier case created a symbolic, if not a legal, hurdle.

Although Nott told Lockwood that if the court had erred she could seek a review from the U.S. Supreme Court, in mid-May 1874 she decided to turn for help to the Congress. Her plan was to lobby for a simply worded proposal that could be transformed into rights-granting legislation. In Illinois, Myra Bradwell and her young legal acolyte, Alta Hulett, had drafted the wording for just such a statute, which was subsequently enacted by the Illinois legislature. It stated, "No person shall be precluded or debarred from any occupation, profession, or employment (except military) on account of sex."[24] Inspired by them, Lockwood made a similar approach to the legislature that governed the federal courts.

She wrote a petition and brief that Benjamin Butler agreed to submit to the clerk of the House of Representatives. In these documents she urged congressional action to ensure "[t]hat, no woman otherwise qualified, shall be barred from practice before any United States court on account of sex or coverture."[25] The brief referred members of Congress to several of its recent statutes, including the 1869 Married Women's Property Act, as evidence of the legislature's position on common law coverture. Lockwood also felt that, without intending to, Nott had given her an opening by insisting that admission to the federal bar "constitutes an office." If this was so, she now wrote, women could hardly be kept from the legal bar as they had already won appointments as postmistresses, in which capacity they were "bonded officer[s] of the Government," and pension agents, also an "office of government."[26] Her brief went on to describe the action of several state courts, "conforming themselves to the new statutes created, and the progressive spirit of the age" that were now licensing women attorneys.[27]

Butler, along with several members of the House Judiciary Committee, worked her request into legislation and on May 25, by a vote of four to three, the committee approved H.R. 3583 and sent it to the full House for a vote.[28] Butler spoke for the bill in floor debate on June 1 and invited questions from his colleagues. Tennessee Representative Horace Maynard pounded away at the issue of married women attorneys. Concerned with the "disabilities arising from coverture," he voted against the bill, as did many others.

Myra Bradwell reported with satisfaction that Butler had maneuvered the bill to the floor where it lost, but with a decent showing of ninety-five "yeas."[29] The Senate proved less tractable. Lockwood had given a copy of the petition to New York Senator Roscoe Conkling, who dutifully submitted it to the Senate clerk. Unlike Butler, he was not a friend of women's rights, and had no intention of using his formidable power on behalf of the petition.[30] On February 16, 1875, a small entry in the *Journal of the Senate* noted, "*Ordered*, That the Committee on the Judiciary be discharged from the further consideration of the petition of Belva A. Lockwood."[31]

Undeterred, she moved on with a new strategy. She knew that the Rules of Practice of the United States Supreme Court permitted an attorney to apply to its bar after practicing for three years before the highest level state, or District of Columbia, court, a requirement she would meet by the autumn of 1876. She reasoned that success with the justices of the U.S. Supreme Court would end resistance to her candidacy in the other federal courts. Proceeding with her plan, Lockwood waited the necessary twenty months and at the end of the required three years, presented her credentials to the justices of the United States Supreme Court. Her good friend and woman suffrage supporter Albert Gallatin Riddle moved her admission.[32]

The nine justices approached by Riddle and Lockwood were men of varied social and judicial beliefs. Most had been members of the Court that rejected Myra Bradwell's appeal. This included Bradley. Unfortunately, Chief Justice Salmon P. Chase, a moderate on the question of women's right to work and the lone dissenter in *Bradwell*, had died. The Court had two new members, Morrison R. Waite and Ward Hunt, who, while riding circuit in June 1873, made headlines as the presiding judge in the (criminal) voting rights trial of woman suffrage leader Susan B. Anthony. Following his insistent instructions, a jury "found" Anthony guilty, after which Hunt fined her for having dared to vote.[33]

Morrison Waite won confirmation as the new chief justice only after the Senate turned back six of President Grant's earlier nominees. Once on the bench, he allied himself with Justice Bradley. He led his Court through a series of seemingly contradictory decisions in the area of racial rights, rejecting the use of all-white juries but disemboweling Reconstruction amendments and federal statutes meant to protect freedmen from vigilantism and to guarantee their voting rights. Two aspects of Waite's jurisprudence might have caused Riddle and Lockwood concern. The chief justice often backed away from judicial intervention in favor of legislative decision making and was also known to use centuries-old English legal concepts as the rationale for his decisions.

On November 6, 1876, Waite announced that the Court had, in fact, voted against the motion to admit Lockwood to its bar. The ruling was brief, concluding tersely that "the Court does not feel called upon to make a change until such a change is required by statute"[34]

Lockwood was a good publicist. She had notified journalists that Riddle would move her admission and encouraged them to cover the story. By the evening of Waite's announcement, articles were being filed far and wide, with one story proclaiming that "the Chief Justice squelched the fair applicant."[35] At the White House that night the First Lady, who had read the newspaper accounts, asked Waite, her dinner guest, "how do you look when you squelch people?"[36] Malvina Harlan, also a guest at the party, reported that Waite had replied with a pained look of embarrassment and a shrug of his shoulders, "Why, I do not know, I'm sure."[37] Waite was anxious to discourage further conversation and careful not to reveal what apparently nobody had discovered, that he and Justices Samuel Miller and David Davis had sided with Lockwood. These three men had voted to approve the motion to admit her, but had been overridden by the six justices whose opinion Waite had announced.[38] In remaining silent about the vote, Waite was honoring the Court's code of confidentiality—although Lockwood eventually found out that Waite and Miller had supported her.[39] He was also, apparently, protecting himself from public ridicule. Malvina Harlan, a lady comfortable with gossip, had pronounced Riddle's motion "unprecedented," and told the table that "the people of Washington generally were laughing in their sleeves over it."[40]

In fact, many people in Washington had no thought of belittling Lockwood. A. G. Riddle represented society that was every bit as solid and respectable as those who had dined with President and Mrs. Hayes. Riddle had come to Washington in 1861 as an Ohio congressman. He served one term and did not seek reelection. A family man, he was now Washington's district attorney. He taught at local law schools and in his spare time wrote plays, biographies, novels, and personal recollections.[41] Riddle was not alone. Many other male attorneys accepted Lockwood's right to compete with them on an equal footing.

Despite this legal setback, Lockwood was not to be stopped. In January 1877 she reigned at the National Woman Suffrage Association meeting in Washington. In a speech on Waite's decision before as many as fifteen hundred NWSA delegates and guests, Lockwood said that it was "the glory of each generation to make its own precedents" and that Blackstone, "of whose works she inferred the judges were ignorant—gives several precedents for women in the English courts."[42] A week later, in an article written for the suffrage publication, *Ballot-Box*, Elizabeth Cady Stanton described Lockwood as the Italian Portia at the bar of Venice. "No more effective speech," Stanton wrote, "was ever made on our platform."[43]

Although Ezekiel Lockwood was quite ill, his wife was not to be underestimated in her determination to change the law. She worked step by step, generating public interest through lectures while privately winning support from male attorneys and creating alliances with members of Congress. She had decided the best chance for change lay with Congress and in January 1877 went back to Capitol Hill, where she won over Missouri Representative John Montgomery Glover. On January 16 Glover introduced legislation that would prohibit discrimination against women attorneys. Titled "An act to relieve the legal disabilities of women," H.R. 4435 was read twice and referred to the Committee on the Judiciary. On the same day, Glover read aloud on the House floor a memorial written by Lockwood as well as petitions of support from Washington lawyers and from leaders of the women's rights movement.[44] Debate and a vote were anticipated.

A national political crisis, however, claimed the short life of H.R. 4435. In the November 1876 presidential contest, charges of election fraud left the country without a confirmed winner. With the country in turmoil, and the future of Reconstruction at stake, Congress established an electoral commission empowered with determining whether Democrat Samuel J. Tilden or Republican Rutherford B. Hayes should be declared president. Massachusetts Representative George Hoar was one of the commission's fifteen members. He was also the person in charge of Lockwood's bill. Distracted by the work of the commission, he ignored H.R. 4435. According to Myra Bradwell, when Hayes was finally selected president the exhausted members of Congress found no time or opportunity to take up the issue of women's rights.[45] Making matters more complicated, Hoar had won a seat in the Senate and left the House.

In these months Lockwood was also visited by a series of domestic crises. Ezekiel died on April 25, 1877. She wrote that he had been "prostrate" for three years.[46] He was three months shy of his seventy-fifth birthday. Business records show that she did not permit herself an extended period of mourning. Six weeks later Hannah Bennett called her daughter to the bedside of her dying father.[47] Lura accompanied Belva to Illinois, where the Bennetts still lived, and together they helped Hannah nurse Lewis Bennett through his last illness. He died on June 26. He was survived by 65-year-old Hannah, four of their children, and several grandchildren. He had farmed land in Illinois since the mid-1850s and left his widow an estate of four or five thousand dollars.[48]

Lura and Belva returned to Washington just before the Great Strike of July 1877, which closed down many railroads and revealed the underbelly of class warfare in a new industrial era marked by extravagance and corruption, and now dubbed "the Gilded Age." At home, they were met with more bad news. Lockwood's sister-in-law, Sarah Hanks Bennett, the wife of her brother Warren, lay gravely ill. Thirty-nine-year-old Sarah had been staying at the Lockwoods' with her teenage daughter, Clara. Before dying she received a promise from Belva that Clara could remain in Washington with her aunt.[49]

These deaths took their toll. Drained physically and emotionally, Lockwood neglected her clients and only with Lura's help did she put her legal practice in order, by autumn again finding time for the stubborn work of lobbying her bill. This paid off when Glover reintroduced "An act to relieve the legal disabilities of women" (renumbered H.R. 1077). It was referred to the House Judiciary Committee, which, on December 7, permitted Lockwood to appear in order to argue its merit.[50]

All signs for passage were promising. The final House vote came on February 21, 1878. The Speaker began the day by calling for committee reports. By arrangement, Judiciary Committee member Benjamin Butler rose to his feet, quickly worked through a list of noncontroversial items, and then indicated that, as instructed by the committee, he had the pleasant task of making a favorable report on H.R. 1077. The bill was read.[51] Its text posed no problem, but several House members objected to the act's broad title. Their concern was easily addressed by insertion of the word "certain" as the legislation was recast, "An act to relieve certain legal disabilities of women."

Butler wanted to push the bill along and, if possible, win immediate House passage. Several readings were required. A preliminary vote—one hundred in favor, sixty-eight opposed—left no doubt that Lockwood and her allies had done their work. Nevertheless, she waited nervously in the visitors' gallery during debate until the final vote showed, "yeas 169, nays 87, not voting 36."[52] The result was thrilling. Three years had passed since Ben Butler had first submitted Lockwood's petition asking for congressional action. In those years she had been rebuffed by both houses of Congress, and by the Waite Court. Now she had the approval of the House.

The next step was to go back to the Senate, which, experience taught her, was the more conservative body on matters of women's rights. Many senators had been open in telling her that they feared her bill would be "an entering wedge for woman suffrage." Others remarked more bluntly, "I am not in favor of women voting and this bill may lead to it."[53] To counter these attitudes, Lockwood sought interviews with each member of the chamber. She discussed with them what she felt it meant to be an American, arguing that women could only be independent if they could pursue work without restrictions. She described to these ambitious men how her career had been held back. She talked about the common law and the age of progress. Most senators met with her. Upstate New Yorker Roscoe Conkling was among the handful who refused. He made it clear that, although originally a New Yorker, Lockwood would get no support from him. She dismissed him as a snob, a man who *might* let people talk to him.[54] Lura thought him just plain old "haughty."[55]

Three weeks after the victory in the House, she received the discouraging news that the Senate's Judiciary Committee, lobbied by Conkling, had given the bill an adverse report. In the view of the majority of the committee members, the power to determine admission to the U.S. Supreme Court bar was reserved to that body, and because no legal obstacle actually prohibited the admission of women, no legislation to remove such disabilities was required.[56] The committee recommended the indefinite postponement of the bill. In Chicago Myra Bradwell was sufficiently alarmed that she wrote a long editorial deploring the decision of the committee, while shrinking from the thought of a Supreme Court "independent and beyond the power and control of Congress."[57]

Lockwood's struggle was matched by the experience of other women attorneys. While Conkling and his colleagues tried to bury the offending bill, on the West Coast California legislators sought to shake off local reform proposed by lawyer Clara Shortridge Foltz. With her colleague Laura de Force Gordon and members of the State Suffrage Society, Foltz spent much of the month of March in Sacramento successfully lobbying a state Woman Lawyer's Bill, which would substitute the word "person" for "white male" in the California Bar code.[58] The expanse of frontier did little to alter the nature of the opposition. Like Lockwood, Foltz and her friends listened to opponents insist that practicing law would move women into the public sphere, "unsex" them, and make them unfit for domestic life.[59]

Despite Foltz and Gordon's victory with state lawmakers, Lockwood knew that her "indefinitely postponed" federal bill was in trouble and, as she had before, turned to men who supported women's rights in order to rescue it. California Republican Aaron A. Sargent was the first senator to come forward, joined immediately by Indiana Democrat Joseph McDonald. On April 22, 1878, the two men offered an amended version of the legislation, "That no person shall be excluded from practicing as an attorney and counselor at law from any court of the United States on account of sex," and asked that, with this new wording, the tabled legislation be placed back on the Senate's calendar. Sargent spoke at some length about women's rights, urging his colleagues to recognize the liberalizing "tendency" of society.[60] He made specific reference to the recent passage of Foltz's bill, and held up a petition of support for Lockwood signed by "the most eminent" male attorneys, 155 of them, in the District.[61] Arkansas Democrat Augustus Garland broke into Sargent's speech, insisting that federal courts had the power to admit women on their own motions, that legislation was unnecessary and an infringement on judicial prerogative.[62] Garland, along with other opponents of the bill, refused to acknowledge that the Supreme Court had earlier ruled against Lockwood.

Pulled from the oblivion faced by most tabled legislation, the amended bill was returned to the hostile Judiciary Committee. On May 20, the bill's opponents again reported adversely on the recommitted bill as well as on Sargent's amendment. Speaking for the committee, Ohio Democrat Allen Thurman repeated Garland's arguments and recommended "indefinite postponement of the bill."[63] Sargent stood and pointedly asked Thurman if the committee "is not aware that the Chief-Justice in deciding against the admission of a lady applicant for admission, said that the Supreme Court would wait for legislation?"[64] Thurman, still hiding behind the sham separation-of-powers argument, insisted that he was not "aware of any remark make [sic] by the Chief-Justice," an improbable reality given public discussion and press coverage so extensive as to have been talked about at a White House dinner party.[65]

The bill had now suffered two adverse reports. The possibility of further action could not have been more remote. But Sargent somehow won agreement from the Senate president pro tempore that the bill would be placed on the calendar.[66] For a week nothing happened. Fearing that he had been deceived, Sargent decided to force the issue. On

May 29, shortly before the noon break, and prior to the scheduled one o'clock consideration of pending appropriations legislation, he asked that the Senate take up Lockwood's bill. No doubt he was hoping that, nearing the end of the session, his colleagues might be sufficiently distracted to give it a quick nod. Instead, opponents argued that there was insufficient time for Sargent's request, forcing him to pretend he sought only a test vote, "to ascertain whether the bill has any more friends."[67] A rancorous exchange ensued between Sargent and members of the Judiciary Committee, during which Sargent lectured those present in the chamber: "If Senators do not like the bill, let them vote it down, and let them discuss it if they please, but, at any rate, I want the bill considered." Minutes later he lost the vote on his motion to debate the bill (twenty-six to twenty-six, with twenty-four absent). He left the Senate saying, "I shall try it again some other time."[68] Shortly after, the legislature recessed for the summer and Lockwood wondered if hers was the curse of Sisyphus.

Lockwood's legal practice was primarily local, but she liked to travel and was more than willing to take clients from outside of the District. In 1878, anxious to expand her practice, she continued her fight to be admitted to the federal courts, while submitting bar applications in Upper Marlborough, Prince George's County, Maryland, and Fairfax, Virginia. While she was successful in Virginia, where she appeared on behalf of the estate of Edward M. Johnson, the circuit court judge in Upper Marlborough, Maryland, rudely refused her.[69] In a letter to Bradwell she described the new "contest" set in motion by Judge Magruder, who had been "offensive and disagreeable" and who had announced to his court, "I pray God that the time may never come when the State of Maryland will admit women to the Bar."[70]

Her experience in these two nearby states illustrated the divided opinion that existed throughout the country about the law, as well as the social conventions, that governed women's progress in the professions and in gaining suffrage. On the one hand, she never failed to win some male legislators, often men whose wives and daughters were active in the cause of women's rights. A. G. Riddle, raised by a single mother, demonstrated an unflinching commitment to women's rights. At critical moments, his outspoken support was sustained by other men who gave her advice, opened their courts to her, or signed petitions. On the other hand, the drawn-out, and still uncertain, debate in Congress, the behavior of Conkling and Thurman, and Judge Magruder, showed the lengths to which men in authority were willing to go to block women's enjoyment of equal professional opportunity, believing her demands would tear apart the comfortable fabric of society.

In the autumn of 1878, the obstacle of Senate opposition remained before Lockwood. The long summer recess had given her time to consider how Sargent had been outmaneuvered, and what could be done about it. There were few new tactical options. The public relations campaign was positive, but bringing woman suffrage leaders to Capitol Hill to support her would only convince Senate fence sitters that her bill was the "entering wedge" they so feared. Having nothing new, she proceeded with the old. She continued to cultivate the press, initiated another petition drive among male attorneys, and caucused with key senators. An otherwise sympathetic journalist described her as putting forward "an unconscionable deal of lobbying."[71]

Lockwood knew that if her bill was to have a chance supporters had to keep it from being sent back to committee. Any hope for victory lay in open floor debate. The final test came on February 7, 1879, a Friday, when her champions in the Senate learned that Allen Thurman, one of the bill's chief opponents, would be out of town.[72] Lockwood was notified and came quickly to the visitors' gallery, where she was joined by her supporters.[73] They listened patiently as the senators attended to other business, including national defense appropriations, the restriction of Chinese immigration, and the creation of a federal Bureau of Public Health. Finally, Senator McDonald stood and proposed that they take up the women lawyers bill.[74] There was a motion to proceed. It passed by a vote of thirty-one to twenty. Some wrangling over rules of procedure followed and then a second motion to read the bill. This motion also passed, on the even stronger vote of forty to twenty.[75] Hearing these votes, Lockwood knew that despite the best efforts of the mighty Conkling and his cronies, the full Senate would now debate the exclusion of women from the federal bar.

Three senators, McDonald, Sargent, and George Hoar, answered for her, defending the bill during floor debate. Sargent had announced his support for a woman suffrage amendment and McDonald, a skilled orator, had won praise from Lura as a man friendly to the cause of woman suffrage who "puts in his oar wherever he thinks it will do the most good."[76]

By contrast, Lura described Senator George Edmunds, their primary opponent that day, as "the fussiest old fossil in the Senate," a man who believed that departing from the practices of yesterday was "diabolical wickedness."[77] In fact, at age fifty-one, Edmunds was hardly an elder statesman or, in all things, a conservative. He was a Radical Republican, a vocal opponent of the Ku Klux Klan, and only two years older than Lockwood. He was admired and powerful. As Washington journalist Emily Briggs observed, "Not a solitary measure passes the Senate that is not licked into shape by the insinuating tongue and all-prevailing mind of vigilant Senator Edmunds."[78]

Edmunds led off debate by reminding his Senate colleagues that the bill had been sent out of committee with an adverse report. McDonald replied that a minority faction had supported it. He then turned the discussion toward a point that a body of lawyers could appreciate. Female attorneys, he argued, like their male counterparts, should have the opportunity to follow their cases through the appeals process. This professional right was "but evenhanded justice" for the client and for the attorney.[79] Aaron Sargent followed McDonald. He rose and held up a petition signed by 160 District of Columbia attorneys: "We, the undersigned attorneys and counselors at law, would respectfully request the passage of House bill No. 1077 entitled 'An act to relieve certain legal disabilities of women.'"[80]

The previous April Sargent had saved Lockwood's bill with an impassioned speech in support of women's rights. As he held the petition, Sargent again sought to carry the day through the fervor of oration:

> [M]en have not the right, in contradiction to the intentions, the wishes, the ambition, of women, to say that their sphere shall be circumscribed. . . . It is mere oppression to say to the bread-seeking woman, you shall labor only in certain narrow ways for your living, we will hedge you out by law from profitable employments, and monopolize them for ourselves.[81]

Hoar rose to second McDonald's argument that legislating bar admission rules for the judicial branch did not violate the constitutional principle of separation of powers. He, too, addressed the unfairness to clients of having to transfer from one attorney to another.[82] Edmunds, sensing that his cause was lost, asked for a vote on a third reading. It carried, thirty-nine to twenty. On that vote, according to the February 7

Congressional Record, and with no further fanfare, there was a third reading and the bill was passed. Lockwood sat in the gallery and smiled.
The bill was sent to the White House where, on February 15, President
Hayes signed it into law. Five years had passed since Lockwood had
first come to Capitol Hill to lobby the legislation.[83]

Lockwood later gave a candid account of the days before the Senate vote:

> I grew anxious, almost desperate, called out everybody who was op-
> posed to the bill, and begged that it might be permitted to come up on
> its merits, and that a fair vote might be had on it in the Senate. I have
> been interested in many bills in Congress, and have often appeared be-
> fore committees of Senate and House; but this was by far the strongest
> lobbying that I ever performed.

Not disagreeing with a reporter who described her work as an "unconscionable deal of lobbying," she wrote, "Nothing was too daring for me
to attempt.[84]

The victory was enormous. Lockwood had pushed a reluctant Congress to enact one of the very first federal measures in support of
women's rights. Her success, never assured, resulted from persistence
and stalwart male allies who emphasized the reasonable nature of the
legislation. It reflected the beginnings of societal recognition of
women's rights, however limited they remained. Her effort, encouraged by the women of the suffrage movement, occurred at a time when
reformers in several states had succeeded in drawing attention to the
unequal nature of married women's right to control their wages and
property. The state bar admission campaigns launched by Bradwell,
Foltz, and Gordon, among others, also signaled lawmakers that Lockwood was not alone in the belief that it was time to lift the legal disabilities that burdened women's employment opportunities.

After the Senate vote, Lockwood held court and sent flowers to the
men who had made it possible—baskets of them to Hoar, McDonald,
and Sargent with boutonnieres to the rest.[85] Myra Bradwell, who, as
Lockwood had written, "started the contest," congratulated her friend
with a lengthy editorial: "Ten years ago the passage of such a law would
have been impossible. . . . Great credit is due Mrs. Lockwood."[86] And
now that the deed was done, Bradwell felt free to link her support for
equality of professional opportunity and woman suffrage: "If women

are allowed to be physicians, clergymen, and last, but not least, lawyers
. . . why should they not be allowed to vote?"[87]

Lockwood waited to make her triumphal appearance at the
Supreme Court. The justices were recessed and not scheduled to recon-
vene until March 3. On that day, at noon, she took a seat near the front
of the courtroom in the place reserved for members of the bar, and *hope-
fuls*. She was dressed in a plain black velvet dress with satin vest and
blue cloth coat, cut "*a l'homme*." Lura, Mary Walker, and business associate Lavinia Dundore accompanied her. Jeremiah Wilson and Samuel
Shellabarger, prominent members of the District bar, sat at her side. An
unusual number of journalists, including the well-known Emily Briggs,
were present. Because of the recess, the justices required four hours to
read aloud what the *Washington Post* described as "the almost endless
grind of decisions."[88]

The candidate waited. Members of Congress entered the chamber.
When the long reading of opinions ended, Lockwood's champion, Senator McDonald, entered the room and warmly congratulated her before
holding a whispered conference with Justice John Harlan. A. G. Riddle
arrived and took up his place next to her. Motions to admit had begun.
Ten male attorneys joined the Supreme Court bar that afternoon.[89]

Finally, signaled by the clerk, Lockwood rose and, accompanied by
Riddle, moved to the inner rail immediately before Chief Justice Waite.
When she stood there was "a bating of breath and craning of necks."[90]
Three years before Riddle had presented her to the Court without success. Speaking in a clear voice, Riddle again said, "I move to admit to
the bar of the court Mrs. Belva A. Lockwood, a member of the bar of the
Supreme Court of the District, in good standing and having an extensive practice in all branches." He referred the Court to the law under
which he made the application and offered "eulogistic" remarks about
his "protégé."[91] Chief Justice Waite asked with a smile if Riddle would
vouch for her character and respectability. Riddle assured the Court
that he would. Waite directed Lockwood to step to the clerk's desk to
take the oath. She gave a graceful bow and stepped to the side, standing behind the other newly admitted lawyers who were busy with the
clerk. At her turn, she took the oath, kissed the Bible, and signed the
name of the first woman to be admitted to practice law before the
Supreme Court of the United States. Family and members of the government pressed around her, cheering loudly as the Court's marshal
called for order.[92]

7

Woman Lawyer

I have been now fourteen years before the bar, in an almost continuous
practice, and my experience has been large, often serious, and many
times amusing. I have never lacked plenty of good paying work; but,
while I have supported my family well, I have not grown rich. . . .
There is a good opening at the bar for the class of women who have
taste and tact for it.

Belva A. Lockwood, 1888

In 1881 American businessman James Densmore sent a letter of advice
to Tina, his married daughter. She and her husband Edward might be
"having a sufficiently happy time of it," but young people get restless
(at least he had), and he believed that Tina ought to consider becoming
a professional woman.[1] He had urged her to read law and now, to encourage her further, he held up Belva Lockwood, recently admitted to
the U.S. Supreme Court bar, as an admirable example of middle-class
female achievement.

Lockwood was by now a recognized member of the Washington
bar, well known to the judges of the D.C. courts. While some other
women lawyers suffered from nerves when speaking in court, or
thought it indelicate to go before the bench, Lockwood was willing,
even eager, to be part of the spittoon-and-boots world of justice. In her
best years, she earned a respectable thirty-five hundred dollars annu-
ally from her practice.[2] In the 1880s, 80 percent of American families
lived on less than five hundred dollars a year.[3] The nearby states of
Maryland and Virginia paid judges an annual salary of slightly more
than three thousand dollars.[4]

Lockwood had eased her way into law in the early 1870s working
alongside Ezekiel, who had given up dentistry and was working as a
notary public as well as a pension and claims agent. This occupation

provided the family with an income while Belva was in law school. She and Lura helped by copying and filing clients' documents, and in this way both women learned about judicial and administrative procedure. Ezekiel also made the necessary connections to win letters of guardianship from the court, another means of earning fees by looking after the finances of minors and the mentally ill.[5] He brought Belva into this work and by 1873 she was accepting cases independent of him.[6] As an agent Ezekiel also pursued land and treaty claims on behalf of Native American clients. This work introduced his wife to an area of law that she later pursued for many years, with considerable drama.[7]

Although he was not an attorney, Ezekiel helped Belva to gain the foothold that was critical to her success as a local attorney. She, however, made the decision of when to strike out on her own. She intended to have a practice in her name and set up an office early in 1873, while still contesting her exclusion from the District bar. Initially, she took real estate cases but then decided that a practice specializing in claims against the federal government, including pensions and bounties (incentives for military enlistment), would be more lucrative.[8] The scope of this practice broadened throughout the 1870s as she successfully fought the men who withheld bar memberships.

Until 1875 the Lockwoods ran her practice out of their rooms at the Union League Hall. Living there provided a convenient and inexpensive, if modest, home and office. The Union League was near to the federal agencies where they filed their clients' papers as well as the buildings that housed the District of Columbia courts. Police Court was held at an old Unitarian Church located at the corner of D and Sixth, NW, three blocks from their rooms.[9] Here people who otherwise knew Mrs. Lockwood as an activist first took their measure of her as an attorney.[10] Minor police cases, probate work, and pension claims provided sufficient business that only a few months after the opening of Lockwood's practice, Lura could advertise her mother's apparent success: "The lady lawyer of Washington has quite an extensive practice, and a branch business and a lady partner in Baltimore."[11] Two months later Lura, well schooled in public relations, wrote that this success "now seems beyond controversy as her office is daily and hourly filled with clients."[12] Against all odds, Lockwood had established herself as a solo practitioner, even arguing that the struggle to be admitted to the D.C. bar had benefited her. "The attention that had been called to me in the novel contest I had made," she wrote, "not only gave me a wide advertising, but drew towards me a great deal of substantial sympathy in the way of work."[13] This was all to the good, as she had entered law at an inauspicious moment. The New York banking house of Jay Cooke failed the week before she was admitted to the D.C. bar, triggering five years of economic turmoil throughout the United States.

Belva's clients were a multiracial group of laborers, painters, maids, tradesmen, veterans, and owners of small real estate properties. She was fortunate to have a network of people who knew her as a teacher, rental agent, landlady, and local activist as well as in the role of Ezekiel's wife. These associations enriched her client base, which she expanded with business cards and a listing in *Boyd's*, Washington's city directory. Perhaps to save money she only rarely took out professional ads in the *Washington Law Reporter*, the local trade paper, but when publishing legal notices in the *Reporter* on behalf of her clients (and at their expense), she made certain that "BELVA A. LOCKWOOD, SOLICITOR" appeared in bold letters at the top of the item.[14]

The fact that Lockwood's clients were largely working-class undoubtedly helped in her success. As a woman she would not have been able, in the words of a female colleague, to make "an extensive acquaintance among business men in an easy, off-hand way, as male attorneys make it in clubs and business and public places."[15] These male networks were denied to her but other channels existed, and she used them to scout for clients. She took cases in the District, Maryland, and Virginia, and was always ready to go further afield. In August 1874 the *Evening Star* reported that she had legal business in the Southwest: "Mrs. Lockwood, the lawyeress, leaves for Texas tomorrow, to be absent some forty days for the purpose of settling up the estate of the late Judge John C. Watrous, of that state, who died some two months ago in Baltimore. Judge Watrous was a large landed proprietor in southwestern Texas."[16] District of Columbia Judge Arthur MacArthur told her that he did not believe that women lawyers could be a success, but the D.C. Supreme Court docket books tell another story: as soon as she was admitted to the Washington bar, the number of her clients increased.[17]

Her goal was a competitive Washington-based legal practice. Initially, after her September 1873 admission to the District bar, she accepted cases that brought her before the Supreme Court of the District of Columbia. Created by Congress (under its constitutional power "to exercise exclusive legislation" over the District), this court was "an unusual hybrid" that had been given most of the trial and appeals authority of other federal courts, but that also heard criminal and civil cases that elsewhere in the United States came before state and local courts. In her first year of licensed practice, she appeared nearly exclusively as plaintiff's attorney in the Law or the Equity division of this court, a pattern that maintained itself to a lesser degree from 1874 to 1885.[18] She argued cases in which damages were sought following allegations of seduction and breach of marriage contract. Like local male attorneys she also had her share of debt and ejectment proceedings, as well as cases involving injunctions, probate proceedings, and trustee appointments. Half of her courtroom equity work, however, centered upon divorce actions. As a woman attorney, she attracted female clients and represented wives as complainants against defendant-husbands. After divorce actions, her most frequent equity work involved injunction proceedings, lunacy commitments, and actions requesting the partition of land. Much of her civil law work did not bring her to court and is not recorded in docket books, but it is likely that, along with the other storefront lawyers of her day, she worked up untold numbers of bills of sale, deeds, and wills in order to stay solvent.

For many people, the postbellum emphasis on gentility made the thought of women working in the criminal courts egregious, even loathsome. Society's morally repugnant dramas played out in criminal court—a place, therefore, off-bounds to *ladies*. Lockwood could have refused criminal cases. Yet, despite her religious rectitude and middle-class aspirations, she did not turn away from criminal cases and criminal court argument.[19] She began with minor offense cases in Police Court in a room teeming with people, many down on their luck, charged with drunkenness or simple assault. By 1875 she had begun to attract clients charged with more serious crimes, representation that brought her before the judges of the criminal division of the D.C. Supreme Court.

From 1875 to 1885 she represented dozens of criminal defendants in this court. They were charged with virtually every category of crime, from mail fraud and forgery to burglary and murder. She won "not guilty" decisions in fifteen jury trials and submitted guilty pleas in nine. Thirty-one of her clients were judged guilty as charged, while five others were found to be guilty of a lesser charge. An entry of *nolle prosequi* ended four cases. She won retrials for several others. She handled most of these cases on her own, with only an occasional male cocounsel. Before the all-male juries of her day Lockwood showed neither the natural female timidity nor the delicacy described by U.S. Supreme Court Justice Joseph Bradley in his *Bradwell* opinion.

After practicing in makeshift space at the Union League building, in 1875 Lockwood took the family to rented rooms at 512 Tenth Street, two doors down from the residence into which the mortally wounded Abraham Lincoln had been brought from Ford's Theater. She conducted business in one of these rooms with Lura and Ezekiel nearby. Although increasingly frail, her husband continued to work as a notary public. His name and seal appear on legal documents filed by his wife up to the month of his death in 1877.[20]

Ezekiel died on April 25. Belva grieved, but five days after his death, she was at her desk petitioning, by letter, for correction of an error in the assessment of a client's taxes.[21] Ezekiel's death was followed by that of her father and her sister-in-law, Sarah. She later wrote letters of apology to clients whose business she had ignored during this sad time, not telling them, however, that although burdened by family tragedy, she had found time to arrange the purchase of a home for her family.[22] The house, at 619 F Street, NW, was a substantial four-story building with twenty rooms. The extended Lockwood clan had lived there prior to its purchase, as renters, and Ezekiel had died there.[23]

Lockwood acquired the property on July 31, 1877, from Alexander W. Russell and Leonidas C. Campbell.[24] She contracted to pay $13,600. She put down a thousand dollars in cash, taking out mortgage loans with Russell and Campbell for the rest; five promissory notes, at 7 percent per annum interest, falling due from three months to six years.[25] In fact, she needed ten years to repay these loans.[26]

The F Street house was a clear statement of Lockwood's now-solid middle-class professional status. Heavily mortgaged, it was undeniably a risky venture, but the purchase made good business sense. The building would be a home, a boarding house, an office, and a long-term investment. (Over the years she would use the property as collateral on loans and business deals. In 1902, when money was tight and she wanted fewer rooms to look after, she turned the basement into a store for rent.)[27]

Although it was not at all fancy, the house made an impression on visitors. In *American Court Gossip*, Mrs. E. N. Chapin told her readers the brick home had nicely furnished parlors "with several good paintings to add their tribute to the lady's taste."[28] The house became the permanent residence of members of Lockwood's extended family, and Catherine, her housekeeper. By 1880 the family included Belva's mother and her niece, Clara Bennett, as well as the recently married Lura and her husband, DeForest Payson Ormes.[29] Lura gave birth to three children, Rhoda, Inez, and DeForest, Jr., at F Street. Rhoda died in infancy in March 1884, and Inez, born nine months later, died there of croup on December 29, 1889.[30] Only DeForest, Jr., born in 1891, survived to adulthood.

Lockwood took over the first floor of the house for her law office, filling the rooms with mahogany and walnut desks and chairs, piled high with books and legal papers.[31] A changing gallery of portraits hung on the walls. An interviewer visiting the office in 1912 reported looking up at "Washington, Martha Washington, Lincoln, Roosevelt and Taft."[32]

In this house Lockwood's public and private lives were intertwined. She staffed her office with family members and, occasionally, a visiting man or woman interested in taking up the law. Twenty-two-year-old William Harrison, a notary, boarded with the family and had a desk in the downstairs office. While a law student, he and Clara courted and, after they married, continued to live at the F Street house.[33] Following his premature death in the mid-1880s, Belva hired her niece, now the mother of a young son, Warren, as an assistant.

The person whose life was most tightly tied to Lockwood's was her daughter, Lura. Except for time away at school, visits to Bennett and McNall relatives, and one trip abroad, she spent her life in homes provided by her mother.[34] She died at age forty-four in a bedroom at F Street, several years after being made a partner in her mother's small law firm.

Mother and daughter began the journey into law in each other's company although Lura dropped out of law school, for reasons she did not record, at the end of the first year. She was twenty-one and spent the remainder of her twenties searching for an occupation and an identity. She was young and unattached but lacked Belva's ability to create opportunity. While her mother toured the South for Greeley and the *Golden Age*, opened a law office, and fought her way into the local bar, Lura worked as a book sewer, and at the Government Printing Office.[35] She was reluctant to identify herself as a legal assistant, although she swore in an affidavit that she had been working in her mother's office "almost continuously since Sept 1873."[36] Her mother was boastful but she was not. She wrote a regular newspaper column about political and social life in the nation's capital for several years before listing herself as a "correspondent" in *Boyd's* and the national census.[37]

Lura married DeForest Payson Ormes on July 3, 1879, four months after her mother's news-making admission to the U.S. Supreme Court bar. She was twenty-nine; Ormes, an East Coast man whose family had lived in Massachusetts and New York, was thirty-five.[38] Although Lura must have hoped that marriage would help her to achieve an identity independent of her mother, at least one Washington newspaper reported the event as "the wedding of Mrs. Belva A. Lockwood's daughter."[39]

Lura's groom was a man of modest talent. Most of his adult life he worked as a pharmacy clerk although he had an interest in the telecommunications industry, worked as an agent of the Southern Bell Telephone Company, and dreamed of becoming a venture capitalist. In 1888 Lockwood told journalist Nellie Bly that DeForest was trying to get up "a stock company in New York for the telautograph."[40]

Although they tried, Lura and DeForest were not able to separate themselves from F Street. Their most notable effort came in the second year of their marriage when they went abroad for eight months, traveling from England to India, on a trip that may have been connected with DeForest's efforts to establish himself in the telegraph and telephone business. In published articles written during the winter of 1881 Lura documented her impressions of London, Versailles, Paris, Cologne, and Naples, as well as their "very slow and tedious" passage on the Suez Canal.[41] By spring she was forwarding her "foreign letters" from India.[42]

After this tour Lura returned to F Street where, while clerking for her mother, she and DeForest began to raise a family. She worked alongside Clara. It was a mutually beneficial arrangement in which Belva provided a home for the two young families whose children, close by in the upstairs living quarters, came to visit and not infrequently got into mischief. Lura's daughter Inez, described by her grandmother as a "wonderfully clever child," on one occasion became so playful that she bumped a lit candle into the curtains, causing legal papers on the nearby desk to burn.[43]

Lura and Clara looked after correspondence, kept accounts, and "booked & jacketed" pension claim applications.[44] Clara eventually moved out of the city, but Lura stayed on and was made a partner. "BELVA A. LOCKWOOD, Attorney and Solicitor" became "BELVA A.

LOCKWOOD & CO., Attorneys and Solicitors." When speaking with Nellie Bly, Lockwood described Lura as a "skilled lawyer [who] takes charge in my absence."[45] In a private communication to the Commissioner of Pensions, Lockwood wrote, "Mrs. Ormes has been practicing as an attorney for some time before the Pension Office."[46] Lura, however, never became a member of the D.C. bar and steadfastly refused to call herself a lawyer. Nevertheless, when she died, Belva, prideful and grieving, wrote once again that her daughter was an "Attorney."[47]

Beside members of her family, Lockwood boarded friends like Mary Walker as well as strangers—tradesmen, government clerks, and artisans—who found their way to the F Street house by word of mouth or after reading her newspaper advertisements. The 1880 census depicts a home bursting at the seams: eighteen people were in the residence. Four were members of her extended family. Visitors and boarders mixed easily, occasionally with comic effect. One night someone confused the room assignments, causing a young man to climb into bed with Susan B. Anthony.[48]

Women came to F Street who hoped to become attorneys. Marilla Ricker arrived in 1877. She came because of Lockwood, and because the D.C. bar admitted women. Raised by a father who taught her to challenge religious and social orthodoxies, Ricker was the widow of a wealthy farmer who, in her home state of New Hampshire, used her status as a property owner and tax payer to promote the cause of woman suffrage. She attended lectures on criminology while living in Europe, and decided to become a lawyer in order to bring change to the criminal justice system. Lockwood's acolyte was smart and quickly went to work as an assistant, reading law and helping with cases. Shortly after her arrival, Lura reported an appearance by Ricker at the D.C. Supreme Court. Calling Marilla "another lady lawyer," she described her as a specialist in criminal law with a strong sympathy for criminals whom she believed to be "morally diseased" (a contemporary term used by progressives to suggest victimization).[49] Ricker was, in fact, an apprentice who, after reading law with Lockwood, also studied with several male attorneys, A. G. Riddle among them. She won admission to the D.C. bar on May 12, 1882, having passed, Lockwood observed, "a very creditable examination with a large class of young men."[50]

Ricker and Lockwood established a close personal relationship that rested on their shared interest in using law for reform purposes as well

as a fondness for public attention. Marilla drew Belva into her campaign on behalf of prisoners' rights, while Belva brought her protégé
into the struggle against employment discrimination. The two women
worked from 1877 until 1882 to overcome the sex discrimination that
prevented Ricker from obtaining an appointment as a notary.[51] After
President Chester A. Arthur granted the appointment, Ricker, "the pris-
oner's friend," used her position as notary to take depositions gratis
from men and women who could otherwise not afford to make a formal
statement.[52]

Emma Gillett, another protégé, came from Wisconsin, despite the
opposition of her family, in order to read law with Lockwood. She apprenticed with her for a year, enrolled in the Law Department of
Howard University, and in June 1883 was also admitted to the D.C.
bar.[53] Gillett took Lockwood as her inspiration but not her model. Less
outgoing than her mentor, and more cautious about her health, Gillett
chose the back office, where she thrived. She refused all jury cases. She
became a Chancery examiner and, like Ricker, won an appointment as
notary public when President Arthur opened the position to women.
She joined a small local law firm headed by Watson J. Newton, where
she stayed for the rest of her career (being made a partner in the late
1890s). At the end of her career, with Washington lawyer Ellen Spencer
Mussey, she revived Lockwood's idea of a professional school for
women and helped to establish the Washington College of Law.[54]

Lavinia Dundore was another woman often seen with Lockwood.
The two women may have first encountered one another in the late
1860s at a meeting of the Universal Peace Union or, somewhat later, at
the NWSA.[55] Lura almost certainly referred to Dundore when she wrote
that her mother had a lady partner in Baltimore. Lavinia, along with
Baltimore agent Kate Harris, worked up pension claim cases for the
Lockwoods.[56] When Belva opened her law practice she regularized the
arrangement, hiring Dundore as a clerk who answered correspondence,
prepared evidence, and kept accounts.[57] Like Ricker, Lavinia boarded at
F Street and joined the coterie of women accompanying Belva at public
appearances. So frequently were Dundore, Lockwood, and Ricker seen
together at the Capitol, the courts, and federal agencies that a local journalist nicknamed them "the three graces."[58]

Dundore shared her friends' strong feelings about workplace discrimination. Late in 1877 she agreed to join their fair employment campaign. While Lockwood was contending with the U.S. Supreme Court

and the Congress, and Ricker was challenging the government to license her as a notary, Dundore was sent up before the judges of the District Supreme Court with an application to become Washington's first woman constable and bill collector.[59] Unlike her friends, Dundore never succeeded. She continued to work at the F Street office until, in June 1879, she testified against Lockwood when a client charged her with demanding an illegal fee in a pension filing.[60] Their relationship soured while Ricker remained a close friend who would later help with Lockwood's 1884 presidential campaign.

Lockwood combined the business of law and the business of running a boarding house in still other ways. In the summer of 1877 Civil War veteran James Kelly came to the law office hoping for help with a pension and a bounty claim. Kelly had been in the army since the 1850s, moving about the country. His wife was dead and he had recently sent for his two daughters, who had been left in California in the care of Catholic nuns. The girls, Elizabeth and Rebecca, came east only to witness their father's mental and physical collapse. By 1879 he required care in the Soldier's Home and in February 1880 Kelly was "adjudged a lunatic." A month later the court appointed Lockwood "committee of the estate" with power to collect and receive the pension money due him from the government. She was charged with the responsibility of furnishing him with necessities, and of looking after his two daughters.

The Kelly daughters, teenagers, had come under her care even before Lockwood's appointment as guardian. James had asked that she watch over them and keep them from the streets. Rebecca and Elizabeth, in some court papers described as "weak minded," proved difficult.[61] Clara later testified that Rebecca never had regular tasks and could not be depended upon.[62] Elizabeth posed more of a problem. Lockwood told a court that she was "too imbecile for self support and required constant supervision to keep her from vagrancy and importuning men."[63] She stayed with Lockwood until 1884, when "she became violently insane and was committed to St. Elizabeth's Asylum."[64] Neither of the girls won the hearts of anyone at F Street but its owner's. Clara, adopted by her aunt and dependent upon her for a home, said, with some exasperation, that Belva would always bear with the girls, "defend and protect them because they had nowhere else to go, quite to the discomfort of other members of her family."[65] In fact, Clara reported, her aunt lost boarders who were not willing to put up with the girls' bad conduct.

The children of Cherokee James Taylor proved easier when put in Lockwood's care. Taylor, a lobbyist for the Eastern Band of Cherokee, first met the Lockwoods in 1875 at the Tenth Street boarding house where Belva cultivated Taylor as a legal client. He gave her his personal legal business while they analyzed the more substantial problem of the Eastern Cherokee, who were negotiating for legal recognition and the right to file with the United States government monetary, treaty-based claims.

Taylor made frequent trips to Washington and sometimes boarded at F Street. On one of these trips, he asked Lockwood to supervise two of his several children. She agreed, taking in John and Dora Taylor in the early 1880s, often for several months at a time. She charged the senior Taylor for their room and board. She looked after their schooling, bought their clothes, and when it was time for them to leave Washington, arranged for their travel to Indian Territory.[66]

The bustling F Street household was situated in the center of downtown Washington, which made it easy for Lockwood to reach the local courts as well as the federal offices and chambers she visited as she expanded her claims, patent, and pensions practice. F Street also put her across the street from the Patent Office and the Bureau of Indian Affairs. Perhaps most fortunate for the Lockwood law firm was the selection of a site barely one block from 619 F Street for the new Pension Building, a handsome red brick structure modeled on the Palazzo Farnese in Rome.[67]

The six hundred block of F Street was, in fact, a hub of legal activity with Washington's legal trade paper, *The Washington Law Reporter*, operating out of rooms at 633 F Street, NW, along with attorney Henry Beard and the Knight Brothers firm. Hosmer & Co. had its office at 629 F, and Andrew Bradley practiced at 635 F. Like Lockwood, they were eager to be near the federal departments as well as the District courthouse on D Street. The walk from F Street to the U.S. Law Library, located in the old Supreme Court chamber at the Capitol, was a pleasant one, but F Street lawyers impatient to conduct business could also travel to the Hill by one-horse tram. Lockwood walked or used public transportation until, in 1881, she shocked Washingtonians by acquiring a bicycle, the first local woman to do so.

The English model bicycle that she purchased was, in fact, an adult's tricycle, a modification of the more dangerous highwheeler. The safer tricycle had recently gained popularity among men but it was not imagined that members of the fair sex would venture onto them. Only a foolishly daring or immodest woman would cycle, out on her own, showing a bit of ankle, provoking verbal harassment. Lockwood was not immodest. She was a practical 51-year-old woman, a health enthusiast who was comfortable with modern technology and unafraid of publicity. She rode several miles daily, going "to the Departments, the Capitol and the Courts," and had acquired the machine after seeing that the male attorneys who rode them were completing their work more quickly.[68]

Columnists immediately noted the spectacle. A reporter for the *Post* described her flying up the Avenue "on her three-footed nag . . . battling the world unaided and alone."[69] An artist's sketch accompanying the article depicted "Mrs. Lady Lawyer" with her "cargo bag of briefs for the Supreme Court or a batch of 'original invalids' for the pension office." Amused by the attention, Lockwood sent back a light-hearted poem: "A simple home woman, who only had thought / To lighten the labors her business had wrought. / And make a machine serve the purpose of feet. / And at the same time keep her dress from the street."[70]

Female cycling was unacceptable to many people because it challenged the morals and manners that ordered society and kept women dependent on men. President Grover Cleveland issued what Lockwood called an edict, telling the wives of his cabinet officers that he did not wish them to ride bicycles.[71] Other pundits declared that the freedom of female cycling caused an "intoxication which comes from unfettered liberty."[72] Large art posters reinforced their pronouncement with images of bare-breasted, abandoned beauties, astride their bicycles. Other wags declared that bicycling ruined the "feminine organs of matrimonial necessity."[73] A few American towns outlawed cycling by women. Dress reformers, however, loved the idea of cycling, believing that it would encourage women "to discard the murderous corset."[74] Susan B. Anthony proclaimed the bicycle a mighty gift that "has done more to emancipate woman than any one thing in the world."[75]

Bicycles were only part of the endless debates women lawyers had over questions of professional decorum, workplace relations, health, and fitness. The best record of their soul searching survives in the letters of a late 1880s women lawyers' correspondence club, a group in which Lockwood participated.

Seven women lawyers and law students at the University of Michigan founded the group in October 1886, calling it the Equity Club. They recruited "Sisters-in-Law" who, like California attorney Laura de Force Gordon, felt a "want of Professional companionship . . . [and] assurances of that close sympathy born of mutuality of interests, which women alone can extend to a woman."[76] Three dozen women trained in law responded to the invitation to participate in a club that operated through the simple device of shared letters.

Lockwood sent off her first and only Equity Club letter on April 30, 1887. Her field was, she wrote, "far from being a dry study, as many have supposed, but on the contrary, possesses a peculiar and fascinating attractiveness."[77] She noted that she had "all and more good paying work than I could attend to without assistance," telling the others that she had taken up and "earnestly" entered into every type of case occurring in civil, criminal, equitable, and probate law.[78] "In the three last orders of cases, I have been markedly successful, and reasonably so in the first."[79] For Lockwood, even such a modest qualification of achievement contrasted with her usual self-promoting public statements, suggesting that she considered these intimate letters private in nature despite their journey through dozens of hands. Unfortunately, she did not analyze why her civil law practice fell short.

Lockwood seldom lost an opportunity to speak on behalf of her reform causes, and this letter was no exception. She made two recommendations urging the elite Equity clubwomen to support the nationalization of state domestic law and to advocate a new curriculum for girls in America's public schools, one that would educate them in the principles of the state domestic law that she wished to nationalize. "Women," she wrote, "have always been the chief sufferers of bad legislation." Referring to guardianship, property, and divorce law, she contended that if schooled early in these "ground principles, a woman would be better able to protect herself and children."[80]

Women lawyers struggled with the public perception that they were mentally and physically inferior and required special treatment to do their job. Equity Club women categorically rejected the idea that they had less talent for law but they acknowledged that their careers might suffer because they were excluded from local fraternal organizations. Mary Green testified that the beneficial influence of her sisters was felt broadly, in particular, in the less agreeable moral atmosphere of the courtroom.[81]

The issues of decorum and performance raised the question of whether, to succeed, women needed to follow the example of men and also pushed the women to interrogate themselves as to whether the "female constitution" permitted women to compete as attorneys. The near-universal answer was "yes."[82] Like Lockwood, most of the Equity Club lawyers did not see themselves as prisoners of the female condition. They did understand, however, as Emma Haddock made clear in one letter, that doing the work of homemaker *and* lawyer caused women's health to fail. Like Lockwood, many of the letter writers practiced regimens for healthful living that included calisthenics and outdoor errands (but not bicycle riding), while in their dress they were sensible women who had accepted many of the teachings of the dress reform movement. Illinois attorney Catharine Waugh was quite specific in her advice. She admonished her Equity sisters to pay more attention to dress, diet, and exercise if they wished to be strong: "My creed includes no corsets, broad, low heeled shoes, reform under garments, dresses in one piece hanging from the shoulders, no tea, little coffee or pork, few pies and cakes, much sleep, a little hoeing in the flower beds and a day in bed when occasion demands instead of sitting and suffering."[83]

8

The Practice of Law

Discussions are habitually necessary in courts of justice, which are
unfit for female ears. The habitual presence of women at these would
tend to relax the public sense of decency and propriety.

Wisconsin Supreme Court, *In re Lavinia Goodell*, 1875

Although a staunch advocate of women's rights, Lockwood practiced
law in the fashion of Washington men with small, street-level firms,
spending her days with a busy mix of clients, paperwork, and court appearances. In the District there were few large law practices. Solo and
partner arrangements dominated on the several streets, including F,
where attorneys clustered, some in rented rooms, others, like Lockwood after 1877, in buildings they had purchased. They belonged to a
profession whose ranks were increasing, making the competition for
clients a constant factor, especially in the areas of debt, deeds, and divorce, along with guardianship, estates, pension claims, and lobbying
private bills before Congress.

Lockwood said that a great part of her "life-work" was "to place my
sister woman on an equality with man."[1] As a political candidate and
lobbyist she was an inventive champion of equal opportunity for
women. Her law practice, however, paid the bills. She wanted to fight
the legal disabilities experienced by women but could not afford to
make sexual bias the sole focus of her work. Still, she managed her
share of poor women clients whose life stories were often like dime
novel plots.

Mary Jane Nichols became Lockwood's client in the winter of 1875.
She had cared for the children of John Adlum Barber until, she alleged,
Barber raped her. In the original bill filed in *civil* court, Lockwood described a "seduction" carried out by Barber against Mary Jane's "will
and earnest remonstrance."[2] She became pregnant with a child born on

January 9, 1875. A month after the original filing Lockwood submitted an amended petition in which she named three instances of rape. Each involved forcible nighttime entry into Mary Jane's room; each sexual attack was accompanied by additional physical assault. The lawsuit asked ten thousand dollars in damages, "in consequence" of the "repeated trespasses, batteries and ill usage," and because Mary Jane had lost her good name, health, and means of earning a livelihood, in addition to incurring the responsibility of caring for Barber's child. What is most interesting about the case is why the two women, lawyer and client, settled on a civil cause of action. Mary Jane had spelled out multiple incidents of rape, a felony, but papers filed by Barber make it clear that he was never charged with a crime.

Mary Jane may have told her story to the police but that Barber was not charged suggests either that she did not, or that she could not produce sufficient evidence. Mary Jane may also have cared less that her employer be imprisoned than that he be made to pay up for her loss of reputation and wages. She was a working woman with practical concerns. In all likelihood Lockwood took it as a civil case because of the fees should she win a settlement, and because she knew that the civil law of seduction was in flux. In Anglo-American law a cause of action for seduction had long been the privilege of fathers and masters (of bound out girls) considered by the law to have a property interest in the young woman. Only in the middle of the nineteenth century did certain states extend this common law right to women, so that *they* could sue their seducers for damages. Even after this change, prevailing legal doctrine (so-called merger doctrine) often preempted a civil suit, prescribing that criminal prosecutions precede or extinguish the sort of private actions brought by Mary Jane.

Lockwood knew that unless Barber was charged and tried in criminal court, legal authority weighed against filing Mary Jane's case.[3] Barber's attorneys, from the local firm of Peter and Darnielle, wasted no time insisting that the absence of a criminal trial precluded the civil suit. Lockwood stood her ground, citing D.C. Judge Andrew Wylie's recent challenge of merger doctrine: "Under the common law a person whose rights have been violated, is not obliged to stand helplessly by and see his private rights merged in the crime against the public."[4] Peter and Darnielle argued that a long line of cases in English and American jurisprudence protected their client from being sued. They did, however, admit a problem. The point of law was not a settled one in the District.

In a written brief they argued that the court should follow the common law as applied by the state of Maryland, as Washington had been a part of that state until 1801.[5]

The case was filed in March 1875. For fourteen months Lockwood and Barber's lawyers lobbed pleas, demurrers, and amended declarations. Over the objections of Barber's counsel, the case was placed on the court calendar. Both sides gave oral argument on May 19, 1876, after which followed more demurrers, pleas, and joinders of issue. Finally, in late September 1876, Lockwood signed an order for discontinuance with the Clerk of the Court. Had John Barber agreed to an out-of-court settlement? There is no record, making it difficult to calculate Lockwood's exact worth to Mary Jane. But her willingness to take the case, and the use of Wylie's opinion, suggest that, only two years out of law school, she was an aggressive and innovative lawyer ready to question received law in an effort to fashion an alternative legal remedy for women like Mary Jane.

The case of client Louisa Wallace provided a different set of circumstances. Described by Lura as "a poor, simple-minded black woman, so weak in mind that she is scarcely accountable for what she does," Wallace was, nevertheless, indicted for infanticide several days after the April 25, 1878, death of her newborn son.[6] At trial the defendant told the court that she had been born a slave in Prince George's County, and was about forty-seven years of age.[7] She had come to Washington during the war, lived for some years with her husband, and worked as a servant.

Court papers filed on May 8, 1878, seeking her indictment, stated that Wallace had been pregnant with a "bastard" child, had delivered a son at her house, and had taken him to the cellar where, it was charged, she secreted the newborn and left him "without nourishment or sustenance."[8] She awaited trial in prison and was arraigned on November 6, 1878, when she entered a plea of not guilty. Lockwood and Washington lawyer James Redington, who joined her as cocounsel, worked on her defense throughout the autumn, submitting to the court the names of defendant's witnesses until December 18, two days before the trial.[9] Among those listed was Lockwood's friend, physician Susan A. Edson, who Lockwood hoped would assist her in raising a reasonable doubt in the minds of the jurors that Wallace's baby had been born alive.

The trial began on December 20. The proceedings moved rapidly, despite many witnesses. By 4:00 P.M. the jury had been charged and sent out to deliberate, a discussion that lasted less than two hours. The all-male jury, rejecting defense contention that the child had been stillborn, found Wallace guilty but in a letter handed to the presiding judge, they urged executive commutation of the stipulated sentence, death by hanging.[10] Lockwood stood next to her client as the verdict was read and later told the press that she would ask for a new trial. Four days later she and Redington filed motions to have the verdict set aside, and for a new trial. They argued technical irregularities and the lack of "sufficient and satisfying evidence" that the child had been born alive.[11] Judge Wylie approved the motion for a new trial, saying that he was obliged to do so because the prosecution had not proved that the child was a bastard.[12] A new indictment was handed down and on April 1 Wallace was arraigned. She was now represented by Lockwood, Redington, and newcomer W. H. Smith.

The second trial lasted several days. The prosecution called as witnesses a number of doctors, anxious to prove that Wallace had given birth to a "child capable of independent existence."[13] Louisa's team again called forward friends and members of her family. Lura later wrote that two of these witnesses, Indian Fannie and Letha Matthews, lied under oath. Caught in the lie, they were later arraigned on the charge of perjury. Lura referred to this as the "disastrous phase" of the trial.

Smith presented the closing argument for the defense. He asked the jurors to pay attention to the "degree of certainty" necessary to establish the truth of a charge and carefully to consider the physiological dimensions of the case. He said that the government needed to show more than evidence that the child had breathed. Before their client could be found guilty of infanticide, the prosecution had to establish that the child had independent life and independent circulation.[14] He told the jury that it was the duty of the government to establish "to your satisfaction and beyond a reasonable doubt" that the child was born alive and that it came to its death by the willful and intentional neglect, or act, of the defendant. If the child died from injuries it sustained during birth that were not intentional, or from a naval cord that unintentionally remained untied, the verdict should be for the defendant.[15]

Sentencing came a week after a guilty verdict.[16] Wallace sat next to Lockwood and Smith as the presiding judge, Randall Hagner, announced that the jurors had again recommended executive clemency, urging that Wallace be sentenced to no more than the ten years' imprisonment permitted in a manslaughter conviction. Hagner, however, showed no compassion. Reacting to the sympathy, in the District and elsewhere, shown to poor women charged with this crime, he began his comments by berating the women of Washington for not attending the trial and acknowledging the important issues raised by the case. "It was an awful fact," he said, "—and it was not appreciated—that this offence was more prevalent here than in any other city."[17] He read an article from a medical journal describing the rise in infanticide. He called the crime atrocious, "evidence of the rudest barbarism," and said that if the child had lived it would not have "come to actual want . . . for there are foundling asylums where infants are cared for."[18] Then he sentenced Louisa to be hanged, arguing that the crime, "if suffered to go unpunished by any country, that country would become a field of blood."[19]

Despite the passion of this speech, Lockwood and her colleagues hoped that the recommendation of the jury would influence President Hayes, who, under the law, had it in his power to commute the capital sentence of anyone convicted in the District's criminal court. Louisa's case was sent to the pardon clerk at the Department of Justice, along with that of at least one other person convicted of murder. On June 16, 1879, four days before the time Hagner had set for her execution, Hayes granted Wallace a conditional pardon, reducing her sentence to the ten years' imprisonment recommended by the jury.

Mary Jane Nichols claimed to have been raped but could not produce the needed witnesses. The paternity of Louisa Wallace's child was never established. In the late nineteenth century the law posed difficult, often impossible, hurdles for women wishing justice, wronged in sexual relations with men. Women's character bore close scrutiny: was she "loose," designing, given to lying? Victimized women could choose to do nothing, to take their sullied names, lost dreams, and out-of-wedlock children and go on with life. Or they could seek satisfaction, as Nichols had, through the use of civil law, public notice, and shaming. A civil action for seduction became popular among women after the Civil War. So did lawsuits for breach of promise of marriage. They were small but important legal weapons used to equalize the bargaining power of women, and Lockwood, enmeshed in women's rights, undoubtedly saw them as instruments to be used in unraveling patriarchy.[20]

Lockwood handled several cases claiming breach of marriage promise. These cases posed evidentiary problems, but Lockwood continued to accept them, and soon after Mary Jane's action she agreed to represent Lucy Walton Rhett Horton.

Lucy was a belle from Alabama with a long name and a small purse. In January 1880 she asked Lockwood to bring a civil suit for twenty thousand dollars on her behalf against John H. Morgan on the cause of seduction and breach of promise of marriage. Lucy claimed that John had seduced her one warm Selma evening, after a ball, down by the river. That was April 1877. Her beau was attractive and the son of one of Alabama's two U.S. senators, John T. Morgan. She became pregnant but had what she termed a miscarriage. Lockwood said Lucy had obtained an abortion. Lucy attempted to hold her beau to his word while still living in Selma. She told Lockwood that "an indictment" had been brought on her behalf in Alabama but that the judge was related to the senior Morgan's wife and had recused himself. No other judge stepped forward to hear the case. Lucy claimed no one wanted to anger the powerful Morgan family.

John H. fled to Washington and the protection of his father. Lucy followed him on at least two occasions. She wanted John to marry her, though she no longer wished to live with him. If he refused, she wanted money and the opportunity to give the world "full notice" of the base nature of his character.[21] Lucy first hired a series of male attorneys to attempt a negotiation on her behalf and, if that failed, a lawsuit. Dissatisfied with the preliminary results, she took after John H. with a pistol. Shots were fired but no one was hurt. Senator Morgan sent his son to Harper's Ferry, West Virginia, for safety while Lucy was indicted on the charge of assault with intent to kill.[22]

The criminal prosecution proceeded slowly. Meanwhile, Lockwood was hired, early in 1880, to continue the civil suit, which was now two years old. Lucy insisted that she should not have to live with the burden of a dishonored life, while Senator Morgan, himself accused of "ruining" several young women, was adamant that his son's affair was nothing more than a youthful indiscretion and opposed both marriage and a settlement.[23] The two sides kept the case before the court for two more years. Then, in November 1881, perhaps after private negotiations, Lockwood filed for dismissal.

Jessie Raymond came to Lockwood—in 1879 or early 1880—for the purpose of bringing a lawsuit. She named Benjamin Harvey Hill as the defendant. Ben Hill was a United States senator from Georgia. He was, according to his biographer, the outstanding southern figure in the Congress.[24] According to Jessie Raymond, he was a sexual predator and the father of a child, Thomas Benjamin, born August 1, 1878. She told Lockwood that she and the married senator had met in November 1877 in the parlor of the Kimball House in Atlanta, Georgia. After this first encounter, Hill obtained her Peachtree Street address and surprised her with a visit.[25] Jessie later testified that the senator seduced her and that an affair ensued. In August their son was born. She apparently attempted legal action in Georgia without success, a fact teased out in a press interview with Hill in which he acknowledged knowing Raymond, having "seen her once in a law office in Atlanta."[26]

Lockwood was well acquainted with Ben Hill. He was a popular and prominent southern Democrat, a man held in high regard for his practical politics and for having helped to bring about a peaceful settlement of the Hayes-Tilden electoral dispute. Lockwood, however, thought him haughty. He had been dismissive of her efforts to open the federal bar to women attorneys and had voted against her bill, and she relished the opportunity to bring this powerful man to justice.

Lockwood first pursued quiet negotiation. Newspaper accounts report that in the initial months of the case Hill gave the 23-year-old Jessie an occasional five dollars, but declared that the whole business was an attempt at blackmail, an assertion, Lura pointed out, that he did not support by asking for Jessie's arrest.[27] He also charged that political enemies had conjured "the conspiracy."[28] These private discussions were not fruitful and on February 27, 1880, Lockwood filed a Notice to Plead in which her client swore that Hill had "debauched and carnally knew [her]; taking advantage of the fact that she was friendless and alone."[29] On March 2 Raymond petitioned the court to waive the docket fee because she was "poor, having no property or means wherewith to pay [the fee] in advance."[30]

Gossip-hungry Washington read eagerly as front-page news articles described the David versus Goliath battle. Lockwood set out to win ten thousand dollars in damages for seduction, and child support, while Hill and his prominent attorney, R. Y. Merrick, sought to bribe Jessie to drop her lawsuit and to discredit Lockwood. It was Gilded Age drama at its best. The client could be unreliable: at one point she accepted Hill's bribe and stated that Lockwood did not have her consent to sue, a statement she later withdrew.[31]

Hill's men and Lockwood's supporters did their best to prosecute the dispute in the press. Hill pounded away at the question of whether

Jessie had authorized Lockwood to bring or continue the suit, while Lura and her mother moved from polite descriptions of the senator to disparaging accounts of his willingness to attack those who stood by the helpless Miss Raymond. In a particularly bitter moment, Lura referred to an unidentified letter alleging that Hill had "ruined several young Washington girls" and frequented houses of ill-fame.[32] In a public letter Lockwood challenged Hill to cease his denunciations of her "in the corridors and ante-rooms of the Senate," while threatening to name the Capitol Hill family whose sixteen-year-old daughter Hill had debauched and to whose members Hill was now dispensing jobs.[33] Jessie, according to reporters, made a daily practice of going to the Capitol or to the senator's residence, where she "contents herself with attracting a crowd and talking loudly to them."[34]

Hill had voted against Lockwood's women lawyers bill but worse yet in her eyes, he had refused all communication with her when she came to Capitol Hill.[35] Lockwood was uncertain whether the contingency arrangement she and Jessie had (most probably) agreed upon would result in the payment of her fees. If need be, however, she was prepared to take her payment in spite, through the opportunity to embarrass Hill. She made this plain in her February 27 Notice to Plead. In it she argued two points: that the court award damages to Jessie and that the matter "may be inquired of by the Country."[36] And in the end, shaming Hill may have been all the payment that Lockwood received. Two separate press accounts, one in late March, another at the end of April, allude to a private settlement and the sight of Raymond, sporting a large roll of bills, boarding a train for Richmond.[37]

Her attorney kept up a spirited fight to defeat the senator's motion to strike the case from the docket, suggesting that the reporters may have been incorrect. In June 1880 Judge Wylie sustained Hill's demurrer and gave judgment for him. He subsequently denied Lockwood's motion to amend her client's declaration, and the case ended. Yet months later reporters were still writing about the case. Apparently, many journalists did not know about Lockwood's personal bitterness toward Hill and could not make sense of her attempt to persuade Judge Wylie not to end the lawsuit after Raymond's disappearance. In February 1881 one journalist wrote,

> Mrs. L. is not to be appeased. She is more the client herself than the client's lawyer. She believes a great wrong was done. . . . The fact sug-

gests that perhaps women lawyers are more valuable than the other kind, or at least more faithful. Their sympathy is easily awakened. . . . Whether they can give way to this sympathy and at the same time preserve the shrewdness which ought to be the first characteristic of all lawyers is a question yet to be decided.[38]

Lockwood did not believe that her actions were guided by *sympathies*. Rather, the high-visibility case offered her the opportunity to hammer away at women's victimization while attacking the reputation of a public official who regularly voted on issues that affected women's lives. Still, it was a messy lawsuit. Raymond was not an easy client, Hill was a powerful man, and there is no record that Lockwood earned a fee. She later tried to capitalize on the public's interest in Hill by preparing a lecture, "Characteristics of Congressmen," but, because of his influence, she was denied rental of the Atlanta opera house and perhaps other lecture halls where she hoped to deliver the talk.[39] She had succeeded in "prosecuting" Hill in the newspapers, but the public slowly lost interest. Hill was diagnosed with cancer and died in August 1882.

Lockwood only infrequently worked with male attorneys. One of these collaborations, *Kaiser v. Stickney*, provided the opportunity for her first oral argument before the United States Supreme Court, the first time that a woman member of the bar participated in argument.[40]

The court heard *Kaiser* on appeal from the Supreme Court of the District of Columbia, on November 30 and December 1, 1880. Lockwood was listed as counsel, along with Mike L. Woods. The case involved the execution of a deed that bound local property for the payment of a twelve-thousand-dollar promissory note. Lockwood had been lawyer for the appellant, Caroline Kaiser, since 1875.[41] With some irony, she tried to use the old and much-criticized D.C. married women's property laws to her client's advantage by arguing that Kaiser, a married woman, could not legally be party to a contract that encumbered her own property. The strategy failed and *Kaiser* was appealed to the U.S. Supreme Court, which, because of the District's unique status, was the court that heard appeals from decisions of the D.C. Supreme Court.

Twenty-one months earlier Lockwood had become a member of the high court bar. Now she stood with Woods, who began their presentation with the same argument made before the D.C. court. He and Justice William Strong fell into a heated discussion of the law.[42] According to the *Evening Star*, which gave the story front-page coverage, Lockwood rose at the conclusion of this exchange and, although she had not been scheduled to speak, asked to be heard. The justices agreed and she spoke for twenty minutes, giving her view of the case.[43] In *Kaiser*, and for some years to come, she stubbornly held to the position that the earlier disabilities imposed on married women by the legal doctrine of coverture should protect them against responsibility for debt.[44] She and Woods did not persuade Waite and his colleagues. They lost their client's appeal and Lockwood left no record indicating that she was able to use this reasoning more effectively in other cases. Still, a woman's voice had finally been heard in legal argument at the highest court in the land.

Unquestionably, by 1880 Lockwood was a celebrity. Even before she argued *Kaiser* people sought her out for public appearances because of her accomplishments. As an engineer of reform, she understood the importance of political theater and willingly participated in noteworthy and attention-getting occasions. One of the most joyful occurred in 1880 when she agreed to propose the admission to the U.S. Supreme Court bar of African-American attorney Samuel R. Lowery.

The son of a slave, Lowery was the first African American from the South to seek this honor. According to Lura, the press corps had learned that a newsworthy event would occur and were present when Lowery and Lockwood entered the courtroom. The journalists were, she wrote, "on the *qui vive*" while the justices, less well informed, "sent out to know what it all meant."[45] Lowery was a Renaissance man, having worked as a minister, teacher, principal, and prize-winning cultivator of silkworms. He was also a lawyer, who had read law with a white Tennessee attorney and been admitted to the bar in Tennessee and Alabama. He and Lockwood may have first met when she toured the South for Tilton, in Washington or through the Universal Peace Union.[46]

Standing before the justices of the nation's highest court, the body that had denied freedom to the slave Dred Scott and had dashed the aspirations of Myra Bradwell and, for a time, Lockwood herself, Lowery and Lockwood became part of a near-unimaginable tableau.[47] Radical Republican Congressman George Julian recognized this, describing the courtroom scene as "a fitting subject for an historical painting."[48] A reporter observed that "it was quite fitting that the first woman admitted to practice before this court should move the admission of the first Southern colored man."[49] The *Havre de Grace Republican* cast the moment as a challenge and an accomplishment: "Who dares say the world is not progressing, when, on the motion *of a woman, a black man* is admitted to practice in the highest court of the land? Shade of Taney!"[50] Everyone was pleased. Nobody commented that the woman in front of the justices was not permitted to vote, or that discrimination and violence against freedmen was increasing.

If the docket books are to be trusted, Lockwood eased out of courtroom work in the mid-1880s. She did not refuse civil and criminal trial work, but in place of courtroom appearances, Lockwood expanded her Civil War pension and bounty claims work—a field that, after the Civil War, attracted thousands of attorneys.[51] Some, like Lockwood, who had learned the ropes early and whose office was in Washington near the Pension Bureau, earned significant incomes from pension filings and pleadings despite federal laws that strictly regulated attorney fees.[52] The Lockwood law office handled seven thousand pension cases from the 1870s through the 1890s.[53]

The Lockwood firm relied on inventive techniques to solicit business. Belva actively used her travels to collect pension claims, carrying in her luggage stacks of handbills advertising the firm of "Belva A. Lockwood & Co."[54] The strategy of soliciting business while on a lecture tour was a successful one, and she wrote home more than once that she was "gathering up and sending home as many claims against the Government as I can find."[55] Back in Washington Lura and Clara would receive the batches of original applications and begin to process them while Lockwood was still out of town.

Because volume lay at the heart of a profitable claims business, agents and attorneys also developed an elaborate system of partnerships and subagents. Professionals in Washington functioned as a hub. They often received unsolicited claims applications from agents living in towns distant from the capital who were not familiar with the peculiarities of the Pension Bureau or knowledgeable about moving an individual claimant's private pension bill through Congress.[56] Lockwood developed her own network of male and female subagents and correspondents.[57]

Lockwood made a good living at pension claims and was respected for her work and her character, but like other pension attorneys, she was not immune from charges of greed and malpractice. She once testified that human nature and the complexities of legal work occasionally led to accusations.[58] In the course of thirty years of pension work, a handful of complaints were filed against her at the Pension Bureau. Most were trivial and easily resolved. One, however, appears to have been true. In a years-long appeal brought by the family of John Heck, whose children she had sheltered, Lockwood was found to have mixed household and pension accounts, and was forced to repay a thousand dollars plus interest.[59]

9

Lady Lobbyist

> What [Mrs. Lockwood] knows from experience about lobbying would make a mighty interesting little book.
>
> *Lockport Daily Journal*, February 17, 1879

Even before becoming a lawyer, Lockwood had tested her skills as a lobbyist, trying to influence suffrage and employment discrimination policy. Before the Civil War the women who lobbied abolition, education, temperance, or suffrage policy appeared before state legislatures but were virtually unseen in Washington. When the fighting stopped, however, female lobbyists descended on the national government and became a common sight on Capitol Hill and at the White House. Government contracts and employment, pensions for widows, claims for war depredations, and the possibility of a constitutional amendment on suffrage brought women to the capital, where they hoped to win the ear of a legislator. They conducted their congressional business in the Rotunda and from the ladies' parlors set aside for them inside the Capitol where, according to Lura McNall certain women gathered, "well dressed, bejeweled, anxious and importunate," their persuasive arts aided by paper, apple, and peanut stands that served to give the rooms a "festive bazar [sic] appearance."[1]

America was of two minds about lady lobbyists. Most observers dismissed them as no better than their male counterparts, widely regarded as shady and self-serving. In *American Court Gossip; or, Life at the National Capitol*, Mrs. E. N. Chapin depicted a gay if cynical political whirl in which spiritualists-turned-lobbyists and blonde widows with "black melting eyes" held "high carnival" in their homes, where wine suppers were "the preparations of an advance on the Congressman who held the purse strings of Uncle Sam."[2]

Neither blonde nor black-eyed, Lockwood lobbied on many matters. In addition to women's rights she buttonholed politicians on matters of pension claims, mining rights, Indian affairs, and foreign policy. As a social cause lobbyist she was unpaid, but when a law client's business required congressional attention, she of course added her time to the bill. On occasion, she made requests that would benefit her practice or a private investment scheme in which she had an interest.[3] She claimed credit for a bill that acknowledged bounties owed to Civil War–era sailors and marines, legislation that aided the men and gave her business as a claims attorney.[4] She was often a foot soldier, useful to reform organizations because of her presence at the capital. She liked the role of the strategist and played it until the end of her life, as she revealed in a 1915 letter to Jane Addams outlining her thoughts for a just postwar settlement.[5] She was a repeat player whose success before Congress with the women lawyers bill was a singular but not unique achievement.

Not surprisingly, women sought Lockwood's help. Illinois reformer Elizabeth Packard was one of the first to approach her, on the rights of mental patients.[6] Packard had been the victim of an extraordinary but lawful involuntary imprisonment at a state hospital for the insane, her admission having been ordered by her minister husband after she had openly challenged him in the matter of his Presbyterian faith. Freed after three years, she emerged a determined reformer who wrote books on the punishing effects of patriarchy and the brutality of the asylum system. She came to Lockwood hoping to promote a "mailbox law" that would guarantee patients a way to send and receive mail, uncensored by staff physicians. In January 1875 the women won a hearing before the postal affairs committee, but the bill Packard proposed, opposed by reformer Dorothea Dix, stalled, and Congress moved on to other legislation.

Marietta Stow, later Lockwood's running mate in the presidential campaign of 1884, enlisted her professional advice in a contest involving marital rights. After Joseph Stow's death, according to his widow, his sizeable estate was needlessly pushed into insolvency by self-interested executors, aided by the local probate court. Stow insisted that she had been cheated out of as much as two hundred thousand dollars.[7] Already a rights activist and not someone to suffer quietly, she went after marital property and estate laws saying they impoverished widows and denied them their fair share for their life's labors.[8] Stow came to

Lockwood with the radical idea of reforming domestic law in the United States by nationalizing it. She called her proposal "An Equal Rights Marriage Property Act." In layperson's language, its six sections described a federal law of marital property, child custody, and estates that would empower women by guaranteeing them half of household resources.[9]

Her arrival, late in 1879, was not well timed. Lockwood was busy with her law practice and her ongoing effort to open government positions to women. Stow presented herself just as Lockwood was hoping to salvage a recent campaign to end male control of the District school board. In July she had petitioned D.C.'s board of commissioners, asking whether there was any legal objection to the appointment of women as school trustees.[10] The petition was part of a national movement to give women a greater voice in education policy: Lockwood was not alone in believing that women performed the largest share of work in educating children and should serve on the boards that administered their schools. Changing minds, however, was not a simple matter. In the same year that she went before the D.C. commissioners, NWSA activist Lillie Blake reported that the governor of New York had vetoed a bill that would have opened his state's school boards to women members.[11]

Lockwood waited several months for the study committee to issue a recommendation on her petition. As expected, the majority recommended that women not become trustees although admitting that women were the "brightest ornament" of the school system, showing more "tact, skill, economy, and devotion than men."[12] There had, however, been disagreement, with the black sheep of the group stating flatly that the appointment of "ladies" would advance the interests of education.[13] The rest of the committee, however, while agreeing that the board of commissioners had the legal power to appoint women, nevertheless strongly recommended that it refuse to do so.[14] In what Lockwood considered a deliberate provocation, the committee voted down two conciliatory reports, instead selecting as its official statement the openly hostile opinion written by Benjamin F. Lovejoy, who accused the activists of wanting the trustee positions for themselves, and who sought to defame them as members of the National Woman's Suffrage Association.[15] Insinuating that the women had nothing better to do than pester officials, Lovejoy also suggested that the petitioners were radicals whose demands did not have the support of the women of Washington. Lockwood tried to speak during the meeting but was refused recognition. After the hearing she confronted Lovejoy and called his report "an unmanly one."[16] She struck back with a written statement calling him a failed journalist and failed attorney who had, in desperation, "contrived to get himself appointed as a school trustee."[17] There was no question that cooler heads needed to prevail just as Stow arrived in town. Lockwood's supporters urged her to keep up the fight against Lovejoy, but she did not yet have a strategy. In time she would decide that it was simply a matter of repeatedly raising the issue and calling out allies, the same approach she had used to win women access to the federal bar.[18]

Stow waited for Lockwood's attention. She hoped for her support as well as her help with members of Congress. The Stow bill interested Lockwood, who, as a leader of the women's movement, supported the expansion of the rights of wives in personal and marital property. In her law practice she had worked with clients who had suffered humiliation and poverty as the result of marital property law that, she said, had the "vestige of heathendom."[19] In early December Lockwood took Stow to the Capitol, where they lobbied the Stow bill but found no enthusiasm for the proposal, one legislators felt certain would antagonize male voters as well the local government officials who jealously guarded the right to control marital and estate law. Only at the last minute did they secure Indiana Congressman Gilbert De La Matyr as sponsor of the bill.

A Methodist preacher, De La Matyr had resigned a ministry in Indianapolis to come to Washington and serve his country. A member of the Greenback Party, he spoke against Gilded Age "money power" and supported legislation that would empower farmers, laborers, and women. On December 9 he presented Stow's bill, H.R. 2623, to his House colleagues. He offered no accompanying comments although, quietly, with Lockwood, he was trying to find a way to make the bill more acceptable. Rather than face the wrath of the states opposed to a federalized code, they proposed a revision that would limit the reach of Stow's proposal, reforming marriage and estate law only in the District of Columbia and the U.S. territories, jurisdictions controlled by the federal government. (They may have envisioned this as a model for future reform.) What happened next is not clear. De La Matyr told the Clerk of the House to record the bill as "An Act to Regulate Estates in the District of Columbia, and the Territories of the United States." As the result of confusion or, perhaps, because Stow did not favor the compromise, the clerk was given, and filed, a handwritten copy that bore the title "An

Equal Rights Marriage Property Act." This document contained the full text of the original proposal for a uniform federal code of marriage property and estates.[20]

The bill was referred to the House Judiciary Committee with hearings scheduled for December 16. Stow, Lockwood, and a handful of women supporters joined members of the committee in a small House conference room where the two lobbyists testified. Stow made her standard arguments while Lockwood argued, more cautiously, for a common marital property law.[21] She said that federal law should recognize marriage as a civil contract in which the property rights of husbands and wives were equal. Then she digressed, telling the startled committee members that young women should not marry until they were able to support a husband: "We have always taught the boy that marriage must not be thought of until he is able to support a wife. What we need in this age, is the same culture for boys and girls."[22] Following this aside, she returned to her defense of the bill, suggesting that "just for a little while," she would like to transform the committee chairman into a woman whose fate was in the hands of the Probate Court, and that he would benefit from being a woman long enough to know "the thorniness of the path along which the gentler sex is obliged to plod its weary way."[23]

Lockwood knew the bill stood little chance of success. Still, she and Stow may have been encouraged by the recent *Reynolds* decision, in which the U.S. Supreme Court upheld the right of Congress to regulate marriage in the Utah territory.[24] Although that legislation had been motivated by the desire to end plural marriage among Mormons, the Court's decision had established the precedent of federal involvement in domestic law. Any optimism that Lockwood mustered, however, was short-lived: the bill died in committee. Stow left Washington not long afterward. She carried with her the satisfaction of having prodded legislators to think about an issue they would rather have avoided. Lockwood was pleased to have testified but unhappy that members of Congress showed no interest in reforming property and estate law in Washington and the territories at a time when a growing number of state legislatures were paying attention to the need for reform.[25] There were, however, other issues to lobby. By the time it was clear that De La Matyr had done as much as he could, she was involved in a new cause: the criminal justice system.

Echoing a concern being raised in many communities, Washington activists said that the District needed to recruit women police officers, a laughable idea in Victorian America.[26] They argued the matter as a question of fair employment. They also contended that women would come forward more readily to report crimes of rape and abuse if precinct houses were staffed with female officers and that there would be less abuse of female suspects if they were not processed by male police. Using the foundation laid down by Sara Spencer's congressional testimony in 1874 and 1877, Lockwood also helped to lobby legislation that would establish, for the first time in the District, a separate reform school for girls to be headed by a female superintendent managing a staff of women.[27] Ironically, the members of the D.C. Board of Commissioners who opposed allowing women on the school board joined in supporting this bill, staff provisions and all.

Success did not come quickly, and required years of lobbying in which bills were introduced and reintroduced.[28] The women played a patient game of public relations, using the press, Congress, and the NWSA, which could always be counted upon for a resolution of support.[29] The District first appointed a woman police matron in 1884. A girls' reform school was approved in 1892, and a separate women's house of detention was opened in 1900.

Lockwood seldom lobbied for causes that enjoyed broad popular support. Like other members of the NWSA she was provocative because her demands for fair treatment and equal opportunity threatened settled arrangements of power, money, and social status. Generally, Lockwood's NWSA colleagues agreed with her when she argued for ending employment discrimination or including women on school boards and other governmental bodies. Her commitment to the cause of the Mormon women of Utah, however, caused worry as some of her activist friends became anxious that their movement could not bear the weight of an issue as contentious as polygamy.

The Church of Jesus Christ of Latter-day Saints (LDS/Mormons) originated in the early-nineteenth-century religious experience of Joseph Smith, whose claims to have seen God and angels were quickly denounced as heresy by more established Christian sects. Smith and his followers experienced harassment that only grew after he claimed a revelation sanctioning plural marriage, the taking of more than one wife by a man. Polygamy was central to Smith's understanding of the way Mormonism would restore the true order of the ancient Church of Christ. Plural marriage strengthened the patriarchal nature of Mormon marriage and reinforced the Mormon emphasis on community, family, and stability over individualism.

After Smith's murder in 1844 by an Illinois mob, his followers moved further west, establishing a colony, called Deseret, in the Great Salt Lake Valley. Under the leadership of Brigham Young, the Mormons established a theocratic government as well as a communitarian economy.[30] In 1850 Congress organized Deseret as the Utah Territory. Young, territorial governor, hoped to bring Utah into the Union as a state. Church leaders quickly discovered, however, that the political, economic, and cultural differences between the Mormons (the largest population in the territory) and the rest of the United States had spawned a politics of intolerance. Officials regarded Mormon polygamists as adulterers. Hoping to gain political ground, the LDS supported the Democratic Party because of its advocacy of states' rights. This action encouraged members of the new Republican Party, at its 1856 convention, to endorse a resolution calling for the abolition of the "twin relics of barbarism," slavery and polygamy. A year later President James Buchanan sent two thousand soldiers west, intent upon replacing Young with a non-Mormon governor.

Anti-Mormon politics fit easily into the larger anti-Masonic, anti-immigrant, and anti-Catholic spirit of mid-nineteenth-century America. In 1862 Congress attempted to eradicate polygamy through an "Act for the Suppression of Bigamy,"[31] sponsored by Vermont Senator Justin Morrill. In theory, the bill honored the right "to worship God according to the dictates of conscience"; in fact, members of Congress argued that polygamy did not deserve the protection of the First Amendment, saying that plural marriage had no valid connection to religious practice and that the legislation regulated marital relations, not religion.[32]

The Morrill bill, despite its enactment, failed for lack of effective enforcement measures. The Utah territorial government, controlled by Mormons, simply ignored its provisions. Then, in 1870, the Utah legislature voted to extend the franchise to the women of the territory.[33] The legislators, in what had now also become a religious war, intended to show that Mormon women, although portrayed as concubines, had more rights and freedom than their sisters in the East.

Congress responded with legislation that would disfranchise plural wives and ban them from serving on juries. This put Lockwood and other members of the NWSA in the position of having to decide whether to defend the right of polygamous women to vote. In 1871 the organization took the courageous step of endorsing the first of many resolutions supporting the right of all Utah women to vote. The Nationals made it clear that they abhorred plural marriage but, perhaps naively, believed that Mormon women did not approve of the practice and could use their vote to cleanse the church of it.[34]

In the early 1870s, while she was in law school and traveling for the *Golden Age*, Lockwood apparently did not concern herself with the Mormon question.[35] A few years later, however, at the January 1876 NWSA convention, she signaled interest. As reported in the local press, on the second evening of the meeting she strode in and reported on activity at the White House and Capitol Hill that did not bode well for the Utah women. She denounced the anti-Mormon "Utah ring" in Congress, and then argued that the Nationals should continue to support polygamous women's right to vote, as they had at previous annual meetings, not because women in Utah would end the reviled practice but because it was a "vested" right.[36] Speaking as an attorney, Lockwood reminded the delegates that Utah had conferred woman suffrage in a constitutional and lawful manner, and that it had been exercised there for five years: "We have not learned that households have been broken up or that babies have ceased to be rocked."[37] On behalf of the resolutions committee, she offered a motion to again support the right of Utah women to vote. The delegates adopted the measure, an action that put the organization in the risky position of defending the democratic rights of a people whose practices they condemned.

The Nationals backed the resolution and authorized Lockwood, Sara Spencer, and Ellen Sargent to form a special committee to "watch over the rights of the women of Utah."[38] The three used this mandate to testify before Congress. The work of the committee continued for several years, operating in the increasingly anti-Mormon political climate encouraged by President and Mrs. Hayes. Late in 1878 Spencer proposed that the NWSA welcome women known to be in plural marriages at its upcoming convention. Lockwood supported this invitation, made to Emmeline B. Wells and Brigham Young's daughter, Zina Young Williams, as did Stanton and Anthony. On January 8 Lockwood hosted a meeting of the executive committee at her F Street house, where it was decided to showcase the Utah representatives and to give them important committee assignments.[39] At the NWSA convention, Wells and Williams were seated on the stage and given the courtesy of an introduction by the venerable Stanton. This occurred just three days after the justices of the U.S. Supreme Court, in *Reynolds v. U.S.*, called polygamy "an offense against society" and declared that the free-exercise-of-religion clause of the Constitution did not protect the Mormons in their practice of plural marriage.[40]

Meanwhile, George Q. Cannon, Utah's congressional delegate, feared retreat on the part of the NWSA just when it appeared that Vermont Senator George Edmunds, an avowed foe of plural marriage, was heading for success with new anti-Mormon legislation. To determine the strength of the NWSA's support, in January 1882 Cannon met with Lockwood and Susan B. Anthony, afterwards reporting to LDS President John Taylor that both women were "ready to render all the aid in their power to fight this [the Edmunds] proposition."[41] The women were particularly alarmed because the initial draft of the legislation called for *all* Utah women to be disfranchised. Sensing that this might be a mistake, the astute Edmunds revised his bill.[42] He narrowed its impact on women by substituting a gender-neutral test that would deny any man or woman in a polygamous relationship the right to vote, hold public office, or serve on juries.[43] The change, calculated to assuage southern states' rights Democrats and silence opposition from the organized suffrage movement, succeeded. Anthony did not argue against the final version of the legislation as she now believed that it protected the rights of *virtuous* women.[44]

Lockwood took a more assertive stance against the Edmunds Act after President Arthur signed the bill into law on March 22, 1882. She did not approve of polygamy, but she believed that the law punished "innocent women for the crimes of men."[45] In part, personal factors influenced her actions. She was developing warm, even admiring relationships with Mormon women and wanted to help them, as well as possibly seeing the Church as a client. At the same time she welcomed an opportunity to criticize Edmunds, who, earlier, had insulted her and voted against home rule for the District as well as her women lawyers bill.[46] The Edmunds Act called for the establishment of a federally appointed, five-person commission to administer the new law. The work of the commission realized the worst fears of the Utah Mormon community. Telegrams arrived in the East describing arrests and the imposition of civil disabilities. Lockwood telegraphed back, "Stand by your guns and resist every encroachment on your liberties. I will do what I can to defend you."[47]

Members of the American Woman Suffrage Association had accepted the Edmunds Act, believing that the loss of voting rights was a fair punishment for being in a plural marriage.[48] Lockwood, however, thought that the Nationals, though chary, might continue to stand with the Mormons, and wanted to lobby the due process issues. When Edmunds, encouraged by the passage of the 1882 bill, again revived the idea of disfranchising all Utah women, she declared her opposition.

In these months Anthony had been working to broaden the appeal of the NWSA. She had been wooing the leaders of the Woman's Christian Temperance Union and promising a more centrally controlled movement, one distracted by fewer "side issues."[49] Lockwood, along with Stanton, Matilda Gage, and other old-timers, had doubts about Anthony's strategy. Lockwood, moreover, was determined that the Mormon question not be dismissed as an issue that might be considered bad for organizational business.

To her credit, Anthony knew that the question of disfranchising all of the women of Utah was too important to ignore. She agreed that Lockwood should speak at the meeting in order to explain Edmunds's plan to strip non-Mormon women, and nonpolygamous Mormon women, of the right to vote. Lockwood began by endorsing the resolution of support for the Mormons, one approved the day before, affirming that the disfranchisement of Utah women for no crime was a cruel display of power and that "this Congress has no more right to disfranchise the women of Utah than the men of Wyoming."[50] Then she delivered a prepared speech, "The Disfranchisement of the Women of Utah."[51] The talk was the angry summation of an attorney whose professional work rested on the important presumption of due process. Lockwood first questioned the constitutionality of the law, telling delegates the commissioners sent by the president had, by their actions, made the law "retroactive contrary to the spirit and letter of the Constitution." Polygamists had been disfranchised before conviction for a crime, as had first wives, women who, under the law, were guilty of no crime. "One would have supposed," she told her audience, "that the matter would have ended there." Looking up from her papers, she made it clear that it had not, and exhorted her listeners to understand that anti-Mormon politics in Congress was driven by "a spirit of tyranny and oppression," a spirit never content, always ready to "inflict some further torture." And that new outrage, she explained, was the legislation to withdraw the right to vote of any woman, Mormon or non-Mormon, living in the Utah Territory.

Congress, Lockwood recalled, had established Utah Territory in 1850 "with all of these peculiarities of a portion of her citizens known to the Government, and not only tolerated, but winked at, and allowed to attain gigantic proportions." And then she landed her blow: "The present strife is a party one, and raised for political effect, and for political ends. The real question at issue is, whether Utah as a State will be Democratic or Republican." She charged that Edmunds, a Republican, had long harbored a prejudice against woman suffrage. With this new measure, he "indulged" that prejudice while cutting off what Lockwood described as Utah women's support for the Democratic Party. Many newspapers covered the meeting and reported the talk as well as the "Utah" resolution. At least one reporter commented that the endorsement put the NWSA in "an attitude not unfriendly to polygamy."[52]

Lockwood repeated her NWSA speech in testimony before the House Judiciary Committee. When none of the pending legislative proposals succeeded she told a reporter, "Now, you must not make me say I defeated them, but they were defeated."[53] Throughout this period she was meeting with Utah's territorial delegate to Congress and corresponding with women leaders in Utah. She was taken up in Utah as a fearless champion and the text of her NWSA speech passed around. After one reading, Apostle F. D. Richards praised her sound constitutional analysis, and commended her courage in speaking before Congress and the suffrage convention on so unpopular a subject.[54] George Q. Cannon also singled her out for staying the course.[55]

At the 1884 annual meeting of the Nationals, despite a six-inch snowstorm, delegates crowded into Lincoln Hall, where they heard Lockwood again speak on the disfranchisement of Utah women. She later said that Anthony had asked her to make the speech, remarking, "If you do not treat that subject, no one else will, as they have neither the knowledge nor the courage."[56] Lockwood began with a lawyerly discussion of due process violations, describing the Edmunds Act and the proposed amendments as witch hunts in the spirit of a religious inquisition.[57] The Mormons, she continued, were decent and loyal people entitled to practice their religion without Washington's "unwarranted usurpation of power."[58] Here, the audience stirred, visibly uncomfortable. Washington, Lockwood said, had pushed forward in this assault because of a "morbid public sentiment intended to oppress a gentle, harmless people."[59] The federal government had no more right to attack the Mormon religion than that of Methodists or Catholics, and it ought to consider that persecution often resulted in the glory of the persecuted (and increased membership for the group). In closing, she pointed to the hypocrisy of married men who carry on long-term affairs. Mormon polygamists, she said, were not so much worse, and "it is profoundly to be hoped that congress will attend to its proper business and let Utah alone."[60]

Lockwood had barely stepped aside when Anthony rushed to the podium. It was her job to introduce the next speaker, but she did not wish to let a moment pass before telling the delegates that the NWSA only concerned itself with invidious legislation that would disfranchise women. Any other laws proposed by Congress to govern Utah and Mormon men, including matters of religion, were "none of our business."[61] The delegates agreed and rewarded Anthony with loud applause. Still on the stage, Lockwood replied sotto voce that she was "sorry not to have sufficient discrimination to see the difference between injustice to men and injustice to women."[62]

Anthony walked away with the lion's share of delegate support but Lockwood was not without allies. Clara Bewick Colby, a NWSA vice-president and the editor of the new *Woman's Tribune*, used her newspaper to defend Lockwood, writing that unjust things were being said about a woman who did not support polygamy but, with others, "holds that Congress has no right to proceed against the Mormons other than by due process of law."[63]

If Colby hoped to explain Lockwood to her critics, and to win exoneration, she failed. Lucy Stone, a leader of the American Woman Suffrage Association who, only a few years before, had praised Lockwood's campaign "against the old fogyism" of the Senate, now found her a reason not to reunite with the Nationals. Shortly after Lockwood's 1884 convention speech, Stone wrote Margaret W. Campbell,

There is a large pressure to have us meet with the Nationals. . . . Now it is not at all my idea that we can or ought to unite. The fact that Belva Lockwood spoke as she did about polygamy in their meeting, shows that we do not want to be with them. But we may be friendly and continue as we always have done to recognize their good work, when it is good.[64]

Despite this criticism, Lockwood continued to lobby Congress on behalf of the Mormons. Edmunds and Nevada Representative George William Cassidy had reintroduced the bill attacked by Lockwood at the convention. Hoping to counter their influence, she walked around an amendment that would negate the proposed disfranchisement of Utah women and testified before the House Committee on Territories that the Cassidy initiative was unconstitutional and if it was enacted, "down will go the liberty of this country."[65] She planned to do more but on March 7 she learned of the death of her former father-in-law, John Mc-Nall, and left to attend his funeral in upstate New York. Four days later, called back to Washington by the death of Rhoda, her infant grand-daughter, Lockwood was stopped in Rochester by a reporter familiar with her recent lobbying. He requested an interview and, although in mourning, she agreed.

Lockwood's support of the Mormons had, by this time, led to rumors that she was a paid agent of the Church. "It is current news," her interviewer said, "that your attitude in regard to the Mormon question, and your opposition to the proposed legislation in regard to it, are based upon the fact that you are employed by the Mormon leaders as their attorney to look after their interests in Congress."[66] He asked her to comment.

Lockwood acknowledged that the Mormons had contacted her in 1882 after federal commissioners began to strike women's names from the lists of voters. Asked again to clarify the relationship, she responded emphatically, "I am not a paid attorney for these people."[67] Lockwood did claim that she and Susan B. Anthony had suggested that the Mormons send money east to help defeat the Edmunds-Cassidy legislation. She remained vague as to the exact sum, or its precise destination, but later said that she had received one hundred dollars, "a collection" sent to her with a resolution of thanks for having spoken on the Mormon question before the Committee on the Territories and at the 1883 NWSA convention.[68]

Whether Lockwood received money from the Mormons mattered only in the way she represented herself before the NWSA and Congress. If the Mormons had retained her as a lobbyist, she was under an ethical obligation to say so. But there is no record to suggest that she was on the LDS payroll, or that she embraced the Mormon cause expecting a financial windfall. Rather, her outspoken commitment reflected her principles and politics, as well as the warm feelings that she developed for the Mormons, several of whom became friends.

That Lockwood would not yield on the Mormon question to the arguments of presidents, preachers, and newspaper editors was not surprising to those who knew her. She pretended a certain disengagement, telling a reporter in 1884 that the anti-Utah legislation was "dreadful, but . . . so to speak, really none of my business."[69] Yet in the same interview, she asserted the importance of speaking out, insisting that Edmunds and Cassidy were powerful agents of antisuffrage politics who must be fought because "to disfranchise the women of Utah affects every woman in the land."[70] And, if truth be told, she did not at all mind opposing them: lobbying permitted her to be a part of the political world that fascinated her and that she wished to influence.[71]

10

Lockwood for President

In view of the fact that France has gone to wreck under the rule of a man, and Great Britain has been secure, in the midst of danger, under the sway of a sad, widowed woman, need we be over much appalled at the idea of a possible lady President in some distant future?

Mrs. H. C. (Sara) Spencer, 1871

In the spring of 1884 Lockwood was fifty-three, in good health, and impatient to do more with her life, finding that the daily fare of small cases and pension filings did not satisfy her appetite for challenge, notoriety, or income. As she faced off against Senator George Edmunds and Congressman George William Cassidy's latest anti-Mormon legislation, Lockwood gave no hint that her yearnings took the form of a political candidacy, but by summer's end, she had become the presidential nominee of the Equal Rights Party (ERP). And by November she had conducted a full campaign for the office, a first for an American woman.

The accounts of Lockwood's nomination, like many political stories, are colored by ego and memory. She was drafted in August 1884, getting the nod from her acquaintance, Marietta Stow, who spoke for the newly formed, California-based Equal Rights Party, and from Stow's activist colleague, attorney Clara Foltz, who later insisted that Lockwood's nomination amounted to nothing more than a lighthearted antic on her and Stow's part, a joke about disfranchised citizens making the nomination.[1] Stow's biographer, however, makes a strong case that the nomination was also part of a serious political strategy devised by Stow to deflect attention from the rebuff given suffrage leaders that year at the Republican and Democratic conventions, and to demonstrate that "the fair sex" could create its own terms of engagement in American party politics.[2] Since 1880 Stow had been stubbornly proposing women for political office as well as urging the establishment of a women's political party. Her intentions were serious and in Lockwood she discovered a committed candidate.

American women's direct engagement in partisan politics began in the 1840s when Whig Party officials encouraged them to participate in the enthusiastic new style of politics that made campaigns popular events. Whig ladies attended rallies, conducted political meetings, wrote pamphlets, and made speeches. In 1844 the party established the first women's campaign clubs to help presidential nominee Henry Clay.[3] Ten years later women took part in the founding of the Republican Party. The issues of slavery, suffrage, and postwar reconstruction further encouraged women's active role in party politics. More women became stump speakers. The boldest of these women stepped forward as candidates. In 1866 Elizabeth Cady Stanton offered herself as a candidate from New York's 8th congressional district.[4] Four years later the flamboyant Victoria Woodhull, by then a New York City newspaper publisher, introduced the nation to the idea of a woman presidential candidate and became the first of her sex to run. She was cast as Mrs. Satan by the influential cartoonist Thomas Nast and campaigned for a short time before her radical views and financial reversals forced her to abandon the race.[5]

Without a female candidate, women took their reform issues to the parties. After the Civil War, suffrage and temperance topped the list. While the Republicans showed only tepid interest, the Prohibition Party, established in 1869, welcomed women who had proven themselves effective opponents of "demon rum" as delegates and committee members. By the early 1880s women were running as candidates for local offices with some frequency, generally for school board trustee or school superintendent, but also as independent or third-party nominees for state senator or governor. A handful won election to school boards.[6] When Stow approached Lockwood in the summer of 1884, American women held full suffrage only in the territories of Utah, Washington, and Wyoming, while fourteen states permitted "the fair sex" to vote in elections dealing with schools. Still thirty-six years from winning the constitutional guarantee of the right to vote, a number of women in the United States were committed members of partisan political communities. Marietta Stow saw no reason why Victoria Woodhull's dream of a female candidacy should not be revived.

Stow, like Lockwood, was a woman given to action. She had returned to California after lobbying unsuccessfully to federalize marital property and probate law. In 1880 she organized the California Woman's Social Science Association (CWSSA) and in 1881 started a newspaper, the *Woman's Herald of Industry and Social Science Cooperator*. She told her readers that the *Woman's Herald* would encourage discussion of equality for women, birth control, eugenics, cooperative enterprise, a shorter work day, the prevention of crime, and the "mischief resulting from a purely masculine form of government in Church and State."[7] Occasionally, Lockwood found her way onto the pages of Stow's paper when the editor discussed the Washington lawyer's opposition to the liquor trade and her healthful practice of bicycle riding.[8]

Many reform women tried to steer a nonpartisan course. Stow did not. She believed in the importance of women's election to political office. Shortly after her return to California, she accepted the Greenback Party's nomination for San Francisco school director. In August 1881 she announced the formation of the Woman's Independent Political Party, whose purpose was to prepare women for political life.[9] Perhaps she hoped to train members as campaign workers because less than a year later Stow announced herself as an independent candidate for governor of California. Using the *Woman's Herald* as the mouthpiece of her campaign, she argued that the "wholly masculine State Household had become littered with party issues and clogged with the debris of party strife."[10] She did not, however, hesitate to present her own candidacy in partisan terms: she was "anti-monopoly, anti-ring, anti-Chinese," in the prime of life, and "unpickled with whiskey and tobacco."[11] Tongue in cheek, she argued that by the codes of chivalry, the honor of the post should be granted to her. More seriously, she insisted that "[w]omen, from Deborah to Victoria, have proved themselves better rulers than men."[12] Not surprisingly she pledged that, if elected, she would abolish local probate courts.

In Oregon, newspaper editor and suffrage leader Abigail Scott Duniway read about Stow's candidacy. Duniway was a thoughtful strategist who opposed the expanding alliance between woman suffrage and temperance organizations because she feared that big liquor money would be called up against the suffrage campaign. Late in the summer she sent Stow a letter in which she termed her candidacy "a very unwise thing." Duniway acknowledged Stow's right to run but feared disaster as there would be "abundant chance for ridicule at the hands of those who are ever ready to sneer at women, deride their abilities and misrepresent their cause."[13]

Duniway conceded that Stow had drawn the attention of the press to the issue of women's right to participate in politics. She also admitted that a female candidacy might increase women's interest in political campaigns and "induce" them to go through the "formality of voting."[14] This, of course, was precisely what Stow intended. With her newspaper, her candidacy, and her various educational women's clubs, including a "Woman's Republic," she hoped to give women the confidence and background necessary to enter politics. She wanted women to insist on their right to vote and furthered the effort by setting up a rump polling place on the front porch of her house. Unlike Duniway, she felt that political theater could create positive momentum and that her completely legal bid for public office demonstrated the irony of *voteless* women candidates.

In the winter of 1884—a presidential election year—activist women across the country were assessing the benefits and shortcomings of the Democratic, Republican, Greenback, and Prohibition parties. Increasingly frustrated by the Republicans' indifference to the suffrage issue, reform women began to break ranks. In doing so they followed the example of temperance leader Frances Willard, who, since 1880, had been making every effort to bring her flock to the Prohibition Party, and Sara Spencer, who had endorsed the Greenback Party. Even Elizabeth Cady Stanton had been heard to say that women had "sat on a limb of the Republican tree singing 'suffrage if you please' like so many insignificant humming-birds quite long enough."[15]

Stow supported the Greenback Party. In the July 1884 issue of the *Woman's Herald*, she described Republicans as "the Stag Party," and berated its leaders for having silenced women at their recent nominating convention. The Greenbackers won her praise for the welcome they had extended to women speakers as well as a campaign platform that emphasized expanded suffrage, cheap money, and fair labor practices. In spite of her endorsement of Greenback candidates, however, Stow continued to believe that women needed their own partisan organization, and that the attention paid to female candidates served the cause of women's emancipation.[16] In the July issue of the *Woman's Herald*, she announced her nomination of West Coast suffrage leader Abigail Duniway as the presidential candidate of a party she baptized with the name "Equal Rights." She listed no vice-presidential aspirant. Instead, below

Duniway's name appeared that of Clara Shortridge Foltz, Stow's nominee for governor of California.

Duniway, who had not been consulted, shot off a letter to Stow from Oregon asking for the removal of her name from the "ballot." She repeated, with admirable civility, her objections to the tactic of running women as political candidates: "Flaunting the names of women for official positions," she repeated, served only to weaken the movement for rights and to give unscrupulous opponents new pretexts for lies, ridicule, and scorn.[17] How, she asked, could "a disfranchised candidate of a disfranchised people" make anything but "a sorry run for any office?"[18]

Using editor's privilege, Stow declared Duniway to be wrong-headed, and insisted women would not be viewed as equals until they were willing to "share and invite scrutiny and comparison."[19] She also recommended in print that Duniway and Foltz organize women's political parties in their respective states, and that Anthony do the same at the national level. Woman suffrage, she wrote, "will have a boom with a practical foundation and tangible superstructure."[20] And then, undiscouraged, Stow continued to search for a presidential candidate.

In August, she hit her mark. Lockwood subscribed to the *Woman's Herald* and had followed the exchange between Stow and Duniway. On August 10 she wrote to Stow in San Francisco, asking rhetorically, and perhaps disingenuously, "Why not nominate women for important places? Is not Victoria Empress of India? Have we not among our country-women persons of as much talent and ability? Is not history full of precedents of women rulers?"[21] The Republicans, she commented, claimed to be the party of progress yet had "little else but insult for women when [we] appear before its [sic] 'conventions' and ask for recognition."[22]

Lockwood, Phoebe Couzins, and several other women had been rebuffed earlier that summer at the Republicans' nominating convention when they appeared before the resolutions committee asking "in vain" that the party support woman suffrage.[23] By the time she wrote her letter on the tenth of August, Lockwood was completely exasperated with the party of Lincoln and maddened by suffrage women who continued to have faith in it. She considered, but openly rejected, Anthony's request that she and other NWSA leaders use their influence to help Republican candidates "out of harmony with real conditions."[24] On August 16 the *St. Louis Post-Dispatch* printed an interview in which Lockwood openly challenged Stanton and Anthony's political leadership. She said that they had every right to come out for Blaine and the Republican ticket but that she could not "see any advantage in standing by the party that does not stand by us."[25] She used the interview to single out Republican leaders in the Senate who had voted to disfranchise the women of Utah and then urged women to join her in supporting the candidacy of Prohibition Party nominee John Pierce St. John. Yet even as she said nice things about the Prohibition Party, in her letter to Stow, Lockwood mused, "It is quite time that we had our own party; our own platform, and our own nominees. We shall never have equal rights until we take them, nor respect until we command it."[26] Playing a coy game of politics, she endorsed St. John while signaling her own availability.

Stow had her candidate. Lockwood had grit, a quality that greatly appealed to Stow, who, on August 23, called a meeting where she read Lockwood's letter and proposed her as the presidential nominee of the Equal Rights Party although she had not asked Lockwood's permission. Stow then recommended Clemence S. Lozier, a New York City physician and suffrage activist, as Lockwood's running mate. Acclamation followed, and letters were sent to the two women. The dispatch to Lockwood read as follows: "Madam: We have the honor to inform you that you were nominated, at the Woman's National Equal-Rights Convention, for President of the United States. We await your letter of acceptance with breathless interest."[27]

Lockwood later said that the letter took her "utterly by surprise," and she kept it secret for several days.[28] On September 3, she wrote to accept the nomination for "Chief Magistrate of the United States" from the only party that "really and trully [sic] represent the interests of our whole people North, South, East, and West. . . . With your unanimous and cordial support . . . we shall not only be able to carry the election, but to guide the Ship of State safely into port."[29] She went on to outline a dozen platform points, and her promptness in formulating policy signaled that she (and the party) intended to be taken seriously about matters of political substance.[30]

The American economy was in an upswing after a period of depression, and there were plenty of issues to discuss. The Civil War had expanded the powers of the federal government, and citizens felt the hand of government in new ways. This satisfied some but displeased others. Patronage remained the mainstay of politics despite the year-old Pendleton civil service reform act. Workers were demanding federal legislation to control powerful new corporations as well as government support of an eight-hour workday. Contentious differences marked positions on tariff and immigration policy. Railroad companies begged for public land. Veterans' pension policy needed reform. Expansionists argued the case for the building of a modern navy. Lasting issues of civil and political rights remained unresolved for African Americans, women, and Native Americans.

Forecasters were predicting another close presidential race. Four years earlier, James Garfield had defeated Winfield Hancock by just forty thousand votes out of nine million cast, and people were again watching the critical states of New York and Indiana. The nearly even division of registered voters between the two major parties caused Democratic candidate Grover Cleveland and Republican nominee James G. Blaine to shy away from innovative platforms. Instead, the two men spent much of their time supporting popular policies that would not cost votes, and trading taunts and insults.[31] That left the business of serious reform to the minor parties and their candidates: Benjamin Butler (National Greenback/Anti-Monopoly), John Pierce St. John (Prohibition), and Samuel Clarke Pomeroy (American Prohibition). Butler, St. John, and Pomeroy variously endorsed an eight-hour workday, the abolition of child and prison labor, a graduated income tax, cheap currency, regulation of corporations, restrictions on the distribution of public land, senatorial term limits, direct election of the president, woman suffrage, and prohibition of the manufacture, sale, and consumption of alcohol. Lockwood joined this group of reform-minded candidates.

The design of Lockwood's platform reflected her practical savvy and her understanding of the sound bite. The platform, she said, should "take up every one of the issues of the day" but be "so brief that the newspapers would publish it and the people read it."[32] Her "grand platform of principles" expressed bold positions and comfortable compromise. She promised to promote and maintain equal political privileges for "every class of our citizens irrespective of sex, color or nationality" in order to make the United States "in truth what it has so long been in name, 'the land of the free and home of the brave.'"[33] She pledged herself to the fair distribution of public offices to women as well as men, "with a scrupulous regard to civil service reform after the women are duly installed in office."[34] She opposed the "wholesale monopoly of the judiciary" by men and said that, if elected, she would appoint a reasonable number of women as district attorneys, marshals, and federal

judges, including the nomination of a "competent woman to any vacancy that might occur on the United States Supreme Bench."[35]

Lockwood did not shy away from taking a position on the thorny
issue of tariffs, although her position did evolve. In her statement of
September 3, she came out in favor of high tariffs in order to "protect
and foster American industries," in sympathy with the working men
and women of the country who were organized against free trade.[36] In
the official platform statement reprinted on campaign literature, however, she modified this position so that the Equal Rights Party might be
identified as middle of the road, supporting neither high tariffs nor free
trade.[37]

Lockwood's membership in the Universal Peace Union was reflected in her foreign policy recommendations. She urged the extension
of commercial relations with foreign countries to promote friendship,
and advocated the establishment of a "high Court of Arbitration" to
which commercial and political differences could be referred.[38] She supported citizenship for Native Americans and the allotment of tribal
land, another position favored by American peace groups. As was to be
expected from an attorney who earned a substantial part of her livelihood doing pension claims work, she adopted a safe stance on Civil
War veterans' pensions. She argued that tariff revenues should be applied to benefits for former soldiers and their dependents; but at the
same time she urged the abolition of the Pension Office, "with its complicated and technical machinery," and recommended that it be replaced with a board of three commissioners. She vowed support for
temperance advocates. She also called for the reform of family law, the
issue that in 1879 had brought Marietta Stow to her:

> If elected, I shall recommend in my inaugural speech, a uniform sys-
> tem of laws as far as practicable for all of the States, and especially for
> marriage, divorce, and the limitation of contracts, and such a regula-
> tion of the laws of descent and distribution of estates as will make the
> wife equal with the husband in authority and right, and an equal part-
> ner in the common business.

Lockwood revised the twelve points outlined in her September 3
letter into an official fifteen-point platform statement that appeared on
campaign flyers below her portrait. The new version expanded certain
statements, used sharper rhetoric, and added several planks, including

a commitment that the remaining public lands of the nation would go to the "honest yeomanry," not the railroads.[39] She stuck to her radical positions of support for woman suffrage and the reform of domestic law, but, in an inexplicable retreat, her earlier promises of an equitable allotment of public positions by sex and any mention of the need for women in the judiciary were absent from the revised statement.

A day after Lockwood accepted the nomination, the Washington *Evening Star* made her candidacy front-page news and reprinted the entire text of her acceptance letter and September 3 platform. Suddenly she was famous.[40] Lockwood was candid with journalists, telling the *Star's* reporter that she would not necessarily receive the endorsement of activist women. Leaders of the American and the National woman's suffrage associations had endorsed Blaine, and Frances Willard had united temperance women with the Prohibition Party. "You must remember," she said, "that the women are divided up into as many factions and parties as the men."[41] In spite of this statement, she did not yet know just how upset NWSA leaders would become as she stole headlines and criticized the Republican Party. Suffrage leaders like Lillie Blake, who was a Democrat, also had harsh words, and she and Lura got into a shouting match, which Lockwood described as "squally," on the pages of the New York *World*.[42] Even the women who nominated her differed with their candidate on important questions of politics. Foltz and Stow supported anti-Chinese policies, while Lockwood attacked the controversial 1882 Chinese Exclusion Act as "anti-Christian and unconstitutional."[43]

Pleased at "the breeze which my nomination has made," Lockwood established campaign headquarters in her home, with Lura taking up the duties of campaign manager.[44] She sent letters to friends and acquaintances in a dozen states asking that they organize ratification meetings and arrange for ballots containing the names of presidential electors pledged to her candidacy. She argued that the opportunity to represent the Equal Rights Party was "a capital one to illustrate practically the ideas for which we have been contending."[45] She pointed out that if women or men electors committed to her are nominated and voted for, "*the votes must be counted* and the matter passes into history as a part of the Campaign of 1884."[46] By Election Day, Lockwood knew of electors pledged to her in at least seven states: Marilla Ricker headed an electoral ticket in New Hampshire, Foltz in California, Amanda M. Best in Maryland, Cynthia Leonard in New York, Leila B. Robinson in Oregon, with yet others in Michigan and Indiana.[47] Clara Foltz claimed that it had been difficult to find California women willing to lend the "dignity" of their names as electors but, in fact, the ERP succeeded brilliantly with a Who's Who list of local women.[48]

Closer to home, on the evening of September 18, party supporters organized a ratification meeting at Wilson's Station, Maryland. They deliberately bypassed the District to make the point that, under a new federal law, neither men nor women could vote in the nation's capital. Notices of the meeting—at an old farmhouse near a railroad station—and how to get there were published in the Washington newspapers and "billed in the streets."[49] Accompanied by her daughter and mother, Lockwood appeared in a black brocaded silk dress, cameo brooch, and gold watch chain, a rather reserved outfit for an appearance whose backdrop included gnarled apple trees, and picnic tables set with lemonade, sandwiches, and cake.

Mr. E. G. Barnard, a Washington family friend who worked at the Treasury Department and boarded with Lockwood, introduced the candidate to the gathering of one hundred supporters, journalists, and "sturdy old farmers of Maryland, who were almost amazed at the audacity of women holding a political convention."[50] Barnard declared that "in this age of progress it was not astonishing to see a woman nominated for the presidency."[51] As he stepped aside, Lockwood stepped forward, a bouquet of goldenrod now attached to her dress, and began her first campaign speech. Placing herself squarely in the role of feisty third-party reformer, she struck out at the Democratic and Republican candidates, accusing them of a "grand scramble" for office in which they offered "the same old platitudes upon which they have been drumming for the last quarter of a century."[52] These parties, she declared, were more concerned with perpetuating their own rule than with "preserving the union or elevating the condition of the laboring classes, enfranchising the women of the country . . . and, above all, rescuing our people from a financial panic, with which the industries of the country are to-day threatened by the contraction of the national currency."[53]

At this rally Lockwood also asserted her legal right to be a candidate, and to hold the office of the presidency. She had earlier told readers of the *Evening Star*, "I cannot vote, but I can be voted for."[54] At Wilson's Station, with her proud mother looking on, she said that there was not a thing in the Constitution that barred a woman's eligibility to become president. The terms laid out by the Framers were clear and she met them: she was a natural-born citizen, more than thirty-five years of age, and a lifelong resident of the United States. When she finished, two supporters were chosen as Maryland electors pledged to the ERP ticket, and the rally ended.

Four days later Lockwood hosted a lively gathering at her F Street house. The parlors were decorated with flags. At the end of one hall Lura had suspended a large piece of canvas on which she had painted an advertisement for her mother and the Equal Rights Party. Thirty people were present, including members of Washington's woman suffrage community and colleagues from the Universal Peace Union.[55] It was at this event that Lockwood and Lura told their friends that the elderly Clemence Lozier had declined the vice-presidential nomination.[56] Days later Marietta Stow agreed to accept the second spot and complete the ticket.

Throughout September the national press spread the story of the Equal Rights Party and its candidates. On the 17th, *Puck*, a mass circulation weekly that featured satiric cartoons, put Lockwood on its cover along with Greenback Party candidate Ben Butler. Artist Frederick Opper drew the lady candidate flying out of a theatrical trap door while Butler, posed and dressed as a buffoon, looked over a caption reading, "NOW LET THE SHOW GO ON! Arrival of the Political Columbine to Join the Political Clown." The costumes and caption identified the two candidates with Columbine and her suitors, Pierrot and Harlequin, stock characters in popular theater.

Three days later the story of the Lockwood candidacy reached thousands more Americans when the enormously popular *Frank Leslie's Illustrated* published an article that contemplated campaigning women with earnest good wishes: "Woman in politics. Why not? . . . Twenty years ago woman's suffrage was a mere opinion. To-day, it is another matter."[57] The article was accompanied by what was essentially an endorsement of Lockwood: a full-page sketch that featured a large portrait of her surrounded by four cameos celebrating women's contributions to the political life of the country.[58] Few readers knew that a woman—Miriam Leslie—controlled the editorial policy of the *Illustrated*.[59] In a short article accompanied by a respectful photograph, *Harper's Weekly* also told its readers about Lockwood's candidacy, saying she possessed "great force of character and indomitable perseverance."[60]

Despite the novelty, even notoriety, of a female candidacy most journalists treated Lockwood with an even-handed professionalism. She encountered no greater mockery than did the male candidates. She had to endure silly lies about hairpieces and sham allegations that she was divorced, but Republican candidate James Blaine was portrayed so harshly that he threatened to sue the publishers of *Puck* while, in cartoons, Cleveland was taunted with cries of "Ma, Ma Where's My Pa" (a reference to his out-of-wedlock child).[61] Thick-skinned, Lockwood later told an audience that a cartoon depicting her with fellow candidate Ben Butler was a "most cherished possession."[62]

Letters poured in for the candidate. They contained "earnest inquiries" about the Equal Rights Party platform and a few nasty bits of character assassination. Lockwood enjoyed one in particular from Elizabeth Cady Stanton admonishing the candidates not to go off "junketing" at public expense.[63] A note from a man included a poem that so amused the candidate she gave it to a reporter for publication:

> O, Belva Ann!
> Fair Belva Ann!
> I know that thou art not a man;
> But I shall vote,
> Pull off my coat,
> And work for thee, fair Belva Ann. . . .[64]

These letters also brought invitations to speak in cities across the country, and in late September she prepared to go on the stump. Her party lacked a campaign chest, but the lady candidate was a curiosity and people were willing to pay to hear her. She received fees for speeches delivered before civic associations and at state fairs. As a middle-class woman without independent income, she had no choice but to make the time she devoted to politics pay. When the election was over, she told reporters that she had a satisfaction denied the other candidates: she had come out of the campaign with her expenses paid and "$125 ahead."[65]

Lockwood also put out an invitation of her own. As an underdog she understood the advantage of debating high-profile candidates. On September 27 she sent a letter to the Democratic Party nominee, Grover Cleveland, summoning all of the presidential candidates to a "convocation."[66] Hoping to establish herself as a high-minded broker in a nasty

campaign, she wrote that the "unseemly, criminations and recrimina-
tions being indulged in by the adherents of the several candidates for
the office to which we have the honor to aspire are not only calculated
to have a deleterious influence upon the masses of the people, but to
bring that exalted position into contempt." She proposed a meeting on
October 10 in Wheeling, West Virginia, with the goal of improving the
conduct of the campaign by establishing a "peaceable armistice."
Drawing upon her knowledge as a member of the Universal Peace
Union, she told Cleveland that similar meetings among European
heads of state had "resulted in good." Reporters dubbed it "Mrs. Lockwood's Brilliant Idea," but there is no evidence that the other candidates acted on her call.

With Lura's help, Lockwood arranged for campaign materials to be
distributed to the public, including several different official portraits,
copies of the ERP platform, posters, and pamphlets. One portrait, cut in
copper plates, was captioned "Our Next President." It was produced in
various sizes and sold in large quantities to help with campaign expenses.[67] It was, perhaps, while waiting to sit for this picture that Lockwood refused to take the small chair made ready by the studio owner.
She spied the one in which fellow candidates Grover Cleveland and
James Blaine had been posed. "Why don't you place me in that chair?"
she asked. "That is the Presidential chair," replied the photographer.
"Well, sir, I will sit in that chair. I think I am able to fill it as well as any
who have occupied it."[68]

Lockwood's earlier experience working in the Greeley presidential
campaign had taught her what needed to be done. On fliers announcing the Equal Rights Party she urged supporters to "ORGANIZE AT
ONCE by calling public meetings, polling the School Districts of your
County, and have at least one Grand Ratification Meeting in each Congressional District."[69] Under the Constitution, she needed presidential
electors pledged to her candidacy, and these materials often mentioned
the "vital importance" of appointing electors who would cast their
votes for her at the meeting of the Electoral College.

In October Lockwood made at least one full campaign circuit, beginning with stump speeches in Baltimore, Philadelphia, and New
York. People who came to hear her were disappointed if they expected
nothing but women's rights talk. She did not believe that the Equal
Rights Party should run a single-issue campaign. The party platform introduced "feminist" ideas, and Lockwood was fond of describing how

women had helped to make the country "blossom as a rose."[70] But the platform also allowed her to address the many other issues that preoccupied Americans. Still, as she wrote in letters to reformer Edward M. Davis, she intended her candidacy to make history in the largest sense—by demonstrating that the Constitution did not bar women from running in elections or holding federal elective office.

Lockwood hoped her candidacy would promote her standing in the women's movement. She had spirited suffrage supporters, women like Gage, Ricker, and Colby, who agreed to be electors on her ticket and who wrote about the campaign. But Susan B. Anthony stubbornly refused to acknowledge Lockwood's effort as a significant contribution to history or the advancement of democracy. The once warm relationship between the two women was giving way in the face of differences over support for the Mormons, and major party politicians, as well as Lockwood's willingness to assert herself and to make independent decisions.

Anthony kept quiet to reporters, a statement in itself, while privately voicing her views. She wrote activist Elizabeth Boynton Harbert:

> Yes—if we women could all pull together! But we can't—each one has a plan & a plea! . . . I feel like letting the "knights of the quill" pronounce upon *Belva's Candidacy*—& we women hold our peace!—They are making good natured items thus far—We have no alternative but to let each one work out her own problem as best she may! I hope no ill to our cause will come from the move—but it has no solid foundation—beyond the woman—Mrs Stowe [sic]—of *Probate Court*-fame—who came east a few years ago.[71]

As head of the NWSA, Anthony believed in a centrally directed organization; she wanted suffrage women to "pull together" according to her plan, one that did not include Lockwood's grandstanding campaign.

Although Anthony did not support Lockwood's candidacy, she did not lack opinions about its themes. A few weeks after writing to Harbert, Anthony went to hear Lockwood give a campaign speech at New York City's Academy of Music. Afterwards, in a note to Elizabeth Cady Stanton, she wrote that the Equal Rights candidate, "*kept too little* on her own specific ground—of *woman & her disfranchised*—her speech was too much like a re-hash of the men's speeches!!"[72] Anthony could not resist adding that Lockwood wore her hair, "ala Martha Washington—save it was no longer a handsome iron gray—*but a dead, dyed brown!!* So human are poor mortal strongminded women!!"

Lockwood often gave a talk entitled "The Political Situation." In the middle of October she spoke in Cleveland, where she appeared before five hundred people at the Opera House. In a loud voice, described as nasal, she attacked the high-tariff position of the Republicans on the grounds that it would injure American commerce. But she then assailed the free-trade policy of the Democrats, arguing that they were "willing to risk our manufacturing interests in the face of the starving hordes of pauper labor in other countries."[73] She applauded the good that capital had done and said that "capital and labor did not, by nature, antagonize, and should not by custom."[74] A few days later in Louisville she returned to this topic, saying her party proposed "to inaugurate a system which encourages the capitalist to invest . . . in business enterprises and insures the workingman certain pay, steady employment and such protections as will lift off his heart that dread of want which to-day crushes out his life and energy."[75] In this interview she also said that she had "grown callous in the rough knocks the world has given me for daring to cull my living outside the beaten track."

Lockwood made the long journey to California in these weeks of campaign travel. Clara Foltz met her in a town near Sacramento. Like Lockwood, Foltz was smart, insistent, self-promoting, and unorthodox. At fifteen she had married a man who turned out to be a poor provider. In 1877, in order to support her five children, she set out to become a lawyer. Like Lockwood, she had to persuade a hostile legislature to open the profession to women. In September 1878 Foltz had passed the bar examination and become the state's first woman lawyer. She was twenty-nine. Four months later, wishing to augment the legal education she had received reading law with a local attorney and aided financially by friends, she registered at the newly chartered Hastings College of the Law. On the third day of lectures the registrar informed her that the directors had decided "not to admit women to the Law School" and she was told to leave.[76] Foltz challenged the directors and in December 1879 California's highest court issued an opinion in her favor, opening the law school to women. Unfortunately, the ruling came too late for Foltz, who was out of funds and had returned to her practice.

By the time of their meeting in 1884, Foltz was a well-known attorney and suffrage activist. She later wrote that their get-together had been carefully planned to permit time for Foltz to tell Lockwood—in private—the "true story" of her nomination: that it had been a prank, and that she and Stow had been surprised to find news of an Equal Rights Party "convention" put on the wire by the Associated Press.[77]

Foltz's recollection, offered thirty-four years after the campaign, is not an account that Lockwood subsequently repeated in public.[78] While for many people the idea of a woman's campaign for the presidency did seem silly or, in Foltz's words, "a good joke," her reminiscence ignores both the events of the summer of 1884, when suffrage women were humiliated at the major party conventions, and Marietta Stow's earlier interest in starting a women's party and nominating women for political office.[79] Lockwood accepted the nomination and privately acknowledged the irony of running for office. She understood, however, whatever the origins of the nomination, the great opportunity she had been handed to awaken the country to the issue of women's rights. She had only to seize the moment. Perhaps what ultimately surprised Foltz was Lockwood's ability to use the nomination for self-promotion while showing, as Stow was fond of saying, that women could help run "the great household of the nation." She made the most of the nomination bestowed on her, lark or not, and Clara admitted that Lockwood was an effective candidate who "carried herself splendidly."[80]

Lockwood enjoyed the opportunity to travel as well as the attention. At one point in the campaign, a railroad company furnished her with an observation car for the trip from Louisville, Kentucky, to New York. Recalling this moment in her "spectacular campaign," she said that "at every station stop I was called out and made an address."[81] She also enjoyed being interviewed; journalists found her frank and cooperative. She continued to be good-natured about the cartoonists who focused on her sex, as well as about the response of the public. In several towns citizens created Belva Lockwood Clubs, in which men meaning to disparage her paraded on city streets wearing Mother Hubbard dresses, a new cut of female clothing with an unconstructed design that freed movement and was considered improper attire out of doors.[82] *Frank Leslie's Illustrated* publicized the Mother Hubbard parades in a blithe article and sketch that poked gentle fun at the candidate.[83] In the same week the editors of *Life* magazine decided that they had ignored Lockwood's campaign too long. Working from the legend of Atalanta, the huntress, and Hippomenes, her suitor, a *Life* cartoonist inked Belva and Ben Butler as the mythological lovers racing to the campaign's "home stretch."[84]

On November 3, the day before the election, Lockwood returned from a campaign tour of the Northwest. Her last stop was Flint, Michigan, where, she told a Washington reporter, a thousand people attended her talk, a larger number than Ohio Congressman Frank Hurd drew the following night. When asked on November 4 where she would await the election news, she replied that her house would be open throughout the evening, "the gas will be lighted," and reporters were welcome to visit.[85]

When the ballots were tallied, the Democratic candidate, Grover Cleveland, was declared the winner, with a projected Electoral College vote of 219 to Blaine's 182. In the popular vote, he squeaked by with a margin of 23,000. Late in the campaign, sensing defeat, the Republicans had funneled money into Butler's third-party campaign, hoping he would spoil the election for Cleveland.[86] Butler polled 175,000 votes, but their distribution among the states did not deny Cleveland the critical Electoral College ballots.[87] Lockwood collected a few thousand votes although she quickly determined that an actual, official count was difficult to establish.

In 1884 the United States had yet to adopt the "Australian" ballot, where all candidates are listed on a single piece of paper. The system then in effect, dating from the early nineteenth century, allowed each party to print and distribute its own ballots containing the names of that party's slate and the electors pledged to it. The ballots were easily identified by eye-catching color and design, and the act of voting often took place in what one political observer described as an "open auction place" in which the elector, journeying to the polls, passed by party ballot peddlers hawking their political wares.[88] At the polling place, the voter deposited the ballot of his chosen party in a box. Some states required that voters sign the back of their ballots, but because the state controlled neither the distribution of ballots nor the administration of the polling place, it was possible to stuff the ballot box as well as to discount or destroy ballots. And that, Lockwood claimed, is precisely what happened.

In a petition sent to Congress in January 1885, she wrote that she had run a campaign, gotten up electoral tickets in several states, and received votes in at least nine of the states, only to determine that "a large vote in Pennsylvania [was] not counted, simply dumped into the waste basket as false votes."[89] In addition, she charged that many of the votes cast for her—totaling at least "4,711"—in eight other states ("New Hampshire, 379 popular votes; New York, 1336; Michigan, 374; Illinois, 1008; Iowa, 562; Maryland, 318; California, 734 and the entire Electoral vote of the State of Indiana") had been "fraudulently and illegally counted for the alleged majority candidate."[90]

Cleveland's margin of votes in New York was only 1,149. Lockwood asked that the members of Congress "refuse to receive the Electoral returns of the State of New York, or count them for the alleged majority candidate, for had the 1336 votes which were polled in said state for your petitioner been counted for her, and not for the one Grover Cleveland, he would not have been awarded a majority of all the votes cast at said election in said state."[91] She also petitioned Congress for the electoral vote of Indiana, saying that at the last moment the electors there had switched their votes from Cleveland to her.[92] In fact, they had not; it was all a prank by the good ol' Indiana boys. As reported by the Indianapolis Daily Sentinel, after their official meeting the electors left a notice for the state auditor notifying him that "a complimentary vote of said Electors be cast for Belva Lockwood . . . and That Hon. James H. Rice be appointed messenger" to carry notice of the vote to her.[93] Either Lockwood did not know it was a joke or, in the spirit of political theater, she played along with the mischief, trying to use it to her advantage.

The electoral votes of New York (thirty-six) and Indiana (fifteen) had been pivotal in the 1880 presidential race. With her petition and credible evidence, Lockwood, perhaps working behind the scenes with congressional Republicans, hoped to derail Cleveland's victory and keep him from becoming the first Democratic president since James Buchanan in 1856. She failed when the legislators ignored her petition, which had been referred to their Committee on Woman Suffrage. On February 11, Congress certified the election of New York Governor Grover Cleveland as the twenty-second president of the United States.[94] In the official count, Belva Lockwood received no electoral votes.

Subsequent interviews suggest that Lockwood was satisfied with the campaign, if not with the vote counting. In a test of democracy, she had run as an acknowledged contender and had spoken her mind. Her talents had been celebrated along with the cause of women. In 1914, when she was eighty-four years old and still not permitted to vote, she was asked whether a woman would one day be president. She replied,

> I look to see women in the United States senate and the house of representatives. If [a woman] demonstrates that she is fitted to be president she will some day occupy the White House. It will be entirely on her own merits, however. No movement can place her there simply because she is a woman. It will come if she proves herself mentally fit for the position.[95]

11

Life on the Platform

No class of public persons, outside of the Christian minister and the press, has greater opportunity to impress his views upon the public than the popular platform speaker.

Belva Lockwood, 1893

Lockwood's life changed as a result of the campaign but not as much as she would have liked. She had long desired an appointment as a public official and hoped that the serious nature of her presidential campaign, along with her professional credentials, might win her consideration. Not surprisingly, in spite of her qualifications, sex prejudice, along with party politics, continued to work against her. She did not accept this quietly.

In 1881 she had requested that President James Garfield appoint her to head the U.S. Mission in Brazil, writing that she was not afraid of yellow fever and had the honor of the acquaintance of the emperor and empress of Brazil.[1] She also claimed to be independent of all political entanglements and qualified for the post by virtue of her knowledge of international law and arbitration. She reminded Garfield that no woman had ever been sent abroad to represent the country "although fully one-half of the population are women."[2] Nothing came of her petitioning.

A few months after the 1884 election, she wrote to the newly inaugurated—and recent rival—Grover Cleveland, again arguing for the appointment of women to public positions. In stark contrast to the respectful letter sent to Garfield, this appeal had the sound of a petulant growl. She began by scolding Cleveland on his recent choice of a reputed womanizer to represent the United States in Turkey: "The selection of S. S. Cox could not have been improved upon. The only danger is, that he will attempt to suppress polygamy in that country by marrying all of the women himself."[3] She further observed that other presidential appointees were incompetent, party hacks, or "a good judge of 'Old Bourbon.'"[4] Although she wanted a consul position, or even one of the appointments for the District of Columbia controlled by the White House, her sarcasm suggests that she expected no offer from Cleveland, who did not make one.

Sex discrimination denied Lockwood the career choices open to her male lawyer friends, several of whom had run successfully for elective office, or had become judges or district attorneys. She was fond of traveling, liked to write, and loved to be in the public eye, so rather than remain within the prison created by this prejudice, she launched a career as a lecturer. Lockwood called it taking to "the platform."[5] She worked for eight years as a professional speaker, represented by the Chicago-based Slayton Lyceum Bureau.[6] With Lura and Clara's assistance, she also maintained her Washington law practice.

The national lecture business that Lockwood joined in the mid-1880s provided audiences with education and entertainment. Aided by the technology of the telegraph, which helped to regularize scheduling, railroads that hustled speakers from town to town, and the public's thirst for information, opinion, and idols, "the platform" permitted authors, clerics, politicians, and reformers to earn fees for delivering stock lectures. In rural churches and cavernous city opera houses, speakers sought to influence public taste and social opinion in a movable celebration of inquiry and free speech. In what became the unifying theme of her life, in the classroom, courthouse, and lecture hall, in newspaper articles, campaign speeches, and letters to presidents, she defended the ideas in which she believed. Unlike some nineteenth-century women who saved their rebellious thoughts for private diaries, she chose the most public methods to express herself.

By late 1884, having run for and lost the presidency, Lockwood was faced with the question of what to do next.[7] There were no high-profile positions available to her in either the women's or the temperance movements. Stanton, Anthony, and Frances Willard, among others, filled those. She earned a good living from her law practice, but she did not grow rich at it and knew that she could not enter the ranks of America's elite attorneys. The rough and tumble worlds of railway and industrial corporate law, a source of great wealth and status for some men, were completely beyond her reach. Faced with the limits of a small practice and the likelihood that she would never become a public official, she took to "the platform" while still working as an attorney. In this way, after the 1884 campaign, she declared that she had no intention of retiring to Washington only to become a quaint political relic, or a nostalgic news item.

The life of the itinerant lecturer suited Lockwood's restless personality and her attraction to situations where she could ply people with opinion. The business end of it earned her speaker fees while the travel permitted her to canvass for new pension and land claims clients. The circuit demanded fortitude, humor, and ingenuity. Temperance leader Frances Willard, who regretted joining the tour, described hotels of "funereal dreariness," "cooked-over cuisine," and "a human snow-bank of folks who have 'paid to get in' and are reckoning . . . whether or not they are really going 'to get their money's worth.'"[8] Elizabeth Cady Stanton, who endured the circuit until 1881, when she was sixty-six, recalled bad conditions but reported with pride that "it was the testimony of all the bureaus that the women could endure more fatigue and were more conscientious than the men in filling their appointments."[9]

Lockwood had barely stopped campaigning when she took up the tour.[10] She revised old lectures and prepared new ones.[11] A newspaper notice placed her in the field late in November and in December, capitalizing on her recent campaign. She drew an overflow audience in Boston, where she spoke, "at racehorse speed," on the subject of intemperance, delighting listeners with attacks on "the poor, weak, sinful apostle of whiskey and tobacco."[12]

Her first tour of the West began early in 1885; she went out carrying a carpetbag filled with notes from earlier lectures, talks whose themes included the American statesman, the status of women, and current politics.[13] In Chicago she had "very good" copper plates made of her portrait, which she used on billboards and in newspapers to advertise her upcoming lectures.[14] In June 1885 she filled engagements in Nebraska, visited with Clara Colby, by now a close friend, and again headed west. On July 6 she arrived in Salt Lake City, the first of four Utah cities in which she was scheduled to speak before a tour of the Pacific Northwest.

Salt Lake was the theological center of the LDS Church and here, as elsewhere in Utah, she was entertained by Mormon leaders who were anxious to pay homage to one of the few public figures who continued to support them against Senator Edmunds.[15] At the home of Mormons Emily and Franklin S. Richards, guests read praise-song poems written in her honor and Lula Green Richards, a founding editor of the *Woman's Exponent*, pointedly censured people who had not been as constant a friend.[16] Later, John T. Caine, Utah Territory's delegate to the U.S. Congress, offered a warm introduction to her lecture.

After her Utah lectures Lockwood stopped at Lake Tahoe for a day of rest. While catching up on political news she read with alarm reports that troops had been ordered to Salt Lake City to prevent a clash between Mormons and non-Mormons. As she pieced together the story, in a protest of Washington's anti-LDS policies, on July Fourth a small group of Mormons had flown the American flag at half-mast. The press had transformed the nonviolent demonstration into an act of treason and spread the story that an outbreak was imminent. Far from home, Lockwood found it difficult to determine what President Cleveland actually knew, but having just visited Salt Lake she felt compelled to tell the president that he was receiving bad information. She wrote to him and then sent a note to John Caine, telling him of her support and enclosing a draft.[17]

Lockwood's letter to Cleveland covered nine handwritten pages. It was thoughtful and diplomatic. She wished to convince him that the deployment of military troops was unnecessary and unwarranted, having been encouraged by opportunists and "a sensational report by the Associated Press."[18] The idea of an outbreak, she wrote, is "absurd." Claiming a mantle of authority, she offered Cleveland her explanation for the incident: "The half masting of the flag was simply intended as an expression of mourning . . . and was without any concert of action." The "sober, industrious" Mormons were reluctant to rejoice on July Fourth, a holiday celebrating freedom and independence, because "the President of their Church [is] under surveillance; their elders and apostles [are] under indictment or in the Penitentiary."

There is no record that the Mormons had asked her to write this letter. Years before she had joined in support of the Mormons because of the assault on Utah women's right to vote, but in this letter, as in her 1884 talk before the NWSA, she emphasized the Mormons' constitutional right to the free exercise of their religion. She brought to Cleveland's attention two recent, troubling statements—one printed in the *San Francisco Chronicle*, one issued by a U.S. federal judge—insisting that the purpose of the 1882 Edmunds Act was "for *the suppression of the Mormon Religion. . . . not to increase morality among the Mormons but to blot out the Mormon Religion.*" She feared fanaticism, on the part of government officials as well as the press.[19] Hoping that the harsh enforcement of the Edmunds Act would not be followed by military intervention, she closed her letter by urging the president to be "prudent" and to show "the same good judgment that you have hitherto manifested in other affairs of State."

Cleveland, only five months in office, chose not to deploy troops. By the first week in August, when Lockwood reached San Francisco after lecturing in Nevada City (California), she knew his course had been "tempered with moderation."[20] Pleased and relieved, in San Francisco she turned her attention from diplomacy to family affairs, trying to make the acquaintance of Mary Lockwood, Ezekiel's twenty-year-old granddaughter.[21] From there her lecture commitments took her to Oregon, Washington Territory, Idaho, and Montana.[22] The late summer months made the work pleasant despite a full schedule that only brought her back to the capital in September. And then, in midautumn, she went off again, leaving Lura and DeForest to look after pension claim filings and to care for family member James Ormes, who had been brought to the house at F Street after suffering a stroke and who died there in November.[23]

During this autumn tour, the Slayton Bureau had once again arranged for Lockwood to speak nightly while making her way toward the Pacific. She advertised a new talk, "Across the Continent and What I Saw," described by one reporter as "a sort of summing up of her observations on her trip . . . in 1884."[24] She claimed to have journeyed nearly seventeen thousand miles during and after her first presidential campaign, and in "Across the Continent" attempted, somewhat awkwardly, to represent the sweep of human accomplishment and the grandeur of the natural wonders that she had seen.[25] The talk permitted her to preach respect for modernity and to pronounce toil and humanity's faculty for reasoning as "the two great motors" that have driven the world forward.[26]

She arrived in Denver on November 11, ready to deliver the talk. Beforehand, several journalists begged interviews. The reporter for the *Daily Denver Times* played to her ego, reporting that she was, "all things considered, the ablest and most consistent advocate of the rights of woman in America. . . . withal a woman to attract attention and command respect."[27] At her request they discussed politics. She commented on the narrow, parochial party loyalties she had noticed in her travels and said she favored subjecting all candidates for office—even those running for the presidency—to a civil service examination. Hoping perhaps for a scoop, the reporter asked her who would be the next women's candidate for the presidency. Lockwood remained coy, answering with a laugh, "That you will have to ask the women. . . . I am not posted. I am not an office-seeker."[28]

Wearing a black cloth dress, her large cameo pin, Spanish lace, and a knitted blue shawl thrown over her shoulders, she also met with a reporter from Denver's *Tribune-Republican* to talk about the outlook for professional women. In this interview she offered an unforgiving appraisal of her sisters, one that ignored the issues of discrimination and domestic responsibility: women, she said, needed to work as much as men, needed to be "educated to work."[29] She thought that there was "a great deal of ability among women; in fact . . . there is nothing they could not accomplish if they were to set about doing things rightly but in most instances they don't do it, and that is just why they fail." She used her profession as an example: "Now take the women throughout the country who are admitted to the bar; they don't practice law." Phoebe Couzins, she told the reporter, "with all her reputation, has practiced very little." She described her own Washington workdays as long, from eight in the morning until eleven at night, only rarely permitting time for "a particularly fine opera . . . or a lecture," and persisted in arguing that any woman who wanted to be successful must "give her time to it as a man does." She did not, however, mention her housekeeper, who kept her home running, or suggest that the workplace, organized with the assumption that working professionals (men) would have wives, might need to be rethought.

In 1883 Henry Ward Beecher, the nationally prominent head of Brooklyn's Plymouth Church, charged seven thousand dollars for seven lectures, at least one of which drew two thousand people.[30] Beecher's reputation as America's finest orator as well as the sensational civil trial in which he stood accused by Theodore Tilton of seducing Elizabeth, his wife, made Beecher an unusual box office draw. Most lecturers, however, including Lockwood, got by charging a nightly fee of thirty to one hundred dollars. Those given to gambling elected a percentage of the house receipts.[31] For most, lecturing was not the road to great wealth. For her hundred-plus nighttime appearances in 1885 Lockwood might have grossed as much as thirty-seven hundred dollars. After paying Slayton and travel expenses, she may have been left with less than two thousand. This was not a puny purse but, considered alongside months of packing and unpacking, forced smiles, missed trains, and repetitious rehearsal of talks, the earnings were hard won. However, together with the pension applications that she collected while on the road, the work provided a significantly larger income than she earned when just practicing law.

There was also, of course, the fickle nature of the public. To sell tickets year after year, regulars on the lecture circuit had to change their topics. After her first trip abroad in 1889 Lockwood added a chatty talk about life in Paris and London, but most of her lectures were on serious topics with titles such as "The Tendency of Parties and Governments" and "The Conservative Force of the College and University with Practical Thoughts on University Extension." She promised nothing personal or sensational. Popular lecturer Kate Field advertised "An Evening with Charles Dickens," "A Musical Folly," and, ominously, "The Mormon Horror."[32] Lockwood responded with a talk entitled, "The Mormon Question: The Other Side." In eight years of touring she allowed herself only one catchy lecture title: "Is Marriage a Failure? No Sir!"

This talk came into her repertoire after a British writer attracted international attention with her radical declaration that the present system of marriage, built on woman's inequality and status as property, was doomed.[33] Lockwood had thought about marriage and divorce more than the average American. She had married young although she would have preferred to continue her education, and had later learned the hard lessons of a widow. She had—with other reformers—argued for the reform of married women's property law and been refused bar admission by judges who insisted that marriage imposed legal disabilities that women attorneys could not overcome. She had supported her friends in Utah against "the anti-Mormon ring" in Congress despite her often-repeated opposition to plural marriage and, during the 1884 campaign, she had urged that a uniform system of marriage and divorce laws be established for all the states. Yet, her lecture on marriage contained few references to any of these experiences and had little of the fire found in the writings of Elizabeth Packard, Marietta Stow, or Elizabeth Cady Stanton. Although she had strong opinions on the subject of women's matrimonial equality, she shielded her "marriage" audiences from her more radical views, some of which only appeared in print or in her "Women of To-day" lecture.

Lockwood used a simple narrative structure in "Is Marriage a Failure?" Falling back on her experience as an attorney and using evidence culled from history, she put wedlock on trial and after cataloguing the abhorrent practices of the past, concluded, apparently to the delight of her audiences, that the Christian religion, in ushering in monogamy, had advanced woman and elevated man.[34] She argued that contemporary marriage worked to the benefit of women: "we have," she said, "virtually taken the marriage contract out of the realm of bargain and sale;—made of it a matter of sentiment, of love, of mutual attraction, of affinity, of respect."[35]

This presentation echoed the zeitgeist of the late nineteenth century, when intellectual and political themes, in the United States, emphasized the inevitable and beneficial march of Western civilization. Modern marriage, shaped by Christianity and Enlightenment ideas of individualism and consent, exemplified this progress: "While marriage," she said, "like law, is an experiment . . . it is undoubtedly, with all its imperfections, the best experiment for the conservation of society yet revealed, or promulgated. Our effort should be to perfect, and not to undermine this system, which has elevated our people above those of heathen nations, and the civilizations of the East."[36] Marriage, she asserted, "conserves . . . the sanctity and purity of republican institutions."[37] Implicit in her analysis was a belief that the institution could contribute to the building of empire.

Lockwood steered a careful course on the lecture platform when she thought caution was appropriate or good for business. She believed that the general public had little interest in women's rights and told a reporter for the *Buffalo News* that while she tried to promote woman suffrage in her lectures, the public "won't stand [for] much."[38] Although she broached the question of female independence in her lecture, "Women of To-day," she left it out of her marriage talk. She did, however, speak her mind about husbands, wives, and self-reliance in an 1888 *Cosmopolitan* article, repeating her argument that girls had "no right to enter [marriage] until able to be self-supporting, and that entered upon, its duties and responsibilities belong as much to her as to the man; so that should death or accident deprive her and her children of the assistance of her life partner, she may be able to take up the business that his hands have dropped."[39] Matilda Joslyn Gage, Lockwood's suffrage colleague, held the Christian Church responsible for the "chains of [woman's] slavery," for opposing women's right to divorce, and for holding woman in a position of "inferiority and subordination."[40] Lockwood, far more conservative than Gage, did not. If she blamed anyone for her dependence as a young widow it was Lewis Bennett, who had not permitted her to obtain the higher education that would have been her armor against adversity.

In the circles in which she lectured, it was also good business to offer a talk on temperance, and Lockwood, a longtime antiliquor activist, obliged. She believed that "the scourge" of alcohol could only be controlled through regulatory legislation and asked why liquor should be any different from deadly poisons whose use was against the law. While it was common to say that drink ruined families, Lockwood also thought it weakened the nation, telling audiences reluctant to replace moral suasion with government regulation that prohibition legislation "will do more for the protection of American industries . . . than our army and our navy."[41] Like a growing number of suffrage reformers, she appealed to her audiences to support woman suffrage because "there is a stronger moral force in the women than the men."[42]

Lockwood's commitment to temperance ran afoul of one small and common habit. Like many women of her day she used nerve tonics and other patent medicines that contained alcohol. Temperance ladies openly purchased these potions, adamant that they were acceptable natural remedies. When towns went "dry," the market for them increased. Opponents of liquor regulation mocked this hypocrisy with wry observations that "the saloon has been transferred to the drugstore," with Lockwood replying that "every honest person knows . . . this is a falsehood."[43] She admitted, however, that there were abuses. The fact was that Americans loved patent medicines.

Lockwood not only testified that she used a tonic that contained alcohol, but late in 1886 she also attempted to capitalize a homeopathic medicine company whose product almost certainly would contain alcohol.[44] The idea may have come from her son-in-law, who had worked as a pharmacy clerk, or she may have been inspired by the phenomenal financial success of Lydia Pinkham, a Massachusetts housewife who made a fortune marketing her "Vegetable Compound" for "woman problems." Pinkham supported temperance; she also permitted substantial quantities of alcohol in her company's most important nostrum. Whatever the inspiration, in 1886 Lockwood decided to use her own fame to compete in the lucrative patent medicine industry, joining with Washington homeopathic physician E. B. Rankin to form the Lockwood Improvement Syndicate. The partners commissioned an original engraving to use on the front of the syndicate's stock certificates. In frank imitation of Pinkham, the artist placed a picture of Lockwood at the center of the image, flanked by drawings of the United States Capitol building and the newly completed Washington Monument. Visually invoking the majesty and authority of the Founding Fathers and the national government, the certificate announced that the company would be capitalized at two million dollars, with shares sold for one dollar.[45]

In December, 1886, the *Woman's Tribune* ran an advertisement for the syndicate. Lockwood was looking for investors. The ad announced that Lockwood, well known in suffrage circles, was president of the venture, whose property consisted of "valuable Patent Rights, Real Estate, and the 'Belva Lockwood and the Homoeopathic Remedies.'"[46] The immediate business plan promised to place remedies prepared by Dr. Rankin before the public. Shareholders were offered a stock certificate that was "a work of art." There is no record that the business succeeded. There are no records of incorporation. A stock certificate that Lockwood mailed to Mary Lockwood Bull, Ezekiel's granddaughter, survived, too striking to be destroyed by Mary or her descendents.[47] Lockwood apparently considered the failure of the syndicate—which occurred quite quickly—a closed chapter and never discussed it. Although Lockwood did not prove herself as a venture capitalist, she continued to support the use of patent medicines that contained alcohol, even going so far as to become one of the many public figures who endorsed them in advertisements. Like the much-admired Clara Barton, Lockwood testified to the benefits of Dr. Greene's Nervura,[48] a "blood and nerve" tonic that was 17 percent alcohol.[49] Greene's promised to make aches disappear and to bring "Vitality and Vigor to All." Lockwood was quoted as owing her good health and strength to its use: "I . . . am pleased to say that it has improved my digestion, relieved the sleeplessness under a great nervous strain, during which I believe that sleep would otherwise have been impossible, and seems in every way to have built up my general health."[50] Americans were self-medicating with alcohol-infused tonics, and Lockwood did not disapprove.

In the good company of women like Barton she had little fear that her endorsements would sour the public image that she shaped and pruned on the lecture circuit. She was not, however, as certain what she wanted the public to know about her increasingly close association with the Mormons, particularly at a time when presidents and pressmen were preaching against them. Thus, in February 1886, after Senator Edmunds had reintroduced legislation, later enacted as the Edmunds-Tucker bill, to repeal the corporate charter of the LDS Church, confiscate many of its holdings, criminally punish adultery, and withdraw suffrage rights from *all* of the women of the Territory, Lockwood signaled opposition to the assault on political and property rights while asking that her correspondence be burned.[51] It is curious that she urged John Caine to destroy her letter of political advice when, in the same month, she willingly "stirred up a hornets nest" at the anti-Mormon Salt Lake *Tribune* by telling a reporter that she thought, "as a rule, the Mormons are ahead of the Gentiles in morals. . . . [They] do not drink, smoke, chew, nor even use coffee and tea, nor frequent saloons or other vile resorts."[52]

In writing Caine, Lockwood used the word "we," again raising the question of whether she was an independent civil libertarian publicly defending Mormon rights, or a lobbyist paid by the LDS Church. Like other groups and businesses the LDS Church employed lobbyists in Washington and invested in efforts to win over the public by countering hostile press coverage.[53] At least one former senator and several powerful railroad men, anxious to secure their position in Utah, lobbied for the Church. In early August, 1887, John W. Young, a Mormon businessman acting as a church agent in Washington, received five thousand dollars from the leadership in Utah to support "several schemes . . . in aid of the cause."[54] He enlisted Lockwood's aid for one of these schemes, a plan to arouse the public and embarrass the federal government by finding non-Mormon bigamists living in Washington who had escaped arrest and prosecution under the Edmunds-Tucker Act. Lockwood searched for bigamists throughout Washington's hot summer months, even calling the attention of the district attorney to a married man residing locally who claimed to be "living in open adultery," but try as she might, did not find a sensitive case.[55] Was she paid for this work? Young, notoriously remiss in accounting for LDS money, left no record.[56] Lockwood never spoke of taking payment and in her 1888 article, "The Mormon Question," reprinted in fifty American newspapers, while describing the recent campaign in the capital to find bigamists, hid her involvement.[57]

It is possible that this article was part of an aggressive public relations campaign carried out by the Church and that she was paid to write it. Only circumstantial evidence exists. Lockwood may have decided to defend Mormons without pay because, in her view, the Edmunds acts were unconstitutional and the disfranchisement of Utah women an "odious" backward step.[58] And although her views on the rights of Mormons were not popular, she was not alone in urging the public to modify its views. Some newspaper editors resisted anti-Mormon sensationalism, and a few members of Congress, mostly southern Democrats, also expressed concern about persecution and the lack of fair play.[59] The NWSA wanted Utah women to vote, and President Cleveland was sufficiently uneasy about several aspects of the Edmunds-Tucker act, including the disfranchisement of Utah's women, that he declined to sign it, instead allowing it to become law without his signature.[60]

Lockwood's support for the Mormon cause came on her terms. She was willing to battle popular opinion about the Church, but she never wavered in her opposition to polygamy, or her support for the right of the women of Utah to vote. In 1888, weighing whether Congress should admit Utah as a state, she did not hesitate to criticize the members of Utah's territorial government, observing tartly, "they tamely submitted to the disfranchisement of their women, and have entirely left them out of their new State Constitution."[61]

When Lockwood published "The Mormon Question" she was fifty-seven and had been "on the tour" for three years. Many women would have thought about retiring, but she showed no sign of slowing down. She kept her hand in politics; found time, despite her travel schedule, to participate in several new organizations committed to women's rights and self-improvement; and became an increasingly prominent spokeswoman for the Universal Peace Union. She was well known and yet she continued to face old problems. The top leadership of the women's movement remained closed to her. She was, perhaps, *too* independent, while for a new generation of activists, she was part of the Old Guard. She had loyal friends like Clara Colby in the suffrage world but no "following." In the twenty years since moving to Washington she had established herself as a champion of women's professional and political rights, but there was now the question of how to maintain her influence. Blocked from a government appointment, or an organization-based position in the suffrage movement, she increased her involvement with the American peace movement.

View of the Capitol, c. 1863. *Reprinted by permission of the Library of Congress.*

One of Lockwood's
less formal photographic
portraits, c. 1880.
*Reprinted by permission of
the National Portrait
Gallery, Smithsonian
Institution.*

Attorney Albert G.
Riddle championed
women's rights. He
motioned to admit
Lockwood to the U.S.
Supreme Court bar in
1879. *Reprinted by
permission of the Ohio
Historical Society.*

Bar admission certificate given by the Supreme Court of the United States to Belva A. Lockwood, March 3, 1879. *Courtesy of the New York State Historical Association Research Library, Cooperstown, NY.*

Lura McNall Ormes helped to run her mother's law practice and for a number of years wrote a "talk of Washington" column. *Courtesy of Mrs. Norma Z. Wollenberg, Town of Royalton Historical Society.*

Mrs Belva Lockwood.

In 1881 Lockwood made the daring decision to ride a bicycle in public. *Collection of Jill Norgren.*

Lockwood's pose became more formal when she ran for the presidency. *Reprinted by permission of the Library of Congress.*

Presidential candidates Benjamin Butler and Belva Lockwood share
the stage in this 1884 *Puck* cartoon. *Collection of Jill Norgren.*

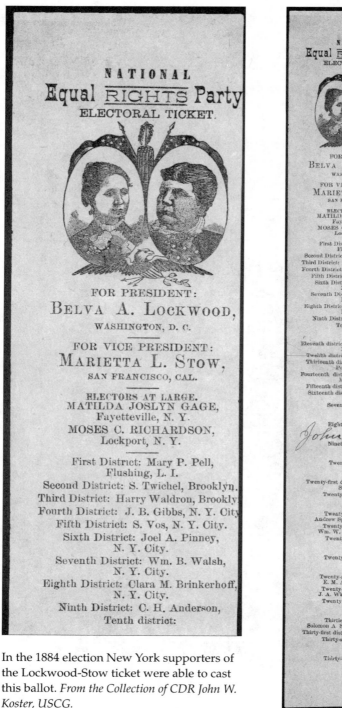

In the 1884 election New York supporters of the Lockwood-Stow ticket were able to cast this ballot. *From the Collection of CDR John W. Koster, USCG.*

When Lockwood tried to capitalize on her fame by starting a homeopathic remedies business ("Lockwood Improvement Syndicate"), she issued stock certificates. *Courtesy of the Bancroft Library, University of California, Berkeley.*

The Henry Slayton Lyceum Bureau managed Lockwood's lecture career for several years. *Reprinted by permission of the National Museum of American History, Smithsonian Institution.*

BELVA LOCKWOOD,
THE EMINENT BARRISTER,
OF WASHINGTON, D. C.,

Who represented the Universal Peace Union at the Paris Exposition, and was their delegate to the International Congress of Peace in that city in 1889, and who was again elected and served as the delegate of the Peace Union to the International Peace Congress in London in 1890—making effective addresses in both congresses, one on "Arbitration" and the other on "Disarmament"—and who is one of the delegates of the Peace Union to the Congress in Rome the present season, is now prepared to favor Churches, Colleges, Teachers' Institutes, and Lecture Committees with any one of the following lectures, viz:

1. **The Paris Exposition and Social Life in Paris and London.**
2. **Is Marriage a Failure? No, Sir!**
3. **Women in the Professions.**
4. **Social and Political Life in Washington.**
5. **Across the American Continent.**
6. **The Tendency of Parties and of Governments.**
7. **The Conservative Force of the College and University with Practical Thoughts on University Extension.**

An advertisement printed after 1890 lists the several topics on which Lockwood was prepared to lecture. *Reprinted by permission of the National Museum of American History, Smithsonian Institution.*

Clara Bewick Colby, editor of the *Woman's Tribune,* was a close friend of Lockwood's. *Reprinted by permission of the Wisconsin Historical Society.*

Lockwood (second from front left) with other officers of the Universal Peace Union. Founder Alfred H. Love is at Lockwood's right. *Reprinted by permission, Universal Peace Union, Swarthmore College Peace Collection.*

American Woman's Republic President Mabel G. Lewis (*left*) with AWR Attorney General, Belva Lockwood (*center*) , and Chaplain, the Rev. Susanna Harris (*right*). *Courtesy of Niagara County Historical Society, Lockport, NY.*

The possibility of hen-pecked husbands was given as a reason to oppose woman suffrage. This cartoon appeared in 1909. *Reprinted by permission of the Library of Congress.*

The day before Woodrow Wilson's inauguration thousands of suffrage women, including Lockwood, put the issue of their voting rights before the nation with an extraordinary procession down Pennsylvania Avenue. *Reprinted by permission of the Library of Congress.*

In 1986 the U.S. Postal Service issued this stamp, honoring Belva Lockwood, as part of its Great Americans series. *Reprinted by permission of the U.S. Postal Service.*

12

Lay Down Your Arms!

War must be stripped of its gaudy attire, its so-called greatness and glory.

Universal Peace Union, 1886

Lockwood's scrappy defense of the Mormons stood in marked contrast to her quiet and dignified work on behalf of world peace. She had joined the Universal Peace Union (UPU) in 1868. It was the most radical peace organization in the United States. Her commitment to the society came without any particular soul searching; rather, she carried within her the optimism of the pre–Civil War period, the evangelical Protestant "fire of the spirit" that had fueled America's earlier enthusiasm for personal and societal salvation. She believed in perfection on earth, and after attending a UPU gathering at the Union League Hall in 1868 had concluded that the group's principles were "in consonance with my own."[1] Those principles combined a belief in living the Christian gospel of love and nonviolence while promoting the prevention of war through concrete policies, including public education, disarmament, and arbitration.[2] This struck her as a blueprint by which a more just and peaceful world might be built, a praiseworthy Christian world.

Lockwood had not opposed the Civil War. After joining the Universal Peace Union she argued that there were alternatives that might have been used to end slavery, such as paying slaveholders to free the people they held in bondage, but during the war she had supported Lincoln and the Union cause, and had organized local women in New York to provision soldiers. Perhaps as Ezekiel's bride, listening to his first-hand accounts of Bull Run and Antietam, she had become more sensitive to the horrors of war. Her second husband had been much affected by his experience as a battlefield chaplain, having accompanied his regiment in the field for two years.[3]

The Universal Peace Union, started in 1867, was a small society intellectually and spiritually connected to the extreme views of an earlier generation of pacifists, particularly William Lloyd Garrison. In 1838 the fiery and controversial Garrison had helped to form the New England Non-Resistance Society (NENRS) after a split with the American Peace Society (APS) over the acceptability of defensive war. Garrison envisioned a radically different society—one that would not discriminate because of sex or race, one governed by the Sermon on the Mount (Matt. 5:38–39).[4] Preaching Christian perfectionism, the belief that humans could achieve sanctification, he argued that men and women must renounce all forms of violence. The NENRS Declaration of Sentiments, authored by Garrison, challenged people not only to disavow force in the most personal aspects of their lives but also, because of the inherent violence of the state, to refuse to serve in the military, vote in public elections, or hold public office. Garrison's revolutionary nonresistance posed a severe test of temperament and action, and attracted few acolytes. The NENRS remained small and marginal within the peace movement although Garrison anticipated Thoreau, Gandhi, and Martin Luther King, Jr.

At the end of the Civil War a number of men and women well known in American communities of conscience came forward, resolved to establish a new peace organization. Quaker Alfred Love assumed a prominent role along with Lucretia Mott, Adin Ballou, leader of the Christian utopian Hopedale Community, and Amasa Walker, pacifist politician and businessman. The society that they formed, which drew on the spirit of the by-then-defunct NENRS, was the Universal Peace Union. Love, a woolens merchant who lived by Garrison's principles of nonresistance, became its president and with the aid of others, including Lockwood, directed it, from Philadelphia, for more than forty years.

Love and his colleagues distinguished the UPU from other peace societies by insisting that peace entailed far more than the absence of war. Peace was a world filled with the spirit of God's love, the millennial kingdom of God on earth in which, where necessary, men and women rejected coercive and unjust secular law, having embraced, in its stead, the higher law of God.[5] A peaceful world, seen in these terms, did not exist as long as inequality and injustice were tolerated. Led by Love, the UPU resisted the temptation to turn inward and to wait for the millennium, instead committing itself to an ongoing critique of government and, critically, to an aggressive program of public education.

At its meetings and in the pages of its publications, the UPU created an open forum for the discussion of justice and contemporary policies of reform.[6]

Love welcomed discussion of provocative issues, including the dangers of a standing army and the evil of capital punishment.[7] The "Indian Question" received extensive coverage in the UPU's monthly newsletter. Women members, with strong support from Love, advocated for women. They wrote articles for the newsletter, whose name changed several times, about suffrage, domestic violence, legal disabilities in marriage, and low wages. UPU men and women called for temperance laws, the abolition of capital punishment, and prison reform. The Union never endorsed a socialist platform but members condemned corporate greed and sympathized with labor, urging, however, arbitrated settlements in favor of strikes.[8]

To a degree, the match between Lockwood and this new peace society was a good one: she was restless, talented, and reform minded. The UPU was a young organization, open to the imprint of members, and appealing in its commitment to social and economic change. She was outspoken, but the UPU constitution guaranteed members "freedom of criticism and dissent."[9] Equally important, the UPU was different from other peace societies in the welcome reception given to women, who became full partners with men in running the organization. Meetings attracted gifted and powerful women. Lockwood's friend, Dr. Mary Walker, attended and spoke at Washington chapter gatherings, as did Josephine Griffing of the Freedmen's Bureau. Susan B. Anthony came occasionally. In 1871 Clara Barton lent her name to the masthead of the association's newsletter. Lavinia Dundore and Lydia Hall became UPU officers. In 1875 Lockwood joined the Union's executive committee, beginning forty years as an officer and the group's Washington lobbyist.

The UPU was an organization whose sympathies lay with Garrisonian nonresistance and Christian anarchy. Lockwood was not a Garrisonian; she was not wary of government. In this stance she was quite different from Love, who did not vote in public elections while she, in the course of her close association with the UPU, eagerly sought employment with the federal government, fought for the right to vote, and twice ran for the presidency. Unlike Love, who in 1888 cited his Garrisonian beliefs in refusing the vice-presidential nomination of the Equal Rights Party, Lockwood believed in working within the system and admired the power of the law. While she understood the state's capacity for violence, she thought that pacifist activists, like activist women, should use, rather than shun, institutions of government to create a more just and nonviolent world. Despite their differences, Love welcomed Lockwood as a colleague. He believed that dissent was valuable and would bring about "a better understanding of God's truth," a view that encouraged debate at UPU meetings and was essential for a member as spirited and independent as Lockwood.[10]

The Universal Peace Union set itself in opposition to all war and had selected a simple motto to champion its ideals: "Remove the Causes and abolish the custom of war, establish the principle and live the principles of peace." Society members promoted the cause of personal and political nonviolence in many of the usual ways: local and national meetings, a monthly newsletter, public lectures, an annual summer "camp meeting" on donated land in Mystic, Connecticut, and persistent lobbying of state and federal officials through personal contact as well as organized petition- and letter-writing campaigns. The UPU also reached out to the international activist community, sending delegates to international meetings, and in 1892 it became an affiliate of the newly formed International Peace Bureau (IPB). Lockwood participated in all of these efforts and was particularly valued for her lectures, lobbying, and international advocacy.

In talks, letters, and published articles Lockwood used the antiwar rhetoric of the nineteenth century. She described combat as "legalized murder," something "brutalizing and debasing," an "animal principal [sic] in human nature controlling the spiritual and the mental."[11] Christian nations, she insisted, should never engage in war. She chose to emphasize practical issues such as the waste and cost of war, and the way war oppressed women and members of the working class: it had been the curse of women living in warlike nations, she would say, to become "the burden bearers . . . the tillers of the soil."[12] Standing armies, she argued, were kept only at great expense to the "industrial classes," which were taxed to support them. In interviews she said that statues honoring military heroes were a bad idea.[13]

She also joined the chorus of reformers who argued that women had the unique power to stop war. She preached equal social and political opportunity for her sex, in part so that women might act according to what she believed were their less aggressive natures. "Men," she wrote, "have long ruled and cannot yet establish peace; they are warriors. Let women have equal rights, and with their pacific influence wars shall be unknown."[14] She suggested that the carnage and cost of the Civil War might have been avoided had woman's advice been asked: "No woman voted a subsidy to maintain it . . . [and] when the great outlay [of blood and treasure] is summed up, including the amount paid and to be paid for pensions," enough would have been spent peaceably to have bought out of bondage every slave.[15]

Interest in the treatment of Native Americans was so strong among members of the UPU that a regular newsletter feature, "The Indian Department," was devoted to the topic. In this column various writers rebuked the federal government for treaty breaking while simultaneously urging support for policies that would end tribal sovereignty and impose upon Indians an "American" way of life.[16] Inexplicably, in the 1870s and 1880s, the dangers increasingly experienced by African Americans did not have the same primacy for members of the UPU.[17] In its newsletter writers condemned the Ku Klux Klan and registered horror at the lynching of former slaves, but the many social and physical manifestations of violence experienced by African Americans, as well as their lack of economic opportunity, did not receive the same attention as Indian affairs, at least not in the UPU's publications.

If the Universal Peace Union was different from other peace societies in its concern with problems of social justice, it was not at all unique in urging cooperation among nations and praising the virtues of binding arbitration and international courts as methods of managing conflict. Immersion by the UPU in this agenda proved critical as it provided a bridge between the group's radical roots and provocative social-justice itinerary, and the mainstream peace movement. Attention to the promise of arbitration marked the UPU as capable of sustaining the demeanor of realpolitik pragmatists *and* evangelicals as its members strove to create a nonviolent world. Lockwood's persistent efforts to establish arbitration courts gave the Union visibility in foreign policy debates.

Lockwood was an avid student of foreign affairs and a great enthusiast of arbitration as a tool of dispute resolution. This came from her training in the law and her recognition of the increasingly interconnected nature of her world. She argued that arbitration should be part of the apparatus of international relations, saying that its use by disputing nations was a "rational and competent substitute for war," a means of relief "from the burdens and disasters of *war*."[18] She readily

joined the coalition of peace advocates who worked to win more specific action from the White House after passage, in 1874, of a concurrent
resolution that "authorized and requested" President Grant to explore
with other nations the possibility of an international system of arbitration.[19] Such action proved to be very slow in coming.

President Grant submitted several international disputes to arbitration but refused to use his office to call an international meeting.
Rutherford B. Hayes, his successor, praised arbitration in his 1877 inaugural address as "a new . . . instrumentality for the preservation of
peace" but ignored pressure for concrete proposals that would for-
malize its use in foreign policy.[20] Lockwood and her friends waited
patiently before deciding that more lobbying was needed. At the
New Year in 1879 she joined Jacob Troth, Daniel Breed, and Chalkley
Gillingham, well-known activists, in petitioning Hayes. Representing
several peace and arbitration groups, the four pleaded with the president to appoint "a Commission to Aid in the Establishment of a Permanent International Tribunal of Arbitration."[21] Hayes made no reply,
causing Lockwood to send off a letter in late February that appealed
to his vanity by eulogizing him as "a President whose whole policy
has been one of peace."[22] Hayes agreed to a series of meetings to discuss the idea of a commission.[23] At one, with several dozen UPU
members present, impatient when the president again begged for
time, Lockwood stepped forward and said imperiously, "Appoint the
Commission!"[24]

Hayes did nothing. Despite evidence to the contrary, Lockwood
tried to put a good face on the failed effort. In a letter read to several
thousand people attending the August 1880 meeting of the Connecticut
Peace Society, one filled with vague but optimistic language, she maintained that "some advance has been made during the administration of
President Hayes."[25] Knowing there would be a new head of state after
the November election, she urged the candidate who prevailed to "take
hold" of the idea of arbitration and, along with Love, wasted no time
lobbying James A. Garfield, the victor. In talks and letters, Lockwood,
now also involved with a new organization called the National Arbitration League, pressed Garfield to acknowledge the value of international arbitration.[26] In a short article she argued that the promotion of a
tribunal of International Arbitration would "shed added luster and
glory" on the incoming administration for having created "a peace
compact that will bless the world," and attacked members of Congress

who, citing the need for economic retrenchment, had refused to appropriate money for arbitration.[27]

Garfield proved receptive to these overtures. Soon after taking office in March 1881 he set in motion plans for an international conference to promote arbitration and to encourage reciprocal commercial relations between the United States and Central and South America. Invitations went out. Then, on July 2, 1881, a disappointed office seeker approached and shot the president as he waited for a train.

The conference, like Garfield, became a casualty of the gunman's bullets and yet support for innovative dispute resolution slowly gained a footing, having found favor with elite politicians, scholars, and businessmen interested in its benefits for U.S. economic expansion. Troth and Gillingham had more than hinted at this when they told Hayes that entrepreneurs were "looking wistfully" at Mexico's commercial markets. Mindful of the Senate's role in foreign policy, the UPU also began looking for allies on Capitol Hill. Lockwood tagged Senator John Sherman, a legislator committed to Garfield's legacy, as someone to lobby. He had been secretary of the Treasury under Hayes and was now one of the most powerful men in the Senate, a respected expert on fiscal policy with an interest in foreign affairs. She found him approachable and joined the ranks of advocates who courted him, hoping that he would promote arbitration.

In 1884, when Cleveland surprised the pundits with his election, Lockwood and Love began, once again, the process of educating a president in the matter of peace policy. Love prepared a fresh policy paper that was, in all likelihood, the outline used by Lockwood in her 28 September 1885 letter to the new president recommending the inclusion of an arbitration clause in all foreign treaties, and the establishment of an arbitration tribunal to be part of the international machinery of conflict resolution.[28] She made a point of saying that arbitration would "enhance our commercial interests," being willing, like Troth and Gillingham, to emphasize arguments based on pragmatic capitalism rather than the teachings of Christ.

The peace and arbitration lobbies settled into a comfortable relationship with Cleveland and Congress. Increasingly, there seemed to be cause for optimism as successful international claims adjustments led the president to tell Congress that the principle of arbitration had received "gratifying confirmation."[29] Articles in the *Peacemaker* reflected with pride on the "marked success" of UPU pressure to lower appropriations in the Army, Navy, and Fortifications legislation.[30] The Peace Union also took credit for bilateral appeals and arguments that had helped to prevent trouble with Canada and England in a long-standing fishing rights dispute while Lockwood continued her work as a UPU loyalist, buttonholing Senator Sherman and other legislators who were sympathetic to the Peace Union's agenda.[31] By November 1887, at a gathering in Philadelphia, she was confident enough about Congress and Cleveland to say that it was an "auspicious time for the establishment of courts of arbitration."[32]

Her comments reflected the very real gains of the movement. By one count, ten bills had recently been introduced in Congress promoting international arbitration while, several weeks before her speech, a delegation from the British House of Commons had arrived in the United States with a petition for the president and Congress endorsing a treaty of arbitration between the two countries.[33] And at the New Year, in an extraordinary public event, multimillionaire industrialist Andrew Carnegie, New York Judge Charles Augustus Peabody, and legal scholar David Dudley Field, whose brother, Stephen, sat on the Supreme Court, appeared in a Senate Foreign Relations Committee room to testify in favor of "pacific means of intercourse among nations."[34] Field gratified Lockwood by saying that he looked forward to the day when international courts would replace the standing armies of the world. Carnegie, the wealthiest man in the hearing room, argued that "crowned heads" could not be trusted, emphasized the importance of satisfactory arbitrators, and, like Lockwood, who was lobbying against several new military spending bills, contended that the peace to be expected would make it unnecessary for the United States to spend "the money of the nation" on armed forces: "If you have ships of war," he insisted, "you will have naval contests. If you have armies you will have battles."[35]

Months later, Lockwood brought the high hopes of her UPU lobbying to a new campaign for the presidency. In May 1888 the Equal Rights Party again nominated her as its candidate. She accepted the nomination, despite earlier protestations of disinterest, and again found herself criticized by some members of the woman suffrage movement.[36] "H.B.B." (Henry B. Blackwell, editor of the *Woman's Journal*) lost no time in writing that the nomination "does not represent any of the large organizations of woman suffragists in this country. . . . [I]t is wholly unauthorized and in no sense representative. . . . [I]t seems premature [for women] to nominate an independent presidential ticket."[37] Matilda Gage also voiced disapproval, telling Elizabeth Cady Stanton that while Lockwood's 1884 campaign had been "really educational," it was "quite ridiculous" to keep up the "presidential idea another year."[38] Journalists complained the candidate was a "Barnum," ever poised to advertise herself, while Susan B. Anthony cattily claimed that her old friend "has not yet reached the years of discretion."[39]

Lockwood was certainly as much of an opportunist as any male politician. She understood the art of self-promotion, but she was deeply interested in politics—the year before she had been part of a failed effort to start an Industrial Reform Party—and knew that public office would never come to women without a fight.[40] By her reckoning, adding her name to the list of candidates, a registry that, by the end of the summer, included incumbent Democrat Grover Cleveland, Republican Benjamin Harrison, and a half-dozen third-party men, was part of an overdue civil rights strategy. The year before she had offered stern advice to the women's movement:

> [T]o gain strength and to get organization . . . put nominees in the field
> *at once* and to keep them there. That is the way that the prohibition
> movement has been carried. It was the policy of the old anti-slavery
> movement and it is the present policy of the labor party. The country
> is prepared to-day for a boldly aggressive movement on the part of the
> women of the country. . . . It is too late to take a weak or vascillating
> [sic] stand.[41]

In fact, by 1888, dozens of women had run for political office, usually at the municipal or county level, most often as school board candidates, and Lockwood was not alone in believing that women should enter partisan politics. "H.B.B.'s" comments suggest, however, that her candidacy failed to win sympathy, much less active support, because she went her own way and did not consult with the head of the American or National suffrage associations in making the decision to accept the nomination. These organizations had plans of action, generally supported major party candidates, and did not want to be upstaged or embarrassed by a woman who was well known nationally. Yet, ironically, Anthony had urged assertive partisan action, saying, "[W]omen never will be heard and heeded until they make themselves a power, irresistible in numbers and strength, moral, intellectual and financial, in all the formative gatherings of the parties they would influence."[42] Sadly, the two women could not agree that Lockwood would be one face of this push into politics, a difference noted by the New York press.[43]

The UPU's Alfred Love had been nominated as Lockwood's vice-presidential running mate. The press warmed to this ticket, quick to appreciate the comic possibilities presented by a candidate named "Love."[44] The choice of Love, a Garrisonian, was peculiar, and it is probable that he was never consulted. When notified, the horror-struck nominee sent off a letter to the Associated Press in which, citing his nonresistant views, he declined the nomination, saying that he could not hold office under a constitution that made the president commander-in-chief and gave Congress the power to declare war. It would not, he wrote, be "clean handed."[45] He also suggested that men "sometimes weigh heavier outside the ballot box-than in it," an observation that must have galled the Equal Rights Party women struggling to win themselves a place at the ballot box that Love had not visited since 1863.[46]

It appears likely that Lockwood suggested, or approved, Love as her running mate blind to his views on office holding. She may have believed that, with no chance of winning, he would be open to the opportunity to use the campaign as a forum for their shared ideas about peace and arbitration as well as social reform and women's rights. Once the campaign was underway, she wrote with considerable displeasure about his decision in a letter to Linda Slaughter, one of the Dakota Territory's most important women reformers and an officer of the NWSA. The campaign, she wrote, needed help: "I expect if you had been put on the ticket as Vice President, the campaign, which I am trying to make lively, would be much more lively than it is. I am getting no assistance from 'Love,' and yet it would seem that to be truly an Equal Rights Party, men and women must work together."[47] She again laid out her stated motive for electioneering: "I intend if possible to get up an Electoral ticket for each State; and thus get up a grand agitation on the woman question, but am not so anxious about the number of votes polled."[48]

In July she traveled to New York, happy to be hosted by Mrs. Cynthia Leonard, who had headed her New York electoral ticket in 1884. Leonard organized a political meeting for Lockwood where supporters weighed how best to present the party's platform of suffrage, temperance, labor and railroad reform, moderate tariffs, and international arbitration while also calculating whether to run candidates for local office.[49]

During this week in New York Lockwood also gave an interview to Nellie Bly, the *World's* "daredevil girl reporter." It was an extraordinary meeting of two self-made trailblazers: the young reporter who feigned insanity and lived in a mental asylum in order to expose abuses seated next to America's first fully fledged woman presidential candidate. The two women spoke in Cynthia Leonard's parlor. Bly immediately took to Lockwood. She liked her handshake, firm, soft, and warm, "worthy of a candidate," and her looks, "a womanly woman . . . intelligent without being manly . . . the beau ideal of a woman with a brain."[50] She also liked that Lockwood was lively.

The two women traveled familiar ground, with Lockwood describing her candidacy as a frank challenge to women: "Men always say, 'Let's see what you can do.' . . . If we always talk and never work we will not accomplish anything."[51] She also said that as part of the Equal Rights Party strategy New Yorker Linda Gilbert, who was well known as an advocate for prisoners, would be nominated for lieutenant-governor while Leonard would submit her name for mayor of New York.[52]

Lockwood revised stock lectures as campaign talks, working in lengthy discussions of the party's platform. A speech in late September at the well-attended Boonville, New York, fair was typical. Barely on her feet after an enthusiastic introduction by a local newspaperman, she condemned the administration in Washington for its "belligerence" in the well-publicized Canadian fisheries dispute.[53] Then she turned to domestic policy and hammered away at the need to use the large federal surplus to build new schools, repeatedly asserting that the health of a democratic republic rested on *politically* educated boys *and* girls. She repeated her belief that women should marry only after acquiring practical skills for the job market to avoid being reduced to the status of "domestic drudge" or "petted doll," a curious sermon to deliver before an audience of hard-working farm wives.

During the 1884 campaign the UPU paid little attention to Lockwood's candidacy. This time, despite Alfred Love's unwillingness to serve on the ticket, the peace group publicized her campaign in its newsletter and invited her to speak at meetings. She used these occasions, one of which included an appearance before several thousand people at the UPU's twenty-second anniversary gathering at Mystic,

Connecticut, to review the party's platform, talking about race relations and "the Canadian question."[54] She called for fair policies toward Native Americans whose land had been taken at insultingly low prices. She was also unabashedly critical of the "misuse and ill-treatment" of Chinese immigrants.[55] Unlike a number of West Coast women's rights activists who encouraged anti-Asian racism, she made a point of praising the Chinese and their contributions.

In discussing race and ethnicity, Lockwood exhibited a particular type of nineteenth-century tolerance: she was willing to open the United States to anyone willing to assimilate into Anglo-Saxon culture. She wanted to see Native Americans "civilize[d], educate[d] and . . . self-supporting."[56] The Chinese deserved no less. She also gave voice to this cultural jingoism in several comments about the annexation of Canada made during and immediately after the campaign.[57] Saying the United States and Canada were tightly bound by geography, railroads, commercial relations, language, and "consanguinity of blood," she argued that Canada must come into the Union because "it is the only possible way in which the constantly recurring difficulties and entanglements of an unprotected frontier . . . can ever be settled"; and "she must come as one of us, come because she wants to come, and with equal rights and privileges. . . . If she comes into the Union it must be a *Consolidation*—her dignity preserved, her rights respected."[58]

Lockwood was not alone in proposing annexation. A number of politicians and businessmen, particularly those from border states, viewed Canada's natural resources and population as a desirable prize. While he was Garfield's secretary of state, James Blaine predicted that a policy of protective tariffs on the part of the United States would leave Canada begging to join the Union. Maine Senator Eugene Hale also agitated the question while Lockwood's friend, John Sherman, sponsored a commercial union bill that passed in the Senate.[59] These men believed that trading with the United States was a privilege to be paid for through consolidation.

Although Lockwood threw herself into electioneering and was well received in most of her appearances, she struggled to attract attention. Local women organized marches and parades but little came of their efforts. Few people sported Lockwood's campaign ribbon, a clever rebus spelling out her entire name with pictures of a bell, a "V," a padlock, and a block of wood.[60] Unlike 1884, this campaign was not first-time news and previously sympathetic reformers, like Gage, found that the candidacy lacked civic value. Four years earlier her political bravado had expressed the optimism of the movement; by 1888, with the woman suffrage movement all but stalled, the campaign drew attention to its failure. When Bly asked if any newspapers were supporting her, Lockwood replied, "no," adding that "there is nothing to make it worth their while."[61] She said, however, that members of Washington's Woman's National Press Association had pledged to write news items about her to include "in their correspondence."[62] Charles Stuart Wells, Lockwood's late-in-the-game running mate, also tried to help by arguing that a vote for their ticket deprived machine politicians of support. There was, he said, another, principled, side to the political equation in which a person "vot[ed] for a moral idea, even if the candidate is not likely to be elected."[63] Wells's point was echoed by editor Emily Bouton, who told Ohio readers that Lockwood was to be admired for her candidacy: "The truth is, she represents a principle which she holds to be a right one . . . in the face of all ridicule. She believes in the ultimate triumph of the law of equality between the sexes."[64]

Lockwood campaigned right up to the eve of the election. When the final tallies reached her, she learned that Benjamin Harrison had earned sixty thousand fewer popular votes than Cleveland but had prevailed in the Electoral College. She sent Harrison the customary congratulatory telegram, only to find herself immediately chastised by a sour editor who accused her of never missing "an opportunity to advertise herself and her law business."[65] In this election, no votes for her appear to have been recorded. She claimed electoral tickets in several states but only a ballot from Kentucky survives.[66]

Lockwood emerged from the campaign hopeful about her country but mixed in her thoughts about the women's movement. A week after the election she wrote a short essay, "Would Women Vote?"[67] She began optimistically by pointing out that twenty-five thousand women in Boston had recently registered to vote "on the school question," demonstrating that they had "political ideas and preferences." Showing annoyance, however, at the lack of support extended to her and the Equal Rights Party by leaders of the women's movement, and unwilling to consider that she made a mistake in accepting the nomination, she cautioned that woman suffrage activists were willing to sacrifice party affiliation to "personal predilections." Women were not necessarily loyal to their sex and would "vote for a male candi-date [rather than] for each other." Still, issues and self-interest might trump prejudice: she thought that members of the Woman's Christian Temperance Union, given the vote, would support a woman prohibi-tionist and that working-class women, "compelled to wrestle with the world for the necessaries of life," would come out to vote in large numbers.

13

The Power of Association

Who would rear . . . our sons and daughters should women be enfranchised and become eligible to office . . . it is only such women as Belva Lockwood who demand the exercise of the ballot.

Opponent of woman suffrage, 1889

Despite her disappointing results in the polls in the fall of 1888, Lockwood was upbeat and, at the beginning of 1889, looking forward to her first trip to Europe. Only days after the election she had signed her name to a letter petitioning permission from the French minister of commerce and industry to hold a Universal Peace Congress in Paris during the International Exposition.[1] The French had been wary of peace radicals and internationalists but now seemed ready to host a meeting of European and North American organizations. It would be the first international peace congress in more than a decade, convening men and women of strong opinion who did not always agree on principle or strategy. The opportunity to go abroad thrilled Lockwood, who made plans to travel with her friend Amanda Deyo, a member of the UPU and one of the first American women ordained as a minister.

On May 13 1889, shortly before leaving for Paris, Lockwood spoke at the UPU's twenty-third annual meeting. She began with stock lecture material on the horrors, and the domestic impact, of warfare. "War," she argued, "for ages has been made attractive and poetical; while its realism, its atrocity, has been studiously concealed and lost in the glamour of victory."[2] As had become increasingly common in the speeches of many UPU leaders in the late 1880s, she warned that the peace of recent years could be destroyed by the new industrial economy. Trusts and combines, she insisted, were an "evil [that] must be legislated out of existence." While she was open and blunt, however, in her condemnation of laboring people preyed upon by capital, she was equally adamant in her opposition to strikes, which she characterized as "miniature wars" that should only be entered into under the very gravest of oppressions. She called, instead, for the use of arbitration. Signaling her interest in issues that would dominate American politics for decades, she also urged government regulation of workers' compensation and hours of labor.

Lockwood departed for Europe after this speech, a new passport carefully tucked into her luggage.[3] She would not return to the United States until early September. She crossed the Atlantic with Deyo, whose chatty letters, sent back to Peace Union headquarters, detailed a calm crossing with time for the study of French and the organization of a shipboard peace meeting.[4]

The women landed at Antwerp on May 26, where they visited local gardens and the city's acclaimed cathedral. Next, they journeyed into Germany on the Rhine River, stopping at Mayence and Heidelberg, then turned west and headed for Paris. They arrived in the French capital on the last day of May and went to their lodgings at 30 Rue de Bassano, a quiet Right Bank street not far from the Champs Elysees.

The newcomers entered a city bustling with the excitement of the international exposition that celebrated the centennial of the French Revolution. To visit the exposition Deyo and Lockwood traveled along the elegant tree-lined boulevards introduced under George Eugène Haussmann's plan for a new Paris and made the short walk across the Seine to the main exposition grounds on the Left Bank. They entered by passing underneath Gustave Eiffel's new thousand-foot tower, which served as a triumphal gateway to the 200-acre site. This marvel of science and engineering rose high above them, its myriad of small, interconnected, and mutually supporting iron struts intended as a symbol of progress representing how people could work together to create a modern liberal democracy through science and technology.[5] Further on, they went into the Galerie des machines, an extraordinary fifteen-acre prefabricated iron structure. Here Lockwood inspected displays of the latest machinery and manufacturing processes. As a patent attorney and ardent cyclist she must have enjoyed this show of human ingenuity although pondering, given her fears about the new industrial economy, whether the world was being changed for the better by industrial science and technology.

Amidst this bustle, the two UPU representatives settled down to work, although fretful about the daily cost, sixteen francs ($3.20), of their lodgings. They set about organizing their exhibit at the fair grounds and began a series of private meetings with European pacifists as well as several local women active in the prison-reform and the so-cial-purity movements. They were called on by the French delegates to the Congress, including the prominent peace leader Frédéric Passy, a former member of the French Chamber of Deputies, who was chairman of the convention's organizing committee.

Lockwood found Paris daunting. After visits to the famous Lemon-nier Professional School for Women, the French House of Deputies, and a gymnastics competition, she wrote in a letter that it took a long time to get around the city—though she was pleased at the modest cost of a carriage ride—and that "there is a great deal of 'how not to do it.'"[6] De-spite their shipboard studies, the two Americans also had difficulty speaking and understanding French. With uncharacteristic humility Lockwood acknowledged that she "felt very small over here with everybody talking French and not able to make myself understood."[7] Surprisingly, she did not take the time to write about Elisa Lemonnier's school, which, established for the purpose of educating girls to support themselves, was exactly the kind of institution Lockwood had long ad-vocated.

The peace meeting opened on June 23 in the Hall of Conferences of the Palais du Trocadero, a Roman-Spanish-Moorish confection of archi-tectural styles erected for an earlier exposition. Lockwood passed into the building through an entrance façade flanked by minarets.[8] Critics had heaped scorn on the building but the public loved it.

Once inside Lockwood watched as Passy brought the first session to order. He planned, during the course of the Congress, to make the case for arbitration as the process of conflict resolution most likely to be accepted by European governments, the method most likely to lead to a continent-wide policy of disarmament. Six hundred people were in the audience, half of whom were representatives of the more than ninety participating peace societies. Lockwood sat on the stage near Passy, pleased that she, and the UPU, had been accorded a place of honor.

Several of the venerable leaders of the European peace movement sat near her, waiting to join Passy in welcoming the delegates. Charles Lemonnier, now in his eighties, was called forward. Passy might have liked to pass over him. Lemonnier argued that lasting peace was im-possible where people were not self-governing and free, and he theo-retically accepted the violence that accompanied liberation campaigns.

He was open in his association with radical republicans and supporters of social reform and had a long history of polarizing the movement. His ideas exposed deep-seated differences, some reaching back decades, that had yet to be resolved, disputes that had impeded the development of an international movement because they did not sit well with more conservative activists, including Passy, who wanted to avoid confrontation with authority.[9] But Lemonnier was too important to be snubbed, and he spoke. Lockwood, closer to Lemonnier on certain viewpoints than to Passy, was also given the opportunity to make a short comment. She was not expected to be controversial and was not, devoting her time to tame praise of France, and Paris, which she called "the city of cities."[10]

On the following day, with the delegates now meeting in the "great hall of the Mayoralty of the 6th Ward, St. Sulpice," Lockwood delivered the paper she had prepared and translated into French.[11] The essay's critical theme was the necessity of international cooperation through new institutions of law and conflict resolution. "Co-operation on both sides of the Atlantic," she said, could replace war with the arbitration of differences, and lead to a general disarmament.[12] Quoting from resolutions recently adopted by the UPU, she urged the establishment of an international court of arbitration and treaties pledging arbitration in place of war. The proposed arbitration system should, she argued, be permanent, unlike the ad hoc adjudications of earlier years. She recommended that the judges of this court be persons capable of bridging the tension between national patriotism and internationalism. In an age of growing nationalism, she said that they must be men "of the largest philanthropy, broadest education and greatest sagacity, who will have at heart not only the good of the countries they represent, but the good of the whole humanity, with a view to durable peace." She stopped short, however, of advocating a permanent staff of salaried adjudicators, an issue that later became one of the reasons for replacing the Hague Tribunal with the World Court.

Lockwood and Deyo carried to Paris the UPU's provocative message that the creation of international institutions need not depend upon the goodwill of national governments. During her talk Deyo declared that "a court of arbitration is the necessity of the hour."[13] She went on to say that if the great nations were not ready for "concert of action," the nongovernmental peace societies gathered in Paris ought to establish an International Tribunal of Mediation, Arbitration, and Conciliation that would stand ready to receive important questions of "social, commercial, political, national and human interest." With Lockwood and certain other delegates, she supported immediate action and intervention that some considered an appropriation of official government authority.

The Congress met for five days. Lockwood was pleased by the fair treatment accorded women, who were encouraged to deliver papers and to speak their minds. She and Deyo wrote home that the meetings were not very orderly yet somehow the participants had discussed many issues, and approved six resolutions. These included support for the principle that justice should regulate the relations between "civilized nations and uncivilized peoples"; annexation only with free consent, and the establishment of a Federation of European States by which to unify the laws of labor, the postal system, and tariffs, as well as criminal and marriage law.[14]

The Universal Peace Congress was only one of many conferences set up to take advantage of people's presence at the Exposition Universelle.[15] Lockwood also attended the meeting of the Interparliamentary Congress, a new association of national legislators who hoped to use their elective positions to encourage international cooperation and disarmament. It was not an open meeting, but she was keen to hear what these representatives had to say. She told Lemonnier of her interest, and he, knowing that she had a journalist's credentials as a member of the small Woman's National Press Association, told her to apply for admission as a reporter.[16] She followed his advice and the conference organizers granted her an observer's seat, making her the only woman present, a fact she reported with pride.[17]

During their five weeks in Paris Lockwood and Deyo also relaxed at several evening "socials," receptions that provided relief from the somber daytime discussions.[18] Lockwood's favorite was a party given by the newly appointed American ambassador to France, Whitelaw Reid, successor to Horace Greeley as the owner and editor of the New York *Tribune*. Much to her delight, Senator Sherman had been invited, and when they saw one another she was able to strike up a "pleasant chat on arbitration," telling him that Passy would like to speak with him.[19] Sherman agreed to a meeting, also brokered by Lemonnier, and an interview was arranged for July 8 at the Hotel Royale. Lockwood was invited, along with Marie Goegg, a Peace Congress delegate from Switzerland who served as interpreter. Sitting together, the senator gave Passy and several members of the French parliament advice on how to approach President Harrison and James Blaine, his secretary of state, suggesting a concrete plan for obtaining a treaty of arbitration between the two nations. He believed that the president, Blaine, and Reid were favorably disposed to the idea of such a treaty but said that "the present instability of French politics" posed certain difficulties.[20] Encouraged by their meeting, the European delegates prepared a petition to send to Harrison.

Amanda Deyo sailed for New York on July 6, leaving Lockwood to spend two additional weeks by herself in the French capital, after which she traveled to London where, on July 20, she installed herself at the Grosvenor Hotel.[21] She had been abroad for nearly two months and expected to stay in England until mid-August. In London she lost no time meeting with British peace movement friends, who organized her visit, beginning with an excursion to the House of Commons to hear debate, after which Felix Moscheles, the British portrait painter and peace leader, made a "grand reception" for her at his home, where he and his wife introduced their American colleague to members of Parliament, lawyers, authors, and artists. Hodgson Pratt, an activist with the English Working Men's Club and cofounder in 1880 of the International Arbitration and Peace Association, also gave a reception in her honor. He arranged for a friend to take her through the Inns of Court and the Court of Queen's Bench, a day of professional touring that ended pleasantly with a sail back on the Thames River, where she saw Queen Victoria entering her carriage.[22]

Despite the touring, Lockwood never forgot that she represented the UPU. Her visits with Moscheles and Pratt had been social, but conversation with them helped her to understand the philosophies and politics that divided the English peace movement. Pratt, a nationalist, was fiercely British and staunchly committed to bourgeois liberalism. Moscheles was far less orthodox in his politics and pursued a cosmopolitan, international life. With Pratt, she discussed the importance of arbitration, industrial cooperation, and international law reform. At the Moscheles home, she listened to the argument for a more ecumenical peace movement.

These meetings required that Lockwood cultivate diplomatic skills, something she enjoyed. Unlike officials of the federal government who repeatedly rebuffed her when she showed an interest in the consular service, Alfred Love, with a business to run and no great love of travel, entrusted her with making political contacts for the UPU. He hoped that she would use her time in London to arrange a meeting with Robert Todd Lincoln, the new U.S. ambassador to England. On July 30 she wrote Love that the ambassador, the eldest son of the slain president, had met with her and listened while she made the case for improving Anglo-American relations.[23]

She had also been instructed by Love to see if an interview with the German emperor, expected in London, was possible. Love had expressed concern about the possibility of war in Europe and wanted her to test the emperor's interest in a German-American arbitration treaty. She wrote back that the emperor was arriving before her ship sailed and that she would prepare an address in German for him. Trying to size up the situation, she told him that "there is a good deal of growling among the crowned heads of Europe" but no immediate danger of fighting.[24]

On August 1, with no letter of introduction, Lockwood wrote to Count Hatzfeldt, the German ambassador to Great Britain, "beg[ging] leave" for an interview of five or six minutes with the emperor.[25] Four days later an aide of Hatzfeldt's replied that it would be impossible to honor her request as "his majesty's time is taken up entirely by previous arrangements."[26] Not to be put off, and determined to be heard, she composed and sent a letter in which she outlined the UPU's philosophy and objectives. She wrote separately that she might send a duplicate copy to Bismarck.[27] Hatzfeldt ignored her.

While Lockwood pursued the emperor, journalists, hoping for a scoop, arrived at her hotel. Editor Henrietta Müller, who wrote under the pen name Helena B. Temple, sat her down for a long session later published in the *Women's Penny Paper (The Only Paper Conducted, Written, Printed and Published by Women)*. Temple thought Lockwood a "very bright and racy talker" whose face, when speaking, "lights up with animation and humour."[28] In repose, she wrote, "it looks full of purpose and concentration." Lockwood chatted amicably with Temple about her family and the condition of women. When asked whether any woman, or woman's book, influenced her as a young girl, she replied that the greatest influence exercised upon her was by her mother, a person of "great spirit." She offered a rare, and perhaps embellished memory of her father, describing him as "a shrewd, intelligent man, much interested in public affairs," a farmer fond of having her read the newspapers to him. She said that her life now left little time for reading literature but that she was "an inveterate newspaper reader" and that she was living proof that a woman could "make a good position and earn a comfortable income as an attorney." Her work, she told Temple, enabled her "to live comfortably, support her family, and save something." She ended by saying she had good feelings about the prospects of all women and offered her much-repeated advice: "Teach girls to be self-supporting and you conquer everything."

Then she suffered a traveler's nightmare. Leaving London for her homeward journey, she misread her ticket and missed the boat in Antwerp. She made new arrangements and arrived in New York on September 3, setting off immediately for a lyceum tour, pleased with the accomplishments of the summer, and bursting with new lecture material advertised as "instructive, entertaining and reformatory."[29]

Lockwood apparently decided, after the 1888 campaign, that she would leave the shaping of women's partisan activity to other reform leaders. She had twice committed her time to the effort of breathing life into the Equal Rights Party and argued for aggressive partisan action on the part of women. Her candidacies had failed to ignite significant support among suffragists, and on her return from Europe nothing happened to convince her that remaining in the game of party politics was a good idea. In some quarters her efforts were honored, but many reform leaders continued to identify her with the unpopular cause of the Mormons or to think of her as a "Barnum" rather than an equal rights visionary. More and more, she had to acknowledge a simple fact: she intrigued people and attracted notice, but she lacked followers.

When she later wrote about running for president she chose not to analyze this failure. It was the case, however, that despite her many years working for suffrage and to overcome employment discrimination, she had not built a base of supporters. This was not surprising as she was working full-time as an attorney. Still, she had not succeeded in using the NWSA, or any of the woman suffrage newspapers, including her own short-lived venture, *Equal Rights*, to build sustained interest in the ways that third-party politics, and women's candidacies, might be used to improve women's lives.

By the late 1880s, the business of organizing women in party politics had, in fact, become increasingly complicated as the number of women's reform organizations expanded. For two decades the fault line among politically active middle-class white women had been defined by the personalities and strategic choices of the National and the

American suffrage associations. Now, however, temperance and religious belief as well as race, class, and regional politics were fueling debate in women's political circles. Lockwood had been on the front line for twenty years, but upon her return from Europe she stepped back and watched the efforts of other leaders struggling to bring women, and their causes, into party politics.

Frances Willard, the charismatic head of the Woman's Christian Temperance Union (WCTU), emerged as the most visible and politically gifted of these leaders. Unlike Lockwood, who made her name as an attorney and combined the duties of her profession with those of reform work, Willard abandoned an early career as an educator and took up full-time work as a champion of temperance. Like Lockwood, she enjoyed public speaking and understood its power. She began to make her mark in 1876 with a talk entitled "The Home Protection Ballot," in which she proposed to change the course of the temperance and suffrage movements by urging their union. Her idea was simple and, she intimated, divinely inspired: addressing the common view that women should not concern themselves with politics, she argued that the *fair sex* must have at least limited suffrage as "a weapon of protection to her home," a defense against loved ones tempted by drink.[30] Men had failed to keep vice and immorality from the kitchen door.[31] Women could do better.

Although criticized by some within the evangelical Christian temperance movement for proposing that women "trail our skirts through the mire of politics," once elected in 1879 as the head of the WCTU Willard set her sights on capturing the agenda of a political party.[32] Abandoning her long-standing support of the Republicans, she endorsed the Prohibition Party and by 1884 had gained sufficient notice that she was asked to second the nomination of John St. John as that party's candidate for president. Her influence grew, but when the Prohibition Party was defeated in the 1888 election, she barely paused before initiating efforts to create a political coalition of reform movement members—agrarians, labor, suffrage, and temperance—that would transform society through a new, populist party.[33]

Willard shared Lockwood's faith that the political system would open itself to women. While head of the WCTU she wrote in her journal, "Had vision in the night of a novel I might write in which a woman becomes Pres't of the United States after a complete Revolution which she leads!"[34] Like Lockwood, Willard understood that action was essential and that piety and vision alone would not defeat demon rum, or bring about the other social and economic reforms that she favored. In creating a faith-based politics for the members of the WCTU she argued that God sanctioned temperance agitation and that women must demand suffrage, not as an individual right but as a religious duty. She ennobled politics for hundreds of thousands of women, sanctifying their partisan activities with a vision of home protection so capacious that it embraced a broad program of labor and education reform as well as significant proposals concerning disarmament and world peace.

Also like Lockwood, Willard faced opposition from many quarters. In 1881 WCTU antisuffragists, led by Annie Wittenmyer, Willard's predecessor, left the organization. Throughout the 1880s Judith Ellen Foster, an influential member of the WCTU and head of its Legislative Department, made spirited attacks on Willard's involvement with the Prohibition Party, and in due course established the rival Nonpartisan Woman's Christian Temperance Union. Many Americans frankly thought that Willard, who espoused total abstinence, was an uncompromising evangelical extremist. But Lockwood, who shared Willard's Methodist faith, was reluctant to criticize her. In an 1888 article Lockwood described the WCTU as having "[come] in and possessed the land," and after Willard died said she was "the peer of the women of her time," a woman who had "virtually made the W.C.T.U. the great Power that it is," a Methodist who "practiced her convictions."[35]

Lockwood was not concerned about the growing power of evangelical women in the suffrage movement, but Stanton, Gage, and Colby, each more religiously liberal than Lockwood, were increasingly alarmed. In 1886 Stanton observed tartly that "most of the women in our movement to-day care more about their religion, the salvation of their souls, than they do about enfranchisement."[36] Stanton was not an atheist, but she had decided, according to a student of her intellectual thought, that the Christian Church and its Bible were "looming obstacles to woman's liberty that needed to be leveled."[37] At several NWSA conventions the trio introduced resolutions critical of the Christian Church, an institution, they told their suffrage sisters, that taught that "woman was an afterthought in creation, her sex a misfortune."[38]

It was natural, given these beliefs, that Stanton would fear the loss of liberality within the NWSA. When Willard's WCTU lobbied for a constitutional amendment recognizing Christ as the "author and head of government," Stanton reared up in opposition, fearful for the future of a secular national government. She shot off a letter to Clara Colby's *Woman's Tribune* in which she insisted that "there is no reason why theological dogmas should be recognized in our National Constitution."[39]

Matilda Joslyn Gage, coeditor of the *History of Woman Suffrage*, and every bit Stanton's match as a philosophically and spiritually curious woman, was also concerned about the conservative direction of national politics and Willard's seemingly unstoppable influence. Writing Stanton, she suggested that a showdown was near: "The great dangerous organization of the movement is the W.C.T.U.; and Frances Willard with her magnetic force, her power of leadership, her desire to introduce religious tests into the government, is the most dangerous person upon the American continent to-day. You and I must stand firm. . . . We must have no religious test for anything."[40]

Lockwood held her tongue as suffrage and temperance colleagues lashed out at one another. She chose a middle course in the 1888 election, supporting temperance while avoiding other, divisive, religious issues. But in 1890 she was asked to take a stand when Gage put out a call for the founding of a new, progressive women's rights organization later named the Woman's National Liberal Union (WNLU). Although several of Lockwood's close friends, including Colby and Ricker, signed the call, she declined while shrewdly arranging to be present at the group's first convention as an observer for the UPU.[41]

Gage and Lockwood had known each other for at least fifteen years when the former put out her call. The two activists agreed that changing women's place in society required more than suffrage rights. Lockwood stressed the importance of education and occupation; Gage, a freethinker, wanted women liberated from the thrall of conservative religion. In her appeal to "liberal-suffrage and other liberal-thought women," Gage denounced the existing women's suffrage organizations for having ceased to be progressive and argued, "A crisis in the nation's life is at hand [because of] the encroachments of 'The Christian Party in Politics.'"[42] She said that suffrage was "valueless" without religious liberty and promised an association devoted to the complete emancipation of women as well as the separation of church and state.

Gage took action after having watched helplessly as more moderate leaders, including Anthony, first wooed Willard and then, in 1889, orchestrated the reuniting of the NWSA with the more conservative American Woman Suffrage Association (forming the National American Woman Suffrage Association). Anthony tried to placate Gage, her old friend and NWSA colleague, but their differences were now too great. With the help of Josephine and William Aldrich, financial backers, Gage started a newspaper called *The Liberal Thinker* and used it to publicize the first meeting of the Woman's National Liberal Union. She scheduled a convention to fall immediately after the February 1890 inaugural of the National American Woman Suffrage Association (NAWSA), hoping, no doubt, to steal a bit of Anthony's thunder and to recruit some of the more liberal members from the newly merged suffrage tent. Leaders of the NAWSA did not take kindly to the news of Gage's denunciation and shortly before the convention, in her usual shorthand, Gage wrote her son Thomas that "Susan & Blackwell counsel or *forbid* attendance upon my con[ference]."[43]

Although Richard Westbrook, a prominent freethinker and longtime supporter of woman suffrage, later charged Gage with holding too tight a rein, the WNLU convention, held in Washington, D.C., was a freewheeling exchange among radicals sufficiently upsetting to local ministers that at least one preached a sermon against the new group.[44] Gage led off with a talk entitled "The Dangers of the Hour." In it she condemned Catholic and Protestant churches, arguing that each sought to expand its power and eventually to end the constitutionally mandated separation of church and state.[45] Hours of heated debate ensued among the hall full of atheists, theosophists, and freethinkers. Lockwood, a church-going Methodist, remained silent until the second day when the focus of the meeting abruptly turned to the reform of the legal system and the need for an office of public defender. William Aldrich and Clara Foltz, who had come to the meeting from California, each addressed the delegates, making impassioned pleas for publicly supported attorneys who would provide a proper complement to the existing system of free juries, witnesses, and courts.[46] Foltz emphasized the importance of the reform for the poor and when she finished Lockwood stepped forward with words of support. She identified herself as a veteran criminal attorney, and told the audience that "perfectly innocent" men and women were often sentenced to time in jail.[47] She went on to talk about an aspect of the question, racial injustice, that Aldrich and Foltz had ignored: "I have known colored men and women too who have lain in jail for years because they had no money. . . . This has happened more times than you could count."[48] Sensitive to the power of first-hand observation, Lockwood then urged the delegates to spend a day at the District's Police Court, where she promised a sober lesson in human rights: "[S]ee what I have seen and know what I have known. . . . fellow men kept on bread and water in solitary confinement."[49]

Although Gage had big plans for the WNLU, it was soon clear that inadequate funding and internal politics would be the death of the organization. She had antagonized Westbrook, who used his influence among freethinkers to question her ability to lead a progressive movement.[50] Routed, Gage went back to writing, saving Lockwood any further need to weigh her interest in the Liberal Union. Instead, out of habit and conviction, Lockwood continued her affiliation with the unified National American Woman Suffrage Association. Despite her independence and unhappy personal relations with Anthony, the community provided by the suffrage movement remained important to her, providing friendship as well as a place to lobby the ideas of the UPU.

14

Pushing for Place

I am beginning to think we are becoming so ring-ridden in the [Na-
tional] that our cause is being injured, and the work and sacrifice of
some of our best workers being paralyzed.

Activist Josephine Kirby Henry, 1899

Matilda Gage's challenge was only one of the power struggles and personality clashes that occurred in the late nineteenth century in the
women's movement. While Gage fought Anthony, J. Ellen Foster stubbornly continued her very public feud with Frances Willard. New York
activist Lillie Devereux Blake repeatedly complained about her treatment at the hands of suffrage colleagues and was "dislodged" several
times from positions of responsibility by people, she said, who wished
to put her "on the shelf."[1] This strife was not without personal cost as
Foster acknowledged in a letter to another activist: "one of the saddest
things in connection with the division in the ranks of the W.C.T.U. has
been the separation in personal friendships."[2]

The once-warm relationship shared by Lockwood and Susan B. Anthony was another casualty of this difficult time, a period in which the failure of old strategies had to be acknowledged and new coalitions created.
For these two women, friendship gave way in the face of differences over
strategy, and self-interest. Lockwood, wearing a mantle of self-impor-
tance as the dean of American women lawyers as well as an active Washington lobbyist, was increasingly willing to assert herself and to incur criticism. Movement leaders may have wished that she would practice law
rather than campaign for political office, but her accomplishments could
not be easily dismissed, and regardless of what Anthony, Blackwell, and
others said, she continued to be a woman of stature within the reform community. She *was* a member of the Supreme Court of the United States bar
and she, alone among them, had run for the presidency.

Yet in the women's movement of the early 1890s, a hydra-headed complex of groups that included the newly formed International and National Councils of Women, the National American Woman's Suffrage Association, the Woman's Christian Temperance Union, the Federation of Women's Clubs, Mother's Clubs, and a scattering of women's professional organizations, Lockwood did not command a national leadership role. Her second campaign for the presidency, almost certainly undertaken to help her lecture career, may also have been intended to improve her standing in the mainstream suffrage movement by enacting her belief that activists should put women nominees in the field. If so, the decision was a mistake, as her candidacy only further antagonized a number of movement leaders who believed she had neither a winning plan nor particularly effective organizational skills.

Years after her death members of Lockwood's family insisted that her loss of position in the suffrage movement was due to Anthony's "tyrannical jealousy," personal feelings that "closed" her out of the inner circle of activists.[3] In fact, Lockwood's outspoken nature and controversial positions had upset a number of powerful suffrage leaders, including Lucy Stone, who had complained about her 1884 speech in support of Mormon rights.[4] Moreover, although Lockwood was convinced that political campaigning was an important way for women to show their interest in partisan politics and to win suffrage, either because of the time her law practice required, or because she did not really grasp the importance of field organizing, she never offered the women's movement a broad (rather than ad hoc) plan of action that identified political positions, candidates, and time tables.

Lockwood and Anthony developed a particularly troubled relationship, each calling the other names.[5] One of the most public snubs occurred in 1888, when Anthony, May Wright Sewall, and Rachel Foster organized the program of speeches for the historic inaugural convention of the International Council of Women scheduled for Washington, D.C. The formation of the council, an important step in establishing global communication and cooperation among women, was precisely the kind of effort that Lockwood would eagerly have boosted. Proposed several years earlier, Elizabeth Cady Stanton's original idea of an International Woman Suffrage Congress had been reworked to embrace broad themes of reform and philanthropy, a concession to younger and more conservative activist women.[6] The gathering stretched over a week in late March with half-day sessions devoted to specific themes—education, temperance, industries, professions, social purity, politics, religion, and law. Although Lockwood was an appropriate person to deliver the talk, "Woman in Law," Ada Bittenbender, an attorney active with the WCTU, was given the honor. Lockwood was also passed over as assignments were handed out in other areas of her expertise. If this were not sufficient reproach, Anthony, Foster, and Sewall left her out of the March 31 pageant, "Conference of the Pioneers," where Stanton, Anthony, and Gage joined Lucy Stone, Henry Blackwell, and Frederick Douglass as well as Senator Samuel C. Pomeroy and Lockwood's mentor, A. G. Riddle, in speaking. The insult intended was so grave that she was not even listed as one of the "pioneers" invited to sit on the stage by the speakers, an honor accorded to the other founders of Washington's Universal Franchise Association.[7] Not someone to hide, Lockwood stayed in the city and chaired a satellite meeting on peace and arbitration organized by Amanda Deyo, revealing nothing of the snub in her dignified report to the UPU.[8]

Time only intensified the differences between Lockwood and Anthony. In 1891 Matilda Gage wrote to Lillie Blake asking if she had heard about a row between the two women: "Were you at the Council. . . ? I hear that Susan and Belva had a fight. What do you know of it? That Susan accused Belva of face-painting, hair-dyeing, and riding on a bicycle! What caused the row? When once Susan hates a person for any cause she omits no method of injuring them."[9]

That their relations were completely ragged was now beyond doubt. Buoyed by the successful merger of the National and American suffrage associations, Anthony had little need for someone like Lockwood, who had never been an obedient foot soldier. Still, in all likelihood, Lockwood's displacement also came from a younger generation of activists willing to elbow aside the older leaders. Marilla Ricker said as much in a letter to Blake: "I saw some years ago that a few of the younger women were inclined to manage matters. Susan Anthony is the only one of the older women who is now to the front, except yourself. . . . Olympia Brown, Phoebe Couzins, Sara Spencer, Matilda Gage, Belva Lockwood . . . and many others were 'frozen out' so to speak."[10]

As it became clear that she could no longer command a significant position within the mainstream woman suffrage movement, Lockwood did not sever her ties to the movement per se, but increasingly worked only with Clara Colby, who, with the founding of the Federal Suffrage Association in 1892, spearheaded a campaign that focused on the right of women to vote in federal elections.[11] After her 1889 trip to Paris and London—where she had been given a warm welcome by European and British peace activists—Lockwood also began imagining a role for herself as an American representative in the newly revitalized international peace movement. At a time when suffrage politics offered few opportunities, this international connection held out the prospect of position—as yet undefined—and community. She seized the possibility of engagement and voiced no concern that the international associations with which she was making cause were far more male dominated than the UPU.

Lockwood's first opportunity to rejoin these new friends came in 1890 with the announcement of a peace meeting in London. She set off on July 2 without a companion. The trip was not without drama as two days out a bad storm broke, with steady "mountains" of sea water washing over a ship already rocking from violent winds. The racks were put on the tables and the portholes closed, while sick passengers huddled in their state rooms.[12] After a day, the winds abated and the passengers "rallied and crawled upon the deck again," too late to celebrate the Fourth of July. Lockwood, a farm woman born with sea legs, reported no discomfort beyond wet feet. At the request of several of the clergymen on board she gave a talk on the peace question, an effort that drew a sizeable crowd to the ship's dining room and considerable applause.

Lockwood had hoped to bring her colleagues at the Universal Peace Congress news that the United States would take the lead in establishing bilateral arbitration treaties, but the actions of the Harrison administration in the spring of 1890 as well as statements by the president, made directly to her at the White House, indicated that the president remained wary of these diplomatic instruments and belligerent in the matter of a long-standing conflict with Venezuela.[13] In fact, the delegates in London, nearly all of whom were men, began the meeting with an airing of old differences. To applause a Frenchman shouted out that he had not come to the meeting to "regulate war, but to declare against it."[14] Cheering filled the hall when yet another delegate announced his total opposition to war. Like the previous year's meeting in Paris, whose disorderly sessions had occasioned comment from Amanda Deyo, there was no shortage of opinion, or spirit.

Yet in the decades since the age of monarchy had slammed up against democratic revolutions and citizen-activists had entered the realm of policy making, certain recommendations for the maintenance of peace had gained prominence. Total opposition to war commanded high moral ground but increasingly peace crusaders spoke about concrete, pragmatic methods of preventing war rather than the scriptural foundation of their pacifism. Arbitration, along with arms reduction, provided the diverse members of the peace community with what one historian described as its "common denominator."[15]

In London Lockwood used statistics and historical examples to make the case for peace. The approach, consistent with her training as an attorney, also acknowledged that arbitration, and, possibly, disarmament, might become a middle ground for politicians. Her talk, titled "Is Any Scheme for Disarmament Practical at the Present Time?" followed this formula, beginning simply, "with the facts and figures before us, it does not seem optimistic or Utopian to declare that disarmament under certain conditions is not only practical but feasible."[16]

This lecture was used as a segue to the presentation of an armaments reduction resolution. Connecting foreign policy with domestic economic questions, the resolution asserted that weapons expenditures caused "general economic disturbance" that stood in the way of healthy forms of capital investment and satisfactory employment.[17] The narrow focus on Europe prompted a call for amendments, and in the discussion that followed a Muslim delegate from Bombay made an eloquent speech, chiding the assembly for insufficient attention to Asia and the desire of people there for peace.

The criticism, more than fair, prompts the larger question of what to think of this congress and the ones that followed each year throughout the 1890s and well into the next century. With hindsight, it must be said that neither this international movement, nor the national societies of which it was composed, won the governmental support at minimum necessary to prevent the Great War that broke upon the world in 1914, or the smaller wars and imperialist actions that preceded it in Asia and the Pacific, South Africa, and Cuba. That history, however, in no way diminishes the insight shared by Lockwood and her colleagues that the chance for peace demanded new institutions of international relations and new ways of thinking about national sovereignty. In London, in 1890, as in Paris months earlier, delegates had only just begun to hammer out the terms of engagement, among themselves and with the governments whose policies they hoped to influence.

After several days of discussion the second annual Peace Congress closed, and Lockwood then donned her own "press hat." Using the credentials issued by the Woman's National Press Association, she was admitted to the annual meeting, in London, of the Interparliamentary Conference, the association of national legislators interested in promoting peace and arbitration. International law expert David Dudley Field, who had presided the week before at the Peace Congress, and Lockwood were among the few observers present from North America. Among other topics, delegates continued to wrangle over whether a permanent international arbitral system could be developed that did not threaten national sovereignty.[18]

After the Interparliamentary Conference, Lockwood attended a two-week adult education program offered by Oxford University. In its third year, enrollment in this summer "Extension Movement" offered "lectures, conversazione, concerts, &c."[19] It was a respectable diversion for a woman traveling alone, one that offered her the possibility of new lecture material. During her session there was a spirited discussion of self-improvement and the politics of adult education, debate rich in its articulation of class bias.[20] When the program ended in mid-August Lockwood made her way back to Liverpool, and sailed for the United States, arriving in Brooklyn on October 25.

The summer of travel ended with a brief trip to the UPU's newly purchased property in Mystic, Connecticut, where the group hoped to erect a Peace Temple.[21] She attended a meeting chaired by Alfred Love and joined in the discussion, prompted by a recent strike of railroad workers, of labor policy, an exchange typical of the UPU's concern for issues of social and economic justice. Lockwood endorsed a set of rules recently drawn up by UPU members, a "bill of rights" to be used in the settlement of differences between workers and owners, and supported a motion that it be sent immediately to the New York State Board of Arbitration in session at Albany. Like Love, she was adamant that all differences between capital and labor could and should be settled by arbitration, and at this meeting insisted that, despite sympathy with the strikers, labor organizations had no right to tie up a railroad. Later in the meeting she reported on the London peace conferences and seconded Amanda Deyo's resolution that the UPU lobby for the repeal of the Chinese Exclusion Act.

Lockwood channeled considerable energy into the peace movement and, in return, found position and intellectual stimulation there. The trips abroad in 1889 and 1890 designated her as a member of considerable standing, a person in whom the UPU invested its scarce treasury.[22]

She did the job well and took on trips to peace meetings in Berne (1892), Chicago (1893), Antwerp (1894), and Geneva (1896) before the demands of caring for her elderly mother, and other family responsibilities, caused her to cut back on travel.

The Peace Union was not, however, the sole focus of her reform activities. With an enthusiasm typical of many late-Victorian, middle-class American women she joined, and in several instances helped to build, a number of organizations, attending meetings of suffrage, self-improvement, and professional associations well into her eighties.[23] She was, in particular, intrigued by the possibility of building a woman's press association. She had long flirted with journalism as a sometime career and was part of a woman's reform culture where writing, editing, or even owning a weekly or monthly newspaper was common.

At the end of her 1884 presidential campaign Lockwood had become copublisher of Marietta Stow's *Woman's Herald of Industry*, renamed *Equal Rights*. It appears that Stow did not require an ownership stake from Lockwood, who thought that, as copublisher, she could extend her influence in the women's right community while giving greater voice to the work of the American peace movement. The two women put out only two or three issues before realizing they were not going to succeed. Why this happened is not clear. Several activist-publishers, including Abigail Duniway at *The New Northwest* (Oregon), Caroline Churchill of the *Queen Bee* (Colorado), Clara Colby at the *Woman's Tribune* (Nebraska; later Washington, D.C.), and Lucy Stone at the *Woman's Journal* (Boston), had found ways to keep their publications afloat.[24] Stow brought to their arrangement an established subscriber base, and the venture, with an editor on either coast, might have provided an interesting bridge between eastern and Pacific suffrage groups. Although neither editor discussed the failure, it seems likely that money was an issue, and that the great distance between the women also created logistical problems.

Stow and Lockwood's collaboration occurred at a time when women journalists, perhaps because of their increasing number, were experiencing fresh discrimination. In 1881 Washington's "lady correspondents," out of "Necessity and Ambition," formed the Ladies Press Club, selecting Emily Briggs as president.[25] The group renamed itself the Woman's National Press Association (WNPA) and, led by Briggs, who wrote as "Olivia," tried to win women journalists access to the

Capitol press gallery, which recently had been declared off-limits to them. She failed to get her sisters by the doorkeeper charged with protecting the male sanctuary, but a purdah-like agreement was struck in which the women were given space, adjoining the men's gallery, but separated by a wire screen and a locked door.[26]

Lockwood joined the WNPA in its earliest days. *Life at the National Capitol* listed her in 1887 as one of the association's eighty members, "women who think as well as write for the leading journals."[27] She went to meetings for the shop talk and camaraderie as well as the lectures on professional issues and current events.[28] She also plumbed the members' goodwill, plying them with requests to cover her presidential campaigns and reform efforts.[29] The WNPA vetted applicants and issued press credentials to serious writers, a process that gained women journalists access to events from which they might otherwise be excluded. Lockwood recognized the importance of equal access if women were going to make their mark in journalism, and as one of the few female members of the International League of Press Clubs, she repeatedly raised the issue of exclusion. She succeeded in winning for "pen women" covering the 1900 Paris Exposition space at writing tables otherwise allotted to men.[30]

Lockwood only dabbled in journalism until her first presidential campaign, when she decided to view her newfound "popularity" as a "call" to newspaper correspondence as well as lecturing.[31] As a writer she became best known in the popular press for her articles about women, beginning with her own story, "My Efforts to Become a Lawyer," published in *Lippincott's Monthly Magazine*. In the same year, 1888, she wrote "The Present Phase of the Woman Question," a spirited defense of education, pluck, and temperance as agents of change. In this essay she commented that "to the moral, sensitive, thinking woman, dependence has always been galling" but claimed that women had now learned "the *sesame*" and predicted real social change that would include a "freer and more exalted womanhood."[32]

The idea of a liberated woman, high-spirited, resourceful, and intelligent, had begun to fascinate the American public. In 1890 Lockwood gave her a face and identity in an article invited by the mass-circulation *Illustrated American*. Shortly, this intriguing woman would be portrayed as the beautiful Gibson Girl, but in Lockwood's "Women of the American Bar," she was presented as the first generation of self-confident professionals, sisters-in-law who had braved the "cold and forbidding" world of law and won admission to the United States Supreme Court bar.[33] It was a sign of Lockwood's prominence as one of the country's first women attorneys that she was asked to make this kind of literary contribution.

One of her most jubilant articles was written in 1893 for the *American Journal of Politics*, a magazine "for Intelligent Men and Women who Read and Think on Vital Questions of the Times." She titled the essay "Women in Politics." Logically, it posed an opportunity to discuss her presidential campaigns and their educational value, but, for reasons she chose not to discuss, she made no mention of her candidacies and downplayed the woman suffrage movement as a "force" bringing women into politics. Instead, taking a forward-looking, modern stance, she highlighted the role of education, labor-saving housekeeping devices, and labor unions as engines of the social change that had opened political life to women. She celebrated the women who, through male balloting, had been elected to the office of school trustee, school superintendent, and even state's attorney. She reported on women who had participated as electors in several of the 1892 presidential nominating conventions, and mentioned two women who had run as candidates for the United States Senate. She also pointed to the presence of women reporters and editors at "every great daily in the country" and to the thousands of "cultured women graduates" coming out of American colleges and universities, and concluded, the year being 1893, that "women in politics have come to stay."[34]

Lockwood also produced a steady stream of essays for the UPU's *Peacemaker*. In this writing she followed her habit of using history and statistics to argue that global interdependence and the advances of civilization demanded, and made possible, the abandonment of war. Her prose was measured and she seldom failed to promote arbitration and to urge the establishment of international courts. On occasion she wrote with an unnerving frankness. One of the most challenging of her UPU essays, "The Other Side," appeared in the winter of 1891. In it she attacked the "sensationalism [and] exaggeration" used to describe the Russian exile system to the American public.[35] She charged a popular lecturer who "dishes out the horrors of Siberian prisons to gaping [American] crowds" with financial self-interest and said another went too far in calling Russia "the monster criminal of the nineteenth century." Russia was, she reminded her readers, a country with which the United States "is on terms of peace, our friend and ally during the late civil war." It was, she admonished, "time to call a halt, to investigate, to look on the other side."

This advocacy, inexplicable to many of the *Peacemaker's* readers, grew out of her desire to see the ratification of a treaty between the United States and Russia then being considered in Washington. She thought that it might be approved if people like her put the actions of Russian authorities in perspective, something she sought to do by writing that American labor and penal practices should be measured against those found in Siberia: "If the horrors of the 'pineries' in the lumber camps of the North, the outrages on the Indians and Chinese in the Northwest, the murders and abuses of the colored people in the South, the atrocities in the convict camps in Georgia and Tennessee . . . were summed up and dished out, with additional embellishments and variations, to Russian audiences . . . the picture might be quite as dark for the United States."

Clearly casting herself as an apologist for the Russians, she asked, "What are the facts?"—and answered that the Russian government, "recognizing that banishment is more humane than hanging, or imprisonment for life, or even for a term, banishes all her criminals alike . . . with a humanity that our government would do well to imitate." These people, she wrote, were known only as exiles, "their manhood is left—they may reform—they may rise again, and they are not necessarily torn from their families." Revealing her own deep sense of self-sufficiency, she summed up, "To every Siberian there is a future if he wills it." Facing the age-old diplomatic choice of carrot or stick, Lockwood advised the higher ground: "Whatever may be the faults of the Russian Government as such, or the defects in the character of the present Czar, we cannot reform them by calling them names. Occupying one-sixth of the inhabitable land of the globe . . . Russia is an ally worth conciliating." To her relief President Cleveland signed what she later described as the "much-abused Russian Treaty."[36]

Lockwood's belief in self-reliance also found sharp expression in several *Peacemaker* essays and editorials on "the Indian Question." After the December 1890 massacre of Sioux at Wounded Knee, she mourned the dead, on both sides, and wrote movingly of the deprivations faced by the Sioux that had caused them to take up the Ghost Dance.[37] She felt that a tragedy as great as Wounded Knee, which had left scores of Sioux women and children dead in the snow, demanded the rethinking of U.S. Indian policy. Few of her Peace Union colleagues, however, anticipated her recommendation: that the Bureau of Indian Affairs (BIA), housed in the Department of the Interior, "turn the Indians over to the War Department."[38] Anticipating the peacekeeping forces of the twentieth century, she argued that "soldiers can be converted to care takers . . . [that] Gen. Miles and Gen. Howard are both kindly, humane and mild mannered men."[39] She insisted that Congress would have shifted responsibility to the War Department long before had the "clamor of would-be friends" not prevented the change.

As a peace activist she needed to defend this startling recommendation and did so by offering the example of the War Department's "admirabl[e]" post–Civil War role in managing the Freedmen's Bureau. Seemingly blind to poverty in African-American communities, and to the role of Reconstruction policy and the Bureau in this outcome, she wrote that freed slaves had started with less than the Indian, having neither land nor annuity, but were now "self-supporting." She proposed management by the War Department, believing—with many others—that the Bureau of Indian Affairs was hopelessly corrupt. She imagined that the War Department could do better, that it could restore "quiet, order and harmony without bloodshed," and break up the "Indian ring," despite the military's role in the deaths at Wounded Knee.[40] The recommendation reflected her judgment as an Indian land claims attorney familiar with the BIA, or naiveté, or both.

A year later she was only somewhat less harsh in her judgment of congressional legislation to remove the Southern Ute from Colorado to arid lands in southeastern Utah. She opposed the plan because of its needless cost as well as its failure to honor established legal agreements. Most of all, however, she objected to the bill because it interfered with a process, "well begun," of assimilating the Indian through exposure to Western education and religion, and the opportunity to farm arable and well-watered land.[41] As was common among the reformers of her day, she refused to entertain the idea that Native Americans might not wish to assimilate.

Self-sufficiency was Lockwood's secular creed. When sick she "braced up" and got the job done.[42] Now in her early sixties, she worked constantly. She lectured, wrote, and directed her law office, a practice increasingly focused on claims against the government. Lura and Clara ran the office when Belva was out of town. In 1890 May Gardner, her sister Inverno's daughter, came to work in the office.[43] May stayed for three years, possibly to assist her aunt and cousin when Lura,

in January 1891, at the age of forty-one, gave birth to a son, DeForest
Lewis Ormes. Family finances fluctuated a great deal in this period,
making Lockwood eager for the passage of the Indian Depredations Jurisdictional Act, legislation transferring the approval of claims from
Congress to the U.S. Court of Claims. When the legislation was signed
into law she lost no time taking out ads announcing that, for the fee—
not to exceed 15 percent—approved by the law, the firm of Belva A.
Lockwood & Co. would "attend promptly to any claim."[44] Reform work
gave her community, and a certain amount of influence, but the practice
of law supported her household.

15

A World's Fair and a Million-Dollar Case

> Women had to battle state-by-state (and territory-by-territory) to be lawyers . . . there are hundreds, maybe thousands, of vivid particular stories, with their displays of nerve and courage.
>
> Barbara Allen Babcock, 1998

In 1893 the United States hosted a world's fair, a coming-of-age party for the nation. Celebrating the four hundredth anniversary of Columbus's first voyage to the Americas, the World's Columbian Exposition had been sold to Congress and bondholders as an overdue salute to the accomplishments of an emerging world power. Cities vied for the prestige of playing host. Congress chose Chicago, and by the time the fair opened on the first day of May a great "White City" had risen on the Lake Michigan shoreline, ready to receive an expected twenty million visitors. The neoclassical confection was a curious site with its lagoon, gondoliers, and beaux arts buildings, an Old World stage set on which to display the latest in scientific achievement and industrial technology.

Lockwood came to the exposition for the opening and again for the month of August. The possibility of using a world's fair to spread the UPU's message of peace had loomed large in her thinking for several years, particularly as she worried about the movement's failure to "reach the masses."[1] Her interest was not unique. Every American reform group understood that the exposition was an opportunity not to be missed, and through exhibits, talks, and free literature, each hoped to promote its cause.

As plans unfolded, the glorification of Columbus and the perceived slighting of Queen Isabella, who had pledged her jewels to fund his expedition, caused spirited discussion among women reformers. Some activists formed the Queen Isabella Association, determined to balance the historical record and to be the exposition's voice of women. Popularly known as the Isabellas, they commissioned a large statue of the queen to counter the publicity given Columbus, and confidently awaited official recognition. They ran afoul, however, of Chicago politics, and other suffrage women, including Josephine Aldrich and Mathilda Gage, who denounced the plan for a statue, citing the queen's support for the Inquisition.[2]

The Isabellas were also challenged by elite women, led by Chicago socialite Bertha Palmer, who, rebuffed in their effort to be full participants with men in the planning of the exposition, accepted the congressional plan of a separate Board of Lady Managers. A pitched battle developed for control of this board and its agenda. The Isabellas, who wanted to put women's accomplishments on view alongside men's, were outflanked in appointments and in the decision to construct a separate Woman's Building where women's contributions to the nation would be presented in a segregated setting.[3]

Lockwood, who had a soft spot for female monarchs and knew women on all sides of this quarrel, endorsed the appointees to the Board of Lady Managers and, surprisingly, said little about women's exclusion from the primary governing body. Pushed aside by the leaders of the women's movement, she was more focused on peace issues, using her time to lobby against military displays and exercises on the fairgrounds.[4] In May 1893, accompanied by Hannah Bailey, a UPU officer who was also head of the WCTU's Peace Department, she traveled to Chicago for the ribbon-cutting ceremonies. The two women set up a permanent peace display and reception area in the Manufactures and Liberal Arts Building.[5] This sprawling structure, which covered more than thirty acres, was a good location housing hundreds of exhibits as well as a popular elevator ride to an observation deck—although the athletic Lockwood later commented that the building's great space made her "foot sore."

American peace activists had long hoped to draw attention to the movement by holding an international congress during the summer of 1893. Lockwood felt strongly about this proposal, believing it would make international pacifism and international law a more vital force in American politics. With Benjamin Trueblood, general secretary of the American Peace Society, she had won over European colleagues fearful about the possibility of U.S. government censorship by providing assurances from fair officials and Secretary of State James Blaine that no speech given at the fair would be "dictated or interdicted by the U.S.

Government."[6] Secure in this pledge, peace activists joined together at the Fifth International Peace Congress in August. During this meeting, Lockwood presented a resolution favoring the establishment of a permanent International Arbitration Court, a measure that called upon the U.S. Congress to empower the president to make overtures to other governments.[7] She said that the question had been under discussion for more than twenty years and that the attitudes of national governments were positive, and argued that the legal framework of treaties and ad hoc arbitration that had evolved in the nineteenth century had successfully prepared the way for such a court, and for peace.

By the time of the Peace Congress the fair was in full swing and to everyone's relief, a great success. Attendance exceeded expectations and the giant ferris wheel, "the wonder of two continents," commissioned as an example of American ingenuity meant to rival the Eiffel Tower, was up and running, its patrons carrying aboard packages of the newly marketed treat, Crackerjacks.[8] Visitors came to the fair by land or water. Many people first viewed the White City from a steamer that ferried them from downtown Chicago. After docking, many women headed off to the nearby Woman's Building, designed in the Italian Renaissance style by 21-year-old Sophia Hayden, a recent graduate of MIT. Crammed with examples of women's achievements in industry, science, and the arts, the juried displays drew overflow crowds, as did the talks that filled its auditorium.

Few sightseers knew about the battle waged by the feisty Isabellas, who, cleverly, sponsored exhibits and talks at their six-story Club House and Congress Hall, a building so close to the fairgrounds that most visitors assumed they had official sponsorship.[9] Lockwood joined in one of these assemblies, a congress of women lawyers, organized by the Isabellas. The gathering, a first-ever convention of female attorneys, was the brainchild of Chicago lawyer Ellen Martin, who believed that her sisters-in-law needed to form an association "to control their representation in the general organizations of women."[10] On August 3 Martin opened the three-day meeting, speaking with optimism about the place of women attorneys in the profession: "Women lawyers have no wrongs to right so far as the bench and bar are concerned, having been almost uniformly well treated by both everywhere."[11] It was a curious conceit at a time when corporate and government legal positions were not open to women and in a year when Lockwood, recently denied admission to the Virginia bar, unsuccessfully petitioned the U.S. Supreme

Court, which, citing *Bradwell*, held that Virginia was completely within its rights to reject her application.[12]

Florence Cronise, a sober, heavy-set, small-town attorney from Ohio, presided over the congress, whose members, before returning home, made the decision to form the National League of Women Lawyers. In her introductory remarks Cronise, an active member of the Equity Club, described the proud history of women's fight to join the legal profession. Two hundred women had trained in law since the late 1860s, many now laboring in a field that, according to the 1890 census, had about ninety thousand male practitioners. A number of the early pioneers—Lockwood, Ada Kepley, Phoebe Couzins, J. Ellen Foster, and Belle Mansfield—were present as well as members of a slightly later but no less impressive generation including Clara Foltz, Carrie Burnham Kilgore, and Mary Ellen Lease.[13] Three—Lockwood, Foltz, and Kilgore—had been admitted to the U.S. Supreme Court bar. During the official program several of the older women reminisced about the early struggle against discrimination, but most of the speakers eschewed the opportunity to discuss personal experience or to engage in women's consciousness raising, talking instead about contemporary legal and political issues. Foster spoke about naturalization and election laws while Lease, the fiery Kansas Populist sometimes dubbed "Yellin' Mary," used a lawyer's perspective to analyze political movements. Foltz, who might have given her public defender speech, chose, instead, a new, esoteric talk titled "Evolution of the Law." Lockwood, speaking just before Foltz on the afternoon of the convention's second day, made the unsurprising decision to use her time before these female opinion leaders to present the case for arbitration and a permanent international court of arbitration.

This choice of topic said a great deal about how Lockwood defined herself and how she wanted others to see her. At the time of the fair, she was an officer of the UPU as well as the president of the National Association for the Promotion of Arbitration, a separate Washington-based group, loosely affiliated with the UPU but one that permitted her to operate free of Alfred Love's control. She was also an enthusiastic recruit to the mission of the Berne-based International Peace Bureau (IPB), a new arm of the peace movement established to link the growing number of groups around the world committed to pacifism. Only months before, she and Baroness Bertha von Suttner, the noted Austrian peace activist, had achieved the distinction of being the only two women elected to the IPB's directorate, permitting them, Lockwood felt, to so-lidify their place in the international peace community among people who paid deference to women as "delegates and fellow workers [as] a matter of course."[14] In Chicago Lockwood wished to advertise her international prominence in the peace movement at a time when her influence in women's rights circles had been eclipsed.

When she left Chicago, Lockwood expressed optimism about the future of the peace movement. She thought her colleagues had done a good job presenting its message and was now quietly testing whether she had sufficient support to be selected as the head of an American IPB bureau.[15] At home in Washington, however, the news was worrisome. Due to ill health, Lura had decided to cut back on work for Lockwood & Co.[16] Nobody, however, expected her sudden death only a few days after the celebration of the New Year. Standing in her bedroom she experienced a fit of coughing and collapsed. Over the signature, "Yours in Sorrow, Belva," her mother wrote Bennett and McNall relatives that the death seemed to be the result of several conditions exacerbated by "grippe."[17] A funeral was held at the F Street house, after which Lura was buried at Washington's Congressional Cemetery next to the two daughters who had died before her.

Lura Ormes had been a quiet, stable presence in her mother's life, a woman who helped to run the house and law firm and, when the moment demanded, Lockwood's political campaigns. She was active in reform causes but, unlike her mother, shied from public roles. Her private favors were recalled fondly by members of the Universal Peace Union who spoke of "unbounded hospitality and marked kindness."[18] She was married to a man who left few footprints, who appears to have deferred to the women of F Street. She was, at the time of her death, forty-four. She had given birth to three children, only one of whom, three-year-old DeForest, survived her.

Lockwood's loss was enormous. Grieving, she said little, accepted condolences, and left no record of how she spent the winter of 1894. In the spring she resumed her reform activities and her legal work. Lura's premature death denied her a daughter and a business partner and for the first time since she had started her law practice in 1873, neither Lura nor Ezekiel sat near her. She was sixty-three, but with her career on the lecture circuit winding down and members of her family to care for she had no choice but to redouble efforts to make her legal work more lucrative. More than ever the financial implications of her determined independence and her apparent disinterest in remarriage after Ezekiel's death dictated her choices. Before Lura's death she claimed to be earning "more than a Congressman's salary" from speaking engagements, boarders, and legal clients.[19] It is unclear whether this figure included Lura's earnings. Belva did not discuss the financial arrangements of their shared law practice; nor did she reveal how, if at all, her son-in-law DeForest helped in meeting the monetary needs of the household. She almost never talked about him.

Although pension claims, each bringing a twenty-five dollar fee, were the backbone of what had become a rather ordinary law practice, Lockwood was hungry for an important, well-paying case.[20] At her age, thoughts of a retirement nest egg were entirely reasonable. But the small size of her firm, a business whose fortunes appeared to be waning, and the fact that she was a woman made the likelihood of realizing a financial coup absurdly low. Still, obstacles had little meaning for her, and there are references throughout her career to clients whose claims, seldom realized, promised the law firm tantalizing compensation through contingency fees.

In 1891 she had jumped into one such case, filing a claim on the estate of Myra Clark Gaines for mother-daughter clients Julietta Perkins and Marie Evans.[21] The Great Gaines Case had achieved legendary status in nineteenth-century American law. The daughter of Daniel Clark, one of the richest men in America, and Zulime Carrière, a French beauty, Myra was raised by friends of her father but kept ignorant of his identity until well after his death. In 1834, at the age of thirty, she made a claim on his estate estimated, in one filing at the U.S. Supreme Court, to be thirty-five million dollars.[22] She fought for recognition as Clark's legitimate heir for fifty years, a legal odyssey that took her to the Supreme Court fourteen times, often represented by America's most prominent attorneys.

When Lockwood entered the case Gaines, whom she knew from her first presidential campaign, had been dead for six years. Gaines's heirs were still struggling to settle her claim and to win distribution of what now amounted to a far smaller estate. The legal brief that Lockwood filed in the Kings County, New York, Supreme Court argued that Gaines had written a will making Perkins her legatee and Evans the executrix, a declaration contested by a number of parties interested in the estate. Lockwood said nothing more about the case until late August 1894 when, on her way to an international peace meeting in Antwerp, she wrote UPU colleagues that she would return to the States in time for the "Gaines Will case, which comes up the third Monday in September."[23] And then, again, silence. Like the dozen other attorneys who had participated in some phase of the Gaines case, most on a contingency-fee basis, Lockwood had gambled that the investment of her time might reap significant reward. She had, however, bet on the wrong parties. In 1897 a New York court brought the case to a close, having ruled against Perkins and Evans.[24]

No lawyer likes to lose a case, but this ruling was a particular blow as Lockwood's financial situation was increasingly precarious. She told Clara Colby of "striv[ing] to stay calm," while bluntly informing distant family members that business was "very dull" and money scarce.[25] Somehow, presumably with the help of philanthropists, she scraped together the funds for a trip to Europe in September 1896 in order to attend international conferences in Geneva, Budapest, and Berlin. She traveled in the company of Frances Graham French, of the Washington, D.C., Bureau of Education. The two women began their tour in Geneva, where, having wrangled official status from the State Department, they represented the United States at the joint Congress of Charities and Congress for the Protection of Children.[26] French gave a paper on the condition of children employed in American factories while Lockwood spoke about Washington's schools, hospitals, juvenile halls, and orphanages.[27] From Geneva the women went to Budapest, where they listened to the closing sessions of the International Peace and Interparliamentary conferences. Eager to better educate the public and extend her reputation, Lockwood had opened, in her F Street home, an American branch of the International Peace Bureau. In Budapest she was anxious to talk with the IPB leaders Frederik Bajer and Elie Ducommun about the success of her reading room as well as her recent antiwar lobbying.[28]

From the Hungarian capital the women journeyed north to Berlin, where they participated in the International Congress of Women.[29] On October 1, awaiting her ship, Lockwood wrote UPU colleagues that she looked forward to returning "to duties and friends, after many days of sight seeing, of interchange of thought, of new plans, etc. etc." With an infuriating lack of explanation and no particular context, she told them, "Our [peace] friends are afraid of socialism, of the social democrats, as they are called, which, as nearly as I can understand, are like the Populists in our country."[30] She sailed home mulling over what she had seen, later concluding, optimistically, "The world over does not differ so much after all and we are constantly getting nearer together."[31]

In fact, this was a period when her hallmark optimism was to be tested. At the Chicago World's Fair she had predicted that the times were ripe for peace despite signs of imperialism from the Pacific to Latin America. She had long argued against Alfred Mahan's call for a modern American navy, labeling the proposed expense a poor use of the country's wealth. She had also heaped scorn on plans to expand the regular army, but it was not until 1895 that she acknowledged the ramifications of the American quest for empire.[32] In that year, while representing the UPU at the Triennial Woman's Council, she delivered a blistering attack on America's military buildup, asking, "Why should we destroy each other?"[33]

Imperialist foreign policy was not confined to the United States. In Europe and Asia the demand for overseas markets, additional territory, and access to raw materials, along with the desire to flex political and military muscle, also overwhelmed arguments for peace. While European nations, and Japan, pursued colonies, in 1898 the United States government, driven forward by capitalists and militarists, forcibly annexed independent Hawaii and went to war with Spain over Cuba and the Philippines. Lockwood wrote European colleagues that she had believed the U.S. "too far advanced to declare war," but unfortunate complications, including the loss of the battleship *Maine* in Havana harbor and false newspaper reports, "[have] developed among our people a very ugly war spirit."[34] Public opinion, stirred to a fever's pitch of prowar nationalism, led zealots to burn UPU president Alfred Love in effigy when his letter to the queen of Spain, urging the grant of independence to her Cuban colony, was misrepresented by the press.[35] Antiwar activists everywhere found themselves under attack. In Washington Lockwood, who used a strategy of attending other reform group meetings to talk about peace principles, was nearly drummed out of a National Congress of Mothers convention because of the bad publicity surrounding Love and the UPU.[36]

In short order the United States triumphed over Spain, a victory that, through the Treaty of Paris, forced Spain to cede the Philippines, Puerto Rico, and the Pacific island of Guam to the United States.[37] Lockwood had felt that war in the Philippines was "very unjust" and, to her credit, at a time when "weak members of the UPU [fell] off," she spoke out even more forcefully about arms control and empire.[38] Amidst the warm reception of Kipling's poem, "The White Man's Burden," she dared to ask, "Have we a right to seize territory because we believe that we can give the people of that territory a better government?"[39] She left no evidence, however, of joining Jane Addams, Mark Twain, or Andrew Carnegie in supporting the new Anti-Imperialist League.

In February 1899 Lockwood tried to put her imprint on history by obtaining a place on the U.S. delegation being sent by President McKinley to the international peace and disarmament conference (Hague I) called by, among others, Tsar Nicholas II. When her effort failed, the ever-loyal Clara Colby complained that the president had selected five *men* (including Alfred Mahan) while ignoring the request of several thousand citizens that Lockwood, a knowledgeable peace activist, be part of the delegation.[40] Whatever her personal disappointment, Lockwood nevertheless worked to raise public awareness of the congress and "rejoiced" at the outcome, which resulted in the creation of a Permanent Court of Arbitration (but no agreement on disarmament).[41] Encouraged by the buzz after the Hague meeting, and anticipating an initiative later advocated by the Carnegie Fund for Peace, she returned to strategic organizational planning, proposing to extend the IPB's "umbrella" functions in the United States by recultivating ties to groups such as the WCTU, the National Congress of Mothers, the National Councils of Women, and the Christian Endeavor Society.[42]

If President McKinley had appointed Lockwood to the U.S. delegation, she would have needed extraordinary arrangements in order to attend. By 1897 her mother, described quite some time before as "a fragile little old lady," had become "too ill to take with me, and too ill to leave behind."[43] The once-inveterate traveler found herself tied to Washington, forced to beg off conferences at home and abroad. In letters of explanation Belva expressed affection for Hannah as well as frustration at the toil of caring for her, responsibilities that increased in August 1899 when Hannah fell over a chair and broke her hip. Generally uncomplaining, Belva now wrote to relatives, "I am so much occupied with Mother, that I hardly get out of the house and she hangs on to me as though she was afraid she would lose me."[44] By November it appeared that Hannah would not regain the use of her legs.[45] It was a difficult time, in which Lockwood's ability to cultivate business and get to the courts may have been limited. Fortunately, the housebound women had the company of eight-year-old DeForest, whose activities, described in one of his grandmother's letters, enlivened the sickroom atmosphere: "Little Forest is at play by me making an electric automobile . . . [which] are getting to be quite abundant in the city."[46]

Inactivity also caused Lockwood to worry that the people who knew her in various reform movements would think she was not pulling her weight or, worse, that they would forget her. In February 1900, as a salve for her ego, she shot off a long letter to the UPU detailing recent accomplishments: large quantities of peace correspondence, a speech on the single tax, congressional lobbying, and a case to be filed shortly in Equity Court. Making certain they did not miss her point, she ended the inventory with the tart observation, "So you see, I am not idle."[47] And, indeed, although she did not often travel outside of the capital in the late 1890s, she ran her office, attended to public relations for the District Suffrage Association, and lobbied support for her selection, as proposed by the Woman's Industrial Relief League, to an unnamed federal position monitoring the treatment of women workers.[48] Yet the occasion of a friend's death pulled her into quiet reflection and she wrote the grieving widower, "I am sitting in sadness & thinking of the past. . . . Many of the friends of our youth have passed away. . . . The summons may come [next] for you and for me."[49]

But it was Hannah, not Belva, who died on July 19, 1900. Her daughter blamed it on Washington's unbearable summer heat. Lockwood's colleagues, who knew Hannah from her years of living at F Street, praised Mrs. Bennett as a "kind friend . . . a loving mother . . . a woman of sterling worth."[50] From all appearances she had been a good mother, a woman who, so many years before, by taking Lura had supported her daughter's extraordinary decision to go to college, and later, lent the dignity of her presence at campaign rallies.[51]

As she celebrated her seventieth birthday three months into mourning the loss of her mother, Lockwood hoped for better days. Her domestic trials, however, were not over. As she later explained to her peace colleague, Elie Ducommun, her son-in-law DeForest took ill and died not long after Hannah. Trying to account for her inattention to IPB business, she wrote, "I have lost two members of my own family during the year . . . both dying at my house . . . much of my time and strength has been taken up in caring for the sick, and the sad duties of burial."[52] She failed to say that "little" DeForest, now orphaned, had become her responsibility and would remain at F Street as her ward.

Unfortunately, her financial situation also remained bleak. She wrote relatives, "I am still working in Patents and Pensions, and a general law business, but my business has been poor for the last 4 years. I am living and supporting my family principally on my rents and my [widow's] pension."[53] She disclosed having "run so far behind" that she had twice had to borrow money to pay her taxes and interest. Why her practice had suffered so much can only be speculated. There was always the question of her sex, and her years away on the lecture circuit may have limited her client base. Lura had been at the helm in the back office and her death, perhaps coupled with some unspoken depression on Lockwood's part, may also have affected the health of the business. Clearly, it was a difficult time for a woman used to success and public notice, but she had by no means given up. She needed a case of truly unusual dimensions, something that would balance the scales of hardship, family tragedy, and a declining career. In 1899 she quietly intimated to relatives that good fortune was on its way, that there was a "deal on hand through which I expect to get myself out of debt and be comfortable."[54] In her portfolio of cases that could only mean the long-lingering Eastern Cherokee claims litigation.

There is no way to determine what Belva Lockwood knew about the legal situation of Native American tribes before the mid-1870s when she met Cherokee James Taylor. Like any educated American she had been taught her nation's history, a sanitized story that sanctified the white man's claim to North America, claims often sealed with treaties, agreements of uncertain worth to Indian nations but of proven financial value to the attorneys called in to sue when these treaties were ignored, or willfully broken.

Lockwood met Taylor shortly after being admitted to the D.C. bar. He was a member of the group of Cherokee living in western North Carolina who had resisted forcible removal to the west by the U.S. government in the 1830s.[55] He was an experienced lobbyist—controversial, ambitious, and smart. He had been representing the Eastern Cherokee since the 1850s, sent by them to Washington to win U.S. recognition of the tribe and, when recognition was granted in 1868, to press treaty-based monetary claims against the United States.[56] He carried a mixed Cherokee-Anglo heritage and was often at odds with traditionalists among the Cherokee.

The earliest evidence of Taylor's involvement with Lockwood occurs in a memorandum dated May 15, 1875. Although signed by Taylor, it was written by Lockwood, who later testified before the U.S. Court of

Claims, "I commenced my labors for the Eastern Cherokees sometime in May 1875, by preparing a long paper to the Commissioner of Indian Affairs in the name of their delegates duly appointed."[57] In this report, she and Taylor set out the grievances under which the Eastern Cherokee had suffered "for so many years," including various monetary claims against the government of the United States and the Western Nation of Cherokees. They asked the commissioner to redress these grievances. When the government did not respond, she filed for an injunction against the United States and the Western Cherokee in the Supreme Court of the District of Columbia, asking for a statement of account between the parties.[58] She acted, with Taylor's approval, because they were "weary with the delay" and hoping to "compel attention to these wrongs."[59]

Lockwood presumably brought suit in the D.C. court as a dodge to the thorny issue of sovereign immunity, the doctrine that protects a government from lawsuits without its consent. In 1863 Congress had specifically exempted treaty-based Indian lawsuits against the United States from the jurisdiction of the Court of Claims, the judicial body established in 1855 to hear all claims against the United States.[60] Indian tribes were denied access on the theory that, like foreign nations, their treaty-based claims were best settled by Congress through bilateral political negotiation.[61] For tribes, resort to the Court of Claims was possible only with the explicit authorization of Congress in the form of a special bill.

The Supreme Court of D.C. made quick work of refusing the lawsuit, claiming a lack of jurisdiction: "the matter and things in controversy, having arisen out of Treaty stipulations, [belong] to the *Executive and to Congress*."[62] This response left Lockwood no choice but to lobby Congress for a special act that would permit the Eastern Cherokee to sue in the Court of Claims, something she did over the course of several years, joined by other—competing—attorneys who, sniffing the possibility of a large contingency fee, had also taken an interest in cultivating the Eastern Cherokee as clients. In 1883, Congress approved a special jurisdictional act and Lockwood, authorized by Taylor and the faction he represented, filed a case at the Court of Claims.[63]

In a well-written legal brief she argued that her client, the Eastern Band of Cherokee Indians, numbering between two and three thousand persons, was suing "the Cherokee Nation, commonly called the Cherokee Nation West, as the real party in interest, and the United States as

Trustee of the fund against which the claim is made."[64] Essentially, she was arguing that the citizens of the Eastern Band, although geographically separated from the Cherokee who had not escaped the U.S. policy of forced removal, were equal tribal members of the Cherokee Nation (West) and must be given an equal share of disputed fees as well as proceeds from land sales, past and present.

Lockwood felt confident of her legal argument, but in a March 1883 letter to Taylor she outlined a problem. Taylor was not in favor with the new governing faction of his tribe and had not provided her with an explicit power of attorney (POA) from a "principle [sic] chief." Without this authorization the Court of Claims would dismiss her from the case. Sounding as optimistic as possible under the circumstances, she told him, "Now our whole business hangs upon one little point, & if you can fix *this point* there is nothing else in our way. . . . [O]ur whole cargo is landed in the Court of Claims. . . . viz . . . *a petition . . . verified by the principle chief of said band*."[65] On the same day James J. Newell, a lawyer now working the case with Lockwood, wrote to Taylor, "Mrs. Lockwood has *filed* the N. C. Cherokee claim . . . and some party should be here to *testify* for the Indians."[66]

As she feared, Taylor's fall from grace did result in the hiring of a new legal team. Nimrod Smith, the new chief of the Eastern Band, signed Washington lawyers Samuel Shellabarger and Jeremiah M. Wilson as tribal counsel, and they promptly filed a motion to end Lockwood's legal representation. She responded by filing additional powers of attorney from subleaders, but in December Chief Justice Charles Drake took her off the case, ruling that she lacked authorization by a principal chief.[67] This left the field open to Shellabarger and his team, who, using a legal theory different from Lockwood's, argued and lost the case.[68]

The story should have ended here. There was, however, a keen sense of justice denied as well as a great deal of money to be claimed. Taylor and Lockwood kept in touch. Taylor moved to Cherokee Nation West, reestablished his standing among the Eastern (Emigrant) Cherokee now living at Cherokee Nation, and, in 1885, again asked Lockwood to represent the Eastern Cherokee.[69] She agreed, monitoring congressional legislation that might affect her clients while looking for new ways to bring a successful lawsuit. In 1887 Congress passed the Dawes Act, legislation meant to "Americanize" the Indian by terminating tribal government, dividing tribally held land into individual allotments, and, not coincidentally, making "surplus" Indian land available to the railroads and white settlers.[70] Two years later Congress opened land near Cherokee Nation West for homesteading; in a single day fifty thousand American settlers swarmed out to claim parcels. Four years later, the United States forced the Cherokee to sell treaty-guaranteed land known as the Cherokee Strip (Outlet) for little more than a dollar an acre.[71]

The only good news in the sale of the Cherokee Strip was a provision calling for a complete financial accounting to be made to the Cherokee Nation of everything due them from the United States under treaties going back to 1817. During floor debate in 1893 one congressman observed that this might involve millions of dollars. The bill's sponsor, aware of long-running disputes over money unfairly withheld from the Cherokee, responded, "That may be true. . . . But. . . . whether the amount be much or little, the Government ought to pay what it owes."[72] A year later Congress learned the price tag of fair dealing when James A. Slade and Joseph T. Bender, government accountants, submitted their report stating that the United States owed the Cherokee people $1,134,248 plus interest at 5 percent.[73] The total amounted to several million dollars. The jubilant Cherokee considered the Slade-Bender judgment *res judicata* (final settlement in a legal proceeding). The U.S. Congress, despite having ordered the report, viewed it as another piece of disposable evidence, and for five years Congress ignored the matter despite constant pressure from tribal delegates. And then, in the winter of 1901, legislators made the decision not to pay up, but to authorize the Cherokee to bring, at the Court of Claims, a finding of fact case, based on the Slade-Bender report.[74]

Taylor and Lockwood saw this as the opening they had long sought. Lockwood was now seventy and determined to not to let other attorneys push her aside in what appeared to be the final phase of judicial decision making. She continued, however, to lack official authorization from a principal chief or tribal council. Attorney Robert Owen claimed this authority, which he used to file a findings-of-fact case on behalf of the Eastern and Emigrant Cherokee Band. Not wasting a minute, Lockwood jumped in to stake a claim for members of Taylor's faction, and for herself. She had maintained ties to the Eastern Cherokee community for two decades. On September 13, 1901, drawing upon this connection with Cherokee citizens friendly to her and to Taylor, and maneuvering skillfully, she entered Owen's case through a motion to intervene. She claimed authorization not from the tribe but from one thousand individual Cherokee who had given her powers of attorney.[75] Unhappy to see her poaching on his case, Owen countered with a motion opposing the intervention. He argued that her clients, if valid members of the Eastern Band, were already covered in the suit and, if not, had no standing to take part. Without explanation, the Court of Claims agreed to Lockwood's intervention. Perhaps the large number of powers of attorney that she submitted (with more coming every day) had convinced the court that the tribal faction served by Owen failed to represent many Eastern Cherokee and that they would not receive fair treatment. Having succeeded, on March 17, 1902, Lockwood triumphantly filed her brief for the intervenors.

The Claims Court heard the multiparty case on March 24, 1902. Weeks later, with no fanfare, the court issued its finding. Without contradicting the conclusions reached by Slade and Bender, the justices "expressed no opinion" as to whether the award should be paid.[76] This threw the Cherokee, once again, into the arms of a Congress reluctant to settle up old debts. In early May, lobbying for a settlement, Lockwood wrote New York Congressman James Sherman, "It now becomes imperative in the interest of good faith with the Cherokees . . . that an appropriation . . . be made."[77]

Members of Congress, however, were still in no hurry to pay up, and in July passed responsibility back to the courts, now recommending a full judicial determination in place of the finding of fact. The Cherokee (East and West) were authorized to bring suit against the United States in the Court of Claims, with the right to appeal to the Supreme Court, upon any claim arising under a treaty with the United States.[78] Seizing the moment, on March 10, 1903, Lockwood filed her case, *Eastern and Emigrant Cherokees v. United States*. Through her own and Taylor's networks, and by subcontracting powers of attorney from local lawyers, she now represented more than five thousand individual Cherokee.[79] The Claims Court consolidated this case with one filed by Owen and a third brought by the Cherokee Nation (West), which was still claiming the award as its own.

The Court of Claims heard arguments in the consolidated case from February 14 to February 21, 1905. Lockwood followed the script established in the undisputed Slade-Bender report, and in letters to Taylor and his son, John, predicted victory:[80] "I had a good time and attention—spoke three times. . . . Nobody spoke against me except McKenna

[sic] of Washington. He thought I had no standing in the Court. His speech . . . fell without comment."[81]

And, finally, there was justice for the Cherokee and a victory for Lockwood. Writing for the majority, Chief Justice Charles Nott, the man who decades before had argued against Lockwood's admission to the Court of Claims bar, ruled that the Cherokee were entitled to the full award, approaching the case as a simple matter of contract of sale. The Cherokee, he said, had lost their land in the East in exchange for a certain amount of money, part of which had never been delivered to them: "This is not the case of a party prosecuting an unliquidated debt, but a case of sale and delivery and nonpayment of the purchase money for the thing sold and delivered."[82] Nott also wrote that the Cherokee who remained east of the Mississippi, as communal owners of the land at the time of the 1835 removal treaty, were fully entitled to their per capita share of the fund. But so, too, he ruled, were Cherokee who had migrated west before the 1835 treaty.[83]

Excited by the ruling Lockwood prematurely predicted a fair distribution of legal fees and wrote to Clara Colby, ecstatic, about the meaning of the large judgment for herself and for the future of women attorneys: "[The judgment] gives me a great reputation as a lawyer, which will help all women, and will give me eventually money enough (I suppose about $50,000) to make my old age comfortable."[84] Although she had an indomitable spirit, the years of near-bankruptcy and waiting had taken their toil; the victory was tonic: "My physical and mental health," observed the now 75-year-old woman, "are better already."[85] Clara was delighted with her friend's success and wrote, in a front-page article, that Belva's triumph "vindicat[ed] the power of woman to take a high place in the legal profession."[86]

Lockwood's work for the Cherokee was not yet over, as she had been correct in predicting an appeal to the Supreme Court. In the autumn of 1905 she prepared for this final showdown, writing yet another legal brief outlining the case presented by her clients. Thirty years had passed since the May 1875 day she had joined James Taylor and "commenced her labors." The brief that Lockwood submitted to the Supreme Court did not differ significantly from her submission to the Court of Claims although she could now cite Nott's approval of the Slade-Bender report.[87]

The Supreme Court began hearing the appeal on January 16, 1906. Lockwood sat at the lawyers' table, still the only woman in a clutch of men. To her right and left were the male attorneys representing the government, the Cherokee Nation, and the Eastern Cherokee Tribe. Looking up she saw nine male justices, among them the affable Chief Justice Melville Fuller; John Marshall Harlan, who, alone, in *Plessy*, had insisted that the Constitution was colorblind; the learned Bostonian Oliver Wendell Holmes; and laissez-faire advocate Rufus W. Peckham, with whom Holmes had jousted, only months before, when arguing that state governments could regulate the hours of work.[88]

Assistant Attorney-General Louis Pradt led off the oral argument, followed by Frederic McKenney for the Cherokee Nation. Lockwood spoke after him.[89] It was later reported that her words came with "great rapidity, but with clearness," the justices following her arguments closely and periodically interrupting with questions.[90] She focused on the rights of the North Carolina Cherokee and the amount of interest that the government owed. Although decades of work were at stake, she showed no nerves and later enjoyed telling John Taylor, "My speech before the Supreme Court has been highly complimented by the Judges."[91]

The Supreme Court handed down its decision three months later, presenting Lockwood's clients with the long-sought victory. Writing for a unanimous court, Fuller affirmed the one-million-dollar Slade-Bender award (plus 5 percent interest) and, agreeing with Lockwood and Owen, reversed the Court of Claims on the critical matter of the right of the Cherokee Nation (West) to share in it.[92] After three decades, using the risky strategy of collecting individual POAs and joining a multiparty lawsuit as an intervenor, Lockwood's clients were about to share in a five-million-dollar award and she, a hoped-for fifty thousand dollars in legal fees. As soon as the court released the opinion she telegraphed the good news to John Taylor, later writing a more detailed letter: "You will see by the Decree . . . that each one of our Eastern & Emigrant Cherokee will get their share."[93] Never forgetting the importance of public relations, she added, "I had a good deal to do with getting the judgment, especially the interest."

After her years of effort Lockwood was anxious to be paid. According to procedure, she would join the other attorneys at the Court of Claims where a formula for the payment of fees would be discussed. She holed up in her office for three days, summing up her expenses and hours—years—of work. As the day of the meeting approached she sent a letter west acknowledging that problems had arisen: "Owen doesn't want the Court to set me aside a fee at all. . . . He thinks that I should collect my fees from my clients. So now we are in a fight for fees, and I have employed an attorney to defend me."[94] There had been decades of work and cash outlays for expenses, and she, like the other eight attorneys, wanted to be paid directly from the award fund to be established by Congress. Owen, however, hoped to freeze her out, forcing her to bill each of her Cherokee clients. The sweet moment of victory had turned into a vicious fight as the attorneys brawled over an expected three-quarter of a million dollars in fees.

16

Aging Soldiers of Cause

Do not go gentle into that good night,
Old age should burn and rave at close of day;
Rage, rage against the dying of the light.

Dylan Thomas, 1951

In the last decade of her life, Belva Lockwood did not so much rage at old age as ignore it, pursuing the same professional and reform work that had long shaped her days. She never abandoned her fight for social and political change and never lost her need for recognition. In a less formal age, she might have been called a tough old bird or, if a man, a relentless warrior.

It was with this spirit of entitlement and fight that she approached the May 1906 meeting to determine the award of attorney legal fees for work in *Cherokee Nation*. Unlike the long-suffering Cherokee, who had been waiting decades for compensation, the lawyers were not patient. Small fortunes were at stake as it was hoped that the Court would approve fee payment at the standard 15 percent. Calculated at that rate the attorneys' share, according to their expense account filings, would be three-quarters of a million dollars.

Although there was more than enough money to go around, Lockwood was justly concerned. Owen had already made his views clear. Once inside the hearing room, she learned that he and the other lawyers, motivated by the desire to maximize their fees, had organized against her, and planned to argue against the assignment of any money to her from the congressional appropriation. During the discussion they pressed this point, claiming that she lacked a power of attorney from any tribal entity and should only expect compensation from the individual families who employed her. Lockwood had angered these men when she successfully intervened in their case, and they now intended to make her pay. Days later they prevailed when the hearing judge decreed that all of the attorneys for the Eastern and Emigrant Cherokee except Lockwood were to share in a 15 percent award, with several assigned as much as one hundred thousand dollars and Robert Owen, double that amount.[1]

With newly hired counsel Lockwood immediately appealed the decree and in late June learned that a compromise was being offered: rather than the fifty thousand dollars she had sought, eighteen thousand dollars would be awarded to her from the lawyers' fee fund, "for actual time spent before Congress and the Court."[2] The amended decree said she was free to collect further compensation from her individual clients but at the rate of 10, not 15, percent.[3] This amended judgment was, in her words, a bitter disappointment, a blow to her ego and her pocketbook.[4] She claimed already to have spent much of the award in the prosecution of the lawsuit, money raised by mortgaging the house on F Street, and now there was an additional three-thousand-dollar legal bill for the appeal.[5]

The money was paid to her on July 5, 1906, although her work on the case was not over. A government roll of Cherokee eligible to share in the five-million-dollar award had to be drawn up, and she needed to make certain that her clients qualified for that list if she was ever to claim the additional fees.[6] Despite her unhappiness, she stopped to send James, now "old and feeble," one thousand dollars.[7] And then she picked up old legal cases as well as reform work that had been dropped in the press of Cherokee business.[8] In August she traveled to Denver for the sixteenth annual meeting of the International League of Press Clubs.[9] Soon after, she and young DeForest sailed for Italy. Although the two often had spent summer vacation time with upstate New York relatives, grandmother and grandson had never taken a long trip together. DeForest was now a suitable companion, a fifteen-year-old described by his "Nannie" as "getting to be quite a large boy."[10] Lockwood's health was good and she looked forward to attending an international peace meeting in Milan.

Socially, the congress proved delightful, with numerous receptions, time to watch King Humbert dedicate the Palace of Fine Arts, and warm applause for delegate Bertha von Suttner, recent recipient of the Nobel Peace Prize. The number of delegates, however, was small, and Lockwood reported that during the meeting the delegates parsed, with little agreement, "abstruse questions of international law."[11] When it ended, she and DeForest visited Rome and in early October sailed home from Naples, stopping at Gibraltar. It was a good voyage, but they had stayed longer than intended and she was anxious to return, having learned by international mail that she was needed in Indian Territory to look after the interests of her Cherokee clients. Before leaving for Europe she had written Clara Colby that there were six thousand Eastern and Emigrant Cherokees "to get on the New Pay Roll under the $5,000,000 judgment."[12] Back from Europe, she settled DeForest in school and left for Muskogee, Indian Territory, hoping to help sort out the increasingly messy state of the government's Cherokee roll, something that would keep her busy for four years.

The hurdles presented by the government proved to be only one of her problems in the aftermath of the Supreme Court's decision, something she came to realize after July 1907 when the family of James Taylor sued her. Taylor had died shortly after the two had visited in November 1906. There had been no sign of a legal problem, or at least none that Lockwood chose to record. She had been representing him in a private North Carolina land claim dispute and knew that his will instructed Frank Rucker, a son-in-law appointed to administer his estate, to retain her to pursue this claim. But seven days before his death, in a codicil to his will, Taylor revoked her employment, saying she had failed to honor a contract to share attorney fees.[13] In his lawsuit Rucker claimed, for the estate, a 50-percent share of the eighteen thousand dollars awarded to Lockwood in the Cherokee case (minus expenses). This amounted to something more than six thousand dollars. Lockwood chose to fight the lawsuit although there was a great deal of evidence that she owed the money. She again hired counsel, and in her initial pleas not only denied the charges but also argued that the estate owed her nearly three thousand dollars for work she had done on Taylor's North Carolina claim.[14]

Balanced against these personal problems was the seemingly endless and discouraging fight for woman suffrage in which she had gamely participated even after her falling out with Anthony. The National's long-time leader had died in the spring of 1906 and the old guard, as well as a talented number of younger leaders, now openly vied for control of the movement and its war chest.[15] For a time the strategy of a national constitutional amendment was downplayed as members of the NAWSA, still the most powerful of the woman suffrage organizations, carried out state-by-state voting-rights campaigns that were tailored to the local politics of race, class, and liquor.[16] Lockwood went along with this by agreeing to lobby Congress when statehood bills were introduced for the territories of Oklahoma, New Mexico, and Arizona. As the proposals came up she urged legislators to support women's right to vote as a condition of joining the Union, and at one point wrote a friend, "I think that we have won out," after a handful of senators told her they would consider putting suffrage in the statehood legislation.[17]

At the same time, she lent her name to several new women's rights organizations whose concerns and strategies differed from those of the NAWSA, including Lillie Devereux Blake's National Legislative League, formed to "labor with the lawmakers" on the diverse legislative issues affecting women.[18] Perhaps because of her friendship with Clara Colby, and the proximity of Congress, Lockwood contributed in more substantial ways to the work of the small Federal Suffrage Association, founded in 1892 and renamed, and revitalized, in 1902 by Colby and Olympia Brown as the Federal Woman's Equality Association (FWEA). The group was born out of frustration with NAWSA's emphasis on state suffrage campaigns.[19] FWEA, of which Lockwood was honorary president and, later, president, promoted the argument made by Judge Francis Minor, who, after the loss of his wife's case at the Supreme Court, insisted that women should at least be permitted to vote for members of the U.S. House of Representatives (senators were not yet directly elected). He argued that by default, and wrongly, states had been permitted to impose restrictions by sex on voters in this federal election and proposed an act of Congress that would establish for women a statutory right to vote for House members, one that would invalidate any state-mandated "males only" qualification.[20] The three women buttonholed and cajoled congressmen for a number of years but, as Brown later admitted, federal suffrage was an idea that never captured the attention of most activists.[21] Still, in March 1908, when Lockwood testified before the Senate Woman Suffrage committee with Anna Shaw and Carrie Chapman Catt, the current and former presidents of NAWSA, she managed several references to the FWEA-sponsored federal suffrage bill knocking about Congress, and concluded her remarks by stating, "only a declaratory law is necessary by the Congress . . . to make women eligible to the ballot."[22]

In July 1908 Lockwood attended the Universal Peace Congress in London representing the UPU and the District of Columbia.[23] The agenda focused on questions of weapons buildup, the treatment of ethnic minorities, and arbitration treaties. Lockwood gave an enthusiastic account of the accomplishments of the five-week-long Central American Peace Conference, held in Washington the previous winter, and offered several resolutions praising its work and that of Andrew Carnegie.[24] Curiously, she did not discuss her recent efforts on behalf of the UPU to win the repeal of capital punishment in the District of Columbia, a practice, she argued, that did not deter crime and was a shameful public spectacle "comparable to a scene in the Cannibal Islands, where human life is taken for food."[25]

At the meeting Lockwood had the opportunity to see first-hand the nasty treatment meted out to her British suffrage sisters who staged a protest at the congress on a day when Chancellor of the Exchequer David Lloyd George made an appearance. After repeatedly calling out, "Why don't you give votes to women," the reformers were shouted down and then dragged out of the building by men who "whack[ed] them with their umbrellas."[26] Before this British suffragettes had said publicly that American suffrage activists were "pretty much asleep." In order to counter this view and to speak against the treatment of the British women, Lockwood claimed a soap box at Hyde Park, where she gave a women's rights speech.[27]

Back at home, she continued to lobby the question of voting rights. Although discouraged by President Theodore Roosevelt's refusal to discuss the issue, she nevertheless called on him to support universal suffrage in the District.[28] But she wrote to Colby, who had left Washington, D.C., to live in Oregon, that there was no point in lobbying the federal suffrage bill. She said that her old friend's time would be better spent poking and prodding the members of the Oregon legislature: "They have the power if they choose to grant suffrage to their women."[29]

Age had not diminished Lockwood's interest in public recognition of her accomplishments and her desire for honors. There were two, in particular, that she coveted. To begin with, she wished her achievements to be acknowledged by her alma mater, now part of Syracuse University. In the winter of 1906, when her success in the five-million-dollar Cherokee case was virtually assured, she wrote to university dean Frank Smalley suggesting herself for an honorary doctor of laws degree.[30] Smalley made no response, forcing Lockwood to bide her time until the winter of 1909 when the dean's office sent out a personal information questionnaire to alumni, permitting her to respond with a compact autobiography. Not bothering to list the many times reporters had turned to her as an opinion leader and symbol of the "New Woman," she thought it sufficient to remark that the New York *Herald* had recently named her the leading woman lawyer in the country. Then, exhibiting her trademark boldness and wry humor, she wrote, "I wish to ask *Syracuse University* to confer on me the Degree of 'L. L. D.' to which I consider myself entitled from my native State, and to do it while I live. Honors do not cheer the dead."[31]

Shortly thereafter, an invitation was extended to her to receive an honorary degree. She traveled north in the summer heat to pick up her prize, a white silk diploma on which was printed, "Belva Ann Lockwood Legum Doctorem Universitas Syracusana, MCMIX."[32] Lockwood immediately began to use "L.L.D." in her correspondence. The honor gave her enormous pleasure, but it paled before the possibility of a far more prestigious award, the Nobel Peace Prize. She believed there was a chance that the selection committee would pay tribute to her grass roots UPU organizing, her work with the International Peace Bureau, and her lobby efforts, before presidents and congressmen, in support of arbitration and international courts. Convinced of the possibility of a Nobel Prize, she spent years doggedly pursuing a nomination.

In his will the Swedish dynamite magnate Alfred Nobel directed that a portion of his fortune be used to establish an international prize for the person "who shall have done the most or the best work for fraternity between nations, for the abolition or reduction of standing armies and for the holding and promotion of peace congresses."[33] Following announcement of his instructions, the once-tranquil world of peace societies erupted with schemes. Peace organization members eyed the prize both as a badge of honor and as a means of replenishing modest treasuries. The Universal Peace Union was no exception.

Neither Lockwood, Love, nor the Universal Peace Union ever received the Peace Prize. Lockwood lobbied for Love and the UPU, and as the years passed, she also attempted to secure the prize for herself.[34] In 1904 Clara Colby backed her friend's candidacy with an item in the *Woman's Tribune* urging that nominators forward Love's *and* Lockwood's names as the precedent had just been established "of dividing the prizes."[35] For several years Lockwood and Love were merely eager. Increasingly, however, their letters reflected frustration and, finally, desperation as the chance of winning appeared ever more remote. The Americans had two strikes against them: their nationality and the UPU's philosophy. In the first five years of the award the prize committee had only selected Europeans as laureates and had shied away from the most radical prophets of nonviolence, including the often-nominated Russian pacifist, Leo Tolstoy.

The selection of President Theodore Roosevelt as the 1906 laureate buoyed Lockwood's spirits. Although Roosevelt had earned a bellicose reputation in the Spanish-American War, his negotiation of the treaty ending the Russo-Japanese War had caused the Nobel committee to look beyond Europe for a recipient. After the announcement of his name, Lockwood thought Love or the UPU stood a chance. But she was wrong, and the next Americans to win were also high-ranking statesmen: cabinet member Elihu Root in 1912 and President Woodrow Wilson in 1919.

Love and Lockwood did not give up easily.[36] In 1910 Lockwood again nominated the UPU for the prize, writing the Norwegian committee that her organization had done "a very large amount of peace work . . . but is now short of funds."[37] Yet, slowly, she and Love began to accept that the influence of the UPU and other grass roots peace societies had waned, and that a new generation of elite men had taken charge of the movement, statesmen and businessmen more concerned with a stable world order than with a world free from war. Lockwood began to feel "frozen out" at every turn and was particularly discouraged after staff at Andrew Carnegie's new peace foundation informed her that the UPU was too small to qualify for grants.[38] This prompted a letter to Love in which she wrote that Carnegie's money "seem[s] to be for the clique or a favored few [while] the Nobel Peace Prizes will all go it seems to European claimants."[39] Airing further disappointment she also told Love that an application—one he had not known about—had been made for her with the Nobel Prize committee by the District of Columbia commissioners. She reported that it had been rejected on procedural grounds, "so that shuts me off for all time."[40]

By 1910 financial solvency had become a perennial issue for the UPU and for Lockwood. In the spring of that year she exposed the fragile nature of her finances to Colby, rebuffing her friend's request for money to restart the now-bankrupt *Woman's Tribune*. "You mistake in thinking me a millionaire. . . . My bank account is exhausted, and none of my court fees for the Past Winter have been paid."[41] Yet her capacity for good humor was evident on her birthday when, speaking with a visiting reporter, she said, "I've never had an eightieth birthday before, and I'll never have another one, so I just said to myself: 'You deserve a day off, and a birthday cake, too!'"[42]

Despite her "day off," at eighty Lockwood remained deeply engaged with the world around her. Two months after her birthday, she offered Colby a long analysis of the British and American woman suffrage movements, writing that the militant tactics of the English women are "not our ways."[43] She thought they were undignified and believed that the American suffrage movement was now better organized and more successful at raising money, in part because "the Press take notice of women speakers here, and help them on."[44] More than ever, she now doubted that a constitutional amendment would succeed; women's voting rights, she told Colby, would come "thro the State Legislatures, or a popular election or both."[45]

In her correspondence and newspaper interviews she continued to give a general, if sometimes disingenuous, accounting of her finances. Reporters were told that her law practice was remunerative while she wrote Colby that, when her court fees were not paid, the household got by on rents and interest, and by practicing "very close economy."[46] She also confided that after her recent return from Oklahoma and the long-awaited distribution of the five million dollars to her Cherokee clients, she had invested all her money in real estate. She did not give specific details, but shortly thereafter land records showed her as the owner of new property as near as the capital's Kentucky Avenue and as far away as Wyoming.[47] The western land, several hundred acres, was almost certainly an attempt to make money from copper and gold mining. Staid and middle-class in many things, she never lost the sense of adventure and attraction to enterprise that, in earlier decades, led her to run for public office and to try her hand at various businesses.

Imagination, ego, and finances also led her, in 1912, to become an officer of the new American Woman's Republic (AWR). The Republic had been conceived by Edward Gardner Lewis, a St. Louis publisher with a flair for understanding, and cultivating, women's interest in self-improvement. It grew out of Lewis's earlier venture, the American Woman's League, a conglomerate whose profits from magazine and newspaper subscriptions supported a host of institutions, including a people's bank, lending library, home industries product exchange, and correspondence course university. The Republic, initially one arm of the

League, was a logical extension of these institutions of aspiration. It was a platform from which Lewis believed women could be trained in civics and from which, at the moment of universal suffrage, they could launch a political party.

Lewis's vision called for a republic, run by and for women, a civic entity that would coexist alongside the government of the United States until women won suffrage and the two republics "merged." It drew inspiration from Marietta Stow's idea for a woman's republic and political party, Lockwood's presidential campaigns, and women's increasingly lively interest in partisan politics and women's parliaments, and it anticipated by a few years suffrage leader Alice Paul's Congressional Union (later the National Woman's Party) as well as the League of Women Voters.[48]

Lewis proposed that the AWR adopt a broad reform agenda addressing suffrage, world peace, education, the protection of children, and the abolition of drink and prostitution. Most audaciously, he established, through the AWR, a "government" to train women in politics and policy so that, educated and experienced through participation, when granted the franchise they would be ready to join men, as a women's voting bloc, in the governance of the United States.[49] Lewis's vision was optimistic and practical although its stated "Caucasians Only" membership policy placed the organization squarely within the mentality of racism found in most white-dominated suffrage and reform associations.

Lockwood had been active in a Washington-based chapter of the American Woman's League and was keenly interested in Lewis's plan to expand the AWR. In June 1912 she traveled to University City, Missouri, near St. Louis, for the first meeting of the Republic. She was fresh from clearing Mary E. Gage, the matriarch of a socially ambitious Washington family, of lunacy charges for threatening to kill Charles J. Bell, a locally prominent banker. The sensational story of an *arriviste* family who thought Bell wished to keep them, and their "handsome daughter," from "the Capital's 400" had captivated Washington wags.[50] Lockwood arrived at the convention happy to report her victory, at the age of eighty-one, against "the legal, medical, and moneyed talent of the District."[51]

Before the meeting she had worked quietly to win support for her election as president of the Republic.[52] Lewis's wife, Mabel, however, wanted the position and, not surprisingly, won it. Lockwood joined her cabinet as attorney general, receiving, for a short time, a monthly salary of two hundred dollars.[53] As a member of the Republic government she traveled, lectured, and helped in organizing new chapters. Several communications, including a letter from Alfred Love asking if she planned to move to St. Louis, suggest that she was expected to spend time in Missouri at meetings of the AWR government. How much remains unclear as she was at home at F Street in October 1912 for an all-day celebration of her eighty-second birthday, taking time to tick off to a reporter her most recent honors and to say that Lella Gardner, a nephew's wife, would write her biography.[54] Asked to comment on the 1912 presidential contenders, she urged Governor Wilson "to speak out frankly" on suffrage so "his real colors" could be seen. "Nobody," she said, "knows just where he stands."[55] She condemned the incumbent William Howard Taft and his fellow Republicans for ignoring "equal rights" women at the party convention while praising former President Theodore Roosevelt because he had finally come out for woman suffrage.

On Election Day she presided over a suffrage meeting in the Red Parlor of the Ebbitt House and later took her turn scanning the returns. The voters of Arizona, Kansas, and Oregon had passed woman suffrage initiatives. Everywhere women were jubilant and, until a final count well after the election, thought Michigan had also declared for woman suffrage.[56] Lockwood wrote to Lella, "Four woman suffrage states at once! Think of it!"[57] Privately, she admitted to Lella that she tired more easily, yet she maintained a schedule that could exhaust a younger person, traveling to Philadelphia and Baltimore for peace and suffrage meetings and in December making the trip to State College, Pennsylvania, to give a talk at one of Lella's clubs.[58] Women's rights were always on her mind. Just before Christmas she wrote Taft, now the lame duck president, urging, with a humorous rhyme, that he appoint Ellen Spencer Mussey or Dr. Clara A. McNaugton as a commissioner: "Then why not a woman / For Commissioner name? / They both Sir are human / With parents the same."[59]

At the New Year she also wrote Lella about "a grand pageant" suffrage women were planning for the day before Wilson's inauguration, a procession to dramatize the demand for a constitutional amendment.[60] "The city," she explained, "is wild about [the idea]. . . . Everybody is in it—Congressmen's wives & Senators—people of high and low degree—the Avenue [Pennsylvania] granted to them . . . the women will sweep the city."[61] She also readied herself for the February 10 unveiling of her formal portrait. She had been sitting for Nellie Mathes Horne, a Boston painter. Horne had posed her in a black academic gown, again suggesting the importance that the honorary degree from Syracuse held for Lockwood. The painting, subscribed by friends, was presented at the New Willard Hotel during an evening billed as "A Tribute to the Progress of Women of the Twentieth Century." The ceremony, reported in many newspapers, pleased her with the portrait immediately going into the federal government's art collection.[62]

After the unveiling, attention turned back to the upcoming woman suffrage march. Activist Alice Paul had convinced the leadership of the NAWSA that a parade the day before the nation swore in its "democratically" elected leader would be a news-grabbing event that could revitalize the fight for a suffrage amendment. Lockwood had attended Paul's first planning session and given "her blessing."[63] The young organizer, who, while living in England, had been arrested and jailed as a participant in the sort of militancy Lockwood scorned, must have convinced her that the "procession" would be peaceful. As March approached Lockwood found herself wooed by different reform sisters anxious for her presence in their group. It was a pleasant change from the years when her political candidacies and poor relations with Anthony had caused some activists to distance themselves from her. The AWR's Susanna Harris wrote that she had ordered a float on which Lockwood would ride as "Justice with a big owl on one side and scales on the other."[64] Hearing this, Washington organizer Nettie Lovisa White sent an impassioned request that Lockwood reconsider: "I am counting on you to ride in my Divisions of the Pioneers [of the voting rights movement] & have provided a seat for you in an electric belonging to a friend."[65] She sweetened the offer by telling Lockwood that she would have a spot on the platform at Continental Hall, "where the procession ends, and our 'Stars' are to deliver speeches."[66]

Despite heckling and shoving from men who opposed woman suffrage, the eye-catching parade, led by lawyer Inez Milholland astride a white horse, was a great success. Washington's *Evening Star* called it a "thrilling pageant [of] modern Amazons marching on to battle."[67] It was reported that Lockwood wore white and purple, the colors of the Woman's Republic.[68] Although Lockwood enjoyed the parade, she wrote Lella surprisingly little about it, telling her only that early spring in the capital, with the many reform organization meetings, "including the Pageant, the Inauguration, the march to the Capitol with petitions for Woman Suffrage for members of Congress . . . is enough to make one crazy."[69] In fact, she was already distracted by an event more important to her. In something of a popularity contest, she had been elected by the women of the AWR as one of twenty "ambassadors" who would, in a sixty-day, all-expense-paid trip, represent the group in Europe at international meetings for the purpose of "laying the foundation for an international Woman's Republic" whose power and influence would put an end to war.[70] Lockwood had been appointed "Dean of the Party" and was not shy in telling Lella that she expected the upcoming two months to be "the crowning glory of my old age."[71]

On May 28 the group sailed from Brooklyn, New York, on the *S.S. Pretoria* hours after an AWR reception in Manhattan. It would be Lockwood's last trip abroad. Although money was tight, she celebrated by purchasing a new black satin dress, "with a handsome lace overdress."[72] The ship landed at Hamburg, after which the delegation made its way to Berlin and Vienna before bringing its peace manifesto to the convention of the International Woman's Suffrage Alliance being held in Budapest. At this meeting Lockwood sat on the platform near Alliance president Carrie Chapman Catt and listened as the AWR's peace resolution was presented and translated into three languages.[73] Afterward, always intrigued by technology, she accepted an invitation to "send out" a peace speech via "megaphone" at the First Hungarian Factory of Music Records.[74] Her talk emphasized the failure of men to bring about arms reductions or to prevent war, and the need, therefore, for women "to form a worldwide government of their own, opposed to war, so strong and influential that the governments of men shall respect it and abide by their dictum."[75]

After Budapest the delegation took its message to the International Exposition at Ghent and the Woman's Exposition being held at Amsterdam. Then they made their way to London where Lockwood read that Alfred Love had just died. In a long letter to his family she praised the man and his work.[76] Back in Washington she learned that the UPU was virtually bankrupt, and needed to sell its property in Mystic, Connecticut, to cover bills and loans.[77] She, too, faced financial problems; she told Clara McNaughton, a friend and FWEA colleague, that her family had overdrawn her bank account while "my small brick house and store are unrented, and some rooms in my house."[78]

In fact, her financial problems were quite severe. After six years in court the Taylor family had won its case against her, and in order to pay them she would have to sell the house at F Street. The lawsuit, instituted in 1907, had been many times delayed, decided, and appealed.[79] In January 1913 she posted a twelve-thousand-dollar bond to stay execution of the judgment. Two weeks later her attorney filed a bill of exceptions while Lockwood again prepared to outwait the Taylor family.

Her strategy combined a lawyer's ability to string matters along in court with the reasonable assumption that she might die before having to pay up. She may have believed that Rucker and the Taylor family would give up. But they did not, and in November 1913, the Court of Appeals of the District of Columbia affirmed the lower court's ruling that she must pay the Taylors. With insufficient funds, and mortgages on her house, she had no choice but to give it over for public auction. Ten days before Christmas, with Lockwood refusing to move out, the building was sold to Charles F. Wilson for slightly less than ten thousand dollars.

During the winter of 1914, still residing at F Street, she cast about for ways to regain possession of the house, which had been resold to the New England Casualty Company.[80] Washington friends sought loans and made public appeals for aid. The *Washington Times* took up her cause, insisting "there must be many of heart and purse large enough to open both without pinching."[81] Lockwood was silent on the subject of the appeals, but for this self-sufficient woman, it must have been a horrifying ordeal. With constancy of character, she kept to her regular routines and interests, and in letters made simple declarations of the likely outcome. At the end of April, before going to Chicago at the request of various women's clubs, she wrote to a relative, "Will probably lose my house."[82] On May 19 she was served with a notice to quit. She continued to stall, and in late June her attorneys filed various motions to block the order of eviction.[83]

At some point during the summer Lockwood realized that legal challenges, venerable age, and public stature would not protect her from the loss of her home. As war was declared in Europe she packed her personal belongings and her law books. By autumn her correspondence bore the address of a rented house with a backyard on nearby Indiana Avenue, where she reestablished her residence and a smaller boarding house. On her eighty-fourth birthday she was interviewed there by an upstate New York reporter. She spoke forcefully about the role of men in starting war. Why not consult the women of the world? she asked: "The burden of the war falls upon them more heavily than anyone else. . . . [G]enerations of women down the years [will] pay the penalty [for this European war]."[84] She said that her convention days were over and that she had closed her law practice. The household was now supported by her widow's pension, rents from her boarders, and a monthly twenty-dollar check from the Home Trust Company, established by Andrew Carnegie to fund pensions for poets, statesmen, teachers, and "other persons of distinction but in need."[85]

Although she would live at least one winter in Florida before her death in May 1917, most of her time after 1914 was spent in Washington keeping up with world events, and the affairs of friends, at local meetings and through letters. Clara Colby and Mary Walker occasionally boarded with her. They did not always pay their rent, but they brought news of the suffrage movement. And for two years beginning in November 1914, she corresponded with Henrik Andersen, a Norwegian-American sculptor half her age who lived in Rome.

Andersen had achieved modest notice as an artist when he, and his work, caught the eye of novelist Henry James. In 1912 he began circulating a master plan for a "World City," a world center of communication whose motto would be "Love—Equality—Peace." James's biographer dismissed it as a sculptor's dream of "a kind of permanent, super–World Fair," while James accused his young friend of harboring "a mania for the colossal," of "MEGALOMANIA," and begged him to "liv[e] in the realities of things."[86]

While James found the idea delusional and utopian, Lockwood thought the plan "one of the grandest ideas of the age," having learned about it when Andersen, his mother, and his sister visited Washington.[87] She pledged to support him when corresponding with members of the international peace community, and immediately tried to solicit interest among her clubwomen friends. An older woman, and a younger man, they played to one another's egos: he praised her as an inspiration to American women; she wrote about him, "It is not the many but the few who move the world."[88] As the war in Europe expanded, they exchanged ever darker thoughts about "this terrible butchery," whether the United States would enter the fighting—Lockwood wrongly thought Wilson a "Peace President"—and whether a United States of Europe might emerge at the conflict's end.[89]

Letters from Clara Colby struck a lighter note, with no mention of the European war. During the winter of 1916, while Lockwood was at the home of friends in St. Cloud, Florida, trying to improve her health, Colby passed along full accounts of suffrage politics and pressed her friend to publicize federal suffrage in the South. They both needed, she said, to "keep the banner flying of women's rights under the original constitution," to explain its difference from the amendment, and to clarify FWEA's difference from the Congressional Union.[90]

The warmth and sun of Florida proved a balm for Lockwood, who returned to Washington full of what she referred to as "lively energy." This good health permitted her to attend a seemingly endless number of meetings. The day before Decoration (Memorial) Day, apologizing that there had simply been no time to write, she sent Colby a letter showing her still in the thrall of the two-day meeting of Taft's League to Enforce Peace. As a member she had attended all but one of the six sessions and stayed until midnight the evening of the banquet, watching a "perfect panic of giving" as the diners rushed to meet a fund-raising goal of three hundred thousand dollars.[91] Many pacifists were critical of the League, whose program did not attempt to outlaw war. League members, however, hoped to limit future conflicts through new forms of diplomacy, perhaps a league of nations, and international policing. Despite her long involvement with the more radical wing of the peace movement, Lockwood apparently liked what she heard and told Colby that the organization could "have a great effect not only on the U.S. but on the world."[92]

Lockwood's next letter to Colby, possibly her last, detailed the ordinary and the extraordinary. She passed on the political gossip, described her attempt to keep schoolchildren from marching in the war-preparedness parade, and inveighed against Congress for using the parade as "cover" to make appropriations for weapons.[93] Then she turned to news of her grandson, DeForest, revealing that he had, against her wishes, joined the National Guard. She wrote that his unit had been mobilized and sent to Arizona to deal with violence along the Mexican border caused by followers of Pancho Villa and government soldiers. She also revealed that he had eloped, marrying Lillian Carter, a Washington neighbor, at St. Paul's Episcopal Church. Adding intimate details, she told Colby he had been obliged "to leave his young wife without staying even an hour." When Lillian, twenty-two, and her husband's Nannie met a few days later, Lockwood found her "a beautiful young woman . . . and very gracious." Although she wrote Clara that "her nose was out of joint & my last prop is gone," she, too, was gracious, giving Lillian a small reception and insisting to Colby that she was "glad" 25-year-old DeForest was married.

Colby, writing back, urged her friend to consider the realities of age: "I would be glad if you would turn your back on roomers . . . and live in comfort in an apartment."[94] Advising Lockwood to sell her heavy law books, she continued, "you will never have the strength to handle [them]. . . . Then it would not be so hard to move."

As well as she knew Lockwood, Colby refused to acknowledge that her friend had no desire for a quiet life. The cloister of an apartment held no appeal for a woman whose natural home was the courtroom and the lecture hall, a woman who loved public notice. It was not surprising that reporters received their usual welcome in October 1916 on Lockwood's eighty-sixth birthday. She regaled them with the history of her legal and political accomplishments, said she was still active in public affairs, and, as if to prove it, described a speech she had given only days before supporting Wilson's reelection. Hand to chin, she posed for a photographer, and invited the room of admirers to share in a cake inscribed "Birthday Greetings—aged 86."[95]

Epilogue

> She has won a place with the few who blazed the trail that other women might walk with greater ease and freedom.
>
> Edith Mosher, "First Day" Ceremony,
> Belva Lockwood Postal Stamp, 1986

In the months after her eighty-sixth birthday Lockwood's health declined. She was ill throughout the winter, worried about money, and, according to friends, not well cared for.[1] She died on May 19, 1917, at George Washington University Hospital. Her death certificate listed the cause as "post-operative shock and age."

When her death was announced, she was praised in newspaper obituaries, remembered as a pioneer in the woman's rights movement, an advocate for peace, and an early candidate for the presidency. At her funeral local clubwomen provided just the sort of pomp that Lockwood had appreciated during her life: the Woman's Christian Temperance Union sent an elaborate floral arrangement to the Wesley Methodist Church, where she lay in state, and a WCTU honor guard watched over her casket. The Reverend Anna Howard Shaw, former NAWSA president, assisted in the funeral service.

The United States had changed in many ways in the course of Lockwood's eighty-six years. Industry had joined agriculture as an engine of the national economy, the needs of each feeding the nation's imperialist impulse. Railroads, the telegraph, the telephone, and the automobile all helped move goods and hastened the pace of life. Citizens and immigrants alike fought to attain middle-class status. Nonetheless, when Lockwood died in 1917 the question remained: Where, exactly, did women fit in modern American society, and what was Lockwood's legacy in extending equality of opportunity to women?

As an attorney and peace leader Lockwood had an impact on American society that was at once tangible and symbolic, and altogether striking in its breadth. No other nineteenth-century woman pioneered women's professional rights and engaged issues of social justice and foreign policy as a member of an international movement for peace. By fighting for the right to join the profession of law, she helped make it possible for other women to make a career of the law.

Lockwood brought a religious zeal and considerable personal energy to the work of uprooting employment discrimination. She believed firmly that women must have the opportunity to care for themselves and to develop their potential. She fought for women's right to become diplomats, journalists, constables, notaries, and school superintendents. In all of these contests—save diplomacy—she eventually prevailed, helping to open vistas and opportunities previously closed to women of her generation and winning universal praise from progressive men and women.

Many reformers, however, parted company with Lockwood when she took the even more daring step of running for the presidency. The personal qualities they had admired when she was battling Congress and "old fogey" judges—her pluck, nerve, and independence of action—suddenly struck them as liabilities. Some of her colleagues believed her to be a "Barnum," more showperson than activist. Other leaders criticized her for being a movement operative who did not know her place. Brushing aside all criticism, Lockwood insisted to the end of her life that her campaigns had been a good idea, providing serious opportunity for public education and dialogue. Her victory in the political sphere was symbolic rather than concrete, but in the context of the nineteenth century, it was no less important for that. And if she was self-promoting, it was in the fashion of politicians, and she thought that this, too, was good.

Lockwood's place in history is defined by the particular nature of her advocacy. In offering herself for action, she bravely subjected herself to public scrutiny and criticism. Throughout her life, weary of talk, petitions, and societal indifference, she stepped forward to seize rights and opportunities granted to men and withheld from women. As a young widow she claimed an education at the cost of three years' absence from her daughter. In postwar Washington, she argued for women's right to vote over the clatter of tin pans tossed by opponents. Her dogged fight to attend law school and win bar privileges for years exposed her to ridicule, while her two presidential campaigns caused many, although not all, of her reform colleagues to turn their backs on her. Her letters to presidents were countless, urging them to open government posts and appointments to women. In her 1899 campaign to win a spot on the U.S. delegation being sent by President McKinley to the Hague peace conference, she said the time for fair play was well past and characteristically offered herself for service.

Her advocacy rested upon a resolute belief that society not only should, but could, do better in realizing fundamental ideals of justice and democracy. As a young woman she had been schooled in early-nineteenth-century ideas emphasizing the possibility of moral and social progress. As an adult her genius lay in shaping that optimism, that "fire of the spirit," into tangible and, at the time, radical examples of the ways women could participate in a society based on equality of opportunity. In this translation of abstraction into action she was far ahead of her peers.

Like all people, Lockwood made mistakes and had flaws. Her decision to run a second time for the presidency caused no harm to her or the suffrage movement but lacked the vibrancy of the first campaign and opened her to charges of foolishness. It exposed the degree to which, despite her achievements and public notice, she was unable to build an organization of any size capable of addressing discrimination against women. She was never described as charismatic and did not successfully cultivate followers even as she was acknowledged as a role model.

The decision to fight the Taylor estate diminished her standing in the legal community and ultimately cost her the house at F Street. Stubborn resolve, a trait that served her well much of the time, in this instance seemed inexplicable as the evidence pointed to contractual obligations to share the Cherokee fee award with her long-time business colleague.

On matters of race policy Lockwood had a mixed record. She was consistently progressive on the question of the Chinese, often in the face of the blatant racism of her West Coast suffrage colleagues. As a member of the Universal Peace Union and as an attorney engaged in claims cases involving Indians, she argued for fair treatment and the recognition of U.S. treaty obligations. At the same time, she approved of late-nineteenth-century legislation such as the Dawes Act, whose intent was the political and cultural destruction of Indian nations. Most perplexing, however, was her failure to take a more aggressive stance with respect to discrimination against African Americans. She drew clients from Washington's black community, counted African Americans among her reform colleagues, and occasionally gave talks to their groups, but she seemed incapable of understanding the disabilities imposed on the freedmen community by racism, and at the very end of her life made the disappointing decision to join the American Woman's Republic, which had a Caucasians-only membership policy.

In her lifetime Lockwood, constitutionally incapable of prolonged pessimism, emphasized the victories. In her old age, even as the United States moved toward war, she spoke of ways to resist militarism. Although the fight for universal woman suffrage had yet to be won, in her last years she celebrated the states that had extended voting rights to women and never doubted that universal suffrage would occur in the near future. And, in fact, as the result of Wilson's need to project a more democratic image around the world, Alice Paul's militancy, Carrie Catt's clearly stated strategies, and, in a final dramatic moment, the influence of a Tennessee legislator's mother on her son's ratification vote, in 1920 the Nineteenth Amendment was approved, granting to women the constitutional right to vote.

It is impossible to know whether Lockwood would have tired of the slow pace of change that followed this victory, and whether she would have become more biting in her thoughts about sex discrimination and women's very slow climb into the profession of law and the world of politics. While Lockwood became a member of the U.S. Supreme Court bar in 1879, Sandra Day O'Connor, the first woman justice on the Supreme Court, was not appointed until 1981. In those more than one hundred years women struggled to enter law schools and to win prestigious clerkships and top law firm positions.[2] In 2006, Justice Ruth Bader Ginsburg was the sole female justice serving on the United States Supreme Court.

Women seeking high public office have also had to contend with deeply engrained attitudes about whether members of the "fair sex" have the abilities necessary to govern. Nearly a hundred years after ratification of the Nineteenth Amendment they remain woefully underrepresented in both the U.S. Senate and the U.S. House of Representatives, as well as in most state legislatures. Connecticut's Ella Grasso was the first woman elected a governor in her own right. The year was 1974, a long fifty-seven years after Lockwood's death.

Belva Lockwood made headlines in the nineteenth century as a trail-blazing attorney and presidential contender. Women have struggled to follow her example but, slowly and surely, they have. Lockwood would not have been surprised at either the extent of the struggle or the successes it achieved. As she said in an 1888 interview, "Equality of rights and privileges is but simple justice," and she very much believed that, in the United States, justice was possible.[3]

Notes

ABBREVIATIONS USED IN NOTES

HWS	Elizabeth Cady Stanton, Susan B. Anthony, and Matilda Joslyn Gage, eds., *History of Woman Suffrage* (1881–1922; reprint New York: Arno, 1969).
IPB/LNL	International Peace Bureau, League of Nations Library, Geneva
LC	Library of Congress
LDJ	*Lockport Daily Journal*
NA	National Archives
NCHS	Niagara County Historical Society
NMAH	National Museum of American History, Division of Social History
NYSHA	New York State Historical Association, Cooperstown (Ormes/Winner Collection)
SCPC	Swarthmore College Peace Collection
SHSW	State Historical Society of Wisconsin, Clara Colby Papers
SU	Syracuse University
UPU	Universal Peace Union

NOTES TO PROLOGUE AND ACKNOWLEDGMENTS

1. Belva Ann Lockwood, "My Efforts to Become a Lawyer," *Lippincott's Magazine*, February 1888, 216.

2. Julia Davis, "Belva Ann Lockwood: Remover of Mountains," *American Bar Association Journal* (June 1979); Madeleine B. Stern, "Belva Lockwood," in *We the Women* (New York: Schulte,1963; reprint Lincoln: University of Nebraska Press, 1994); Julia Hull Winner, "Belva A. Lockwood: That Extraordinary Woman," *New York History*, October 1958.

3. The biography project was underway by November 4, 1912, when Lockwood wrote to Lella, "I am exceedingly glad that you like your job for 2 reasons. 1st I desire the biography to be presentable and to do me justice without flattery and 2nd I wish you to make some money out of it." Lockwood to Lella Gardner, Papers of Belva A. Lockwood, SCPC.

4. Lockwood had given Lella certain documents while they worked on the biography and Lella said that her aunt had promised that she might have

the rest upon her death. Years later Lella wrote to Ellen Starr Brinton, "in the end she died suddenly, and altho I went at once, I found that [DeForest] had scooped the office all [not legible] and given it to the Salvation Army, *so he said*." Gardner to Brinton, 20 October 1944, DG OOO, Records, SCPC.

5. Belva Lockwood to Lella Gardner, 27 March 1912: "I have *3 or 4 good size scrapbooks, and a lot more papers*." Papers of Belva A. Lockwood, SCPC. Lockwood's grandson kept one of the scrapbooks, but the rest have been lost. Correspondence between Lella Gardner and Ellen Starr Brinton, June 16, 1938, February 3, 1939, February 10, 1939, and October 20, 1944, DG 000, Records, SCPC. In the 1960s he distributed the Lockwood papers in his possession among several archives.

6. Letter from Ellen Starr Brinton to Lella Gardner, 16 June 1938, DG 000, Records, SCPC. In this letter Brinton writes that DeForest "greatly regretted the destruction of Dr. Lockwood's papers."

NOTES TO CHAPTER I

1. "Belva Lockwood's Ancestry." Materials collected by Mrs. Emma Cramer, author's files.

2. William Wyckoff, *The Developer's Frontier: The Making of the Western New York Landscape* (New Haven, CT: Yale University Press, 1988), 59–60.

3. Belva A. Lockwood to Mrs. Emily A. Greene, 28 November 1907, private collection, author's files.

4. Belva Lockwood to Lella Gardner, 5 January 1913, Papers of Belva A. Lockwood, SCPC; in the same collection, Lockwood to Gardner, 7 April 1912.

5. William Pool, ed., *F. N. Trevor Landmarks of Niagara County New York* (D. Mason & Co., 1897), 267.

6. Carol Sheriff, *The Artificial River: The Erie Canal and the Paradox of Progress, 1817–1862* (New York: Hill and Wang, 1996).

7. In 1912 Lockwood recalled to Lella Gardner how her father moved the family from farm to farm and that she and Rachel were born in Griswold Street, Niagara County, Inverno, in Royalton, and Warren and Cyrene, "in Erie Co. in the country." Letter of 7 April 1912, Papers of Belva A. Lockwood, SCPC.

8. Julia Hull Winner, *Belva A. Lockwood* (Lockport, NY: NCHS, 1969), 1.

9. Harold B. Johnson, "Interview with Belva Lockwood," *Watertown Daily Times*, November 7, 1914. Newspaper archives, Scrapbooks, 22:40.

10. "Belva Lockwood," (New York) *Sun*, August 27, 1888, 4.

11. Belva A. Lockwood, "My Efforts to Become a Lawyer," *Lippincott's Magazine*, February 1888, 216.

12. Belva A. Lockwood, "The Women Who Tried to Vote," *LDJ*, May 13, 1871, 1.

13. John McNall, a lifelong Methodist, gave the couple a large Bible, now in the possession of the Royalton Historical Society, in which Belva inscribed her wedding date.

14. Lockwood, "My Efforts," 216.

15. "Obsequies. John McNall," *LDJ*, March 10, 1884, 3.

16. Lockwood, "The Women Who Tried to Vote," 1. Relatives believe that the couple lived on the corner of Chestnut, Ridge, and Gasport Roads. Pat Stepien, "Famous Belva Lockwood Still Recalled by Kin Here," *Gazette*, October 3, 1976, clipping, Lockwood files, NCHS.

17. Lockwood, "My Efforts," 216–17.

18. Ibid., 217.

19. New York Census Schedule, 1850, Royalton, Niagara County, M-432, Roll 560, 308. She presumably paid off the mortgage on their property as well as outstanding personal debts with the sale of this real estate. Later she wrote that "it needed all of [my] active energy to straighten out the affairs of [my] husbands [sic] estate, with the half-digested plans which his enfeebled condition had prevented his carrying out." Belva Ann Lockwood, "Belva A. Lockwood." Autobiographical manuscript sent to Susan B. Anthony for Johnson's New Universal Cyclopaedia, 24 July 1876, in the Papers of E. C. Stanton and S. B. Anthony, 18: 938–41, LC.

20. Lockwood, "Belva A. Lockwood." Autobiographical manuscript sent to Susan B. Anthony.

21. Ibid.

22. Lockwood, "My Efforts," 217. Her coursework consisted of geometry, German, anatomy, physiology, and bookkeeping. Lockwood, "Belva A. Lockwood." Autobiographical manuscript sent to Susan B. Anthony.

23. Lockwood, "My Efforts," 217.

24. Lockwood, "Belva A. Lockwood." Autobiographical manuscript sent to Susan B. Anthony.

25. Lockwood, "The Women Who Tried to Vote," 1.

26. Lockwood, "My Efforts," 217.

27. Ibid., 217.

28. In 1834 Oberlin College initiated coeducational classes. Later, it was claimed that "the true origin of co-education in the United States of America" lay in the Methodist seminaries, which, "without making any extraordinary pretentions about it . . . introduced this co-education." "Alumni Reunion," June 22, 1875, 35–36, Belva Lockwood Papers, SU.

29. Lockwood, "My Efforts," 218.

30. Belva Lockwood, "An Alumna Tells of Life in Our University in 1856–7," March 21, 1895, 1. Belva Lockwood Papers, SU.

31. Ibid., 1–2.

32. Ibid., 2; also, "Report of Mrs. B. A. McNall, Alumnus of Genesee College," June 1867. Belva Lockwood Papers, SU.

33. Lockwood, "My Efforts," 218.

34. Ibid., 218–19. A number of prosuffrage women lectured in central and western New York while Belva was in college, and she may also have heard Lucy Stone, Ernestine Rose, and the Reverend Antoinette L. Brown. See Ann D. Gordon, ed., *The Selected Papers of Elizabeth Cady Stanton and Susan B. Anthony*, vol. 1, *In the School of Anti-Slavery, 1840–1866* (New Brunswick, NJ: Rutgers University Press, 1997), 1:291.

35. Lockwood, "An Alumna Tells," 3.

36. She took the job on the advice of her college president although, in later autobiographical essays, she claimed to have "formed" other plans. Lockwood, "My Efforts," 218.

37. Untitled typescript manuscript. Lockwood files, NCHS.

38. Lori D. Ginzberg, *Untidy Origins: A Story of Woman's Rights in Antebellum New York* (Chapel Hill: University of North Carolina Press, 2005), ch. 1.

39. Whitney R. Cross, *The Burned-Over District: The Social and Intellectual History of Enthusiastic Religion in Western New York, 1800–1850* (New York: Harper, 1950), 3–4.

40. "Report of Mrs. B. A. McNall."

41. Methodist women had nearly equal rights in church communion and had preached at meeting in western New York, Cross, *Burned-Over*, 237, 177. Early in his ministry John Wesley encouraged women to engage in public good works. Earl Kent Brown, "Women of the Word," in Hilah F. Thomas and Rosemary Skinner Keller, eds., *Women in New Worlds* (Nashville, TN: Abingdon, 1981), 69–70.

42. Elite Washington women of the early Republic used salons for "petticoat politicking." Both Federalists and Democrats brought women to meetings to demonstrate the importance of virtue to the survival of the Republic. See Catherine Allgor, *Parlor Politics* (Charlottesville: University Press of Virginia, 2000) and Rosemarie Zagarri, "Gender and the First Party System," in Doron Ben-Atar and Barbara B. Oberg, eds., *Federalists Reconsidered* (Charlottesville: University Press of Virginia, 1998), 118–34.

43. Margaret Fuller, *Woman in the Nineteenth Century* (New York: Norton, 1971), 171.

44. Elizabeth Cady Stanton, Paulina Wright Davis, and Lucinda Chandler wrote that they drew upon Fuller's "Conversations" as a model for their activities. Charles Capper, *Margaret Fuller* (New York: Oxford University Press, 1992), 290–97, 306.

45. Joan Hedrick, *Harriet Beecher Stowe* (New York: Oxford University Press, 1994), 11.

46. Geoffrey C. Ward, *Not for Ourselves Alone: The Story of Eizabeth Cady Stanton and Susan B. Anthony* (New York: Knopf, 1999), 65–68.

47. Utica *Evening Herald* editorial reprinted in Ward, *Not for Ourselves*, 68.

48. Gordon, *Selected Papers*, 1:376.

49. Lockwood, "My Efforts," 219.

50. Ibid., 219.

51. Ibid., 219.

52. Ibid., 219; Ward, *Not for Ourselves*, 81.

53. Lockwood, "My Efforts," 219.

54. Illinois Census Schedule, 1860, Douglass, Iroquois County, M-653, Roll 231, 310, lines 30–34. Inverno, her sister Rachel, thirty-one, and her brother, Warren, twenty-seven, lived with their parents, according to this census.

55. Lockwood, "My Efforts," 220.

56. Anne Firor Scott, *Making the Invisible Woman Visible* (Urbana: University of Illinois Press, 1984), 68.

57. Miriam R. Levin, *Defining Women's Scientific Work* (Dartmouth, NH: University of New England Press, 2004); Kathryn Kish Sklar, *Catharine Beecher: A Study in American Domesticity* (New York: Norton, 1976).

58. Lockwood, "My Efforts," 219–20. Beecher published *Physiology and Calisthenics: For Schools and Families* (New York: Harper & Brothers, 1856) and *Calisthenic Exercises, for Schools, Families, and Health Establishments* (New York: Harper & Brothers, 1856).

59. "Belva Lockwood Ran in 1888 Presidential Election," *Tioga County Courier*, November 16, 1988, 2–3.

60. Mike Gulachok, "McEnteer Portrays Belva Lockwood," *Tioga County Courier*, March 10, 1993, 2.

61. Lockwood, "The Women Who Tried to Vote," 1; "Report of Mrs. B. A. McNall."

NOTES TO CHAPTER 2

1. Henry Adams, *The Education of Henry Adams: An Autobiography* (1907; reprint New York: Modern Library, 1996), 256.

2. Adams, *Education*, 44.

3. Mary Clemmer Ames, *Ten Years in Washington* (Hartford, CT: Worthington, 1875), 67.

4. James H. Whyte, *The Uncivil War: Washington during the Reconstruction, 1865–1878* (New York: Twayne, 1958), 16.

5. Adams, *Education*, 253.

6. Ibid., 256.

7. Alan Lessoff, *The Nation and Its City: Politics, "Corruption," and Progress in Washington, D.C., 1861–1902* (Baltimore, MD: Johns Hopkins Press, 1994), 7.

8. Ibid., 8.

9. Belva A. Lockwood, "My Efforts to Become a Lawyer," *Lippincott's Magazine*, February 1888, 221. Late in life Lockwood told a reporter that she moved to Washington because the *Evening Star*, its newspaper, was a good recommendation for the city. "Belva Lockwood Is 86 Years Old," *Evening Star*, October 23, 1916, 10.

10. Robert M. McWade, "Mrs. Lockwood Tells of Suffrage Move's Growth," *Woman's National Daily*, (n.d.). Papers of Belva A. Lockwood, SCPC.

11. "Educational," *Evening Star*, September 4, 1866, 1.

12. Lockwood, "My Efforts," 221.

13. Donald A. Ritchie, *Press Gallery: Congress and the Washington Correspondents* (Cambridge, MA: Harvard University Press, 1991), 146.

14. 71 U.S. 2 (1866); *Evening Star*, March 7, 1866, 2.

15. McWade, "Mrs. Lockwood Tells."

16. Goldsbury and Russell's *The American Common-School Reader* (1844).

17. Lockwood, "My Efforts," 221.

18. Ibid., 221.

19. "Educational," 1.

20. Allen C. Clark, "Belva Ann Lockwood," 35–36, *Records of the Columbia Historical Society* (1935), 207. The Union League building was built with funds contributed by the National Council of Union Leagues. Michael W. Fitzgerald, *The Union League Movement in the Deep South* (Baton Rouge: Louisiana State University Press, 1989), 1–36.

21. "Report of Mrs. B. A. McNall, Alumnus of Genesee College," June 1867. Belva Lockwood Papers, SU.

22. For Lockwood's account of this application, see "My Efforts," 221.

23. Ibid., 221. Lockwood's aspirations were not completely misplaced. In this period William Dean Howells, born poor and without connections, won an appointment, at the age of twenty-four, as American consul to Venice after writing Abraham Lincoln's campaign biography.

24. Julia Hull Winner, *Belva A. Lockwood* (Lockport, NY: NCHS, 1969), 96.

25. Wesley United Methodist Church, Washington, D.C., "Record of Members in Full Connection."

26. Lockwood to Dr. McNaughton, 28 December 1901, Donohue Rare Book Room, University of San Francisco.

27. Agnes Wright Spring, ed., *A Bloomer Girl on Pike's Peak, 1858* (Denver Public Library: Western History Department, 1949).

28. Ames, *Ten Years in Washington*.

29. General George Thomas made the appointment over the protests of his superiors and his men.

30. The payment of taxes occasionally qualified a man for suffrage. Alexander Keyssar provides an excellent overview of the political development of suffrage in *The Right to Vote* (New York: Basic Books, 2000).

31. Keyssar, *Right to Vote*, 87–88.

32. Congress has the authority to make law for the District of Columbia. U.S. Constitution, Article I, section 8, clause 17.

33. Cowan was a Republican who, according to a December 12, 1866, editorial in the *New York Tribune*, had "abandoned his party, has been repudiated by his State, and may well be casting about for some new issue by which to divert attention."

34. *Congressional Globe*, 39th Cong., 2d Sess., December 11, 1866, 55.

35. *Congressional Globe*, 39th Cong., 2d Sess., December 11 and 12, 1866, 56, 66, and 83.

36. *Congressional Globe*, 39th Cong., 2d Sess., December 12, 1866, 79.

37. Ibid., 79.

38. Act of January 8, 1867, ch. 6, 14 U.S. Stat. 375.

39. *HWS*, 3:809.

40. "Knox," *LDJ*, January 11, 1878, 2.

41. "Dentistry, Dr. Lockwood," *Evening Star*, August 11, 1866, 1.

42. E Street Baptist Church of the City of Washington, D.C., *Articles of Faith with the Covenant, Rules of Church Order, and Discipline with a List of Members* (Washington, DC: Judd & Detweiler, 1869); *Fitzhigh v. Gaskins*, RG 21, Equity, NA.

43. "Humphreys' Adminx. v. The U.S. Chief" (autobiographical sketch), 6, Papers of Belva A. Lockwood, SCPC.

44. James H. Lockwood, "Early Times and Events in Wisconsin," in Lyman Copeland Draper, ed., *Collections of the State Historical Society of Wisconsin* (Madison, WI: The Society, 1903), 2:153.

45. http://searches.rootsweb.com (history of Galena).

46. "General Affidavit of Chas. Alexander," Belva Lockwood Application for Pension, 28 November 1890, Box 37469, Bundle 249912, NA.

47. "Ezekiel Lockwood," *Evening Star*, April 26, 1877, 4.

48. Lockwood, "My Efforts," 222.

49. "Additional Evidence Affidavit." Ezekiel Lockwood, Pension File, Box 37469, Bundle 249912, NA.

50. Clark, "Belva Ann Lockwood," 206.

51. James Densmore to his daughter, Tina, 16 June 1881, original in possession of Christopher Densmore, West Chester, PA.

52. "Petition of E. Lockwood, agent of Charles Rosenfield," *Journal of the Senate*, 41st Cong., 2d Sess., 1870, 66, 378, and 543.

53. The address of the Union League Hall was 481 Ninth Street. As a result of renumbering, the address changed to 432 Ninth Street. See *Boyd's City Directory for Washington, D.C.* (1869), 51–52.

54. Lockwood, "My Efforts," 222.

55. *HWS*, 3:810–11.

56. Lockwood, "My Efforts," 222.

57. Ibid., 222.

58. Andrea Moore Kerr, *Lucy Stone: Speaking Out for Equality* (New Brunswick, NJ: Rutgers University Press, 1992), 81, 86.

59. B. A. Lockwood, "Christmas Week in Washington," *LDJ*, December 30, 1872, 2.

60. Clark, "Belva Ann Lockwood," 209.

61. Belva Ann Lockwood, "Belva A. Lockwood." Autobiographical manuscript sent to Susan B. Anthony for Johnson's New Universal Cyclopaedia, 24 July 1876. The Papers of E. C. Stanton and S. B. Anthony, 18:938–41, LC. A passing comment by family friend Allen Clark suggests that local people thought Ezekiel had lost his identity when he married Belva, becoming "Mrs. Belva A. Lockwood's husband." Clark, "Belva Ann Lockwood," 207.

NOTES TO CHAPTER 3

1. Men like Ezekiel occasionally chaired the meetings. "Universal Franchise Association," *Evening Star*, November 1, 1869, 4.

2. Holmes was a statistician who wrote reports at the Bureau of Education. Agnes Wright Spring, ed., *A Bloomer Girl on Pike's Peak, 1858* (Denver Public Library: Western History Department, 1949), 61–62.

3. Allen C. Clark, "Belva Ann Lockwood," 35–36, *Records of the Columbia Historical Society* (1935), 207.

4. Ibid., 207.

5. *HWS*, 3:809; Clark, "Belva Ann Lockwood," 207.

6. Belva A. Lockwood to Dr. Clara McNaughton, 28 December 1901, Clara McNaughton Papers, Donohue Rare Book Room, University of San Francisco; Robert M. McWade, "Mrs. Lockwood Tells of Suffrage Move's Growth," *Woman's National Daily*, (n.d.), Papers of Belva A. Lockwood, SCPC.

7. *HWS*, 3:809; Clark, "Belva Ann Lockwood," 209.

8. Clark, "Belva Ann Lockwood," 208–9. After several years, the members of the UFA started referring to the group as the "Equal Rights Association."

9. *HWS*, 3:809. For membership lists see Belva A. Lockwood, "Woman's Suffrage Work in the District of Columbia," *Peacemaker* 21 (August 1902),183 and *HWS*, 3:810–11.

10. *HWS*, 3:809.

11. Ibid., 809, 811. Letters of Josephine Griffing, Rare Books and Manuscripts, Columbia University.

12. "Local News," *Evening Star*, January 13, 1871, 4.

13. "American Anti-Slavery Anniversary," *Standard*, May 13, 1865, 2.

14. Stanton to Phillips, 25 May 1865, in Theodore Stanton and Harriet Stanton Blatch, eds., *Elizabeth Cady Stanton* (New York: Arno Press, 1969), 2:104–5.

15. Ellen Carol Dubois, ed., *The Elizabeth Cady Stanton–Susan B. Anthony Reader* (Boston: Northeastern University Press, 1992), 90.

16. The Fourteenth Amendment, Section 2, provided only modest protection for political rights by requiring that, as a condition for readmission to the Union, the former Confederate states enfranchise their male ex-slaves or face a proportional decrease in their congressional representation. This is the first time that a reference to gender appears in the federal Constitution.

17. Massachusetts Senator Henry Wilson proposed a more radical amendment that would have prohibited discrimination in voting and holding office on account of race, color, nativity, property, education, or creed. It failed because of prejudice and concern over transformation of the relationship between the national government and the states. Alexander Keyssar, *The Right to Vote* (New York: Basic Books, 2000), 95.

18. Elizabeth Cady Stanton, "The Sixteenth Amendment," in Ann D. Gordon, ed., *Against an Aristocracy of Sex: The Selected Papers of Elizabeth Cady Stanton and Susan B. Anthony* (New Brunswick, NJ: Rutgers University Press, 2000), 237.

19. Anthony letter, 4 June 1869, in Gordon, *Aristocracy of Sex*, 247–48.

20. Ellen Carol DuBois, *Feminism and Suffrage* (Ithaca, NY: Cornell University Press, 1978), 185.

21. Between 1863 and 1869 proposals to enfranchise African Americans were defeated in fifteen northern states and territories. Keyssar, *Right to Vote*, 89–104.

22. Gordon, *Aristocracy of Sex*, 238.

23. Ibid., 240.

24. Letter of Lucy Stone, 6 October 1869, in DuBois, *Feminism*, 196.

25. Helena B. Temple, "Interview, Mrs. Belva A. Lockwood," *Women's Penny Paper*, October 5, 1889, 1.

26. Belva A. Lockwood, "The Women Who Tried To Vote," *LDJ*, May 13, 1871, 1.

27. Lockwood may have been a member of the Independent Order of Good Templars, a militant temperance organization. See Mrs. E. N. Chapin, *American Court Gossip; or, Life at the National Capitol* (Marshalltown, IA: Chapin & Hartwell, 1887), 33.

28. Belva A. Lockwood to National Working Men's Convention, 14 August 1869, Mary Edwards Walker Papers, SU.

29. Lois Beachy Underhill, *The Woman Who Ran for President: The Many Lives of Victoria Woodhull* (Bridgehampton, NY: Bridge Works Publishing, 1995), 196.

30. "Woman Suffrage," *Evening Star*, January 19, 1870, 4.

31. "Local News: Women's Rights," *Evening Star*, January 18, 1870, 1.

32. "Woman Suffrage," January 19, 1870, 4.

33. Ibid., 4.

34. Ibid., 4.

35. Ibid., 4.

36. Kepley was the first woman to receive an American law degree.

37. I. M. Hamilton to Josephine Griffing, 5 November 1870. Griffing Letters, Columbia University.

38. Like other suffrage women, Lockwood lectured occasionally under the auspices of the International Workingmen's Association, but there is no evidence that she was an active member. Timothy Messer-Kruse, *The Yankee International: Marxism and the American Reform Tradition, 1848–1876* (Chapel Hill: University of North Carolina Press, 1998), 39.

39. Mary Clemmer Ames, *Ten Years in Washington* (Hartford, CT: Worthington, 1875), 372, and Cindy Sondik Aron, *Ladies and Gentlemen of the Civil Service* (New York: Oxford University Press, 1987), 70–71.

40. Aron, *Ladies and Gentlemen*, 6.

41. 14 U.S. Stat. 207.

42. *HWS*, 3:814 and 2:348.

43. *Journal of the House of Representatives of the U.S.*, 41st Cong., 2d Sess., March 21, 1870, 497, 500; *Congressional Globe*, 41st Cong., 2d Sess., Part III, 1870, 2094; Belva A. Lockwood, "Woman's Suffrage Work in the District of Columbia," *Peacemaker* 21 (August 1902), 183.

44. *HWS*, 3:811–12.

45. "Belva Lockwood, 82 Years Young, Who Started the Disturbance," (New York) *World*, November 3, 1912, N5.

46. *Congressional Globe*, 41st Cong., 2d Sess., Part V, June 11, 1870, 4353.

47. *Congressional Globe*, 41st Cong., 2d Sess., Part V, June 10, 1870, 4330.

48. Ibid., 4331.

49. *Congressional Globe*, 41st Cong., 2d Sess., Part V, June 11, 1870, 4353.

50. Ibid., 4353. All references in this paragraph to Arnell's speech of June 11 are found on this page.

51. 16 U.S. Stat. 250.

52. Aron, *Ladies and Gentlemen*, 83–85.

53. Lura McNall, "Our Washington Letter," *LDJ*, September 15, 1875, 2.

NOTES TO CHAPTER 4

1. Harold B. Johnson, "Interview," *Watertown Daily Times*, November 7, 1914, Newspaper archives, Scrapbooks, 22:40.

2. Arabella Mansfield became the first woman lawyer in America in 1869 when Iowa admitted her to its bar; Charlotte E. Ray was the first African-American woman to complete law school. See Virginia D. Drachman, *Sisters in Law: Women Lawyers in Modern American History* (Cambridge, MA: Harvard University Press, 1998); Karen Berger Morello, *The Invisible Bar: The Woman Lawyer in America, 1638 to the Present* (New York: Random House, 1986); J. Clay Smith, Jr., "Black Women Lawyers," *Howard Law Journal* 40, no. 2 (1997).

3. Elmer Louis Kayser, *Bricks without Straw: The Evolution of George Washington University* (New York: Appleton-Century-Crofts, 1970), 49–50, 124, 128, and 130. Lockwood wrote that after the rejection by Columbian, she applied unsuccessfully to Georgetown University Law School. "Humphreys' Adminx. v. the U.S. Chief" (autobiographical sketch), 1, Papers of Belva A. Lockwood, SCPC.

4. Eighteen hundred and seventy, District of Columbia Census Schedule, 3rd Ward, M-593, Roll 124, 356. In addition to the Lockwoods, the household included Lura, Jessie, and employee George Woods, identified as "Black." After the closing of McNall's Seminary, Lura found a position sewing books and, still later, worked as a government clerk. *Boyd's City Directory for the District of Columbia*, 1871 and 1872.

5. Lockwood, "Old Homeweek Speech," in "McEnteer Portrays Belva Lockwood," *Tioga County Courier*, March 10, 1993, 2.

6. Belva Ann Lockwood, "My Efforts to Become a Lawyer," *Lippincott's Magazine*, February 1888, 222.

7. Ibid., 222.

8. Kayser, *Bricks*, 165.

9. Lockwood, "My Efforts," 222.

10. Ibid., 222.

11. Kayser, *Bricks*, 143–44.

12. Lockwood, "My Efforts," 222; "No Ladies Admitted," *Evening Star*, October 26, 1869, 4.

13. "Mrs. Dr. Lockwood's Application," *Evening Star*, October 28, 1869, 4.

14. Belva A. Lockwood, "The Women Who Tried to Vote," *LDJ*, May 13, 1871, 1. It is likely that Jessie died of typhoid fever.

15. Ibid., 1.

16. Lockwood, "My Efforts," 222. In 1954 National merged with George Washington University (once Columbian College, later Columbian University.).

17. Lockwood completed classes in the spring of 1872. Lockwood to Julia Ward Howe, 21 March 1887, Howe Papers, Chapin Library of Rare Books, Williams College.

18. Lockwood, "My Efforts," 222–23. Lura was enrolled in the program in May 1871. She did not, however, complete the course of study. Lockwood, "The Women Who Tried to Vote," *LDJ*, May 13, 1871, 1. As late as June 1871, Belva expected Lura to finish. Lockwood to Isabella Beecher Hooker, 17 June 1871, Stowe Center Library, Hartford, CT. Susan A. Edson and Caroline B. Winslow attended in the first quarter. The class also included one African-American man, William T. Greener. "Humphreys' Adminx.," 3, Papers of Belva A. Lockwood, SCPC.

19. Lockwood, "My Efforts," 223.

20. Ibid., 223.

21. Ibid., 223.

22. Ibid., 223.

23. So called by Lord Coke. Steve Sheppard, ed., *The History of Legal Education in the United States: Commentaries and Primary Sources* (Pasadena, CA: Salem Press, 1999), 1:292.

24. E.g., New Hampshire from 1842 until 1872. Robert Steven, *Law School: Legal Education in America from the 1850s to the 1980s* (Chapel Hill: University of North Carolina Press, 1983), 9.

25. "Female Lawyers," *Evening Star*, April 23, 1872, 4.

26. Lockwood, "My Efforts," 223.

27. Ibid., 223.

28. Ibid., 223.

29. "Women as Attorneys in Washington," *Chicago Legal News*, April 20, 1872, 220.

30. Lockwood, "My Efforts," 223.

31. Ibid., 223.

32. "Theodore Tilton," *The Golden Age*, September 14, 1872, 5.

33. Lockwood, "My Efforts," 223.

34. Robert C. Williams, *Horace Greeley: Champion of American Freedom* (New York: New York University Press, 2006), 274–78 and 299–307.

35. Ellen Carol Dubois, ed., *The Elizabeth Cady Stanton–Susan B. Anthony Reader*, rev. ed. (Boston: Northeastern University Press, 1992), 107.

36. "Campaign Notes," *The Golden Age*, August 24, 1872, 5.

37. *Woman's Journal*, October 19, 1872, 1.

38. Ibid., 1.

39. B. A. Lockwood, "The Old North State," *The Golden Age*, August 17, 1872, 3. She did not remind her readers that Greeley had been one of the men who, believing Jefferson Davis should be tried or released from prison, had posted bail bond for him in 1867. Williams, *Horace Greeley*, 272.

40. "Campaign Notes," 5; B. A. Lockwood, "Canvassing for 'The Golden Age,'" September 14, 1872, 3.

41. Mrs. B. A. Lockwood, "Southern Immigration," *The Golden Age*, October 12, 1872, 2.

42. Ibid., 2.

43. Lockwood, "Southern Immigration," 2.

44. Rebecca Edwards, *New Spirits: Americans in the Gilded Age, 1865–1905* (New York: Oxford University Press, 2006), 23–29.

45. Belva A. Lockwood, "Women of Washington," *The Golden Age*, December 21, 1872, 2.

46. Daniel R. Ernst, with Laura A. Bedard, *The First 125 Years: An Illustrated History of the Georgetown University Law Center* (Washington, DC: Georgetown University Law Center, 1995), 9–10. The law department at Georgetown opened in 1870. It was a night school.

47. Lockwood, "My Efforts," 224.

48. Lura McNall, "Our Washington Letter," *LDJ*, February 10, 1872, 1.

49. Lockwood, "My Efforts," 224.

50. Ibid., 224.

51. Belva Lockwood, "Humphreys' Adminx. v. the U.S.," 6.

52. Lockwood to Grant, 3 September 1873. Dreer Autograph Collection, the Historical Society of Pennsylvania.

53. Lockwood, "My Efforts," 224.

54. Virginia G. Drachman, *Hospital with a Heart* (Ithaca, NY: Cornell University Press, 1984).

55. Brooke Kroeger, *Nellie Bly* (New York: Random House, 1994), 196.

56. Lockwood, "My Efforts," 224.

NOTES TO CHAPTER 5

1. *HWS*, 3:31.

2. *HWS*, 3:28.

3. Ibid., 29, 35.

4. Lois Beachy Underhill, *The Woman Who Ran for President* (Bridgehampton, NY: Bridge Works Publishing, 1995), 66–69.

5. *New York Herald*, April 2, 1870, reproduced, in part, in Underhill, *The Woman Who Ran for President*, 77–79. Woodhull's biographers differ as to whether she originated the idea of conducting the campaign. Underhill at 57 and Barbara Goldsmith, *Other Powers* (New York: Knopf, 1998), 212.

6. Underhill, *The Woman Who Ran for President*, 98–99.

7. *Act to enforce the Right of Citizens of the United States to vote in the several States of this Union*, 16 U.S. Stat. 140; also, Eric Foner, *A Short History of Reconstruction* (New York: Harper & Row, 1990), 195–96; and "The Memorial of Victoria C. Woodhull," December 19, 1870, reprinted in Madeleine B. Stern, ed., *The Victoria Woodhull Reader* (Weston, MA: M & S Press, 1974), n.p.

8. "Woman's Right to Vote," *Evening Star*, January 11, 1871, 1.

9. "Memorial of Belva A. Lockwood and Others, with the Moral and Constitutional Argument in Support of the Same," written January 21, 1871, and submitted to the Senate by Samuel C. Pomeroy of Kansas on January 23, 1871, Rare Book Division, LC. Similar language, but not identical in wording, occurs in a second essay by Lockwood, Caroline Winslow, and Susan A. Edson, "Memorial of Citizens of the District of Columbia in Favor of Impartial Suffrage, and Asking to Have That Right Secured in the Bill Reorganizing Government for the District," RG 46, Box 157, NA.

10. Lockwood, et al., "Memorial of Citizens of the District," 5.

11. "Memorial of Belva A. Lockwood and Others, with the Moral and Constitution Argument in Support of the Same," 4. All quotations in this paragraph are from this page of the memorial.

12. *An act to provide a Government for the District of Columbia*, February 21, 1871, ch. 62, 41st Cong., 3d Sess. See Section 7, referring to "male citizens."

13. *HWS*, 3:812.

14. Report No. 22 of the U.S. House of Representatives on the Memorial of Victoria C. Woodhull, January 30, 1871, in Stern, *The Victoria Woodhull Reader*, n.p.

15. Ibid.

16. A. G. Riddle, "The Right of Women to Exercise the Elective Franchise under the Fourteenth Article of the Constitution" (Washington, DC: Judd & Detweiler, January 11, 1871), 13–14, in *History of Women*, reel 406, item 2935, LC.

17. *HWS*, 2:496.

18. "A New Phase of the Woman Question," *Evening Star*, April 14, 1871, 2.

19. "Want to Vote," *Evening Star*, April 14, 1871, 4.

20. "Demonstration at the Board of Registration Yesterday," *Daily National Republican*, April 15, 1871, 4.

21. "'Grace Greenwood'" on the Woman Question and 'The Star,'" *Evening Star*, April 17, 1871, 2; "The Would-be Women Voters," *National Republican*, April 15, 1871, 2; "The Ballot and Wages," *National Republican*, April 19, 1871, 2.

22. "To the Ladies of the District," *Evening Star*, April 16, 1871, 2.

23. "Woman Suffrage: The Ladies Hold a Meeting," *Daily National Republican*, April 19, 1871, 4.

24. *Congressional Globe*, 39th Cong., 2d Sess., December 11, 1866, 63, 65.

25. "Woman Suffrage in Washington," *Woman's Journal*, April 29, 1871, 129.

26. "Woman Suffrage: The Ladies Hold a Meeting," 4.

27. "Election Results," *Evening Star*, April 20, 1871, 1.

28. "Female Balloteers," *National Republican*, April 21, 1871, 1.

29. "Second Edition: Later Returns," *Evening Star*, April 20, 1871, 1.

30. "Female Balloteers," 1.

31. *Sara Spencer v Martin, et al.*, RG 21, Law 8467, NA; and *Sarah E. Webster v. Griffin, et al.*, RG 21, Law 8468, NA. Mrs. Griffing also brought suit, according to the *Woman's Journal*, May 6, 1871, 137. Her death in 1872 ended that lawsuit. There is no explanation as to how the plaintiffs were chosen or why Lockwood was not one of them.

32. Webster and Spencer sued to recover five hundred dollars from the board of registration members and twenty-five hundred dollars from the judges of election in her district. "Transcript of Record in case of Sarah E. Webster v. E. W. W. Griffin & others," RG 267, Appellate Jurisdiction Files 6206–7, NA; "Have Women the Right to Vote?" *Evening Star*, April 24, 1871, 1.

33. Lockwood to Dr. Mary Walker, 29 July 1871, Belva Lockwood Papers, SU.

34. "Woman's Rights: Registration and Equal Pay," *Morning Chronicle*, July 15, 1871.

35. Ibid.

36. Lockwood to Walker, July 29, 1871.

37. "Woman's Suffrage in the Supreme Court of the District of Columbia: Argument of the Counsel for the Plaintiffs; Opinions of the Court" (Washington, DC: Judd & Detweiler, 1871), 4, Rare Books and Special Collections, LC.

38. A. G. Riddle, "Suffrage Conferred by the Fourteenth Amendment. Woman's Suffrage in the Supreme Court of the District of Columbia in General Term, October 1871. Sara J. Spencer vs. The Board of Registration, and Sarah E. Webster vs. The Judges of Election. Argument of the Counsel for the Plaintiffs with the Opinions of the Court" (Washington, DC: Judd and Detweiler, 1871), 5–6, in *History of Women*, reel 406, item 2936, LC.

39. Riddle, "Suffrage Conferred," 35–56. Riddle refers to the problems that Myra Bradwell's lawyer, Matthew Carpenter, had created with his particular interpretation of the Fourteenth Amendment, 25, 30.

40. "Opinion of the Court" in Riddle, "Suffrage Conferred," 69.

41. Ibid., 72. Docket book records for the two cases show that a denial was issued on September 13, 1871, and that, after an appeal for a rehearing was filed, the original denial was sustained on November 11, 1871, RG 21, Supreme Court of the District of Columbia Docket Book, vol. 9, NA.

42. Susan B. Anthony, *An Account of the proceedings on the trial of Susan B. Anthony, on the charge of illegal voting, at the presidential election in Nov. 1872, and on the trial of Beverly W. Jones, Edwin T. Marsh and William B. Hall, the inspectors of election by whom her vote was received* (1874). Rare Books and Special Collections, LC. As part of New Departure direct action, Marilla M. Ricker of New

Hampshire unsuccessfully attempted to vote in March 1870. Nannette E. Gardner registered and "voted unquestioned" in the April 3, 1871, election in Detroit, Michigan, *HWS*, 2:586–87 and 3:406. On women voting before the New Departure, see Ellen Carol Dubois, "Taking the Law into Our Own Hands," in Marjorie Spruill Wheeler, ed., *One Woman, One Vote* (Troutdale, OR: New Sage Press, 1995), 86.

43. Ellen Carol DuBois, *The Elizabeth Cady Stanton–Susan B. Anthony Reader* (Boston: Northeastern University Press, 1992), 103–4.

44. Memo No. 22, *Sarah E. Webster vs. E. W. W. Griffin, et al.*, RG 267, United States. Supreme Court File, Appellate Jurisdiction Case 6206 and 6207, NA. Riddle and Miller may have hoped for a dismissal *sua sponte* (for inaction).

45. *Bradwell v. Illinois*, 83 U.S. 130 (1873).

46. *Bradwell*, 139.

47. It is significant that the *Slaughter-House Cases*, 83 U.S. 36 (1873), dealing with the right to labor of men, produced a 5–4 vote, whereas the vote in *Bradwell*, rejecting the claims of a woman, was 8–1.

48. For Riddle's comments on Carpenter, see Riddle, "Suffrage Conferred," 25–30.

49. Jane M. Friedman, *America's First Woman Lawyer* (Buffalo, NY: Prometheus Books, 1993), 22. There is uncertainty whether Bradwell gave permission to Carpenter to argue that the Fourteenth Amendment did not enfranchise women.

50. Friedman, *America's First Woman Lawyer*, 22–23.

51. *Minor v. Happersett*, 88 U.S. 162 (1875). In their brief the Minors also presented a First Amendment argument. Philip B. Kurland and Gerhard Carper, eds., *Landmark Briefs and Arguments of the Supreme Court of the United States: Constitutional Law* (Arlington, VA: University Publications of America, 1975), 7:245–46.

52. *Minor*, 178.

53. Susan B. Anthony to Isabella Beecher Hooker and Olympia Brown, 4 January 1875, in Ann D. Gordon, ed., *The Selected Papers of Elizabeth Cady Stanton and Susan B. Anthony*, vol. 3 (New Brunswick, NJ: Rutgers University Press, 2003), 29.

NOTES TO CHAPTER 6

1. "Mrs. Lockwood's Victory," *Chicago Legal News*, March 2, 1878, 191.

2. Lockwood, "My Efforts to Become a Lawyer," *Lippincott's Magazine*, February 1888, 225.

3. Ibid., 225.

4. Ibid., 225.

5. Editor, "Mrs. Lockwood's Application for Admission in the Court of Claims," *Chicago Legal News*, April 11, 1874, 233; Marion T. Bennett, *The United States Court of Claims, a History: Part I—The Judges, 1855–1976* (Washington, DC: Committee on the Bicentennial of Independence, 1976), 40.

6. Lockwood, "My Efforts," 225.

7. Ibid., 225. Bradwell reprinted the Court of Claims opinion along with her editorial. *Chicago Legal News*, May 23, 1874, 277–78, 281.

8. Hendrik Hartog, *Man and Wife in America* (Cambridge, MA: Harvard University Press, 2000), 115–22.

9. *In re Mrs. Belva A. Lockwood, Ex Parte*, 9 Ct. Cl. 346, 347 (1873).

10. Ibid., 347.

11. "An Act regulating the Rights of Property of Married Women in the District of Columbia," April 10, 1869, 16 U.S. Stat. (1871), 45.

12. "An Act prescribing the Form of enacting and resolving Clauses of Acts and Resolutions of Congress, and Rules for the Construction thereof," February 25, 1871, 16 U.S. Stat. (1871), 431.

13. 9 Ct. Cl. 346, 348.

14. Lockwood, "My Efforts," 225.

15. J. Clay Smith, Jr., *Emancipation: The Making of the Black Lawyer, 1844–1944* (Philadelphia: University of Pennsylvania Press, 1993), 43.

16. 9 Ct. Cl. 346, 352.

17. Lockwood, "My Efforts," 226.

18. Lura McNall, "Our Washington Letter," *LDJ*, May 20, 1874, 2.

19. "Mrs. Lockwood, and the Late Associate Knott of the Court of Claims Now Retired" [sic], 2–3. Papers of Belva A. Lockwood, SCPC.

20. Lockwood, "My Efforts," 226.

21. *Bradwell v. Illinois*, 83 U.S. 130, 141 (1873).

22. Jane M. Friedman, *America's First Woman Lawyer: The Biography of Myra Bradwell* (Buffalo, NY: Prometheus Books, 1993), 29.

23. "Mrs. Belva A. Lockwood," *Chicago Legal News*, May 4, 1872, 236.

24. Harvey B. Hurd, ed., *The Revised Statutes of the State of Illinois, 1874* (Springfield: Illinois Journal Co., 1874), 169.

25. *Journal of the House of Representatives*, May 18, 1874, 982; Belva Lockwood, "Brief, Sustaining Petition of Belva A. Lockwood," May 1874, Records of the U.S. Senate, Sen. 41-48A, A-J6, Box 101. Misdated May 1884, NA.

26. Lockwood, "Brief, Sustaining Petition of Belva A. Lockwood," 3.

27. Ibid., 2–3.

28. H.R., *Minutes*, December 9, 1873–March 3, 1875, Committee on the Judiciary, 43rd Cong., 1st & 2d Sess., May 25, 1874.

29. *Congressional Record*, House, 43rd Cong., 1st Sess., June 1, 1874, 4447–48.

30. *Journal of the Senate of the United States*, 43rd Cong., 1st Sess., May 25, 1874, 610.

31. *Journal of the Senate of the United States*, 43rd Cong., 2d Sess., February 16, 1875, 273.

32. Lockwood, "My Efforts," 226–27, where she offers a convoluted explanation of this decision.

33. Susan B. Anthony, *An Account of the Proceedings on the Trial of Susan B. Anthony on the Charge of Illegal Voting at the Presidential Election in Nov. 1872* (Rochester, NY: Daily Democrat and Chronicle Book Print, 1874), Rare Book Room, LC, 65–66.

34. Supreme Court of the United States, *Minutes*, November 6, 1876.

35. Malvina Shanklin Harlan, *Some Memories of a Long Life, 1854–1911* (New York: Modern Library, 2002), 100.

36. Ibid., 101.

37. Ibid., 101.

38. Papers of Morrison R. Waite, November 6, 1876, Docket Book, Container 30, Manuscript Division, LC.

39. Lockwood, "My Efforts," 227. Myra Bradwell mocked the Court's mulish love of English precedent. *Chicago Legal News*, February 10, 1877, 169.

40. Harlan, *Some Memories*, 100.

41. He published *The Life, Character, and Public Services of Jas. A. Garfield* (Cleveland, OH: W.W. Williams, 1883). His unpublished texts are found at the Western Reserve Historical Society, Cleveland, Ohio.

42. *HWS*, 3:64.

43. Ibid., 3:65.

44. *Congressional Record*, House, 44th Cong., 2d Sess., January 16, 1877, 661–62; "Women's Right to Practice in the U.S. Courts," *Chicago Legal News*, February 10, 1877, 169; Lura McNall, "Our Washington Letter," *LDJ*, January 30, 1877, 2.

45. "Mrs. Lockwood's Victory," *Chicago Legal News*, March 2, 1878, 191.

46. Lockwood, "My Efforts," 227.

47. "Affidavit of Lura McNall," 2, *In re Estate of James Farr*, RG 21, Old Series Guardianship Case 2578, NA.

48. Eighteen hundred and seventy Illinois Census Schedule, M-593, Roll No. 231, 310, lines 11–12 and M-653, Roll No. 231, 310, lines 30–34.

49. "Died: Bennett," *Evening Star*, July 10, 1877, 3.

50. H.R., *Minutes*, October 31, 1877–March 3, 1879, Committee on the Judiciary, 45th Cong., 1st, 2d, & 3d Sess., December 7, 1877, 41.

51. *Congressional Record*, House, 45th Cong., 2d Sess., February 21, 1878, 1235.

52. Ibid., 1235.

53. "Belva Lockwood, 82 Years Young," (New York) *World*, November 3, 1912, N5.

54. Ibid.

55. Lura McNall, "Our Washington Letter," *LDJ*, May 8, 1878, 2.

56. *Congressional Record*, Senate, 45th Cong., 2d Sess., March 18, 1878, 1821.

57. "Shall Women Be Admitted to Practice Law in the Federal Courts?" *Chicago Legal News*, March 23, 1878, 215.

58. Barbara Allen Babcock, "Clara Shortridge Foltz: 'First Woman.'" *Arizona Law Review* 30 (1988): 687.

59. Ibid., 688.

60. *Congressional Record*, Senate, 45th Cong., 2d Sess., April 22, 1878, 2704.

61. Ibid., 2704.

62. Ibid., 2704.

63. *Congressional Record*, Senate, 45th Cong., 2d Sess., May 20, 1878, 3558.

64. Ibid., 3558.

65. Ibid., 3558.

66. Ibid., 3559.

67. *Congressional Record*, Senate, 45th Cong., 2d Sess., May 29, 1878, 3889.

68. Ibid., 3889–90.

69. "Was Mrs. Belva A. Lockwood Admitted to Practice Law in the State of Virginia?" *The Law Student's Helper* 1 (1893): 200. Lockwood writes that she was admitted in the summer of 1878, but the certificate of admission that she submitted to the editor is dated 21 September 1879, http://www.stanford.edu/group/wlhp/profiles/belvalockwood.shtml.

70. "Mrs. Lockwood's Case," *Chicago Legal News*, November 16, 1878, 70–71; Lura McNall, "Our Washington Letter," *LDJ*, October 23, 1878, 2.

71. Item from the *Springfield Republican* found in Lucy Stone's 1878 diary but incorrectly dated 1877. National American Woman Suffrage Association Collection (NAWSA), Reel 12, Manuscript Division, LC. She had support from Richard T. Greener, the Acting Dean of the Law Department of Howard University, who invited her to lecture, "to pay a slight tribute to your success in a difficult profession under extraordinary disadvantages." Greener to Lockwood, 7 December 1878, quoted in Julia Winner, *Belva A. Lockwood* (Lockport, NY: NCHS, 1969), 18.

72. *Congressional Record*, Senate, 45th Cong., 3d Sess., February 7, 1879, 1083.

73. H. B. B., "Women's Lawyers in the United States Supreme Court, February 22, 1879" (possibly the diary of Harriet Butler), 1, NAWSA, Reel 12, Manuscript Division, LC.

74. *Journal of the Senate*, February 7, 1879, 45th Cong., 3d Sess., 230–37.

75. Ibid., 236.

76. Lura McNall, "Our Washington Letter," *LDJ*, May 1, 1878, 2.

77. Lura McNall, "Our Washington Letter," *LDJ*, April 12, 1878, 2.

78. Emily Edson Briggs, *The Olivia Letters* (New York: Neale Publishing Co., 1906), 344–45.

79. *Congressional Record*, Senate, February 7, 1879, 1082–83.

80. Ibid., 1082–83.

81. Ibid., 1084.

82. Ibid., 1084–85.

83. 20 U.S. Stat. 292 (1879).

84. Lockwood, "My Efforts," 229; "The Surprise," *LDJ*, February 17, 1879, 2. Mary Walker may have written this *LDJ* article.

85. "Woman's Right to Practice before the United States Supreme Court," *LDJ*, February 11, 1879, 2; Lura McNall, "Our Washington Letter," *LDJ*, February 18, 1879, 2.

86. "Admission of Women to the Bar," *Chicago Legal News*, February 15, 1879, 179.

87. Ibid., 179.

88. "Mrs. Lockwood's Victory," *Washington Post*, March 5, 1879, 1.

89. "The Courts," *National Republican*, March 4, 1879, 3.

90. "Mrs. Lockwood's Victory," 1.

91. Ibid., 1.

92. Lura McNall, "Our Washington Letter," *LDJ*, March 6, 1879, 2; "Mrs. Lockwood's Victory," *Woman's Journal*, April 12, 1879, 118, and *Washington Post*, March 5, 1879, 1.

NOTES TO CHAPTER 7

1. James Densmore to Tina Densmore, 16 June 1881, 2. Original in the possession of Christopher Densmore, West Chester, Pennsylvania.

2. Julia Hull Winner, *Belva A. Lockwood* (Lockport, NY: NCHS, 1969), 97.

3. Thomas G. Shearman, "The Owners of the United States," *The Forum* 8 (November 1889): 265.

4. Charles C. Jones, *The Necessity for Increasing the Salaries of the Judicial Officers of Georgia* (Macon, GA: J.W. Burke & Co., 1885), 14 and appendix.

5. Evidence is spare but Ezekiel was acting as an agent as early as December 1869. *Journal of the Senate*, 41st Cong., 2d Sess., December 22, 1869, 66, March 16, 1870, 378, and April 25, 1870. Early evidence of his work as a guardian appears in RG 21, Old Series Guardianship Case 2141, NA. In 1870 he gave up his dental practice. He sold his instruments and rented his office to a local man, James M. McCauley. *Ezekiel Lockwood v.*

John J. Callahan, Administrator of James M. McCauley, RG 21, Law Case 11854, NA. In 1871 Ezekiel changed his listing in *Boyd's City Directory* from "dentist" to "claim agent."

6. RG 21, Old Series Guardianship Case 2578, NA.

7. Belva A. Lockwood to Dr. Mary Walker, 29 July 1871, Belva Lockwood Papers, SU.

8. Virginia G. Drachman, *Women Lawyers and the Origins of Professional Identity in America: The Letters of the Equity Club, 1887–1890* (Ann Arbor: University of Michigan Press, 1993), 58; "Belva Lockwood, 82 Years Young," *The World*, November 3, 1912, 5.

9. Police Court was established in 1870 to give the D.C. Supreme Court relief in matters of minor criminal offenses. Act of June 17, 1870, 16 Stat. 153.

10. Belva Lockwood to Dr. Mary Walker, 28 September 1871, Belva Lockwood Papers, SU.

11. Lura McNall, "Our Washington Letter," *LDJ*, September 3, 1873, 2.

12. Lura McNall, "Our Washington Letter," *LDJ*, November 21, 1873, 2.

13. Belva Ann Lockwood, "My Efforts to Become a Lawyer," *Lippincott's Magazine*, February 1888, 224.

14. *Washington Law Reporter*, February 4, 1878, 39.

15. Drachman, *Women Lawyers*, 113.

16. "Local News," *Evening Star*, August 17, 1874, 4.

17. Lockwood, "My Efforts," 224.

18. Jeffrey Brandon Morris, *Calmly to Poise the Scales of Justice: A History of the Courts of the District of Columbia Circuit* (Durham, NC: Carolina Academic Press, 2001), xvii. In the Anglo-American system, equity law follows from the principle that no right should be without an adequate remedy. For a more detailed summary of Lockwood's cases, see Jill Norgren, "Before It Was Merely Difficult," *Journal of Supreme Court History* 23 (1999): 25–27.

19. Lockwood is listed as the sole attorney of record in 80 percent of her criminal cases.

20. RG 21, Equity Case 4840, NA.

21. Belva A. Lockwood to D.C. Board of Commissioners, 30 April 1877, RG 351, Register of Letters Received, vol. 8, NA.

22. Belva A. Lockwood to Edward M. Davis, 13 August 1877, Joseph Rubinfine, Catalogue 63/64, sold into a private collection.

23. Board of Health, District of Columbia, Certificate of Death, Ezekiel Lockwood.

24. District of Columbia Recorder of Deeds, Liber 862, Folio 453–54, recorded August 2, 1877. Julia C. Russell, wife of Alexander, owned the property and consented to its sale.

25. District of Columbia Recorder of Deeds, Liber 862, Folio 448, recorded August 2, 1877.

26. RG 21, Equity Case 10677, NA. The trust on 619 F Street was released in the late 1880s. District of Columbia Recorder of Deeds, Liber 1588, Folio 384.

27. Winner, *Belva A. Lockwood*, 99.

28. Mrs. E. N. Chapin, *American Court Gossip; or, Life at the National Capitol* (Marshalltown, IA: Chapin & Hartwell, 1887), 32.

29. In the 1880 Census Hannah Bennett's name appears as a resident of Lockwood's household in the District of Columbia as well as that of her eldest daughter's (Rachel Bennett Robinson) Onarga, Illinois, household. As was customary, Hannah visited back and forth. Microcopy T-9, Roll No. 123, 255, line 45 and T-9, Roll No. 214, 291, line 38. Rachel's husband, James, had been born in Canada in 1833. His occupation is given as livery/stable keeper.

30. Inez Ormes, "Certificate of Death," Record No. 69811, Washington, D.C. Rhoda's name, followed by "1884–1884," is inscribed on the Ormes family tombstone at Washington's Congressional Cemetery. The exact day and month of her birth is not known. She died the second week of March 1884.

31. Lella Gardner to Ellen Brinton, 7 July 1938, DG 00, Box 10, Records of the SCPC.

32. "Belva Lockwood, 82 Years Young," N5; Affidavit of Clara B. Wagner, (n.d.), 4, RG 21, Equity Case 7177, NA.

33. Harrison is described as a law student in Lura's wedding announcement: "Marriage of Miss Lura McNall," *Evening Star*, July 5, 1879, 4. Testimony that he was a clerk and notary in Lockwood's office is found in the complaint of Charles Pealing, January 27, 1881, and October 13, 1881, RG 15, Law Division, Pension Claims File, Attorneys, 1862–1933, Box 329, B. A. Lockwood, NA. From 1880 to 1884 Lockwood's business letters and documents show Harrison's notary seal and signature. Lockwood motioned his appointment as U.S. Commissioner and Examiner in Chancery. RG 21, General Term Minutes, 1863–1893, 4: 183; his October 1881 D.C. bar admission is noted here at 164.

34. Lura and DeForest Ormes may have lived in New York for a year in the early 1880s.

35. "Lura McNall," *Boyd's City Directory*, 1871, 1874.

36. Petition of Betsey Foreman, RG 21, Old Series Guardianship Case 2578, NA.

37. She wrote for the (New York) *Lockport Daily Journal*. Her wedding announcement indicates that these "letters" were also published in Maryland and Indiana. "Marriage of Miss Lura McNall," *LDJ*, July 8, 1879, 2.

38. The 1880 District of Columbus Census Schedule gives DeForest's age incorrectly as thirty-four; the 1900 D.C. Census lists DeForest, Sr., as age fifty-six, born April 1844 in Massachusetts.

39. Reprinted as "Marriage of Miss Lura McNall," *LDJ*, July 8, 1879, 2.

40. Nellie Bly, "Woman's Part in Politics," *The World*, August 12, 1888, 13; also, Lura McNall, "Our Washington Letter," *LDJ*, December 27, 1879, 2.

41. Laura [sic] McNall, "Our Antipodes," *LDJ*, June 7, 1881, 4. Lura's first "Letter from Europe" appears in the *LDJ*, January 5, 1881. They continue at regular intervals, concluding with two filed from Bombay and published on June 7 and June 15, 1881.

42. Lura McNall, "India," *LDJ*, June 15, 1881, 2.

43. Bly, "Woman's Part in Politics," 13; *In re Estate of James Kelly*, December 6, 1894, 4–5, RG 21, Equity Case 7177, NA.

44. Complaint of William Ward, Sworn Statement of Clara B. Harrison, September 24, 1887, 1, RG 15, Law Division, Pension Claims Files, Attorneys, 1862–1933, Box 329, B. A. Lockwood, NA.

45. Bly, "Woman's Part in Politics," 13.

46. Letter of B. A. Lockwood, 23 October 1886, RG 15, Law Division, Pension Claims File, Attorneys, 1862–1933, Box 329, NA.

47. Lura McNall Ormes, Certificate of Death, Washington, D.C., Record No. 94,122.

48. J. Nat Steed, "A Half-Century in Washington: Personal Adventures with the Great and Near Great," 1–2, Belva Lockwood File, Historical Society of Washington, D.C.

49. Lura McNall, "Our Washington Letter," *LDJ*, November 21, 1877, 2.

50. Belva A. Lockwood to Julia Ward Howe, 21 March 1887, Howe Papers, Chapin Library of Rare Books, Williams College, describing the work of women attorneys. In 1891 Ricker became a member of the U.S. Supreme Court bar.

51. "Women as Notaries," *National Republican*, December 20, 1877, 1.

52. In 1884 Ricker was appointed to the quasi judicial position of U.S. commissioner and examiner in Chancery. In New Hampshire, she brought the challenge that opened the state bar to women lawyers. Still struggling to open high-level government service to women, in the late 1890s she made an unsuccessful request of President William McKinley to appoint her to a diplomatic post in South America. *Ricker's Petition*, 66 N.H. 207, 29 Atl. 559 (1890); John Reid, *Chief Justice: The Judicial World of Charles Doe* (Cambridge, MA: Harvard University Press, 1967), 161–62 and 284–85.

53. Virginia G. Drachman, *Women Lawyers and the Origins of Professional Identity in America: The Letters of the Equity Club, 1887 to 1890* (Ann Arbor: University of Michigan Press, 1993), 96.

54. Grace Hathaway, *Fate Rides a Tortoise: A Biography of Ellen Spencer Mussey* (Chicago: John C. Winston Co., 1937), 107–8. Mussey and Gillett began with the idea of a program for women but quickly made it coeducational. In 1876 Lockwood and eight Washington women had incorporated a school

called the Women's National University to provide women, in a nonhostile environment, "a thorough knowledge of Science, law, Divinity and Medicine." Incorporation Certificate, June 30, 1876, Acts of Incorporation, Liber 2, Folio 105, D.C. Archives and Records Center; Belva Lockwood to Matilda Gage, *Ballot Box*, September 1876, in *The Papers of Susan B. Anthony*, Scrapbook, Microfilm 3570, Reel 18, LC.

55. Dundore was active in the UPU and attended its meetings in Washington as early as February 1868, *Bond of Peace*, Microfilm 13.1, SCPC.

56. Claim of Margaret Pote, RG 15, Law Division, Pension Claims File, Attorneys, 1832–1933, Box 329, B. A. Lockwood, NA.

57. Answer of L. C. Dundore, *Smith v. Dyer*, 6–7, RG 21, Equity 5874, NA.

58. Allen C. Clarke, "Belva Ann Lockwood," *Records of the Columbia Historical Society* 35 (1935), 215.

59. Lura McNall, "Our Washington Letter," *LDJ*, January 3, 1878, 2; *HWS*, 3:72. During her account of Dundore's unsuccessful attempt to become a constable at the January 1878 NWSA convention, Lockwood told the membership that women were ready for open rebellion. She offered an explicit and radical dare. Women, she argued, would only get their rights if they took them, and to get them it might be necessary to carry out a "domestic insurrection." She suggested that "young women refuse to marry, and married women refuse to sew on buttons, cook, and rock the cradle until their liege-lords acknowledge the rights they are entitled to." *HWS*, 3:3.

60. Letter of Lavinia C. Dundore, June 26, 1879, stating that she was present when the attorney demanded of the pensioner an illegal fee in complaint of Margaret Pote, RG 15, Law Division, Pension Claims File, Attorneys, 1862–1933, Box 329, B. A. Lockwood, NA.

61. Brief of the Committee, 3, RG 21, Equity Case 7177, NA.

62. Affidavit of Clara B. Wagner, 4. Rebecca is listed in *Boyd's* as living at 619 F Street in 1881 and 1882, occupation "servant."

63. Brief of the Committee, 3.

64. Brief of the Committee, 4.

65. Affidavit of Clara B. Wagner, 3–4.

66. "In Acct with Belva A. Lockwood, Exhibit 8," *Rucker v. Lockwood*, Filed Sept. 12, 1907, 1–2, RG 21, Equity 49662, NA.

67. Pamela Scott and Antoinette J. Lee, *Buildings of the District of Columbia* (New York: Oxford University Press, 1993), 183–86. It was completed in 1887 and is now the National Building Museum.

68. Belva A. Lockwood to Mrs. J. W. Stow, 4 November 1882, reprinted in *Woman's Herald of Industry*, January 1883, 4.

69. "Familiar Characters: Mrs. Belva Lockwood and Her New Tricycle," *The Post*, March 5, 1882, (n.p.), Belva Lockwood File, Historical Society of Washington, D.C.

70. "Belva Mounts Her Pegasus," *The Post*, March 7, 1882, (n.p.), Belva Lockwood File, Historical Society of Washington, D.C.

71. Winner, *Belva A. Lockwood*, 94.

72. Terry Precision Cycling Catalogue, Fall 2001, "Unfettered Liberty" and "Celestial Cycle," 36.

73. Lisa Larrabee, "Women and Cycling: The Early Years," in Frances E. Willard, *How I Learned to Ride the Bicycle* (1895; reprint Sunnyvale, CA: Fair Oaks Publishing, 1991), 86.

74. Robert A. Smith, *A Social History of the Bicycle* (New York: McGraw-Hill, 1972), 66.

75. Ida Husted Harper, *Life and Work of Susan B. Anthony* (1898; reprint North Stratford, NH: Ayer Co., 1998), 2:859.

76. Drachman, *Women Lawyers*, 50.

77. Ibid., 57.

78. Ibid., 58.

79. Ibid., 58; Lockwood to Julia Ward Howe, 21 March 1887, 3. Howe Papers, Chapin Library of Rare Books, Williams College.

80. Drachman, *Women Lawyers*, 59.

81. Ibid., 164.

82. Ibid., 101, 156, and 159.

83. Ibid., 175.

NOTES TO CHAPTER 8

1. Lura McNall, "Washington Letter," *LDJ*, April 13, 1880, 2.

2. *Nichols v. Barber*, Original Bill, March 16, 1875, 1, RG 21, Law 13854, NA.

3. Defendant's Brief, RG 21, Law 13854, NA, 1.

4. Joinder in demurrer, August 28, 1875, 1, RG21, Law 13854, NA.

5. Defendant's Brief, 13854, 2–3.

6. Lura McNall, "Our Washington Letter," *LDJ*, June 17, 1879, 2.

7. "Charge of Child Murder," *Evening Star*, April 3, 1879, 4.

8. True bill, May 8, 1879, 2, RG 21, Criminal 12529, NA.

9. The Freedmen's Bureau provided legal aid to former slaves, raising the possibility that these attorneys were being paid through a publicly funded program. Maxwell Bloomfield, *American Lawyers in a Changing Society, 1776–1876* (Cambridge, MA: Harvard University Press, 1976), 345–46.

10. *U.S. v. Louisa Wallace*, United States Marshal's Office, Jurors' Recommendation, December 20, 1878, RG 21, Criminal 12529, NA.

11. Motion for a new trial, 1, RG 21, Criminal 12529, NA.

12. "Convicted of Murdering Her Infant," *Evening Star*, January 24, 1879, 4.

13. *U.S. v. Wallace*, Warden's Return: Witness List, March 28, 1879, RG 21, Supreme Court of the District of Columbia, Criminal Case 12845, NA.

14. "Prayer of deft.," April 4, 1879, 2–3, RG 21, Criminal Case 12845, NA.

15. Ibid., 3–4.

16. "The Child-Murder Case," *Evening Star*, April 5, 1879, 4; "The Conviction of Louisa Wallace," *Evening Star*, April 7, 1879, 4.

17. "Another Death Sentence," *Evening Star*, April 12, 1879, 4.

18. Ibid., 4.

19. Ibid., 4.

20. Reform of the criminal as well as civil law code was debated in Washington in this period. Lura McNall wrote that legislation had been proposed to make rape a capital offence in the District, commenting that "something should be done for the protection of those ladies who are forced to be out at night." *LDJ*, March 9, 1880, 2.

21. *Horton v. Morgan*, Lucy Horton to Mr. Jno. H. Morgan, 17 January 1878, 2, RG 21, Law 20954, NA.

22. *U.S. v. Lucy W. R. Horton*, Docket Book No. 13271, RG 21, NA.

23. *Horton v. Morgan*, Stenographer's transcript, Jan. 31 and February 4, 1880, 33, RG 21, Law 20954, NA.

24. Haywood J. Pearce, Jr., *Benjamin H. Hill* (1928; reprint New York: Negro Universities Press, 1969), 308.

25. Affidavit, February 20, 1880, reprinted by Lura McNall in her March 13, 1880, *LDJ* column.

26. "Jessie Raymond's Charge against Hon. B. H. Hill," *Evening Star*, March 3, 1880, 1.

27. Lura McNall, "Our Washington Letter," *LDJ*, March 3, 1880, 2.

28. "The Hill-Raymond Scandal," *Evening Star*, April 16, 1880, 1.

29. *Raymond v. Hill*, Notice to Plead, February 27, 1880, 1, RG 21, Law 21680, NA.

30. *Raymond*, Declaration, affidavit & notice to plead, March 2, 1880, RG 21, Law 21680, NA.

31. "Jessie Raymond," *Evening Star*, March 4, 1880, 4.

32. Lura McNall, "Our Washington Letter," *LDJ*, March 9, 1880, 2.

33. "A Sharp Letter," *Syracuse Standard*, reprinted *LDJ*, March 17, 1880, 2.

34. "The Raymond-Hill Scandal," *Evening Star*, March 23, 1880, 1.

35. Lura McNall, "Our Washington Letter," *LDJ*, March 15, 1880, 2. Hill acknowledged the snub, "Mrs. Lawyer Lockwood's Allegations against Senator Hill," *Evening Star*, March 13, 1880, 1.

36. *Raymond v. Hill*, Notice to Plead, February 27, 1880, 2, RG 21, Law 21680, NA.

37. "Jessie Raymond and Tommy," *Evening Star*, March 26, 1880, 1; "A Denial from Senator Hill," *Evening Star*, April 23, 1880, 1.

38. Item from the *Elmira Free Press*, reprinted *LDJ*, February 26, 1881, 2.

39. Ibid., 2.

40. *Kaiser v. Stickney*, 131 US clxxxvii Appx. (1889: "Cases Omitted"); U.S. Supreme Court Transcript of Record No. 90, *Kaiser v. Stickney*, Vol. IV, Part 2 (1880); Mike L. Woods, Brief for Appellant, Caroline Kaiser, author's files; Aravindra Seshadri, "Kaiser v. Stickney," http://www.law.stanford.edu/library/wlhbp/papers05/Lockwood_li-Seshadri05.pdf.

41. Kaiser owned buildings on Tenth Street quite near where the Lockwoods had lived.

42. "A Woman Case in the Supreme Court," *Evening Star*, December 2, 1880, 1.

43. Ibid.; *Rough Minutes of the Supreme Court of the United States, 1790–1985*, November 30 and December 1, 1880, vol. 56, RG 267, NA.

44. In 1882 Belva infuriated District Judge MacArthur by attempting to use her marriage to Ezekiel as a defense against a monetary judgment. "Verdict against Mrs. Lockwood," *Evening Star*, January 5, 1882, 4; generally, see the publications of Richard H. Chused.

45. Lura McNall, "Our Washington Letter," *LDJ*, February 11, 1880, 2.

46. Lowery's name is occasionally noted in the UPU's newsletter. See, *Peacemaker* 6 (1886–87): 126.

47. *Dred Scott v. Sandford*, 19 Howard 393 (1857); *Bradwell v. Illinois*, 16 Wallace 130 (1873).

48. *HWS*, 3:174.

49. *National Republican*, February 4, 1880, 1.

50. Reprinted in "Our Washington Letter," *LDJ*, February 11, 1880, 2.

51. Lockwood referred to herself as Dr. E. Lockwood's "partner and successor," letters of 18 and 20 March 1880, RG 15, Pension Claims File, Attorneys, 1862–1933, Box 329, "B. A. Lockwood," NA.

52. *United States v. Hall*, 98 U.S. 343, 353–55 (1878); 20 Stat. 243, June 20, 1878, and 23 Stat. 98, July 4, 1884.

53. "Belva Lockwood Is 86 Years Old," *Evening Star*, October 24, 1916, 10. In contrast, claims baron George E. Lemon said his law firm had processed fifty thousand filings and appeals. *Report of the House Select Committee on Pensions, Bounty, and Back Pay, House of Representatives*, 46th Cong., 3d Sess., vol. 1983, January 26, 1881, 390.

54. "The New Pension Bill Passed!" Letters to the Members of the Bull Family (BANC MSS 80/77z), Bancroft Library, University of California, Berkeley.

55. Virginia G. Drachman, *Women Lawyers and the Origins of Professional Identity in America* (Ann Arbor: University of Michigan Press, 1993), 57.

56. Veterans' pensions were granted by the Bureau of Pensions and by special acts (private bills) of Congress. From 1885 to 1887, "40 percent of the

legislation in the House and 55 percent in the Senate consisted of special pension acts." Morton Keller, *Affairs of State* (Cambridge, MA: Harvard University Press, 1977), 311.

57. For example, Belva Lockwood to Judson Grippen, Esq. (March 12, 1890). RG 15, Law Division, Pension Claims File, Attorneys, 1832–1933, Box 329, "B. A. Lockwood," NA.

58. Statement about Attorneys fee, January 19, 1898, 3, John Heck file, RG 15, Pension Claims File, Attorneys, 1832–1933, Box 329, "B. A. Lockwood," NA.

59. Ibid., Lockwood statement, March 1898, 2–3.

NOTES TO CHAPTER 9

1. Lura McNall, "Our Washington Letter," *LDJ*, March 16, 1878, 2.

2. Mrs. E. N. Chapin, *American Court Gossip; or, Life at the National Capitol* (Marshalltown, IA: Chapin & Hartwell, 1887), 31.

3. "A bill for the relief of Belva A. Lockwood," *Journal of the Senate*, 48th Cong., 1st Sess., 1283; "Petition of E. C. Curtiss, B. A. Lockwood, H. J. French to make Mineralogical and Geological investigations on Goat Island California," (n.d.); and "Petition," February 9, 1874, H.R. 43-A-H15.3, Committee on Public Lands, Various Subjects, Jan. 1874–Feb. 1874, NA.

4. "War Department—For the Payment of Bounties to sailors and marines," ch. 130, 18 Stat. 390 (1875).

5. Lockwood to Jane Addams, 17 January 1915, Papers of Belva A. Lockwood, SCPC.

6. Barbara Sapinsley, *The Private War of Mrs. Packard* (New York: Kodansha International, 1991); Mrs. E. P. W. Packard, *The Mystic Key; or, The Asylum Secret Unlocked* (Hartford, CT: Lockwood-Brainard Co., 1879), 133.

7. Donna Schuele, "In Her Own Way: Marietta Stow's Crusade for Probate Law Reform within the Nineteenth-Century Women's Rights Movement," *Yale Journal of Law and Feminism* 7 (1995): 281–85. Schuele demonstrates that Stow's figure was incorrect.

8. Mrs. J. W. Stow, *Probate Confiscation: Unjust Laws Which Govern Woman* (1876; reprint New York: Arno Press), 256.

9. In "Original Bills and a few other items considered, December 12, 1879–January 7, 1880," H.R. 2623, 46th Cong., 2d Sess. Stow's proposal was, however, introduced as "An Act to Regulate Estates in the District of Columbia and in the Territories of the United States."

10. Lura McNall, "Our Washington Letter," *LDJ*, September 25, 1879, 2.

11. "The Women's Convention," *National Republican*, January 22, 1880, 4.

12. "Our Public Schools," *Evening Star*, November 12, 1879, 4.

13. Ibid., 4; Belva A. Lockwood, "Women as Trustees," *LDJ*, November 18, 1879, 2.

14. "Our Public Schools," 4.

15. Lockwood, "Women as Trustees," 2.

16. "Our Public Schools," 4.

17. Lockwood, "Women as Trustees," 2.

18. *HWS*, 4:571–72.

19. Testimony of Belva A. Lockwood, December 16, 1879, in Behalf of the Widow's and Orphan's Bill, reprinted in *Woman's Herald of Industry*, December 1884, 2.

20. "Original Bills and a few other items considered, December 12, 1879–January 7, 1880."

21. Testimony, 2.

22. Ibid., 2.

23. "Work at the Capitol," *Washington Post*, December 17, 1879, 1; "Washington News and Gossip: Married Women's Rights," *Evening Star*, December 17, 1879, 1.

24. *Reynolds v. United States*, 98 U.S. 146 (1879).

25. Nancy F. Cott, *Public Vows: A History of Marriage and the Nation* (Cambridge, MA: Harvard University Press, 2000), in particular, 52–55 and 168–69.

26. *HWS*, 3:73.

27. "An Act to Establish a Reformatory Institution for Girls in the District of Columbia," in "Original Bills and a few other items considered, December 12, 1879–January 7, 1880." 46th Cong., 2d Sess., NA; Lura McNall, "Death of Judge Edmunds," *LDJ*, December 19, 1879, 2.

28. Lockwood to Dr. Clara McNaughton, 28 December 1901; Women's Suffrage Collection, Gleeson Library, University of San Francisco; *HWS*, 4:571.

29. *HWS*, 3:152.

30. Leonard J. Arrington, *Great Basin Kingdom* (Salt Lake City: University of Utah Press, 1993); and Howard R. Lamar, *Far Southwest, 1846–1912*, rev. ed. (Albuquerque: University of New Mexico Press, 2000).

31. Act of July 1, 1862, ch. 126, 1, 12 Stat. 501 (1862) (repealed 1910).

32. Edwin Brown Firmage and Richard Collin Mangrum, *Zion in the Courts* (Urbana: University of Illinois Press, 1988), 134–35; Sarah Barringer Gordon, *The Mormon Question: Polygamy and Constitutional Conflict in Nineteenth-Century America* (Chapel Hill: University of North Carolina Press, 2002), ch. 2.

33. In 1870 voting citizens of a U.S. territory cast ballots in local elections, for members of the territorial legislature, and for the territorial delegate to Congress.

34. Lola Van Wagenen, *Sister-Wives and Suffragists* (Ph.D. thesis, New York University, 1994), 6.

35. In the early 1870s, a number of Lockwood's Washington colleagues were adamant in their support of Mormon women. Van Wagenen, *Sister-Wives*, ch. 3; on Aaron Sargent's position, see *Congressional Globe*, January 16, 1873, 42nd Cong., 3d Sess. (Part 1), 646; and *Congressional Record*, February 28, 1876, 44th Cong., 1st Sess. (Part II), 1328.

36. "The Suffrage Movement," *National Republican*, January 29, 1876, 1; *HWS*, 3:5.

37. *HWS*, 3:6.

38. *HWS*, 3:5.

39. "National Woman Suffrage Association," *Evening Star*, January 9, 1879, 4.

40. *Reynolds*, 98 U.S. 146.

41. George Q. Cannon to John Taylor, 14 January 1882. John Taylor Presidential Papers, Church of Jesus Christ of Latter-day Saints Archives, Salt Lake City, Utah (hereafter LDS Church Archives).

42. Van Wagenen, *Sister-Wives*, 344–45.

43. "An act to amend . . . in reference to bigamy, and for other purposes," ch. 47, 8, 22 U.S. Stat. 30, March 22, 1882, in particular, section 8.

44. Van Wagenen, *Sister-Wives*, 344–45.

45. Belva A. Lockwood, "The Disfranchisement of the Women of Utah," *Woman's Exponent*, June 15, 1883, 12.

46. Emily Edson Briggs, *The Olivia Letters* (New York: Neale Pub. Co., 1906), 345.

47. "The Mormon Question," *Deseret Evening News*, March 29, 1884, 3. Lockwood and attorney Phoebe Couzins expressed interest in serving on the commission but President Arthur declined to consider either woman.

48. Van Wagenen, *Sister-Wives*, 349–50.

49. Ibid., 370–71; Ellen Carol Dubois, *Woman Suffrage, Women's Rights* (New York: New York University Press, 1998), 161.

50. "The Woman Suffrage Convention," *Evening Star*, January 24, 1883, 3. While the daily newspapers reported the full list of approved resolutions, the list subsequently published in the *HWS* does not include the resolution passed in support of the voting rights of Utah women. *HWS*, 3:256. The editors may have chosen to omit the resolution or may simply have made an error. There is no evidence to support one explanation over the other.

51. Reprinted in *Woman's Exponent*, June 15, 1883, 12ff. Quotations in this and the following two paragraphs are from this article.

52. *Chicago Inter Ocean*, February 1, 1883, cited in Beverly Beeton, *Women Vote in the West* (New York: Garland, 1986), 70.

53. "The Mormon Question," *Deseret Evening News*, March 29, 1884, 3.

54. Lockwood, "The Disfranchisement of the Women of Utah," 14.

55. George Q. Cannon to John Taylor, 30 January 1883. John Taylor Presidential Papers, 1877–1887, LDS Church Archives.

56. "Mrs. Lockwood's Speeches," *Woman's Exponent*, April 1, 1884, 164.

57. Ibid., 164.

58. Ibid., 164.

59. "Seeking Freedom," *National Republican*, March 6, 1884, 2.

60. "Mrs. Lockwood's Speeches," 164; "Seeking Freedom," *National Republican*, March 6, 1884, 2.

61. "Seeking Freedom," 2. Anthony maintained her commitment to the right of every woman, whether "Mormon or Gentile," to vote, and as late as 1890, at the last executive session of the NWSA, urged that the Nationals not go back on this record of support. Private communication from Ann Gordon to the author.

62. "Seeking Freedom," 2.

63. "Item," *Woman's Tribune*, April 1, 1884, 2.

64. Stone to Campbell, April 1884, Records of the NWSA, Reel 12, Manuscript Division, LC.

65. "The Mormon Question: An Interview with Mrs. Belva A. Lockwood," *Rochester Democrat and Chronicle*, March 12, 1884, reprinted in *Deseret Evening News*, March 29, 1884, 3.

66. Ibid., 3.

67. "The Mormon Question: An Interview," 3.

68. "Mrs. Lockwood's Speeches," *Woman's Exponent*, April 1, 1884, 164. Also, Charlotte Godbe to President Woodruff, 5 February 1889, reprinted in Madsen, *Battle for the Ballot*, 141 and the Franklin D. Richards Diary, February 9, 18, and 27, 1884, LDS Church Archives.

69. "The Mormon Question: An Interview," 3.

70. Ibid., 3.

71. At age eighty-two she warned family members that an upcoming visit would be a short one as Congress was in session and the groups she represented needed her. Lockwood to Lella Gardner, 1 December 1912, Papers of Belva A. Lockwood, SCPC.

NOTES TO CHAPTER 10

1. Clara Shortridge Foltz, "Belva A. Lockwood: First Woman Presidential Candidate," *Women Lawyers' Journal*, January 1918, 27–28.

2. Sherilyn C. Bennion, *Marietta and the Spirit of Reform* (unpublished manuscript, author's files), 276–94.

3. Jo Freeman, *A Room at a Time: How Women Entered Party Politics* (Lanham, MD: Rowman & Littlefield, 2000), 33.

4. She received only twenty-four votes but her act, asserting woman's right to run for office, caused wide discussion. Theodore Stanton and Harriot Stanton Blatch, eds., *Elizabeth Cady Stanton* (New York: Arno Press, 1969), 2:114–15.

5. Barbara Goldsmith, *Other Powers* (New York: Knopf, 1998), ch. 27; Lois Beachy Underhill, *The Woman Who Ran for President* (Bridgehampton, NY: Bridge Works, 1995), chs. 22–25.

6. "Scissors," *Woman's Herald of Industry*, January 1883, 1; R. Davis, *Woman's Republic: The Life of Marietta Stow, Cooperator* (CA: Pt. Pinos Editions, 1980), 164–68. Laura de Force Gordon campaigned for the California state Senate in 1871.

7. "Seven Reasons for Publishing *The Herald*," *Woman's Herald of Industry*, September 1881, 1.

8. "Letter of Belva A. Lockwood," *Woman's Herald of Industry*, May 1882, 4; "Tricyclies," *Woman's Herald of Industry*, June, 1882, 5; "Letter of Belva A. Lockwood," *Woman's Herald of Industry*, January 1883, 4.

9. "Woman's Republic," *Woman's Herald of Industry*, October 1881, 1, 6.

10. "Mrs. J. W. Stow Independent Candidate for Governor of California," *Woman's Herald of Industry*, July 1882, 1.

11. Ibid., 1.

12. Ibid., 1.

13. "Comments of the Press," *Woman's Herald of Industry*, September 1882, 4.

14. Ibid., 4.

15. Melanie Susan Gustafson, *Women and the Republican Party, 1854–1924* (Urbana: University of Illinois Press, 2001), 56.

16. "Comparison," *Woman's Herald of Industry*, July 1884, 1.

17. "Please Take It Down," *Woman's Herald of Industry*, August 1884, 1.

18. Ibid., 1.

19. "Stow's Response to 'Please Take It Down,'" *Woman's Herald of Industry*, August 1884, 1.

20. Ibid., 1.

21. Belva A. Lockwood, "How I Ran for the Presidency," *National Magazine*, March 1903, 729.

22. Ibid., 729.

23. Ibid., 729; "Three of a Kind," *St. Louis Post-Dispatch*, August 16, 1884, 1. Lockwood told the *Post-Dispatch* that the Republicans received the resolution with "nothing but derision."

24. Lockwood, "How I Ran," 729.

25. "Three of a Kind," 1.

26. Lockwood, "How I Ran," 729. In a 1914 interview, Lockwood repeated that she had written to Stow to challenge Stanton and Anthony's endorse-

ment, on behalf of suffrage women, of Blaine. Harold B. Johnson, "Interview," Watertown (New York) *Daily Times*, November 7, 1914. Newspaper archives, Scrapbooks, 22:40.

27. "Woman's Presidential Campaign," *Woman's Herald of Industry*, October 1884, 1. Stow and Eliza C. Webb signed the letter.

28. Lockwood, "How I Ran," 729.

29. Madeleine B. Stern, "Two Unpublished Letters from Belva Lockwood," *Signs* (Autumn 1975), 274.

30. Belva A. Lockwood to Marietta L. Stow . . . and members of the National Equal Rights Party, 3 September 1884. This letter contains her initial platform proposals, later modified. Reprinted in Madeleine B. Stern, "Two Unpublished Letters," 274–75; also, Manuscripts Division, Department of Rare Books and Special Collections, Princeton University Library.

31. For example, the Republicans devoted ten pages of their election primer to polygamy, a favorite issue with northern voters who approved of government intervention in Utah. Republican National Committee, *The Republican Campaign Text Book of 1884* (New York, 1884), 98–107, Campaign Material, 1880–88, Political History Collection, NMAH.

32. Lockwood, "How I Ran," 730.

33. Stern, "Two Unpublished Letters," 274.

34. Ibid., 274.

35. Ibid., 275.

36. Ibid., 274.

37. The modified fifteen-point platform is reprinted in Lockwood, "How I Ran," 730–31.

38. All quotations in this paragraph are found in the September 3, 1884, platform. Stern, "Two Unpublished Letters," 274–75.

39. Lockwood, "How I Ran," 730–31.

40. Lockwood wrote, "The secret was out and next morning I was famous." Ibid., 732.

41. "Platform and Interview," *Evening Star*, September 4, 1884, 1.

42. Lockwood, "How I Ran," 732.

43. "The American Prohibitionists: Mrs. Belva A. Lockwood," *Evening Star*, February 23, 1884, 8. Stow described herself as a supporter of anti-Chinese policies when she announced as a candidate for governor. "Mrs. J. W. Stow," *Woman's Herald of Industry*, July 1882, 1. Foltz also had anti-Chinese positions. Barbara Allen Babcock, "Clara Shortridge Foltz: Constitution-Maker," *Indiana Law Journal* 66 (1991): 853–54.

44. "Mrs. Lockwood and Her Campaign," *Evening Star*, September 13, 1884, 1.

45. Lockwood to Edward M. Davis, 7 September 1884, State Historical Society of Wisconsin. Davis was the reform-minded son-in-law of Lucretia Mott.

46. Lockwood to "Friend Davis," 20 September 1884, State Historical Society of Wisconsin.

47. Lockwood, "How I Ran," 733.

48. Foltz, "Belva A. Lockwood," 28.

49. Lockwood, "How I Ran," 732.

50. Ibid., 732.

51. "Belva Is Ratified," *National Republican*, September 19, 1884, 1. According to *Boyd's City Directory* E. G. Barnard boarded with her at 619 F Street from 1881 until 1887.

52. "Belva Is Ratified," 1.

53. Ibid., 1.

54. "For Belva and Reform," *Evening Star*, September 17, 1884, 1.

55. "Ratifying Mrs. Lockwood's Nomination," *Evening Star*, September 23, 1884, 1.

56. Lozier issued a statement from her home in New York on September 19 indicating that Lockwood had put her name forward without permission and that, while she appreciated the "kind intentions of the friends who have made use of her name," she did not see the "need of a special Woman's suffrage ticket when all the candidates for president are friendly to woman suffrage." "Will Not Run with Belva," *Baltimore American*, September 20, 1884, 1.

57. "Woman in Politics," *Frank Leslie's Illustrated Newspaper*, September 20, 1884, 72, 74–75.

58. Ibid., 72.

59. In 1880 Miriam Folline Leslie, a journalist, inherited her husband's publishing empire. She legally changed her name to "Frank Leslie" and directed the business for fifteen years. She supported women's rights and in her will left nearly half her $2 million estate to Carrie Chapman Catt for "the furtherance of the cause of Woman's Suffrage." Madeleine B. Stern, "Miriam Florence Folline Leslie," *Notable American Women* (Cambridge, MA: Harvard University Press, 1971), 394.

60. "Mrs. Belva Lockwood," *Harper's Weekly*, September 20, 1884, 621, 615 (photo).

61. Cover cartoon with the caption, "Another Voice for Cleveland," *Judge*, September 27, 1884.

62. "Suffrage Would Be a Blessing," Belva Lockwood, Sophia Smith Collection, Smith College, (n.d.), possibly the *Baltimore American*.

63. "Mrs. Lockwood and Her Campaign," *Evening Star*, September 13, 1884, 1.

64. "Poem," *Evening Star*, September 26, 1884, 4.

65. "Mrs. Lockwood's Campaign Closed," *Evening Star*, November 5, 1884, 4.

66. "Mrs. Lockwood's Brilliant Idea," *Evening Star*, September 29, 1884, 1. All quotations in this paragraph are from this article.

67. Lockwood to Lella Gardner, 9 May 1913, 1, Papers of Belva A. Lockwood, SCPC.

68. "Belva Lockwood's High Self-Esteem," *Cincinnati Commercial Gazette*, October 19, 1884, 6.

69. Women's Suffrage Collection, Gleeson Library, University of San Francisco.

70. "Belva Lockwood's Canvass," *Evening Star*, October 13, 1884, 1.

71. Susan B. Anthony to Elizabeth Boynton Harbert, 6 October 1884, Elizabeth Boynton Harbert Collection, Huntington Library, San Marino, California.

72. Susan B. Anthony to Elizabeth Cady Stanton, 23 October 1884, in Ann D. Gordon, ed., *Selected Papers of Elizabeth Cady Stanton and Susan B. Anthony*, vol. 4, *When Clowns Make Laws for Queens, 1880–1887* (New Brunswick, NJ: Rutgers University Press, 2006), 371–74.

73. "Belva Lockwood's Canvass," 1.

74. Ibid., 1.

75. "An Honored Guest," *Louisville Courier Journal*, October 15, 1884, 6.

76. Barbara Allen Babcock, "Clara Shortridge Foltz: 'First Woman,'" *Arizona Law Review* 30 (1988): 699–700.

77. Foltz, "Belva A. Lockwood," 28.

78. Lockwood, "How I Ran"; "Suffragists in Parade March 4," newspaper clipping, probably dating from 1913, Papers of Belva A. Lockwood, SCPC. Caroline B. Winslow, Lockwood's colleague at the Universal Franchise Association, understood that the campaign was a parody with serious intentions. She wrote,

> The nomination . . . of Belva A. Lockwood . . . may be the huge joke
> Belva and her friends are disposed to make it. But it may be the beginning of that which will grow into a mighty controlling political
> party. Many controlling forces have had a very insignificant commencement. Who can read the future? The movement cannot be said
> to be without principles or issues.

Caroline B. Winslow, "Tall Oaks from Little Acorns Grow," *Alpha*, October 1884.

79. Foltz, "Belva A. Lockwood," 27.

80. Ibid., 28.

81. Johnson, "Interview," 40.

82. Although most Mother Hubbard clubs satirized Lockwood and her political aspirations, she later wrote that at least one of them performed "creditable" political work. Lockwood, "How I Ran," 733; also, Sharon E. Wood, *The Freedom of the Streets* (Chapel Hill: University of North Carolina Press, 2005), introduction.

83. "A Belva Lockwood Club," *Frank Leslie's Illustrated*, November 1, 1884, 169, 171.

84. "Atalanta Lockwood and Hippomenes Butler in the Home Stretch," *Life*, October 30, 1884, 243. The story of Atalanta was set down by the Roman

poet Ovid. *Judge*, another mass circulation magazine, acknowledged her candidacy with the cartoon, "The New Ticket: The Campaign Is Now Open," October 11, 1884, 5. This was followed by a cover cartoon, "No Mash Here," and short article, "Belva Lockwood," in which Lockwood is described as smart and admirable but "unfortunate in living some two or three hundred years before the world is ready for her." October 18, 1884, 3.

85. "Belva Confident," *Evening Star*, November 4, 1884, 1.

86. James T. Havel, *U.S. Presidential Candidates and the Elections: A Biographical and Historical Guide* (New York: Macmillan, 1996), 2:57.

87. Cleveland polled 4,874,986 votes, while Blaine received 4,851,981. In the presidential election of 1880 the Greenback Party was accused of trying to win advantage by polling sufficient votes in critical states to send the election to the House of Representatives. See, "The Possible Danger," *Lockport Daily Journal*, June 14, 1880, 2.

88. Jerrold Glenn Rusk, *The Effect of the Australian Ballot Reform on Split Ticket Voting, 1876–1908* (Ph.D. thesis, University of Michigan, 1968), 17, 22.

89. Lockwood, "How I Ran," 733.

90. "Petition of Belva A. Lockwood of the Equal Rights Party for President . . . ," 2, RG 46, Records of the Senate, Box 101/Sen 48-A-J, NA. Referred to the Committee on Woman Suffrage, January 12, 1885; "How The State Voted," *Baltimore American*, November 6, 1884, 4.

91. "Petition of Belva A. Lockwood," 3.

92. Ibid., 3–4.

93. "Casting the Vote," *Indianapolis Daily Sentinel*, December 4, 1884, 5.

94. *Congressional Record*, House, February 11, 1885, 1532.

95. Johnson, "Interview," 40.

NOTES TO CHAPTER 11

1. Reprinted in "Belva A. Lockwood," *LDJ*, April 26, 1881, 4.

2. Ibid., 4.

3. Lockwood to Grover Cleveland, 4 April 1885, Grover Cleveland Papers, Series 2, reel 9, LC.

4. Ibid.

5. Lockwood to Lella Gardner, 5 January 1913, Papers of Belva A. Lockwood, SCPC.

6. David Ward Wood, ed., *Chicago and Its Distinguished Citizens: Progress of Forty Years* (Chicago: Milton George & Co., 1881), 134. Slayton published speaker information in a magazine sent out to selection committees.

7. Anne M'Dowell, "Women's Department," (Philadephia) *Sunday Republic*, March 14, 1880.

8. Richard W. Leeman, *"Do Everything" Reform: The Oratory of Frances E. Willard* (New York: Greenwood Press, 1992), 14.

9. Elizabeth Cady Stanton, *Eighty Years and More* (1898; reprint Boston: Northeastern University Press, 1993), 260, 262; "Belva's Pluck," *LDJ*, March 4, 1885, 2.

10. Item, *LDJ*, February 26, 1881, 2.

11. Lockwood to Darwin C. Pavey, 24 September 1884, Chicago Historical Society.

12. Item, *LDJ*, December 24, 1884, 2; Lockwood to Darwin C. Pavey, Esq., 8 March 1885, Schlesinger Library, Radcliffe College.

13. Lockwood to Pavey, 24 September 1884. Her lectures, "Commercial Reunion of the North and the South," and "Women as Guardians and Administrators," do not appear to have been popular and appear on few advertisements.

14. Lockwood to Lella Gardner, 9 May 1913, Papers of Belva A. Lockwood, SCPC.

15. "Mrs. Lockwood's Visit," *Woman's Exponent*, July 15, 1885, 29; "Mrs. Lockwood Is Coming," *Woman's Exponent*, July 1, 1885, 2.

16. "Mrs. Lockwood's Visit"; Melinda Evans, "Belva Lockwood and the Mormon Question," www.law.stanford.edu/library/wlhbp/papers/Mevans_lockwood.pdf.

17. Lockwood to John T. Caine, 23 July 1885, John Thomas Caine Collection, Utah State Historical Society; Edward Leo Lyman, *Political Deliverance: The Mormon Quest for Utah Statehood* (Urbana: University of Illinois Press, 1986), 27, 31.

18. Lockwood to Grover Cleveland, 23 July 1885, U.S. Department of the Interior, Territorial Papers of Utah, 1850–1902, LC. Pages 6–8 of the rough draft sent to Caine are found in the John Thomas Caine Collection, Utah State Historical Society. Subsequent quotations come from the final draft of the letter to Cleveland. On the role of William Nelson, AP correspondent, see Lyman, *Political Deliverance*, ch. 3.

19. Lockwood to Cleveland, 23 July 1885.

20. Ibid.

21. Lockwood to Miss Mary Lockwood, 4 August 1885, Bull Family Collection, Bancroft Library, University of California.

22. Lockwood to Caine, July 23, 1885.

23. James Ormes, District of Columbia Death Certificate 49395. He was, in all likelihood, DeForest's father or uncle.

24. "Short Talk with Belva," *Daily Denver Times*, November 12, 1885, n.p.

25. Untitled notes, typed from the original, probably "Across the Continent," NYSHA, 68.

26. Ibid., 72.

27. "Short Talk with Belva."

28. Ibid.

29. "Women as Bread Winners," *Denver Tribune-Republican*, November 12, 1885, n.p. All quotations in this paragraph are from this article.

30. Jean M. Ward and Elaine A. Maveety, eds., *"Yours for Liberty": Selections from Abigail Scott Duniway's Suffrage Newspaper* (Corvallis: Oregon State University Press, 2000), 223.

31. Account page, January 18, 1886, Slayton Lyceum Bureau, Belva Lockwood Papers, NCHS, Lockport.

32. "Notes about Women," *Woman's Tribune*, September 1885, 2.

33. Belva A. Lockwood, "On Marriage," NYSHA, 104.

34. Ibid., 62.

35. Ibid., 71.

36. Ibid., 117.

37. Ibid., 105–6.

38. "Our Belva, the Ex-Candidate for the Presidency in Buffalo but Skips Niagara," *Buffalo News*, loose clipping, n.d., author's files.

39. Belva A. Lockwood, "The Present Phase of the Woman Question," *Cosmopolitan*, March–October 1888, 468–69.

40. Matilda Joslyn Gage, *Woman, Church, and State* (1893; reprint Aberdeen, SD: Sky Carrier Press, 1998), 292–96. Gage wrote to Lockwood, "No hell is so great as that of an uncongenial marriage!" Lockwood, "On Marriage," unnumbered page, back of file.

41. Lockwood, "The Present Aspect of the Temperance Question," 26, NYSHA.

42. Ibid., 40.

43. Ibid., 5*″″″. (Lockwood used stroke markings and asterisks as she added and amended lecture material.)

44. Before this venture, late in 1884, Lockwood had joined Marietta Stow in recasting the *Woman's Herald of Industry* as a more explicitly feminist newspaper, renaming it *Equal Rights*. They published several issues but failed to attract readers and in July 1885 the paper ceased publication. Item, *Woman's Tribune*, July 1885, 2.

45. Lockwood to Mary Lockwood, 11 October 1886, Bull Family Collection, Bancroft Library, University of California.

46. Advertisement, "The Lockwood Improvement Syndicate," *Woman's Tribune*, December 1886, n.p.

47. The only example I have been able to find hung for many years on the living room wall of one of Mary Lockwood Bull's descendents. This certificate has now been placed in the Bull Family Papers, Bancroft Library, University of California.

48. "Clara Barton Indorses Dr. Greene's Nervura," Warshaw Collection of Business America, Patent Medicines—Manufacturers, NMAH; "Greene's Nervura Cures Belva A. Lockwood," Lockwood Papers, NCHS, Lockport.

49. A. Walker Bingham, *The Snake-Oil Syndrome* (Hanover, MA: Christopher House, 1994), 32, 50.

50. "Greene's Nervura Cures Belva A. Lockwood."

51. Act of March 3, 1887, 24 Stat. 635 amending 22 Stat. 30; Lockwood to John T. Caine, 14 February 1886, John T. Caine Collection, Utah State Historical Society; Sarah Barringer Gordon, *The Mormon Question* (Chapel Hill: University of North Carolina Press, 2002), 183; Lyman, *Political Deliverance*, 26–32.

52. "Belva A. Lockwood, and 'Mormon' Mothers," *Woman's Exponent*, March 1, 1886, 150.

53. Lyman, *Political Deliverance*, ch. 3; letters of Charles W. Penrose, 27 August 1887 and 30 December 1887, http://www.jfs.saintswithouthalos.com/pri/cwp_1887media.htm.

54. Wilford Woodruff to John W. Young, 6 August 1887, First Presidency Letterpress Copy Books. The Church of Jesus Christ of Latter-day Saints Archives, Salt Lake City, Utah (hereafter LDS Church Archives). The letter was accessed in 2005 on jfs.saintswithouthalos.com/First Presidency Letterpress Copy Books; John W. Young to Woodruff, Cannon & Smith, 20 August 1887, John W. Young Papers, LDS Church Archives.

55. Lockwood to John W. Young, 6, 9, and 26 September 1887, John W. Young Papers, LDS Church Archives.

56. Lyman, *Political Deliverance*, 72.

57. Belva A. Lockwood, "The Mormon Question." The article appeared with different titles in many U.S. newspapers; Franklin S. Richards to Wilford Woodruff and George Q. Cannon, 28 February 1888, Franklin S. Richards Correspondence, Utah State Historical Society.

58. Belva A. Lockwood, "The Disfranchisement of the Women of Utah," reprinted in *Woman's Exponent*, June 15, 1883, 12.

59. Lyman, *Political Deliverance*, 22–23.

60. Act of March 3, 1887. 24 Stat. 635, 641.

61. Lockwood, "The Mormon Question." In 1896, after becoming a state, Utah reinstated woman suffrage.

NOTES TO CHAPTER 12

1. Belva A. Lockwood, "Arbitration and the Treaties," August 1897, Papers of Belva A. Lockwood, SCPC, 3–4.

2. Charles DeBenedetti, *The Peace Reform in American History* (Bloomington: Indiana University Press, 1980), 60.

3. Ezekiel Lockwood's Compiled Civil War Record, RG 94, NA.

4. Henry Mayer, *All on Fire: William Lloyd Garrison and the Abolition of Slavery* (New York: St. Martin's Griffin, 1998), 250.

5. Thomas F. Curran, *Soldiers of Peace* (New York: Fordham University Press, 2003), 11; Mayer, *All on Fire*, 224–26.

6. I thank Wendy E. Chmielewski for this insight in her paper, "Yours, for Radical Peace: The Universal Peace Union, 1866–1913," Conference on Social and Political Movements, Indiana Association of Historians, February 1998, 2–3.

7. Mayer, *All on Fire*, 249–50.

8. When Andrew Carnegie suggested that employee wages rise or fall according to company profits, the UPU endorsed the plan. *Peacemaker* 5 (1887): 121.

9. Curran, *Soldiers of Peace*, 112.

10. Ibid., 113.

11. *Peacemaker* 6 (1886): 213.

12. *Peacemaker* 8 (1889): 8–9.

13. "Mrs. Belva Lockwood Opposes Statues to Heroes and Cadet Corps," *Washington Post*, (n.d.), Belva Lockwood file, NCHS, Lockport.

14. *Peacemaker* 7 (January 1888): 131.

15. Belva A. Lockwood, "My Efforts to Become a Lawyer," Lippincott's Magazine, February 1888, 220. She had previously included this argument in her peace talks, e.g., *Voice of Peace* 8 (April 1882): 194.

16. Letter of L. Dundore and Belva A. Lockwood, 21 August 1878, *Voice of Peace* 5 (October 1878): 111.

17. African-American lecturer and author Frances Watkins Harper was a prominent UPU member.

18. "Publications," December 12, 1889, UPU, Reel 13.3; "Petition" from Jacob M. Troth, Daniel Breed, Belva A. Lockwood, and Chalkley Gillingham to Rutherford B. Hayes, January 15, 1879, Misc. Letters of the Department of State, 1784–1906, RG 59, NA.

19. Resolution of June 17, 1874, *Voice of Peace* 5, no. 12 (March 1879): 182.

20. Rutherford B. Hayes, "Inaugural Address of March 5, 1877," http://www.ukans.edu/carrie/docs/texts/23haye1.htm.

21. "Address Presented to President Hayes by a Committee of the District of Columbia Peace Society," *Voice of Peace* 5, no. 12 (March 1879): 182.

22. Lockwood to R. B. Hayes, 27 February 1879, Misc. Letters of the Department of State, 1784–1906, RG 59, NA.

23. "Progress of the International Arbitration Movement," *Voice of Peace* 6, no. 1 (April 1879): 9.

24. "Official Report of the Thirteenth Anniversary of the Universal Peace Union," *Voice of Peace* 6, no. 3 (June 1879): 33, 41.

25. Letter of Belva Lockwood, *Voice of Peace* 7, no. 8 (August 1880): 126–27.

26. In 1880 Lockwood, Daniel Breed, and ex-governor Frederick P. Stanton, among others, created the organization to influence public opinion. A

short while later it was announced that "the National Arbitration League is . . . doing the work formerly performed by the [Washington UPU] branch." *Peacemaker* 1, no. 1 (1882): 39.

27. B. A. Lockwood, "International Arbitration," *Voice of Peace* 8, no. 1 (April 1881): 10.

28. Lockwood to Cleveland, 28 September 1885, Manuscripts Division, Series 2, Reel 20, LC.

29. President Grover Cleveland, Annual Message to Congress, December 8, 1885, http://www.presidency.ucsb.edu/site/docs/sou.php.

30. *Peacemaker* 5, no. 1 (1886): 40; "Twentieth Annual Report," *Peacemaker* 5 (1886): 40.

31. *Peacemaker* 5 (1886): 41.

32. *Peacemaker* 6 (1887): 126.

33. "International Arbitration," Senate, Misc. Doc. No. 141, 50th Congress, 1st Session, June 18, 1888, 24–27; "The Bills before Congress," *Peacemaker* 5 (1886): 39.

34. Misc. Doc. No. 141, 18–19.

35. Ibid., 15–16.

36. "Belva Thinks She Will Win," (New York) *World*, July 12, 1888, 1.

37. "Belva Lockwood's Nomination," *Woman's Journal*, May 1888, 158.

38. Matilda Joslyn Gage to Elizabeth Cady Stanton, 13 July 1888, reprinted in the *Woman's Tribune*, August 18, 1888.

39. "People Talked About," (New York) *World*, November 10, 1888, 4; "People Talked About," *World*, August 26, 1888, 4.

40. "Mrs. Lockwood's New Party," *Evening Star*, December 17, 1887, 9. In this interview, she said that party members wished to discuss industrial reform and a remedy for existing industrial evils, ideas associated with Benjamin Butler's defunct Greenback–Anti Monopoly Party, which also anticipated the Populist Party of the 1890s. Lockwood thought the Industrial Reform Party (IRP) would draw support from followers of Henry George. The IRP also supported "the abolition of the liquor traffic and granting of woman suffrage."

41. *Woman's Tribune*, May 1887; Papers of E. C. Stanton and S. B. Anthony, Roll 25:205, Manuscripts Division, LC.

42. Ida Husted Harper, *Life and Work of Susan B. Anthony* (1898; reprint North Stratford, NH: Ayer, 1998), 2: 641.

43. "Belva Lockwood," (New York) *Sun*, August 27, 1888, 4.

44. Item, (New York) *World*, May 17, 1888, 4.

45. Alfred H. Love to N. S. Chapin and C. Leonard, 27 October 1888, reprinted in *Peacemaker* 7 (1888): 86–87.

46. Ibid., 86–87.

47. Lockwood to Linda Warfel Slaughter, 16 July 1888, Benjamin and Linda Slaughter Papers, State Historical Society of North Dakota.

48. Ibid.

49. Lockwood did not support "measures to . . . stop the immigration of the scum of Europe and Asia . . . cheap foreign labor," and ignored the delegates' call for heavy taxation of foreign landlords. "Platform of the Equal Rights Party," *Woman's Tribune*, October 27, 1888.

50. "Woman's Part in Politics," (New York) *World*, August 12, 1888, 13.

51. Ibid., 13.

52. "Mrs. Leonard to Run for Mayor," (New York) *World*, October 18, 1888, 3; "Three Women Wish to Vote," *World*, October 10, 1888, 1.

53. "Belva Lockwood's Address," (Boonville, NY) *Herald*, September 20, 1888.

54. "Arbitration," *Peacemaker* 7 (October 1888): 68–69. The UPU picnic grove at Mystic was a popular summer meeting place.

55. "Belva A. Lockwood as Presidential Candidate," *Peacemaker* 7 (1888): 84.

56. Ibid., 84.

57. "Belva A. Lockwood as Presidential Candidate," 85.

58. "Official Report of the Twenty-Second Anniversary of the Pennsylvania Peace Society, December 5, 1888," *Peacemaker* 7 (1888–89): 136.

59. *Congressional Record*, Senate, 50th Cong., Sess. 1, August 7, 1888, 7286, and September 18, 1888, 8670–71.

60. Belva Lockwood 1888 campaign ribbon with pin. New York, Dobkin Collection. There were also lampooning songs, including "Belva, Dear, Belva, Dear," (New York) *Morning Journal*, July 29, 1888, writings, and ephemera.

61. "Woman's Part in Politics," (New York) *World*, August 12, 1888, 1. Perhaps to compete with Bly, the New York *Sun* published a "sketch of the character and career of Mrs. Belva Lockwood," August 27, 1888, 4.

62. "Woman's Part in Politics," 1.

63. "Mrs. Lockwood's New Candidate," (New York) *World*, October 29, 1888, 2.

64. Emily S. Bouton, "Some Talks: Mrs. Belva A. Lockwood," *Toledo Weekly Blade*, December 20, 1888, Papers of Belva A. Lockwood, SCPC.

65. "People Talked About," (New York) *World*, November 10, 1888, 4.

66. "Electoral Ticket of the Equal Rights Party, State of Kentucky, 1888." Papers of Belva A. Lockwood, SCPC.

67. Belva A. Lockwood, "Would Women Vote?" November 12, 1888, General Manuscripts, Rare Books and Special Collections, Princeton University. All quotations in this paragraph are found in this article.

NOTES TO CHAPTER 13

1. "Universal Congress of Peace, in Paris, 1889," *Peacemaker* 7 (1888): 127–28.

2. "Address of Mrs. Lockwood," *Peacemaker* 8 (1889): 8–12. All quotations in this paragraph are found in these pages.

3. General Records of the State Department, M1372, Passport Applications, 1795–1905, RG 59, NA.

4. "From Our Delegates," *Peacemaker* 8 (1889): 4–7.

5. Miriam Levin, *When the Eiffel Tower Was New* (South Hadley, MA: Mt. Holyoke College Art Museum, 1989), 23.

6. "Letters from Our Delegates in Europe" *Peacemaker* 8 (1889): 21, 24.

7. Ibid., 21.

8. Norma Evenson, *Paris: A Century of Change, 1878–1978* (New Haven, CT: Yale University Press, 1979), 128.

9. Sandi E. Cooper, ed., *Internationalism in Nineteenth-Century Europe* (New York: Garland, 1976), 159–62.

10. "Opinions of the Press," January 29, 1892, 2, Lockwood/Ormes Collection, NMAH.

11. While in Paris Lockwood distributed a paper, titled "International Arbitration," along with a brief French translation, "Discours prononcé par Madame Belva A. Lockwood," Bibliothèque de Documentation Internationale Contemporaine, Nanterre, France; "Letters from Our Delegates in Europe," *Peacemaker* 8 (1889): 21. The name of the translator is not given.

12. "Address of Mrs. Belva A. Lockwood," *Peacemaker* 8 (1889): 29–30. All quotations in this paragraph are found in these pages.

13. "Address of Rev. Amanda Deyo," *Peacemaker* 8 (1889): 28.

14. "Letters," *Peacemaker* 8 (1889): 23; "A Frenchman's View of the Recent Peace Congresses," *Peacemaker* 8 (1889): 63–64.

15. Lockwood and Deyo also attended working sessions of the International Congress for the Works of Women and the Ligue internationale de la paix et de la liberté, an organization Lemonnier had helped to found.

16. "Letters," *Peacemaker* 8 (1889): 24.

17. Ibid., 46.

18. "Mrs. Belva A. Lockwood's Report," *Peacemaker* 8 (1889): 45–46; "The Great Peace Congress," (New York) *World*, July 21, 1889, 17.

19. "Letters," *Peacemaker* 8 (1889): 24.

20. Ibid., 24–25, 48.

21. Ibid., 26.

22. Ibid., 46–47.

23. Ibid., 47.

24. Ibid., 47.

25. Belva A. Lockwood, "Emperor William and the Peace Union," *Peace-maker* 8 (1889): 81.

26. Ibid., 81.

27. "Letters," 47.

28. "Interview," *Women's Penny Paper*, October 5, 1889, 1. All quotations in this paragraph are from this article.

29. Item, *Peacemaker* 8 (1889): 78.

30. Frances E. Willard, *Autobiography of an American Woman* (Chicago: Woman's Temperance Publishing Association, 1892), 351.

31. Suzanne M. Marilley, "Frances Willard and the Feminism of Fear," *Feminist Studies* (Spring 1993): 131.

32. Richard W. Leeman, *"Do Everything" Reform: The Oratory of Frances E. Willard* (New York: Greenwood Press, 1992), 13.

33. Ruth Bordin, *Woman and Temperance* (Philadelphia: Temple University Press., 1981), 131–33.

34. Carolyn De Swarte Gifford, *Writing Out My Heart: Selections from the Journal of Frances E. Willard, 1855–96* (Urbana: University of Illinois Press, 1995), 375.

35. Belva A. Lockwood, "The Present Phase of the Woman Question," *Cosmopolitan*, March–October 1888, 470; Belva Lockwood, "Life and Times of Frances E. Willard," undated lecture written after 1910, Lockwood/Ormes Collection, NMAH.

36. Kathi Kern, *Mrs. Stanton's Bible* (Ithaca, NY: Cornell University Press, 2001), 53, citing a letter sent to Antoinette Louisa Brown Blackwell, 27 April 1886.

37. Kern, *Mrs. Stanton's Bible*, 96; Elizabeth Cady Stanton; The Revising Committee, *The Woman's Bible* (1895; reprint Seattle: Coalition Task Force on Women and Religion, 1974).

38. Kern, *Mrs. Stanton's Bible*, 97.

39. Ibid., 124.

40. Ibid., 124.

41. At the meeting, Gage read a letter from Love, who urged, "Take the radical peace movement into your convention." Matilda Joslyn Gage, ed., *Woman's National Liberal Union: Report of the Convention for Organization, Febru-ary 24th and 25th, 1890* (Syracuse, NY: Masters and Stone Publisher, 1890), 59.

42. Gage, *Woman's National Liberal Union Report*, 3.

43. Matilda Joslyn Gage to Thomas Clarkson Gage, 22 February 1890, Gage Collection, Schlesinger Library.

44. Matilda Joslyn Gage to Thomas Clarkson Gage, 7 March 1890, Gage Collection, Schlesinger Library. The sermon was preached at Washington's Sixth Presbyterian Church after which, in the same letter, Gage wrote her son,

"I am glad of it. I wish to compel thought and attract attention to the new step. I did not at first think of attacking the *foundations* of the church itself— but . . . one day . . . knew it was right."

45. Gage, *Woman's National Liberal Union Report*, 41.

46. "Hon. William F. Aldrich," *Peacemaker* 16 (1898): 154–56. The need for public defenders was being discussed in socialist and utopian circles; Aldrich had written about the idea in the January 1890 issue of *The Liberal Thinker*. After listening to Foltz, Aldrich abandoned the model that would have the public defender replace all paid criminal defense lawyers in favor of a public officer who would serve the poor. Barbara Allen Babcock, "Inventing the Public Defender," *American Criminal Law Review* (October 2006).

47. Gage, *Woman's National Liberal Union Report*, 78.

48. Ibid., 78.

49. Ibid., 78.

50. Evelyn A. Kirkley, *Rational Mothers and Infidel Gentlemen* (Syracuse, NY: Syracuse University Press, 2000), 110–13.

NOTES TO CHAPTER 14

1. Grace Farrell, *Lillie Devereux Blake* (Amherst: University of Massachusetts Press, 2002), 150, 162–72.

2. J. Ellen Foster to Linda Slaughter, 14 May 1892, Benjamin and Linda Slaughter Papers, State Historical Society of North Dakota.

3. Lella Gardner to Ellen Starr Brinton, 10 May 1943, DG 000, Records, SCPC.

4. Lucy Stone to Margaret W. Campbell, 5 April 1884, NAWSA Collection, Reel 12, Manuscript Division, LC.

5. Anthony wrote cattily about Lockwood's dyed hair while Lockwood referred to Anthony as having been "soured" by life. Anthony to Elizabeth Cady Stanton, 23 October 1884, in Ann D. Gordon, ed., *Selected Papers of Elizabeth Cady Stanton and Susan B. Anthony*, vol. 4, *When Clowns Make Laws for Queens, 1880–1884* (New Brunswick, NJ: Rutgers University Press, 2006), 371–74; Lockwood, "My Efforts to Become a Lawyer," *Lippincott's Magazine*, February 1888, 219.

6. May Wright Sewall, *Genesis of the International Council of Women and the Story of Its Growth, 1888–1893* (Indianapolis, IN: April 1914), 6; Ellen Carol Dubois, ed., *The Elizabeth Cady Stanton–Susan B. Anthony Reader* (1981; reprint Boston: Northeastern University Press, 1992), 175–78.

7. Program of the International Council of Women, March 25 to April 1, 1888, 10, Woman Suffrage Collection, NMAH; Susan B. Anthony to Rachel G. Foster, 11 November 1887, Anthony-Avery Papers, University of Rochester.

8. "Report of Our Delegation to Washington, April 20, 1888," *Peacemaker* 6 (1888): 208–10.

9. Matilda J. Gage to Lillie Devereux Blake, 14 March 1891, L. D. Blake Papers, Missouri Historical Society.

10. Marilla Ricker to Lillie Devereux Blake, 31 May 1899, L. D. Blake Papers, Missouri Historical Society.

11. Olympia Brown, ed., *Democratic Ideals: A Memorial Sketch of Clara B. Colby* (Federal Suffrage Association, 1917), ch. 6.

12. "Letters from Belva A. Lockwood, One of Our Delegates to Europe," *Peacemaker* 9 (July 1890): 35–36.

13. Belva A. Lockwood to Benjamin Harrison, 20 June 1890, Benjamin Harrison Papers, LC; "Editorial Department": "Action of the U.S. Congress and Venezuela," *Peacemaker* 9 (1890): 11–12 and 14–16. Lockwood sent background correspondence and copies of the 1890 "Concurrent Resolution to Invite Arbitration," which she referred to as the Sherman Resolution, to the president.

14. "The Universal Peace Congress, London, July 14 to 19," *Peacemaker* 9 (September 1890): 45–46.

15. Sandi E. Cooper, *Patriotic Pacifism* (New York: Oxford University Press, 1991), 8, 61.

16. Reprinted, "Universal Peace Congress"; *Proceedings of the Universal Peace Congress, Held in the Westminster Town Hall, London, from 14th to 19th July, 1890* (London: Office of the Congress, 1890), 197–98.

17. "Universal Peace Congress," 50.

18. Belva A. Lockwood, "The Inter-Parliamentary Conference on International Arbitration, of London," *Peacemaker* 9 (1890): 61.

19. "Visitor's Ticket, Third Summer Meeting of University Extension and Other Students in Oxford, August 1890," Lockwood Papers, NCHS, Lockport.

20. "The University Extension: Third Summer Meeting in Oxford," *Oxford University Herald*, August 9, 1890, 5, Belva A. Lockwood Collection, New York State Library, Albany; "Mrs. Belva Lockwood Talks," *New York Times*, Aug. 26, 1890, 8.

21. "Twenty-Third Anniversary of the Connecticut Peace Society," *Peacemaker* 9 (1890): 80.

22. Published appeals for funds, correspondence, and finance committee reports suggest that much of this travel was financed by the UPU treasury with individual delegates, when possible, contributing personal funds. See "Generous Mrs. Lockwood," *Peacemaker* 10 (1892): 148; "Appeal for Funds for the Fifth Universal Peace Congress, Chicago, 1893," *Peacemaker* 11 (1893): 176; "Committee on Finance, Entry 133—Belva A. Lockwood Expenses of trip to Europe peace convention," UPU, Letters, Reel 13.7, 47, SCPC.

23. Lockwood to Lella Gardner, 30 April 1913, Papers of Belva A. Lock-

wood, SCPC; E. A. Rend, M.D., to Mrs. Belva Lockwood, 20 April 1913, Lock-wood/Ormes Collection, NMAH.

24. Sherilyn Cox Bennion, *Equal to the Occasion: Women Editors of the Nine-teenth-Century West* (Reno: University of Nevada Press, 1990).

25. Elizabeth V. Burt, "Introduction," in Burt, ed., *Women's Press Organizations, 1881–1999* (Westport, CT: Greenwood, 2000), xvii. Neither Burt nor I have found many records from these early women's press associations.

26. Elizabeth V. Burt, "A Bid for Legitimacy: The Woman's Press Club Movement, 1881–1900," *Journalism* 23, no. 2 (Summer 1997): 74; Donald A. Ritchie, *Press Gallery* (Cambridge, MA: Harvard University Press, 1991), ch. 8.

27. Mrs. E. N. Chapin, *Life at the National Capitol* (Marshalltown, IA: Chapin & Hartwell, 1887), 127.

28. Aurelia Hadley Mohl to Mrs. Linda W. Slaughter, 1 March 1888; Lockwood to Linda Slaughter, 13 April 1888; Lockwood to Slaughter, 16 July 1888, each in the Benjamin and Linda Slaughter Collection, Historical Society of North Dakota.

29. Lockwood also helped to form the Federation of Woman's Press Clubs. Lockwood to Linda Slaughter, 30 October 1891, Benjamin and Linda Slaughter Collection, Historical Society of North Dakota; "Federation of Woman's Press Clubs," *Woman's Tribune*, November 21, 1891, 308–9. Lockwood opened the meeting, held at the offices of the *Woman's Journal*, and was elected the group's auditor. Colby, Lucy Stone, and Frances Willard, among others, were present. Also, "Report of the Woman's National Press Association," *Woman's Tribune*, November 21, 1891, 312.

30. Patricia G. Holland and Ann D. Gordon, eds., *The Papers of E. C. Stanton and S. B. Anthony* (Wilmington, Del.: Scholarly Resources, 1991), Microfilm 39: 764.

31. "Mrs. Belva Ann Lockwood," in Frances E. Willard and Mary A. Livermore, eds., *A Woman of the Century* (1893; reprint New York: Gordon Press, 1975), 469.

32. Belva A. Lockwood, "The Present Phase of the Woman Question," *Cosmopolitan*, March–October 1888, 467, 470.

33. Belva A. Lockwood, "Women of the American Bar," *Illustrated American*, July 26, 1890, 45.

34. Belva A. Lockwood, "Women in Politics," *American Journal of Politics*, April 1893, 387.

35. Belva Ann Lockwood, "Editorial Department: The Other Side," *Peacemaker* 9 (1891): 190–93. Quotations in this and the two subsequent paragraphs are found in this article.

36. Belva Ann Lockwood, "The Russian Treaty," *Peacemaker* 12 (July 1893): 8; Belva A. Lockwood, "Editorial Department: Peace Notes," *Peacemaker* 10 (1892): 128–29.

37. Belva Ann Lockwood, "The Indian Scare," *Peacemaker* 9 (December 1890): 108.

38. Belva Ann Lockwood, "The Indian Question," *Peacemaker* 9 (1890): 148.

39. Ibid., 148.

40. Ibid., 148–49.

41. Belva Ann Lockwood, "The Removal of the Utes from Colorado," *Peacemaker* 10 (1892): 166.

42. "Mrs. Lockwood's Departure for Europe," *Peacemaker* 10 (1892): 55.

43. Lockwood to Mary Bull, 6 January 1893, Bull Family Letters, Bancroft Library, University of California.

44. Advertisement, "Indian Depredation Claims," *Woman's Tribune*, May 23, 1891; Larry C. Skogen, *Indian Depredation Claims, 1796–1920* (Norman: University of Oklahoma Press, 1996), 114–17, 210–13.

NOTES TO CHAPTER 15

1. "The Lecture Field," *Peacemaker* 11 (1893): 181; "Mrs. Lockwood's Departure for Europe," *Peacemaker* 10 (1892): 55.

2. Matilda Joslyn Gage, ed., *Woman's National Liberal Union, Report of the Convention for Organization* (Syracuse, NY: Masters & Stone, 1890), 63.

3. Jeanne Madeline Weimann, *The Fair Women* (Chicago: Academy Press, 1981).

4. Lockwood, "Women in Politics," *American Journal of Politics* (April 1893): 387; "The World's Fair and a Military Parade," *Peacemaker* 9 (December 1890): 106; "Item," *Woman's Tribune*, September 12, 1891, 292.

5. Lockwood to Elie Ducommun, 1 June 1893, IBP, Box 27, LNL.

6. "The Peace Congress at Berne," *Peacemaker* 10 (1892): 75; "Peace Congress," *Woman's Tribune*, October 1, 1892, 1.

7. Belva A. Lockwood, Paper presented at the Congress of Law Reform and the Fifth International Peace Congress, August 7 and 14, 1893, 2, Papers of Belva A. Lockwood, SCPC.

8. Norman Bolotin and Christine Laing, *The World's Columbian Exposition* (Washington: Preservation Press, 1992), 29, 156.

9. Weimann, *The Fair Women*, 67.

10. "Women Lawyers at the Isabella Club House," *Chicago Legal News*, August 26, 1893, 451.

11. Ibid., 451.

12. *In re Lockwood*, 154 U.S. 116 (1893). Virginia admitted her in 1894: "Mrs. Lockwood Will Practice," *New York Times*, October 2, 1894, 4.

13. "Queen Isabella Association," *Chicago Legal News*, August 5, 1893, 421 (conference program).

14. "The Peace Congress," *Peacemaker* 10 (1892): 75; "Peace Congress," *Woman's Tribune*, October 1, 1892, 1. Lockwood titled the talk "Present Attitude of the Nations toward International Arbitration."

15. For another view, see Sandi Cooper, *Patriotic Pacifism* (New York: Oxford, 1991), 93; "The National Association for the Promotion of Arbitration, of Washington, D.C.," *Peacemaker* 12 (1894): 153.

16. Item, *Peacemaker* 12 (1894): 153.

17. Lura Ormes died January 7, 1894; Lockwood to "Mrs. Ed. Robinson & R. Cordelia McNall, Lockport, N. York." Lockwood Papers, NCHS, Lockport.

18. "Sorrow and Sympathy," *Peacemaker* 12 (1894): 141.

19. "Lawyers in Petticoats," *Chicago Daily Tribune*, April 5, 1890, 9. In addition to this income she owned the house on F Street, valued at twenty thousand dollars, and "a snug homestead in Anacostia, back of Frederick Douglass' place, which is worth $5,000." Ibid.

20. Ibid., 9. Lockwood said that her largest legal fee in seventeen years of practice had been five hundred dollars, and that most of her fees had been far smaller.

21. In the Matter of the Probate of the Last Will and Testament of Myra Clark Gaines, Deceased, Brief of Belva A. Lockwood, of Counsel for Appellants Perkins and Evans, Supreme Court, Kings County, NY, General Term.

22. Elizabeth Urban Alexander, *Notorious Woman: The Celebrated Case of Myra Clark Gaines* (Baton Rouge: Louisiana State University Press, 2001), 4.

23. "Letters from Our Delegates to Antwerp," *Peacemaker* 13 (1894): 44. In order to continue her representation of Perkins and Evans in Surrogate's Court, Lockwood successfully applied for New York State bar membership, denied to her years before (in 1880); "Mrs. Lockwood Gains Recognition," *Washington Post*, May 11, 1893, 1; Christine Sebourn, http://www.stanford.edu/group/WLHP/papers/Stoneman.htm.

24. Alexander, *Notorious Woman*, 243; *Julietta Perkins and Marie P. Evans v. Gaines Administrators*, New York Supreme Court Reports, 74 Hun 95; 83 Hun 225; and 84 Hun 520.

25. Lockwood to Clara Colby, 15 and 17 August 1894, SHSW; Lockwood to Geo. M. Bull, 18 June 1895, Bull Family Letters, Bancroft Library, University of California.

26. Officially, IIe Congrès International d'Assistance et IIe Congrès International de la Protection de l'Enfance. The State Department pointedly refused to pay their expenses. Lockwood to Wm. W. Rockhill, 1 August 1896, Records of the State Department, Misc. Letters, 1784–1906, RG 59, NA; "Letters from Belva A. Lockwood, September 7, 1896," *Peacemaker* 15 (1896): 62.

27. "Report of Belva A. Lockwood," November 25, 1896, RG 59, NA.

28. Lockwood, "Third Report of the American Branch Peace Bureau," April 20, 1895, [sic] *Peacemaker* 13 (1894): 10–11. William Aldrich contributed

"some forty or more volumes" to this peace library. *Peacemaker* 15 (1896): 31. She extended her involvement with non-American peace groups by also joining Princess Gabrielle Wiszniewska's Paris-based League for International Disarmament.

29. "Letters," *Peacemaker* 15:62.

30. "Letters from Belva A. Lockwood, Anvers, October 1, 1896," *Peacemaker* 15 (1896): 88.

31. Ibid., 88.

32. Belva A. Lockwood, "Our Fighting Force," *Peacemaker* 13 (1894): 109.

33. Belva A. Lockwood, "The Growth of Peace Principles and Methods of Propagating Them," 28 February 1895, 9, Papers of Belva A. Lockwood, SCPC.

34. Lockwood to Fredric [sic] Bajer, 19 April 1898, IPB, Box 10/6, LNL.

35. Alfred Love to Elie Ducommun, 7 July 1898, IPB, Box 199, LNL.

36. "Letter from Belva A. Lockwood," *Peacemaker* 17 (1898): 9.

37. Belva Lockwood to "Dear Friend," 7 April 1898, IPB, Box 236, LNL.

38. Belva Lockwood to Elie Ducommun, 21 May 1901, IPB, Box 178, LNL.

39. W. J. Colville, "The White Man's Burden," *Peacemaker* 17 (1899): 168–70; Lockwood to the Pennsylvania Peace Society, 23 November 1898, *Peacemaker* 17 (1898): 116.

40. Resolution of February 7, 1899, D.C. Federation of Women's Clubs, IPB, Box 236/7, LNL; "The Czar's Conference," *Woman's Tribune*, April 22, 1899.

41. Lockwood, Letter, 17 May 1899, *Peacemaker* 17 (1899): 228; Lockwood, Letter, 7 February 1900, *Peacemaker* 18 (1900): 176; Cooper, *Patriotic Pacifism*, 97–103. Cooper describes this court as "the grandparent of the World Court of the twentieth century."

42. Lockwood to Elie Ducommun, 10 June 1899, IPB, Box 178, LNL.

43. "Lawyers in Petticoats," 9; Lockwood to Munsey Bull, 19 November 1899, Bull Family Letters, Bancroft Library, University of California.

44. Lockwood to Emily Arvilla Green, 27 August 1899, private collection (copy in author's files).

45. Lockwood to Bull, 19 November 1899.

46. Lockwood to Green, 27 August 1899.

47. "Letter from Our Vice President, Belva A. Lockwood," *Peacemaker* 18 (1900): 175–76.

48. Lockwood to Clara Colby, 15 January 1899, SHSW.

49. Lockwood to Wm. G. Richardson, 24 March 1899, Collection of Mrs. Harry McAvoy, Courtesy of Norma Wollenberg.

50. "In Sympathy," *Peacemaker* 19 (August 1900): 34.

51. Lockwood to Gaston Moch, 16 August 1900, IPB, Box 82/13, and Lockwood to Bajer, 20 August 1900, IPB, no box number, each at the LNL.

52. Lockwood to Ducommun, 21 May 1901, IPB, Box 178, LNL.

53. Lockwood to Munsey Bull, 19 November 1899.

54. Ibid.

55. Jill Norgren, *The Cherokee Cases* (Norman: University of Oklahoma Press, 2004), chapters 1–3; John R. Finger, *The Eastern Band of Cherokees, 1819–1900* (Knoxville: University of Tennessee Press, 1984).

56. Finger, *Eastern Band*, 118; Jerry L. Clark, "The Indian Countryman; or, The Life and Times of James M. Taylor, Cherokee," unpublished, 1986, author's files.

57. *Band of Eastern Cherokees vs. The Western Nation*, Exhibit A, Statement of Belva A. Lockwood, April 20, 1885, 1, Ct. Cl. General Jurisdiction 13828, RG 123, NA, hereafter, Statement of Belva A. Lockwood.

58. *Cherokees of North Carolina v. Cherokees of Indian Territory* (also called *Eastern Cherokees v. Western Cherokees*), Equity 4627, RG 21, NA; Statement of Belva A. Lockwood, 2–3.

59. Statement of Belva A. Lockwood, 2.

60. Act of March 3, 1863, ch. 92, sec. 9, 12 Stat. 765, 767; Act of February 24, 1855, ch. 122, sec. 1, 10 Stat. 612.

61. *Congressional Globe*, 62:124, April 12, 1862.

62. Statement of Belva A. Lockwood, 9.

63. Suit was brought under section 5 of the Deficiency Bill, 47th Cong., 2d Sess., approved March 4, 1883.

64. *Eastern Band of Cherokee Indians v. Cherokee Nation of Indians and the United States*, Brief for Plaintiff, Ct. Cl. 13606, 1, RG 123, NA.

65. Lockwood to James Taylor, 11 March 1883, Taylor Papers, Duke University.

66. J. J. Newell to James Taylor, 11 March 1883, and Lockwood to James Taylor, 12 March 1883, each in Taylor Papers, Duke University.

67. *Eastern Band of Cherokee Indians v. The Cherokee Nation West and the United States*, 19 Ct. Cl. 35, 37–39 (1883); Finger, *Eastern Band*, 145–46.

68. *Eastern Band of the Cherokee Indians v. The United States*, Brief for Plaintiff, Ct. Cl. 13828, 20, RG 123, NA; *Eastern Band of Cherokees v. U.S.*, 20 Ct. Cl. 449 (1885); *Eastern Band of Cherokee Indians v. U.S. and Cherokee Nation*, 117 U.S. 288 (1885).

69. Power of Attorney to Lockwood, April 23, 1885, Taylor Papers, Duke University. The two signed another contract and POA in 1897 to prosecute cases relevant to the Slade-Bender report. Lockwood-Taylor agreement of March 8, 1897, Donohue Rare Book Room, Gleeson Library, University of San Francisco.

70. The General Allotment (Dawes) Act, 24 Stat. 388.

71. William T. Hagan, *Taking Indian Lands: The Cherokee Commission* (Norman: University of Oklahoma Press, 2003), ch. 7.

72. *Congressional Record*, H.R., 52nd Cong., 2d Sess., January 14, 1893, 572.

73. H.R. Ex. Doc. 182, *Moneys Due the Cherokee Nation* (the Slade-Bender Report), 53rd Cong., 3d Sess., Serial 3323.

74. Sen. Doc. 215, *Memorial of Eastern or Emigrant Cherokees*, 56th Cong., 1st Sess., Serial 3858, 15–16; Sen. Doc. 163, *Moneys Due the Cherokee Nation* (Letter to the Senate and House from the Attorney-General, Dec. 2, 1895), 56th Cong., 1st Sess., Serial 3852; *Congressional Record*, Senate, 56th Cong., 2d Sess., February 20, 1901, 2682; also, S. 3681, 56th Cong., 1st Sess, *in* Ct. Cl. Cong. 10386, RG 123, NA; Sen. Doc. 282, 305, and 308, 56th Cong., 1st Sess., Serial 3868.

75. Owens filed Ct. Cl. Cong. 10386. For Lockwood's filing see Ct. Cl. Cong. Jurisdiction Docketbook, vol. 2 (May 4, 1900–July 1, 1902), 196, RG 205, NA.

76. *Eastern Cherokees v. U.S.*, Statement, Ct. Cl. Cong. 10386, April 28, 1902, 7.

77. Lockwood to James S. Sherman, 2 and 9 May 1902, RG 233, HR57A-F14.2, Box 28, NA.

78. Act of July 1, 1902. 32 Stat. L. 716 and Act of March 3, 1903, 32 Stat. L. 996.

79. *Eastern and Emigrant Cherokees v. United States*, Findings of Fact and Brief, Ct. Cl. 23212, 12, RG 123, NA.

80. Findings of Fact, Ct. Cl. 23212, 33; *Amended Petition*, September 2, 1903, Ct. Cl. 23212, 5, Papers of Belva A. Lockwood, SCPC; Eastern and Emigrant Cherokees, Reply Brief, Ct. Cl. 23212, November 9, 1904, 11, RG 123, Box 1693, NA.

81. Lockwood to James Taylor, 26 February 1905, reprinted in Transcript of Record, *Lockwood v. Rucker*, U.S. Ct. of Appeals, D.C., 2519, 20. RG 276, NA. Lockwood should have written Frederic D. McKenney.

82. *Cherokee Nation v. United States*, 40 Ct. Cl. 252, 323 (1905).

83. Ibid., 40 Ct. Cl., 328–32.

84. Lockwood to Colby, 18 May 1905, SHSW.

85. Ibid.

86. "A Woman Lawyer's Triumph," *Woman's Tribune*, May 13, 1905, 1.

87. *Eastern and Emigrant Cherokees*, Brief, Supreme Court of the United States (1905), 30, Papers of Belva A. Lockwood, SCPC.

88. *Plessy v. Ferguson*, 163 U.S. 537 (1896); *Lochner v. New York*, 198 U.S. 45 (1905).

89. U.S. Supreme Court, *Minutes*, January 16–18, 1906, RG 267, M215, Roll 24, NA.

90. "Woman to Highest Court," *The Sun*, January 18, 1906, Scrapbook, RG 267, NA.

91. Lockwood to John M. Taylor, 7 May 1906, Taylor Papers, Duke University.

92. *United States v. Cherokee Nation*, 202 U.S. 101, 132 (1906). While waiting, Lockwood appeared at the Court on April 16, 1906, to show support for attor-

ney Sarah Herring Sorin on the occasion of her admission to the Supreme Court bar.

93. Lockwood to John M. Taylor, 5 May 1906, Taylor Papers, Duke University. The following quotation is also from this letter.

94. Lockwood to John M. Taylor, 5 May 1906, Taylor Papers, Duke University.

NOTES TO CHAPTER 16

1. *Eastern Cherokee v. U.S.*, 45 Ct. Cl. 104 (1909–10), 136–37.

2. *Rucker v. Lockwood*, Bill of Exception, April 1909, D.C. Supreme Court, Law 49662, Box 786, RG 21, NA, reprinting May 28, 1906, decree.

3. *Rucker v. Lockwood*, Defendant's Pleas & Answer, D.C. Supreme Court, Law 49662, RG 21, NA.

4. Ibid.

5. Lockwood frequently mortgaged and remortgaged her house. See *Rucker*, Defendant's Pleas.

6. *Rucker*, Bill of Exception, Deposition of William Taylor.

7. *Rucker*, Defendant's Pleas.

8. Lockwood to Clara Colby, 18 May 1905, SHSW.

9. Lockwood to Clara Colby, 16 August 1906, SHSW. Lockwood served on its governing board.

10. Lockwood to Clara Colby, 31 August 1906, SHSW.

11. Belva. A. Lockwood, "From One of Our Delegates to the 15th Universal Peace Congress," *Peacemaker* 25 (1906): 209.

12. Lockwood to Colby, 16 August 1906.

13. Taylor-Lockwood Contract of March 8, 1897, Taylor Papers, Gleeson Library, University of San Francisco.

14. *Rucker*, Defendant's Plea.

15. Carrie C. Catt to Mrs. Clara B. Arthur, 4 January 1909, Woman's History, NMAH.

16. Catt to Arthur, 4 January 1909.

17. Lockwood to Clara W. McNaughton, 22 January 1905, McNaughton Papers, Gleeson Library, University of San Francisco; Lockwood to Alfred Love, 12 February 1905, UPU, Reel 13.7, SCPC.

18. Katherine Devereux Blake and Margaret Louis Wallace, *Champion of Women: The Life of Lillie Devereux Blake* (New York: Fleming H. Revell Co., 1943), 207–13.

19. Olympia Brown, ed., *Democratic Ideals: A Memorial Sketch of Clara B. Colby* (Federal Suffrage Association, 1917), 58, 72. Colby spent many years living in Washington, D.C., while married to Leonard W. Colby, a lawyer. When they divorced and Clara moved west, she and Lockwood maintained their

friendship through visits and letters in which they discussed reform issues and exchanged family news. For a discussion of Colby's life, contributions, and family life, see Kristin Mapel Bloomberg, *Suffrage, Scandal, and Sacrifice: The Life of Clara Bewick Colby* (Lincoln: University of Nebraska Press, forthcoming); her letters to Lockwood are at the SHSW; and Clara Colby to Captain R. H. Pratt, 17 October 1902, Richard Henry Pratt Papers, Beinecke Rare Book and Manuscript Library, Yale University.

20. Brown, *Democratic Ideals*, 60.

21. Ibid., 63, 68–70, 76–77.

22. Senate, *Hearing before the Select Committee on Woman Suffrage on Joint Resolution (S.R. 47)*, Doc. 409, March 3, 1908, 6, 60th Cong., 1st Sess.; Lockwood to Clara Colby, 4 April and 4 May 1908, SHSW.

23. Records of the Commissioners of the District of Columbia, Entries 169299–169301, June 1908, RG 351, NA.

24. Clara Bewick Colby, "A-Foot with My Vision: Number 6. The Peace Congress," *Woman's Tribune*, October 10, 1908, 1.

25. Lockwood to Hon. Charles F. Scott, 31 March 1908, Papers of Belva A. Lockwood, SCPC.

26. Colby, "A-Foot with My Vision."

27. Lockwood to Colby, 17 January 1908; Belva Lockwood, "Extracts from letter to A. C.," *Peacemaker* 27 (September 1908): 213.

28. Lockwood to Clara Colby, 18 November 1908, SHSW.

29. Lockwood to Clara Colby, undated (probably early November 1908), SHSW.

30. Lockwood to Frank Smalley, 28 February 1906. Belva Lockwood Papers, Syracuse University Archives. Syracuse, following the practice of British universities, which awarded master's degrees to undergraduate alumni after a wait of three or four years, had given Lockwood a master of science degree on June 25, 1872. Communication from Edward L. Galvin, Archives Director, to author, December 20, 2000.

31. Belva Ann Bennett Lockwood, Questionnaire Response, no date, 4, Belva Lockwood Papers, SU.

32. Royalton Historical Society, Royalton, New York. After receiving this degree, she traveled to Owego for Tioga County's Old Home Week celebration, where she was an honored guest. Mike Gulachok, "McEnteer Portrays Belva Lockwood," *Tioga County Courier*, March 10, 1993, 7.

33. Alfred Nobel, *Last Will and Testament*, November 25, 1895, http://www.hotchkiss.k12.co.us?HHS/nobelnov/nobel.htm.

34. Letters of Alfred H. Love, 17 March 1900 and 30 May 1900, UPU, Reel 13.7, SCPC; Belva A. Lockwood, *Peacemaker* 22 (March 1903): 54–55; Lockwood to Le Norske Nobel Komite, 5 December 1905, Lockwood to the Nobel Committee of the Norwegian Parliament, 10 December 1907, and Lockwood to the

Nobel Committee of the Norwegian Parliament, 24 January 1910, each found in the Archives of the Nobel Institute, Oslo, Norway; Lockwood to Alfred H. Love, 15 March 1912, UPU, Reel 13.19, SCPC; Alfred H. Love to Lockwood, 27 September 1912, UPU, Reel 13.7, SCPC.

35. Item, *Woman's Tribune*, February 6, 1904, 1.

36. "The Nobel Peace Prizes," *Peacemaker* 28 (January 1909): 20.

37. Lockwood to the Nobel Committee, 24 January 1910.

38. Lockwood to Love, 15 March 1912.

39. Ibid.; Love to Lockwood, 27 September 1912, 28 January 1913, and 2 April 1913, UPU, Reel 13.7, SCPC; Lockwood to Andrew Carnegie, 14 December 1910, Andrew Carnegie Papers, LC.

40. Lockwood to Love, 15 March 1912; but see, "Syracuse Alumnae Seeks Nobel Peace Prize," *Syracuse Daily Journal*, May 19, 1914, 1.

41. Lockwood to Clara Colby, 24 March 1910, SHSW.

42. "Eighty Years Old Is Mrs. Lockwood," 1910 clipping, Papers of Belva Lockwood, SCPC.

43. Lockwood to Clara Colby, 1 January 1911, Clara Colby Papers, Huntington Library, San Marino, CA.

44. Ibid.

45. Ibid.

46. Ibid.

47. In 1910, D.C. deed books show that she acquired 444 Kentucky Avenue, SE, Square 1062, Lot 62. In 1914 she signed this parcel over to her grandson. In 1913 she purchased, with Washington lawyer A. E. L. Leckie, land that had been part of the Wind River Indian Reservation. RG 49, Serial Patent File 309095-7, NA. Her grandson and heir sold the property to Mary Leckie Roberts. Supreme Court of the D.C., Estate of Belva A. Lockwood, Probate No. 24037. After she bought the Wyoming land Lockwood urged women weary of "the drudging city life" to take up light farming. Clipping, "Women Are Urged to Seek Country," *Washington Herald*, March 17, 1913, Papers of Belva A. Lockwood, SCPC.

48. Elisabeth S. Clemens, *The People's Lobby* (Chicago: University of Chicago Press, 1997), 202.

49. Michael Cohen, "Votes and More: The Rise and Fall of the American Woman's Republic," unpublished graduate seminar paper, Harvard University, 27 February 2003, 28–29, author's files.

50. "U.S. Marshals Seek Mrs. Gracie," *Washington Herald*, April 13, 1912; Lockwood to Lella Gardner, 7 April 1912, Belva A. Lockwood Papers, SCPC.

51. "In the matter of the Mary Gage case," 1912, Papers of Belva A. Lockwood, SCPC.

52. "Capital Woman Boomed for Republic Presidency," undated clipping, Papers of Belva A. Lockwood, SCPC.

53. Lockwood to Lella Gardner, 30 April 1913, Papers of Belva A. Lockwood, SCPC; "2000 Out for Park Suffrage Meetings," *Ohio State Journal*, August 1912 clipping, Papers of Belva A. Lockwood, SCPC; Lockwood to Lella Gardner, 11 August 1912, Papers of Belva A. Lockwood, SCPC.

54. Alfred Love to Lockwood, 10 April 1913, UPU, Reel 13.7, SCPC; "Letter from Belva A. Lockwood," *Peacemaker* 31 (Sept. 1912): 195.

55. "Belva Lockwood, 82 Years Young," (New York) *World*, November 3, 1912, N5.

56. Wallace Irwin and Inez Milholland, "Two Million Women Vote," *McClure's Magazine*, January 1913, 241.

57. Lockwood to Lella Gardner, 10 November 1912, Papers of Belva A. Lockwood, SCPC.

58. Lockwood to Lella Gardner, 1 December 1912, 30 December 1912, and 5 January 1913, Papers of Belva A. Lockwood, SCPC.

59. Lockwood to President Taft, 13 December 1912, Taft Papers, Series 6, reel 372, case no. 170GQ, LC; "Woman Suggested for the Vacancy on Supreme Bench," undated clipping (published after the October 14, 1911, death of Justice John Marshall Harlan), Papers of Belva A. Lockwood, SCPC.

60. Lockwood to Gardner, 5 January 1913.

61. Lockwood to Lella Gardner, 12 January 1913, Papers of Belva A. Lockwood, SCPC.

62. Lockwood to Gardner, 30 April 1913. In 1917 it went to the National Portrait Gallery.

63. Alice Paul Interview, November 1972 and May 1973, Regional Oral History Office, University of California, Berkeley.

64. Julia Winner, *Belva A. Lockwood* (Lockport, NY: NCHS, 1969), 100.

65. Nettie Lovisa White to Lockwood, 15 February 1913, Lockwood/Ormes Collection, NMAH.

66. Ibid.

67. "Suffrage Crusaders in Thrilling Pageant Take City by Storm," *Evening Star*, March 3, 1913, 1.

68. Winner, *Belva A. Lockwood*, 100. Lockwood continued to testify in support of federal suffrage. H.R., *Hearings on H.R. 26950 (Woman Suffrage)*, 1913, 20.

69. Lockwood to Gardner, 30 April 1913.

70. "Ambassadors Leave for Buda Pesth," *Woman's National Weekly*, May 31, 1913, California Colony Section, 1.

71. Lockwood to Gardner, 30 April 1913.

72. Lockwood to Lella Gardner, 13 May 1913, Papers of Belva A. Lockwood, SCPC.

73. Mildred S. McFaden, "A Glimpse of Picturesque Buda Pesth," *Woman's National Weekly*, August 9, 1913, clipping, Papers of Belva A. Lockwood, SCPC.

74. Belva A. Lockwood, "Megaphone." Undated speaking notes, Ormes/Lockwood Collection, NMAH.

75. Ibid.

76. Lockwood to the Love Family, 20 July, 1913, UPU, Reel 13.18, SCPC.

77. Arabella Carter to Lockwood, 4 March 1914, UPU, Reel 13.7, SCPC.

78. Lockwood to Clara W. McNaughton, 4 August 1913, Women's Suffrage Collection, Gleeson Library, University of San Francisco.

79. *Rucker v. Lockwood*, Mandate, Court of Appeals of the District of Columbia, Law 49662, February 10, 1910, recording judgment made April 2, 1909, RG 21, NA.

80. District of Columbia Recorder of Deeds, December 16, 1913, Liber 3667, folio 335; January 8, 1914, Liber 3674, Folio 274.

81. "Belva Lockwood in Dire Need," *Woman's Journal*, April 4, 1914, 111, reprinting an appeal printed in the *Washington Times*. In an age before pensions and Social Security such appeals were not uncommon. In 1913, friends tried to raise money for Clara Colby, who was nearly destitute. Lockwood to Clara McNaughton, 10 October 1913, Women's Suffrage Collection, Gleeson Library, University of San Francisco.

82. Winner, *Belva A. Lockwood*, 101.

83. *Rucker v. Lockwood*, Notice to Quit, Supreme Court of the District of Columbia, Law 49662, May 19, 1914; Petition, June 22, 1914; Order of the Court, June 22, 1914; Motion to Vacate and Discharge Rule and Dismiss Petition, June 25, 1914, RG 21, NA.

84. Harold B. Johnson, "Interview," *Watertown Daily Times*, November 7, 1914, Newspaper archives, Scrapbooks, 22:40

85. Robert M. Lester, *Home Trust Company, 1901–1943* (Carnegie Corporation of New York, June 1, 1943), 11; Cuno H. Rudolph to Home Trust Co., 21 May 1917, Home Trust Pension Papers, Rare Book and Manuscript Collection, Columbia University.

86. Leon Edel, *Henry James: A Life* (New York: Harper & Row, 1985), 675–76.

87. Lockwood to Henrik Andersen, 3 December 1914, Henrik Andersen Papers, LC.

88. Andersen to Lockwood, 30 November 1914 and Lockwood to Andersen, 3 December 1914, Henrik Andersen Papers, LC.

89. Lockwood to Andersen, 8 August 1916, and Andersen to Lockwood, 9 September 1916, Andersen Papers, LC.

90. Clara Colby to Mrs. L. Brackett Bishop, 18 February 1916, and Colby to Lockwood, 21 February 1916, SHSW.

91. Lockwood to Clara Colby, 29 May 1916, SHSW.

92. Ibid.

93. Lockwood to Clara Colby, 7 July 1916, SHSW. Subsequent quotations in this paragraph cite to this letter.

94. Clara Colby to Lockwood, 17 July 1916, SHSW.

95. "Belva Lockwood Is 86 Years Old," *Evening Star*, October 24, 1916, 10.

NOTES TO EPILOGUE

1. Ellen Burroughts Foster to Olympia Brown, 29 March 1917, Olympia Brown Papers, Reel 8, Schlesinger Library.

2. Timothy L. O'Brien, "Why Do So Few Women Reach the Top of Big Law Firms?" *New York Times*, 19 March 2006, Business Section (online).

3. "Lady Candidate," November 23, 1888, newspaper clipping, SCPC.

Index

About the Author

Jill Norgren grew up in Stamford, Connecticut. She received her B.A. from the University of Pennsylvania and her Ph.D. from the University of Michigan. She is Professor Emerita of Government and Legal Studies, John Jay College of Criminal Justice and the Graduate Center, the City University of New York. She is also the author of *The Cherokee Cases: Two Landmark General Decisions in the Fight for Sovereignty* and coauthor of *Partial Justice: Federal Indian Law in a Liberal-Constitutional System* and *American Cultural Pluralism and Law*. She writes on U.S. politics and law and has a particular interest in the history of American women. Her articles have received awards from the American Society for Legal History and the United States Supreme Court Historical Society. She wrote much of this book while a fellow at the Woodrow Wilson International Center for Scholars in Washington, D.C.